LPIC-1 IN DEPTH

Michael Jang

Course Technology PTR

A part of Cengage Learning

COURSE TECHNOLOGY
CENGAGE Learning™

Australia, Brazil, Japan, Korea, Mexico, Singapore, Spain, United Kingdom, United States

COURSE TECHNOLOGY
CENGAGE Learning™

LPIC-1 In Depth
Michael Jang

Publisher and General Manager, Course Technology PTR:
Stacy L. Hiquet

Associate Director of Marketing:
Sarah Panella

Manager of Editorial Services:
Heather Talbot

Marketing Manager:
Mark Hughes

Acquisitions Editor:
Megan Belanger

Project/Copy Editor:
Karen A. Gill

Technical Reviewer:
Elizabeth Zinkann

Editorial Services Coordinator:
Jen Blaney

Interior Layout Tech:
Bill Hartman

Cover Designer:
Mike Tanamachi

Indexer:
BIM Indexing & Proofreading Services

Proofreader:
Melba Hopper

For product information and technology assistance, contact us at
Cengage Learning Customer & Sales Support, 1-800-354-9706

For permission to use material from this text or product, submit all requests online at **cengage.com/permissions**. Further permissions questions can be e-mailed to **permissionrequest@cengage.com**.

CBT Nuggets is a registered trademark of The CBT Nuggets, LLC.
Linux is a registered trademark of Linus Torvalds in the U.S. and other countries.
All other trademarks are the property of their respective owners.

Library of Congress Control Number: 2009924619

ISBN-13: 978-1-59863-967-4

ISBN-10: 1-59863-967-6

Course Technology, a part of Cengage Learning
20 Channel Center Street
Boston, MA 02210
USA

Cengage Learning is a leading provider of customized learning solutions with office locations around the globe, including Singapore, the United Kingdom, Australia, Mexico, Brazil, and Japan. Locate your local office at: **international.cengage.com/region**.

Cengage Learning products are represented in Canada by Nelson Education, Ltd.

For your lifelong learning solutions, visit **courseptr.com**.

Visit our corporate Web site at **cengage.com**.

Printed in the United States of America
1 2 3 4 5 6 7 11 10 09

For Randy Lembke

Acknowledgments

Books like this are the product of hard work by every member of a team. I want to thank everyone involved in the development of this book. Megan Belanger showed the insight and flexibility that allowed me to write this book using open source products. Elizabeth Zinkann is, as always, a marvelous technical editor and most excellent friend. Karen Gill showed wonderful patience as the project editor and did a terrific job as copy editor. And, of course, this book would not have been possible without all of the hard work of Bill Hartman, Melba Hopper, Kevin Broccoli, and Mark Hughes.

Most importantly, all the work I do is worth it because of the love, patience, and support of my wonderful wife, Donna. Because we have both been widowed, we've shared the worst of times. But today, she is my happiness.

About the Author

Michael Jang (LPIC-2, RHCE, UCP, LCP, Linux+, MCP) is a full-time writer, focused on open source operating systems and associated certification exams. His experience with computers dates back to the days of jumbled punch cards. His other books on Linux certification include *RHCE Red Hat Certified Engineer Linux Study Guide*, *RHCT Red Hat Certified Technician Linux Study Guide*, *Ubuntu Certified Professional Study Guide*, *Mike Meyers' Linux+ Certification Passport*, and *SAIR GNU/Linux Installation and Configuration Exam Cram*. Michael's other Linux books include *Ubuntu Server Administration*, *Linux Annoyances for Geeks*, *Linux Patch Management*, *Mastering Fedora Core 5*, and *Mastering Red Hat Enterprise Linux 3*.

Contents

Introduction

As I write this book, the Linux community is more hopeful than ever. Even bad economic times don't discourage Linux users, because that's when the cost advantages of Linux get more attention. But with difficult economic times, resumes are being filtered for a number of elements, including certification.

When hiring managers look at resumes, they look for experience first. But before many hiring managers even get a look at a resume, human resource managers look for certifications. When they look for certifications, they look for candidates who have passed the exams of the LPI (Linux Professional Institute). With the possible exception of the Red Hat certifications, the LPI certifications are the most respected in the industry. However, because the LPI exams are distribution-neutral, they qualify candidates beyond just the Red Hat distribution.

There are three levels of LPI Certifications (LPIC), plus one affiliated certification, as listed in Table I.1.

Table I.1 LPI Certifications

Certification	Description
LPIC-1	Level 1; Exams 101, 102
UCP	Ubuntu Certified Professional; requires LPIC-1 certification plus the LPI 199 exam
LPIC-2	Level 2; Exams 201, 202
LPIC-3 (Core)	Level 3; Exam 301
LPIC-3 (Specialty)	Level 3; Exam 301 and one other of the following LPI level 3 exams: 302, 303, 304, 305, or 306

As suggested by the title, this book is focused on the LPIC-1 certification. In overview, per http://www.lpi.org/eng/certification/the_lpic_program/lpic_1, to pass the LPI 101 and 102 exams, a candidate should be able to do the following:

◆ Work at the Linux command line

◆ Perform easy maintenance tasks: help out users, add users to a larger system, backup & restore, shutdown & reboot

◆ Install and configure a workstation (including X) and connect it to a LAN, or a stand-alone PC via modem to the Internet

In contrast, take a quick look at the overview for the LPIC-2 certification, per http://www.lpi.org/eng/certification/the_lpic_program/lpic_2:

◆ Administer a small to medium-sized site

◆ Plan, implement, maintain, keep consistent, secure, and troubleshoot a small mixed (MS, Linux) network, including a

   ◆ LAN server (samba)

   ◆ Internet gateway (firewall, proxy, mail, news)

   ◆ Internet server (Web server, FTP server)

◆ Supervise assistants

◆ Advise management on automation and purchases

This should give you a basic feel for the depth of knowledge required for the LPIC-1 certification.

Before this time, the LPIC-1 certification was more focused on system administrators. The April 2009 revision of the associated LPI 101 and 102 exams brought in topics of wider interest. In other words, no longer do you need to be qualified as a junior-level Linux system administrator to pass the LPI 101 and 102 exams. You just need to be an expert Linux user, also known as a "power user."

To this end, details of the Linux kernel; the installation of software packages from source code; and services such as Apache, Samba, and DNS have been moved to the LPIC-2 certification exams 201 and 202. Older hardware topics, such as UPS (Uninterruptible Power Supply) and IRQ (Interrupt Request) ports, have been dropped. However, a greater understanding of the boot process, more detailed networking configuration, system logging, Linux provisions for the disabled, internationalization, and basic SQL commands are now part of the LPI 101 and 102 exams.

LPI certifications are considered active for five years. After five years, you can retake the certification exams at the same or higher levels to keep your certification active. For example, if you qualify for the LPIC-1 certification in 2009, your certification is considered active until 2014. If you pass the LPIC-2 exams before 2014, your LPIC-1 certification is also kept active while the LPIC-2 certification is active.

 NOTE

Do not rely on "braindumps." When a question is found on a braindump site, LPI reserves the right to replace such questions in the exam pool.

Suggested Linux Distributions

The LPI exams are vendor neutral. As such, they can include questions for all current Linux distributions—at least current at the last revision time of the exams, April 2009. In practice, the LPI exams are focused on Red Hat and Debian-based Linux distributions.

I've selected CentOS 5 and Ubuntu Hardy Heron to represent these two distribution types. CentOS 5 is based on the same source code used for Red Hat Enterprise Linux 5, the enterprise-level distribution of Red Hat. I chose CentOS 5 because Red Hat Enterprise Linux 5 is difficult for readers to keep up-to-date for more than 30 days without significant costs, which is one of the reasons why the CentOS project exists. The Hardy Heron release of Ubuntu is the latest one available as of this writing with "Long Term Support," which makes it more suitable for the enterprise, in the same way that Red Hat Enterprise Linux does. I refer to these distributions throughout the book as the "selected distributions."

 NOTE

Although Red Hat Enterprise Linux uses open source software, Red Hat is able to protect its distributions through its trademarks, such as its "shadowman" picture of the man in the red hat. Red Hat complies with open source licenses by releasing the source code for virtually all of its packages. CentOS uses the same open source software packages used and released by Red Hat, omitting Red Hat trademarks. In that way, CentOS 5 does not violate Red Hat trademarks and is functionally identical to Red Hat Enterprise Linux 5. However, I'm not a lawyer, and I'm not making legal representations regarding open source software.

To download these distributions, you need to access what's known as an ISO file. The file that I recommend you download for both distributions is more than 4GB in size, so a high-speed connection is recommended. You can download CentOS 5 from one of the worldwide mirrors listed at

```
http://www.centos.org/modules/tinycontent/index.php?id=30
http://www.centos.org/modules/tinycontent/index.php?id=31
http://www.centos.org/modules/tinycontent/index.php?id=32
```

Likewise, you can download Ubuntu Hardy Heron from one of the worldwide mirrors listed at https://launchpad.net/ubuntu/+archivemirrors.

 NOTE

Although I recommend that you download a DVD, some mirrors may have only CDs available. While you can use CDs, they may require significant downloads of additional software.

To illustrate, one common archive is available from the Argonne National Laboratory at http://mirror.anl.gov. It includes links to download a number of Linux distributions using the HTTP (Hypertext Transfer Protocol), FTP (File Transfer Protocol), and rsync protocols. DVDs for both distributions are not available from all mirrors. If you prefer the FTP protocol, you can download the CentOS 5 and Ubuntu Hardy Heron releases from the following respective sites:

```
ftp://mirror.anl.gov/pub/centos/5.2/isos/i386/
ftp://mirror.anl.gov/pub/ubuntu-iso/DVDs/ubuntu/hardy/release/
```

The latest release available as of this writing of the selected distributions is CentOS 5.2 and Ubuntu Hardy Heron 8.04.2. These are actually updates of CentOS 5 and Hardy Heron 8.04. If you see a later update such as CentOS 5.3 or Hardy Heron 8.04.3, downloads of such are acceptable for this book.

Alternatively, if you do not have access to a suitable high-speed connection, these distributions are available from third parties in CD and DVD formats. Some vendors are listed on the CentOS site at http://www.centos.org/modules/tinycontent/index.php?id=24. Others are listed on the Ubuntu site at http://www.ubuntu.com/getubuntu/purchase.

 NOTE

It's also possible to get Ubuntu Live CDs for free by request at https://shipit.ubuntu.com. However, because such CDs are shipped from Europe, delivery typically takes several weeks to other continents such as North America.

After the noted ISO files are downloaded, you can "burn" them to appropriate media (CD or DVD) with Linux commands such as cdrecord (which can work on both CDs and DVDs); however, the details may be beyond the capabilities of excellent LPIC-1 candidates. (Commands such as cdrecord are not part of the LPIC-1 objectives.) So it's acceptable to burn such media with Linux GUI tools such as Nautilus or K3b, or even equivalent Microsoft Windows or Apple Macintosh tools.

Alternatively, if you have access to virtual machine options such as VMware, Virtualbox, Parallels, Xen, KVM, and so on, you may be able to use the downloaded ISO file directly on that virtual machine, without having to "burn" the image to physical media. Details are as varied as the range of available virtual machine options.

The installation process for both CentOS 5 and Ubuntu Hardy Heron is straightforward. Both GUI and text-based installation options are available. Official guides are available online at http://www.centos.org/docs/5/ and https://help.ubuntu.com/8.04/.

What You'll Find in This Book

This book covers every objective for the LPIC-1 certification. It supports candidates who are studying to pass both LPI 101 and LPI 102 exams. It includes 15 chapters; the first eight chapters focus on the requirements of the LPI 101 exam. It also includes four sample exams (two each for the LPI 101 and LPI 102 exams).

 NOTE

The command-line prompt shown in this book is slightly different from what you'll see in either the CentOS 5 or the Ubuntu Hardy Heron releases. Because their default prompts differ from each other, this book just assumes the more common command-line prompt for a regular user, as shown here:

$

However, in most cases, the command-line prompt reflects that associated with administrative users. Although that prompt also varies between the CentOS 5 and Hardy Heron releases, this book assumes the more common command-line prompt for a root administrative user, as shown here:

#

For the latest detailed objectives, navigate to http://www.lpi.org. As of this writing, the current objectives for LPI exams 101 and 102 can be found at http://www.lpi.org/eng/certification/the_lpic_program/lpic_1/exam_101_detailed_objectives or http://www.lpi.org/eng/certification/the_lpic_program/lpic_1/exam_102_detailed_objectives. Check them yourself against Table I.2 to make sure you're studying the latest objectives. Table I.2 includes direct quotes of the objectives as of this writing. Because the LPI exams are international, Table I.2 includes spelling, capitalization, and grammar that may be in conflict with standard written American English.

The total objective weight for each exam is 60. Normally, you'll see 60 questions on each exam. The table also includes objectives and subobjectives. For example, objective 101 covers "System Architecture," with a weight of 8. It consists of objective 101.1, "Determine and Configure Hardware Settings," with a weight of 2; "Boot the System," with a weight of 3; and "Change Runlevels and Shutdown or Reboot System," also with a weight of 3.

Table I.2 LPIC-1 Objectives, by Chapter

Exam	Topic	Subtopic	Description	Weight	Chapter
101			Exam 101	60	1–8
	101		System architecture	8	1
		101.1	Determine and configure hardware settings	2	1
		101.2	Boot the system	3	1
		101.3	Change runlevels and shutdown or reboot system	3	1
	102		Linux Installation and Package Management	11	2–3
		102.1	Design hard disk layout	2	2
		102.2	Install a boot manager	2	2
		102.3	Manage shared libraries	1	2
		102.4	Use Debian package management	3	3
		102.5	Use RPM and YUM package management	3	3
	103		GNU and UNIX Commands	26	4–6
		103.1	Work on the command line	4	4
		103.2	Process text streams using filters	3	5
		103.3	Perform basic file management	4	4
		103.4	Use Debian package management	4	5
		103.5	Create, monitor, and kill processes	4	6
		103.6	Modify process execution priorities	2	6
		103.7	Search text files using regular expressions	2	5
		103.8	Perform basic file editing operations using vi	3	6
	104		Devices, Linux Filesystems, Filesystem Hierarchy Standard	26	7–8
		104.1	Create partitions and filesystems	2	7
		104.2	Maintain the integrity of filesystems	2	7
		104.3	Control mounting and unmounting of filesystems	3	7
		104.4	Manage disk quotas	1	8
		104.5	Manage file permissions and ownership	2	8
		104.6	Create and change hard and symbolic links	2	8
		104.7	Find system files and place files in the correct location	2	8

Table I.2 Continued

Exam	Topic	Subtopic	Description	Weight	Chapter
102			Exam 102	60	9–15
	105		Shells, scripting, and data management	10	9
		105.1	Customize and use the shell environment	4	9
		105.2	Customize or write sample scripts	4	9
		105.3	SQL data management	2	9
	106		User interfaces and desktops	8	10
		106.1	Install and configure X11	2	10
		106.2	Setup a display manager	2	10
		106.3	Accessibility	1	10
	107		Administrative tasks	12	11
		107.1	Manage user and group accounts and related system files	5	11
		107.2	Automate system administration tasks by scheduling jobs	4	11
		107.3	Localisation and internationalisation	3	11
	108		Essential system services	10	12
		108.1	Maintain system time	3	12
		108.2	System logging	2	12
		108.3	Mail transfer agent (MTA) basics	3	12
		108.4	Manage printers and printing	2	12
	109		Networking fundamentals	14	13, 14
		109.1	Fundamentals of internet protocols	3	13
		109.2	Basic network configuration	2	13
		109.3	Basic network troubleshooting	3	14
		109.4	Configure client-side DNS	2	14
	110		Security	9	15
		110.1	Perform security administration tasks	3	15
		110.2	Setup host security	3	15
		110.3	Securing data with encryption	3	15

Who This Book Is For

This book is designed to help those Linux professionals who want to pass both LPI 101 and LPI 102 exams. Because LPI assumes that qualified candidates have significant experience with the Linux operating system, this book assumes that readers have at least one year of experience with Linux.

Although it is possible for someone new to Linux to pass the LPI exams, these exams assume that you already know how to install Linux. In fact, installation is not even a requirement for the LPI exams, because it is assumed that you are beyond that stage of Linux experience.

The LPIC-1 certification is the first step in the LPI series of certificates, as described in Table I.1.

How This Book Is Organized

This book is organized for the most part sequentially, per the aforementioned LPIC-1 objectives. There are 10 main objectives associated with the latest LPIC-1 exams. Chapters 1 through 8 cover objectives 101 through 104, which are associated with LPI exam 101. Chapters 9 through 15 cover objectives 105 through 110, which are associated with LPI exam 102.

Each chapter includes two review questions for each objective weight. For example, Chapter 15 covers Topic 110: Security. The subobjectives in this topic have a total weight of 10. Therefore, you'll see 20 questions in Chapter 15.

This section includes numerous quotes from the detailed objectives, per http://www.lpi.org/eng/certification/the_lpic_program/lpic_1/exam_101_detailed_objectives and http://www.lpi.org/eng/certification/the_lpic_program/lpic_1/exam_102_detailed_objectives.

Chapter 1, "System Architecture," starts with a brief overview of the LPIC-1 exams. With respect to hardware, it expects LPIC-1 candidates to "be able to determine and configure fundamental system hardware." It covers the boot process, in the expectation that "candidates should be able to guide the system through the booting process." It also covers what you need to know to change runlevels, manage processes, and set a new default runlevel.

Chapter 2, "Configure a System for Linux," illustrates examples of appropriate disk partition schemes. It goes into detail about interactions with both the GRUB (Grand Unified Bootloader) and LILO (Linux Loader) boot loaders. It also describes how you can find the shared libraries that executable programs depend on.

Chapter 3, "Package Management Systems," goes into detail on the software package systems originally built for Debian and Red Hat Linux. It also describes the use of the dpkg and apt-* commands for Debian-style packages, as well as the rpm and yum commands for Red Hat-style packages.

Chapter 4, "Command Lines and Files," is focused on how you can manage files from the command-line interface. Based on the bash shell, you "should be able to interact with shells and commands using the command line." This chapter also illustrates how you can "use the basic Linux commands to manage files and directories."

Chapter 5, "Command Filters and Pipes," covers how to take advantage of text streams as databases with appropriate filters. With the right redirects, you'll learn more about the concepts of standard input, standard output, and standard error. In the same vein, you need to know "how to manipulate files and text data using regular expressions" such as the grep and sed commands.

Chapter 6, "Processes, Priorities, and Editing," covers the basic operation of the vi text editor. It also helps you "manage process execution priorities" as well as "perform basic process management."

Chapter 7, "Manage and Maintain Filesystems," is focused on the nitty-gritty of filesystem management. When you're finished with this chapter, you "should be able to configure disk partitions and then create" regular and swap filesystems on hard disks. Once a partition is written, you should "be able to maintain a standard filesystem, as well as the extra data associated with a journaling filesystem." Of course, a filesystem is not useful until you have control over how that filesystem is mounted and unmounted.

Chapter 8, "File Permissions and More," will help you understand how to manage disk quotas as well as how to "control file access through the proper use of permissions and ownership." Specialized files include hard and soft links. Search tools such as find and locate navigate through the FHS (Filesystem Hierarchy Standard).

Chapter 9, "Shells, Scripting, and Data Management," describes how you can "customize shell environments to meet users' needs," as the environment relates to profiles. The shell scripting sections, "Manage the Shell Environment" and "Write Simple Shell Scripts," describe standard Linux scripts, along with the basic commands used in such scripts. LPI candidates should also know the basics of data manipulation using SQL (Structured Query Language).

Chapter 10, "The GUI Desktop Environment," covers the basics of configuring Linux for a graphical desktop. From what you see in this chapter, you "should be able to install and configure X and an X font server." In addition, you should know how to set up appropriate login screens with XDM (X display manager), GDM (GNOME display manager), and KDM (KDE display manager). Finally, you should understand the basic accessibility technologies associated with the Linux GUI.

Chapter 11, "Administrative Tasks," covers the basics of Linux system administration. You'll see how "to add, remove, suspend, and change user accounts," how to "automate system administration tasks" with the cron and at daemons, as well as how to localize a system for different languages and time zones.

Chapter 12, "Essential System Services," shows you how to maintain an accurate system time using NTP (Network Time Protocol). It describes the basic configuration of system log services and associated files. This chapter also shows you the basic facts of MTAs (mail transfer agents) covered on the exam. Finally, it describes basic configuration and troubleshooting issues associated with CUPS (Common UNIX Printing System).

Chapter 13, "Basic Networking," addresses the fundamentals of how Linux systems communicate. As suggested by the objectives, "candidates should demonstrate a proper understanding of TCP/IP network fundamentals." In this chapter, you'll also see how to "view, change, and verify configuration settings on client hosts."

Chapter 14, "More Network Fundamentals," covers the basic commands used "to troubleshoot networking issues on client hosts." Separately, it also covers how you can "configure DNS on a client host."

Chapter 15, "Security Administration," addresses "how to review system configuration to ensure host security in accordance with local security policies." When you're finished with this chapter, you "should know how to set up a basic level of host security." Finally, you'll learn the basics of SSH (Secure Shell), as well as how to set up associated private and public data keys.

Appendix A, "Chapter Review Question Answers," includes answers to the review questions listed at the end of each chapter.

Appendix B, "LPIC-1 101, Sample Exam 1," includes a complete simulation of the 60-question LPIC-1 101 exam.

Appendix C, "LPIC-1 101, Sample Exam 2," includes a second complete simulation of the 60-question LPIC-1 101 exam.

Appendix D, "LPIC-1 101, Sample Exam 1 and 2 Answers," includes the answers to both sample LPIC-1 101 exams.

Appendix E, "LPIC-1 102, Sample Exam 1," includes a complete simulation of the 60-question LPIC-1 102 exam.

Appendix F, "LPIC-1 102, Sample Exam 2," includes a second complete simulation of the 60-question LPIC-1 102 exam.

Appendix G, "LPIC-1 102, Sample Exam 1 and 2 Answers," includes the answers to both sample LPIC-1 102 exams.

Appendix H, "About the CD," introduces four videos on several LPIC-1 topics provided by CBT Nuggets, with instructions on how to play those video nuggets on a Linux system. These topics address the command line and SSH (secure shell).

How to Prepare for the LPIC-1 Exams

This book is designed to be read from beginning to end. In some respects, the book may appear to repeat topics, because some of the same commands are covered in multiple chapters. Such topics are covered in multiple exam objectives, and as such, you can expect to see more questions on each topic.

If you're already supremely confident about the topics in a chapter, read at least the "Key Terms" section from that chapter and answer the review questions. Be aware: a term that is defined in the "Key Terms" in an early chapter is not repeated in the Key Terms of later chapters. For example, because GRUB is defined in Chapter 1, you'll find its definition only in the "Key Terms" section of that chapter, even though it's also covered in Chapter 2. For your convenience, the index at the back of the book uses bold page numbers to indicate where each term is defined.

How to Become LPIC-1 Certified

To become LPIC-1 certified, you must do the following:

1. Register at https://www.lpi.org/eng/certification/register_now for an LPI ID number, which is required before signing up for an exam.

2. Select an exam. If you're reading this book, you're considering the LPI exams 101 and 102. To qualify for the LPIC-1 certificate, you need to pass both exams.

3. Read the LPI exam policies at http://lpi.org/eng/certification/policies. They cover exam renewal, recertification, exam retakes, and the disciplinary process at http://lpi.org/eng/certification/disciplinary_procedure.

4. Schedule an exam through one of three channels: Pearson VUE (http://www.vue.com), Prometric (http://www.2test.com), or one of the major trade shows and conferences where LPI makes exams available. Sometimes Linux user groups may also sponsor LPI exam events.

5. Take and pass the LPIC-1 101 and 102 certification exams.

 NOTE

If you take an LPI exam from someone other than Pearson VUE or Prometric, you may take the exam in paper and pencil format. You'll get an exam booklet and a test sheet, with ovals and blank lines, similar to the paper and pencil format of the Scholastic Aptitude Test or the ACT exams.

There are now 60 questions each for the LPI 101 and 102 exams, which matches the total objective weight for each exam. If you get a 60-question exam, you'll have 90 minutes to complete the exam.

LPI reportedly has a permanent pool of several hundred questions for each exam. So the exam you see is likely to include few duplicates to the exam that your colleagues may have seen.

LPI exam scores range from 200 to 800. To pass, you need a score of 500. Per http://www.lpi.org/index.php/eng/certification/faq/faq_on_exams, "The number of correct questions required to achieve a score of 500 varies with the overall difficulty of the specific exam that is taken."

On occasion, you may get more than 60 questions on an exam. In that case, you'll have additional time. Only 60 of the questions count toward your score. The remaining questions are "beta" questions, under consideration by LPI for inclusion in the permanent pool of available questions. Unfortunately, there is no way to identify the difference between a graded question and a beta question.

The questions on LPI exams may follow one of three formats: multiple choice single answer, multiple choice multiple answer, and fill-in-the-blank. The following is an example of a multiple choice single answer question:

1. Which of the following commands lists files in the current local directory?

   A. ls

   B. dir

   C. list

   D. cmd

The answer is A: the ls command.

Next is an example of a multiple choice multiple answer question:

2. Which of the following are command line console text editors? Choose two.

   A. vi

   B. emacs

   C. gedit

   D. OpenOffice.org Writer

The answers are A and B: the vi and emacs editors.

The following is an example of a fill-in-the-blank question:

3. Enter the command that navigates to the /etc directory. _____

The answer is cd /etc. If you're taking the exam at a PC, you'll have to type in the answer. If you're taking the exam in paper and pencil format, you'll have to write the answer on a line to the right of the lettered answers.

For more information about all available certifications from the Linux Professional Institute, please visit http://www.lpi.org.

To contact LPI with any questions or comments, call (916) 357-6625 or send an e-mail to info@lpi.org. The LPI mission statement is to "promote and certify essential skills on Linux and Open Source technologies through the global delivery of comprehensive, top-quality, vendor-independent exams."

Although LPI is a not-for-profit based in Canada, exams are delivered worldwide in a number of languages, including English, German, Japanese, French, Chinese, Spanish, and Portuguese.

LPI exams are specially developed to measure competencies of actual Linux professionals. For this reason, the LPI exams include fill-in-the-blank questions, where spelling and syntax matter. In addition, although the multiple choice multiple answer and multiple choice single answer questions are not unprecedented, the questions include, per https://www.lpi.org/eng/certification/faq/faq_on_exams, "obscure options for commands."

The contents of this training material were created for the LPI Certification Level 1 (LPIC-1) 101 and 102 exams covering LPIC-1 certification objectives that were current as of April 1, 2009.

The Linux Professional Institute has not reviewed or approved the accuracy of the contents of this training material and specifically disclaims any warranties of merchantability or fitness for a particular purpose. LPI makes no guarantee concerning the success of persons using any such "Authorized" or other training material to prepare for any LPI certification exam.

On the Day of the Exam

The LPIC-1 exams are surprisingly difficult. So once you have the skills, make sure you have a clear head on the day of the exam. Make sure you've eaten an appropriate meal. Each test center has different policies on whether you can take snacks or (caffeinated) beverages into the exam room. If you feel the need for such help, call the exam center.

If you want a last-minute review, reread the objectives. Then reread key terms from each chapter. And good luck!

PART I

LPI Exam 101

Chapter 1

System Architecture

After completing this chapter, you will be able to

■ Select appropriate Linux distributions

■ Use a variety of commands and files for hardware detection and management

■ Take advantage of the features in the GRUB boot loader menu

■ Describe the boot process in detail

■ Manage services and runlevels like a responsible administrator

Introduction

The first topic in the objectives for the Linux Professional Institute Certification Level 1 (**LPIC-1**) is **System Architecture**, the high-level overview of the organization of Linux and how it interacts with hardware. In this book, you'll systematically examine each topic as defined in the objectives for Exams 101 and 102, as defined at http://www.lpi.org.

In the past, the **Linux Professional Institute** (LPI) assumed that candidates for its LPIC Level 1 exams had at least a year's worth of experience with Linux. If you pass this exam, you're qualified as a Linux power user, at least according to the developers of the LPI exams. Because these exams assume some level of experience, this book is designed for people with at least a few months of Linux experience at the **command-line interface**.

In this chapter, you'll examine each topic, command, utility, and file, as specified in the LPIC-1 objectives, in three areas, which correspond to objective topics 101.1, 101.2, and 101.3. Under "Determine Hardware and Configure Settings," you'll examine the Hardware Abstraction Layer (HAL), find currently detected hardware, and manage peripherals. In the "Boot the System" section, you'll see how to make best use of the boot loader menu and understand the boot process. In the "Service Setting Management" section, you'll learn the responsible methods for managing services.

 TIP

This chapter addresses three objectives in the LPI exam: 101.1 ("Determine and Configure Hardware Settings"), 101.2 ("Boot the System"), and 101.3 ("Change Runlevels and Shutdown or Reboot System").

A Brief Overview of Linux and the LPI Exams

Linux owes its success to the efforts of a community. Although it was originally built as a clone of UNIX, it has grown. As an open source operating system, it is distributed without license fees. That can lead to significant savings over the hundreds of servers and thousands of desktops in a typical enterprise. But this savings would not be significant unless Linux worked. And it does work. It's enterprise ready. It's also the platform for enterprise-intensive applications. And now it's the standard platform for **Apache**, the most popular Web server on the Internet.

Enterprises that use Linux are looking for qualified people. One way that hiring and human resources managers filter through resumes is to look for users who are certified in Linux. To this end, the Linux Professional Institute develops the most popular vendor-neutral Linux certification exams.

Current Requirements

This book focuses on the detailed objectives listed at http://www.lpi.org. Because none of the topics are suitable for an introduction, I jump directly into the requirements in each chapter. I assume that you have some experience with Linux, so some of the terms in this chapter may seem foreign if you have no Linux experience.

The listed objectives cover both the LPIC-1 101 and 102 exams. Exam 101 covers LPI topics 101 through 104. Exam 102 covers LPI topics 105 through 110. Different weights, totaling 60 for each exam, are assigned to each topic and subtopic. As noted in the Introduction, each exam includes 60 questions.

Target Distributions

The LPI exams are vendor neutral. The objectives include commands available from two Linux package types, developed for the **Debian** and **Red Hat** distributions. Out of the hundreds of Linux distributions available, I chose two for this book.

First, to represent the Debian style of Linux distributions, I've selected Ubuntu (http://www.ubuntu.com). Sponsored by **Canonical**, **Ubuntu** is perhaps the most popular Linux distribution in use today. Its releases are representative of the Debian-style Linux distributions, and they are much more popular than the Debian distributions from which it has been developed. The most stable release of an Ubuntu Linux distribution available at the time of this writing is **Hardy Heron**; because it was released in April 2008, it is also known as 8.04, based on the year (2008) and month (04) of the release.

Second, to represent the Red Hat style of distributions, I've selected CentOS (http://www.centos.org). Whereas Red Hat releases the most popular Linux distribution in the enterprise, Red Hat requires a subscription to get updates. And that can be expensive. Fortunately, Red Hat releases virtually all the package components of Red Hat Enterprise Linux under open source licenses. **CentOS**, the Community ENTerprise Operating System, takes this source code and strips out Red Hat logos to avoid trademark issues to create a compatible distribution. The most stable release of CentOS Linux available at the time of this writing is known as CentOS 5, which is based on the source code released by Red Hat for Red Hat Enterprise Linux 5. It was first released in mid-2007. (I'm actually using CentOS 5.2, which mirrors the second major update to Red Hat Enterprise Linux 5, also known as version 5.2.)

Over the lifetime of this exam, there will be numerous distributions released with more features. However, it is almost certain that some of these new features will go beyond what is covered in the current LPI exams.

For more information on the objectives and how they're covered throughout the book, see the Introduction. I also include detailed information on how you can download the target distribution releases: Ubuntu Hardy Heron and CentOS 5.

Determine Hardware and Configure Settings

Linux once had problems detecting whole categories of hardware. **Winmodems**, which use Microsoft driver libraries, were difficult to configure. Wireless cards took a lot of work to configure. But today, these problems are in the past.

With HAL, Linux detects most hardware automatically—as soon as each component is connected. HAL is documented on modern Linux filesystems in directories such as /sys and /proc. With the right commands, you can learn a lot about currently detected hardware, whether it's part of the motherboard or connected as PCI (Peripheral Component Interconnect) or USB (Universal Serial Bus) cards. For those hardware components where drivers are not installed, you'll learn how to install them and confirm that they're properly loaded.

NOTE

This section is focused on LPI Exam 101 Objective 101.1, "Determine and Configure Hardware Settings."

The Hardware Abstraction Layer and the Daemon

HAL is the software that lies between the physical hardware and the body of the operating system. The LPI objectives suggest that you need a conceptual understanding of the four major components of HAL: sysfs, udev, hald, and dbus. It also suggests that you need a basic understanding of the use of the /sys, /proc, and /dev directories.

HAL works through a kernel device manager that listens to connectors for events, especially when hardware is installed and removed. When such events are detected, the **udev** system creates (or removes) appropriate devices to enable communication between the operating system and hardware. The hardware abstraction layer daemon (**hald**) maintains that database of hardware currently connected to the system. Finally, the **dbus** system enables communication between hardware as documented and actual running processes.

The System Filesystem and /sys Directories

HAL documents settings in a virtual filesystem, known as the system filesystem (**sysfs**). First implemented for Linux kernel 2.6, it's populated in several different categories, in appropriate subdirectories as described in Table 1.1.

Although additional directories may be included in the /sys directory filesystem, the subdirectories shown in the table include the common elements as documented in the original sysfs specification. For more information, see http://www.kernel.org/pub/linux/kernel/people/mochel/doc/papers/ols-2005/mochel.pdf.

Table 1.1 Virtual /sys Subdirectories

/sys Subdirectory	Function
block/	Contains subdirectories for each block device, such as hda for the first PATA (Primary ATA) hard drive
bus/	Includes subdirectories for hardware connections, from those which connect via ACPI (Advanced Configuration and Power Interface) to USB
class/	Represents every device class registered with the kernel
devices/	Contains the hierarchy of detected devices
firmware/	Includes objects associated with firmware drivers
module/	Specifies directories for each loaded kernel module

The /proc Directories

The /proc directory is a virtual filesystem, populated dynamically during the boot process. Whenever there's a change to hardware, it's written dynamically to files in the /proc directory and subdirectories. For example, take a look at the /proc/cpuinfo file. The file shown in Figure 1.1 displays detection data for two CPUs. In this case, it's an expression of the dual-core

```
processor       : 0
vendor id       : GenuineIntel
cpu family      : 6
model           : 15
model name      : Intel(R) Core(TM)2 CPU       T7200  @ 2.00GHz
stepping        : 6
cpu MHz         : 1000.000
cache size      : 4096 KB
physical id     : 0
siblings        : 2
core id         : 0
cpu cores       : 2
fdiv bug        : no
hlt bug         : no
f00f bug        : no
coma bug        : no
fpu             : yes
fpu exception   : yes
cpuid level     : 10
wp              : yes
flags           : fpu vme de pse tsc msr pae mce cx8 apic sep mtrr pge mca cmov
pat pse36 clflush dts acpi mmx fxsr sse sse2 ss ht tm pbe nx lm constant_tsc arc
h_perfmon pebs bts pni monitor ds_cpl vmx est tm2 ssse3 cx16 xtpr lahf_lm
bogomips        : 3999.11
clflush size    : 64

processor       : 1
vendor id       : GenuineIntel
cpu family      : 6
:
```

FIGURE 1.1 *Linux detects two CPUs on this system.*

CPU on the laptop being used to write this book. If you read the contents of the /proc directory, you'll see a bunch of numbers, which correspond to the **process identifier** (PID) numbers associated with running processes. A few other interesting settings are listed in Table 1.2.

Table 1.2 Virtual /proc Files

/proc File	Description
cmdline	Top-level root directory information defined in the **boot loader** configuration file
cpuinfo	Detailed information on all detected CPUs; multicore CPUs are detected as if they are separate CPUs
dma	Allocated DMA (Direct Memory Addresses)
iomeom	Assigned I/O (Input/Output) memory
interrupts	Occupied IRQ (Interrupt Request) ports
meminfo	Detailed information on memory allocation
modules	Information on loaded kernel modules
mounts	Currently mounted filesystems
partitions	Assigned partition devices with block sizes

You can change some kernel settings through files in the /proc directories. For example, there are specific /proc directory files that control IP packet forwarding—for IP version 4 as well as IP version 6 addresses. The following command, run as the administrative root user, activates IP version 4 packet forwarding until the next reboot:

```
# echo "1" > /proc/sys/net/ipv4/ip_forward
```

Although the file and associated directive vary by distribution, they're controlled during the boot process by a setting in the /etc/sysctl.conf configuration file.

For most distributions, the key directive has been net.ipv4.ip_forward, which is a Boolean variable. In other words, if this is set to 1, packet forwarding for IP version 4 networks is enabled—at least as soon as the changes to this file are read with the **sysctl** -p command. It's also implemented the next time this Linux system is started.

The udev System and the /dev Directory

The udev system is the device manager for Linux operating systems associated with kernel version 2.6. It works as the manager of files in the /dev directory.

Files in the /dev directory fall into several categories. When block devices are detected, they're assigned a /dev/ file for communication. For example, drives, partitions, volumes, and

RAID (Redundant Array of Independent Disks) arrays may all have their own device files in the /dev directory. Several loop devices are available in this directory for mounting images. Many terminal devices are shown in /dev for terminal consoles, such as the command-line consoles available from the first six terminals.

Many of these files are created as appropriate hardware is detected; for example, if the first SATA drive on the local system has 10 partitions, the udev system detects these partitions and creates the /dev/sda1 through /dev/sda10 device files.

One important part of device management is partition management, especially as it relates to the partition that contains the /boot directory. Although the /boot directory is normally configured on a separate partition, it can also be included on the same partition as the top-level root directory (/). However, it's generally not configured on a RAID array or a logical volume.

Set the Correct Hardware ID for Different Devices, Especially the Boot Device

To identify the partition with the /boot directory, run the mount command. From the following output, you can identify /dev/sda1 as the partition device associated with the /boot directory.

```
/dev/sda1 on /boot type ext3 (rw)
```

If no such output exists with the mount command, make sure the contents of the /boot directory are available, with a command such as ls /boot. Under those circumstances, the /boot directory would be included in the partition or volume with the top-level root directory. In that case, you'd look for output similar to the following:

```
/dev/hda2 on / type ext3 (rw)
```

This means that the hardware device file with boot files is /dev/hda2, which corresponds to the second partition on the first PATA hard drive.

The dbus System

The dbus system enables IPC (interprocess communication), with a focus on desktop applications. Hardware features that prompt for actions on a graphical desktop environment work through dbus. The dbus system enables graphical desktop environments to automatically mount devices such as USB keys—or even start appropriate multimedia applications when a digital media device such as an iPod is detected.

Currently Detected Hardware

Every systems administrator needs to know how to find detailed information for just about every detected hardware component. But there are modest limits on what Linux (or any operating system) can detect. Linux tools don't read the manufacturer of the lights on a physical system because a light (or power connector) doesn't have an internal chip that includes information about its identity.

You can learn a lot about the devices connected to the local system with various list commands—including the hardware resources associated with each device. The lsmod command lists currently loaded modules; many are device drivers that enable communication with different hardware components. For example, the lsmod | grep cpu command, as shown in Figure 1.2, can reveal a lot about the functionality associated with the CPU.

```
michael@UbuntuHH:~$ lsmod | grep cpu
acpi_cpufreq         10796  1
cpufreq_stats         7104  0
cpufreq_ondemand      9740  1
cpufreq_userspace     5284  0
cpufreq_powersave     2688  0
cpufreq_conservative  8712  0
freq_table            5536  3 acpi_cpufreq,cpufreq_stats,cpufreq_ondemand
processor            36872  4 acpi_cpufreq,thermal
michael@UbuntuHH:~$ ▌
```

FIGURE 1.2 *The modules listed with the* lsmod *command can reveal more.*

Then there's the lspci command, which can reveal important details of hardware connected through the PCI bus. The output shown here, from the last line of output on my laptop system, is a good sign for the use of my wireless card; it even identifies the manufacturer, model, and revision level of the card.

```
0c:00.0 Network controller: Intel Corporation PRO/Wireless 3945ABG Network Connection
(rev 02)
```

If there were some problem with the wireless card, more information is available with the -v or even the -vv switches. For example, the lspci -v command reveals the following about the same wireless card—including associated hardware resources:

```
0c:00.0 Network controller: Intel Corporation PRO/Wireless 3945ABG Network Connection
(rev 02)
     Subsystem: Intel Corporation Unknown device 1020
     Flags: bus master, fast devsel, latency 0, IRQ 220
     Memory at efdff000 (32-bit, non-prefetchable) [size=4K]
     Capabilities: [c8] Power Management version 2
     Capabilities: [d0] Message Signalled Interrupts: Mask- 64bit+ Queue=0/0 Enable+
     Capabilities: [e0] Express Legacy Endpoint IRQ 0
```

Not only should that be enough information to find an available Linux driver for that card, but it provides information on the IRQ, memory footprint, power management, and more.

Similar to lspci is the lspcmcia command. The difference is that it's focused on cards currently inserted into a PC Card slot. It doesn't work on the newer "Express Cards"; cards in those slots (which have a different form factor relative to PC Cards) can generally be detected with the lspci command.

Also similar to lspci is the **lsusb** command. From this excerpt of the output, we can see a couple of USB devices connected through Bus 005.

```
Bus 005 Device 009: ID 05ac:1262 Apple Computer, Inc.
Bus 005 Device 008: ID 04e8:1623 Samsung Electronics Co., Ltd
Bus 005 Device 001: ID 0000:0000
```

Running the lsusb -v command yields more information, including the mass storage characteristics of both devices. As you might suspect, the first device is an iPod, and an lsusb -v command provides information on audio input and output characteristics.

 TIP

Before disconnecting a USB (or an **IEEE 1394**) media device such as a portable hard drive, make sure that partitions from that drive are not mounted. Otherwise, any data currently being transferred between drives may be lost.

Finally, prepare to be overwhelmed with information. The **lshal** command displays all devices connected and detected via HAL. When I try this command on my laptop and desktop systems, I see about 120 devices on each. Detected devices include those revealed in the output to the lspci and lsusb commands.

The **lshw** command provides similar information—focused on internal system components. It should either be run from the root account or with the sudo lshw command. It's in a more useful format for regular administrators. Figure 1.3 reveals just the start of detected capabilities of the motherboard.

```
ubuntuhhserver
    description: Desktop Computer
    product: PROD00000000
    vendor: OEM00000
    width: 32 bits
    capabilities: smbios-2.3 dmi-2.3 smp-1.4 smp
    configuration: boot=normal chassis=desktop cpus=0 uuid=00000000-0000-0000-00
E0-00004CE3D106
  *-core
      description: Motherboard
      product: K8M800-8237
      physical id: 0
    *-firmware
        description: BIOS
        vendor: Phoenix Technologies, LTD
        physical id: 0
        version: 6.00 PG (09/07/1905)
        size: 128KiB
        capacity: 448KiB
        capabilities: isa pci pnp apm upgrade shadowing cdboot bootselect sock
etedrom edd int13floppy360 int13floppy1200 int13floppy720 int13floppy2880 int5pr
intscreen int9keyboard int14serial int17printer int10video acpi usb agp ls120boo
t zipboot biosbootspecification
:
```

FIGURE 1.3 *The lshw command says a lot about the motherboard.*

NOTE

The LPIC exams assume that you've logged in as the root user. However, many administrators don't trust the practice and follow the Ubuntu model, in which all administrative commands are prefaced with the sudo command. When authorized, sudo gives regular users nearly full administrative access, also known as superuser permissions. For more information, see Chapter 15, "Security Administration."

LOG IN AS ROOT

Although the LPIC-1 exams assume that a user is logged in as the root administrative user, many Linux gurus dislike the practice. In fact, default Ubuntu installations do not include a password for the root user. To log in as a root user in Ubuntu, log in as the first regular user and run the sudo su command. Next, enter your user password. Then enter the su - command to assume root account settings.

If you see the hash mark (#) in place of the dollar sign ($) as the command prompt, you're logged in as the root user. If desired, you can then run the passwd command to create a password for that user.

If you don't log in as the root user, you may need to specify the full directory path to many administrative commands. For more information, see Chapter 4, "Command Lines and Files."

Out of respect for those who log into the root account only when necessary, I specify the regular user prompt ($), where the use of the administrative account makes no difference.

Peripheral Management

Courtesy of HAL, you can deduce a lot of information about most components connected to the local system. Most peripherals are also included in the output to the lshal command. However, this information does not extend to all external peripherals, such as printers.

Peripherals are components connected to a computer system that do not contribute to—and are not part of—the system core architecture. The definition of peripherals is fuzzy; for example, some believe that graphics cards are integral to the system core architecture. Peripherals as expressed in the LPI objectives are devices that can be installed and removed and are driven by modules that can be listed with the lsmod command.

Not all such peripherals are "hotplug" devices; in other words, you have to power down a system before removing (or installing) internal peripherals such as **PATA** (Parallel Advanced

Technology Attachment) or **SATA** (Serial Advanced Technology Attachment) hard drives. In the words of the LPI objectives, such peripherals are "coldplug" devices.

 NOTE

The LPIC-1 objectives include a reference to system configuration "without external peripherals such as keyboards." Although such configurations are common for servers, they may require a specialized setting in the BIOS boot menu described later in this chapter. Remote configuration is also possible with the SSH service described in Chapter 15.

Peripheral Driver Management

Although Linux has made excellent progress with hardware, it doesn't detect and configure all peripherals. For that matter, Microsoft Windows, especially Vista, has a similar (or greater) degree of difficulty working with hardware. Sometimes the driver just needs to be added, or perhaps a conflicting driver needs to be removed.

With the same techniques, peripherals can be enabled and disabled. In other words, to disable a peripheral, you can remove the associated driver module; to enable that peripheral, you would load the appropriate driver module. All the commands in this section are located in the /sbin directory.

As an example, I'll demonstrate on one of my virtual machines. The **rmmod** command is the standard for removing modules. Let's look at the applicable modules. The following is the output of the lsmod | grep pcnet32 command.

```
pcnet32      35141  0
mii           9409  1  pcnet32
```

The pcnet32 module, a standard driver for a network card, depends on the mii module. This module drives the "Media Independent Interface," which regulates network communication. You could try to remove the mii module with the rmmod mii command, but that would lead to an error message pointing to the dependency. You could also remove the pcnet32 module, but that may not take care of the dependency. You can avoid such issues by removing both modules simultaneously.

Now try to reverse the process; the **insmod** command is designed to insert a module in the current configuration. But if you try to run the insmod pcnet32 command, you might receive the following message:

```
insmod: can't read 'pcnet32': No such file or directory
```

To make that command work, you'd have to cite the full path and the full name of the module. But with dependencies, that doesn't always work. That's one reason for the development of the **modprobe** command. It's sort of like the yum or apt-get commands for package management (see Chapter 3, "Packet Management Systems") in that it incorporates and loads dependent modules. To install `pcnet32` and `mii` modules simultaneously, all you need to run is the `modprobe pcnet32` command. Alternatively, to remove both modules, run the `modprobe -r pcnet32` command.

Different Types of Mass Storage Devices

Various mass storage devices are available. There are the standard internal devices, specifically hard drives and CD/DVD drives. Floppy drives, where they still exist, are also internal drives. Then there are the external drives; with current technologies, they're primarily connected through USB and IEEE 1394 ports. Let's examine each of these options.

 NOTE

IEEE 1394 is a standard of the Institute of Electrical and Electronics Engineers, more commonly known by its trade names: FireWire and iLink.

Internal Hard Drives

Internal hard drives are the primary storage medium for most computers today. The three major drive types are PATA, SATA, and **SCSI** (Small Computer Systems Interface). This section is focused on the devices as a whole; for more information on partitions, see Chapter 2, "Configure a System for Linux."

PATA drives are the new name for drives based on the old IDE (Integrated Drive Electronics) interface, also known as ATA (Advanced Technology Attachment) drives. Until relatively recently, most PCs used PATA drives. Such PCs typically included up to four PATA drives, connected to a primary and a secondary controller. You could connect up to two drives to each controller. One connector on each controller was designated as the master; the second connector on each controller was designated as the slave. Device files were allocated based on their position, as described in Table 1.3.

Table 1.3 PATA Device Files

Device File	Controller	Position
/dev/hda	Primary	Master
/dev/hdb	Primary	Slave
/dev/hdc	Secondary	Master
/dev/hdd	Secondary	Slave

Although hard drives or CD/DVD drives can be configured with PATA interfaces, some PATA drives may be associated with other device files. For example, many CD/DVD drives, even when attached to PATA primary or secondary controllers, are assigned device file /dev/scd0. In some cases, even PATA hard drives may be assigned SATA drive device files.

Despite the name, each SATA drive is connected to different ports on a motherboard. However, although the latest SATA standards are backward compatible with the latest SCSI drives, SATA is designed for regular PCs. The device files associated with SATA drives are more straightforward; the first SATA drive is given device file /dev/sda; the second SATA drive is given device file /dev/sdb; and so on.

SCSI drives are serial in nature; in other words, one serial drive is connected directly to a controller; the second serial drive is connected to that first drive. As such, they follow the same device file protocol as SATA drives; the first SCSI drive on a system is /dev/sda; the second SCSI drive is designated /dev/sdb; and so on.

External Mass Storage Devices

There are other types of mass storage devices. Common options are housed externally and connected with either a USB or IEEE 1394 cable. In either case, the device is configured as if it were a serial device. For example, when I attach a portable USB hard drive and then a USB key on my desktop system, the two are configured as /dev/sdd and /dev/sde, respectively.

Boot the System

The LPI exam objectives cover two major boot loaders: **GRUB** and LILO. These are acronyms for the Grand Unified Boot Loader and the Linux Loader. But the acronyms aren't important. GRUB is the default boot loader for the major Linux distributions today. So you'll focus on GRUB, as well as how you can take advantage of the GRUB Boot Loader menu. You'll learn about the boot process, along with how it's documented in various log files. You will examine a basic LILO menu in Chapter 2.

 NOTE

This section is focused on LPI Exam 101 Objective 101.2, "Boot the System." Part of this section overlaps with Objective 102.2, "Install a Boot Manager," at least with respect to the "Interact with the boot loader" knowledge area.

Use the GRUB Boot Loader Menu

Many Linux distributions now hide the GRUB boot loader menu during the boot process. If you don't do anything, the only evidence you'll see of a boot loader menu is a message like the following. The message flashes by in less than 5 seconds, unless timeout is set to 0 in the /boot/grub/menu.1st configuration file described shortly.

```
Press 'Esc' to Enter the Menu...
```

 NOTE

The terms "boot loader" and "bootloader" are used interchangeably; both are used in Linux documentation. The remainder of this book will use "boot loader" unless otherwise specified by the output to a command or utility.

A GRUB menu appears; one example is shown in Figure 1.4. The GRUB menu is commonly password protected. If a message suggests that you need to press **p** to enter a password, you'll have to either find or disable that password. The steps to do this are beyond the scope of the LPI exam.

```
Ubuntu 8.04, kernel 2.6.24-16-virtual
Ubuntu 8.04, kernel 2.6.24-16-virtual (recovery mode)
Other operating systems:
Ubuntu 7.10, kernel 2.6.22-14-server (on /dev/sdb1)
Ubuntu 7.10, kernel 2.6.22-14-server (recovery mode) (on /dev/sdb1)
Ubuntu 7.10, memtest86+ (on /dev/sdb1)




    Use the ↑ and ↓ keys to select which entry is highlighted.
    Press enter to boot the selected OS, 'e' to edit the
    commands before booting, or 'c' for a command-line.
```

FIGURE 1.4 *A typical GRUB menu.*

There are three basic options at the main GRUB menu. Unless you've never installed a new kernel, chances are good that you'll have at least two options available to highlight. These options in the main GRUB menu window are either different kernels, or different operating systems. If you highlight an option and press Enter, the system boots into the selected kernel.

The two other options appear below the menu window. The e command allows you to edit the stanza of directives associated with the highlighted option. The c command starts a command line at a grub> prompt, which supports the use of selected commands, some of which you'll examine in Chapter 2. However, the LPI objectives suggest that you also need to know how to "provide common commands to the boot loader and options to the kernel at boot time."

 NOTE

Some distributions include a fourth GRUB menu option, an a command that directly accesses the kernel command line. This is useful for booting into a different runlevel such as 1 for single user mode.

Change GRUB Boot Loader Options

If errors during the boot process prevent Linux from booting, examine the target stanza to look for errors.

No changes made through the GRUB menu are permanent. The next time this system is booted, the original configuration is restored. Permanent changes require editing the GRUB configuration file, typically the menu.1st file in the /boot/grub/ directory.

Let's examine the following GRUB stanza:

```
root (hd0,0)
kernel /vmlinuz-2.6.18-92.1.18.el5 ro root=/dev/VolGroup/LogVol00 rhgb quiet
initrd /initrd-2.6.18-92.1.18.el5.img
```

First, be aware that there are two different meanings for the word root in this stanza. The first line, root (hd0,0), specifies the location of the /boot directory, which contains critical boot files, such as the Linux kernel and the **initial RAM disk**. The (hd0,0) looks for these files on the first partition of the first configured hard drive. If it were (hd0,2), it would look for the /boot directory on the third partition of the first hard drive.

For clarity, I'll split the explanation of the second line into two parts. The kernel directive looks for the Linux kernel. The first forward slash assumes the kernel is in the top directory of the partition, as defined by the root (hd0,0) directive. The file that follows is the file name of the actual Linux kernel.

The ro mounts the top-level root directory that follows. This particular directive would work if that directory were mounted as a logical volume, on the device file /dev/VolGroup/LogVol00. If the top-level root directory were mounted on a regular partition, you'd see a device file such as /dev/sda2, which would point to the second partition on the first SATA or SCSI hard drive on the local system. The rhgb and quiet specify a Red Hat Graphical Boot with many boot messages hidden.

NOTE

One common option for booting into single user mode is based on editing the kernel line from a target GRUB menu option. On most distributions, to access single user mode, add the number 1 after the end of the line. Although it's not covered in the LPIC-1 objectives, the Upstart system has changed this on the latest Ubuntu distributions; a "recovery mode" is made available in the GRUB menu that supports access to single user mode. Other distributions may have variations; for example, SUSE Linux requires the root administrative password to access single user mode.

Finally, the initrd line specifies the location of the initial RAM disk, which is a temporary filesystem booted to enable the booting, mounting, and configuration of the actual Linux operating system.

You can also access the GRUB command line from this screen by pressing c. (Linux is so case sensitive that an uppercase C doesn't work even in current GRUB menus.) At the grub> prompt, type help to see a list of available commands. The objective from this command line is to enter those commands required to boot an operating system. So from the sample stanza previously described, try the root (hd0,0) command. If it's a partition formatted to one of the standard Linux filesystem formats, you'll see the following output:

```
(hd0,0): Filesystem type is ext2fs, partition type 0x83
```

This is the output you'll see if the partition is mounted to either the Linux second extended (ext2) or third extended (ext3) filesystems. Try the same command with different numbers. You'll learn more about how GRUB works with partitions.

If it is in fact the filesystem for the /boot directory, you'll be able to confirm it with the next command. Start with the kernel / command, and press the Tab key. If successful, the command completion features will list all files in the current directory. If it's the right directory, you'll find the kernel and initial RAM disk files here. With the help of command completion, problems related to spelling or typing errors should be kept to a minimum.

Review the Boot Process

The boot process starts when a system is powered up and is essentially done when you're able to log into the local system. The first parts of the boot process happen before it touches any part of the Linux operating system. As suggested by the objectives, you need to "demonstrate knowledge of the boot sequence from BIOS to boot completion." To that end, you should understand the basics of the **BIOS** (Basic Input/Output System), the workings of the boot loader, when Linux loads the kernel, as well as the first process, known as **init**. The previous section included detailed information on the boot loader.

The system BIOS works first through the Power-On Self Test (POST) to test for proper connections of detected components such as RAM and internal cards. If there's a problem such as a loose connection, you may hear a beep. Details are almost as varied as the motherboard configurations that are available; fortunately, they are beyond the scope of the LPI exams.

Modern BIOS systems take advantage of the ACPI specification, which is the standard not only for power management but for the information received when devices are detected. The alternative Advanced Power Management system is essentially obsolete today. However, if you have trouble booting a Linux system due to a legacy device, it may be possible to disable ACPI either in the BIOS or during the Linux boot process. Fortunately, details of the many varied BIOS menus are beyond the scope of the LPI objectives. Disabling ACPI is an option covered in Chapter 2.

Hardware data is collected and can be customized through the BIOS menu. Access to such menus is often hidden; access keys such as Esc, F2, and Delete are manufacturer specific. Key options include the boot sequence, network boot access, and password protection. You could boot from a "Live CD" to start a fully functional version of several Linux distributions. But in most cases, the BIOS hands off the boot process to the first 512 bytes of the first or second hard drives—specifically, in a region known as the **MBR** (Master Boot Record) of such drives. If the standard Linux GRUB boot loader is properly configured, a pointer in the MBR reads information from the GRUB configuration file, normally /boot/grub/menu.lst. For more information on configuring this file, see Chapter 2.

If Linux is booted through GRUB, the selected kernel is associated with a stanza of settings. As described in the previous section, it loads a kernel as well as an initial RAM disk located on the /boot directory. HAL also works during the boot process to detect hardware and load drivers as needed. Then the init process is started, followed by the services at the default runlevel, as described later in this chapter.

 NOTE

For at least a couple of major Linux distributions, init is being replaced. Because the Upstart system is designed as a drop-in replacement for init, the developers behind the LPI exam chose to keep Upstart out of the 2009 exam revision. The Hardy Heron release of Ubuntu Linux, and even Red Hat's Fedora 11 are configured with Upstart, so you'll need to rely on the CentOS 5 system (or another older distribution) to learn init, especially related files such as /etc/inittab. The init files are described in more detail later in this chapter.

Boot Process Log Files

If you want to know more about what happens during the boot process, read the log files. The messages that relate to the boot process are stored in the /var/log/dmesg log file. Because this is the kernel ring buffer, events that change the kernel or related modules are also recorded in this file. For a cleaner view of the messages that occur just during the boot process, run the **dmesg** command.

Although system logs are discussed in Chapter 12, a quick reading of the associated /etc/syslog.conf configuration file confirms that a number of standard messages are sent to the /var/log/messages file, a common "catch-all" logging file.

Take a look at the /var/log/dmesg file. Compare it side by side with the output to the dmesg command. If you've just booted Linux, the contents of these files will be nearly identical. They commonly include messages associated with fundamental parts of the local system, such as the BIOS, CPU, RAM, power management, motherboard busses, USB hubs, and hard drive controllers.

Service Setting Management

The way that services are started (or stopped) depends on a concept known as **runlevels**. After Linux starts the init process, it begins booting services that are configured in the default runlevel. The way runlevels are configured varies by distribution. Further variations have been introduced with the Upstart daemon. Although Upstart is not part of the LPI objectives, it is the default for the latest releases from both Ubuntu and the Fedora Project. I summarize Upstart features in this section.

Organized Runlevels

Seven different runlevels are typically configured on a Linux distribution. In most cases, they are numbered 0 through 6. Not all runlevels are used. Different Linux distributions do assign the same functionality to three runlevels:

◆ **Runlevel 0.** Known as the halt runlevel. Services as configured in the /etc/rc0.d/ directory are executed. These services along with the /sbin/halt command are executed, courtesy of the /etc/init.d/halt script.

◆ **Runlevel 1.** Also known as single user mode. Services as configured in the /etc/rc1.d/ directory are run. When a system is booted into this runlevel, it starts a single command-line prompt for the root administrative account. In many Linux distributions, runlevel 1 provides root-level administrative access without password protection. Security associated with runlevel 1 is an important issue, which is why access to the init command is limited to users with administrative privileges.

◆ **Runlevel 6.** Another name for reboot mode. Services as configured in the /etc/rc6.d/ directory are executed. These services, along with the /sbin/halt command, are executed.

Outside of these runlevels, the defaults diverge for the major Linux distributions. The distributions associated with Red Hat packages, including SUSE Linux, configure two default runlevels: 3 for a text console and 5 for a GUI login screen. The distributions associated with Debian packages, including Ubuntu, configure runlevel 2 as the default.

Default runlevels for standard Linux distributions can be configured in the /etc/inittab configuration file. It's a standard file explicitly cited in the LPI objectives.

Manage by Runlevel

Services are started and stopped whenever a system moves between runlevels. Such actions may kick off users who are logged into a service. Responsible administrators therefore need to know how to alert users before shutting down a service. Administrators also need to know how to move a system to single user mode; as specified in the LPI exam objectives, that corresponds to runlevel 1.

Alert Users Prior to Shutdown

Any change in runlevels would kick off any user who is logged into a local server. Hints on how to send a message to users are available in /etc/inittab configuration files. For example, the following directive from an older version of /etc/inittab from a Fedora 10 system points to a message that's sent to users, two minutes before an actual shutdown:

```
pf::powerfail:/sbin/shutdown -f -h +2 "Power Failure; System Shutting Down"
```

As suggested by the man page for the shutdown command, the shutdown -k command can be used to send warning messages. For example, if at 12:50 p.m. I run su -c '/sbin/shutdown -k 13:00 "This system is going down, please logoff.", users will see the following message:

```
Broadcast message from user@localhost.localdomain
        (/dev/pts/0) at 12:50
This system is going down for maintenance in 10 minutes!
This system is going down, please logoff.
```

Courtesy of the -k switch, the system doesn't actually shut down. It does help notify connected users, though. You can then proceed with a desired action such as a shutdown, a reboot, or another change of runlevels, such as a move to single user mode.

Move to Single User Mode

Single user mode can help the administrator solve a number of problems. Lost administrative passwords generally do not matter in this mode. Only one user is connected to a system when it's in single user mode. To navigate to this mode, you can use the init or **telinit** commands. However, this action kicks off any currently logged on users, so a responsible administrator first sends a warning. The previous section described one way to send that warning.

It's easy to bring a system to single user mode. Just run the `init 1` or `telinit 1` command. The process on Ubuntu systems, starting with the Hardy Heron release, is a bit more complex; any move to runlevel 1 brings up the recovery menu shown in Figure 1.5. You'd also see this menu if Recovery Mode were selected from the GRUB menu during the boot process. From that menu, to actually start runlevel 1, select the Drop to Root Shell Prompt option.

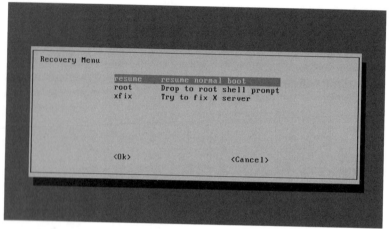

FIGURE 1.5 *Single user mode is a recovery mode.*

Shut Down and Reboot from the Command Line

As suggested earlier, there are `shutdown` and `init` commands that can bring a system to the shutdown or reboot runlevels. Some of this is intuitive; the `shutdown` and `reboot` commands to shut down and reboot a system. The `shutdown -r 2` command shuts down and then reboots the system, in two minutes.

Alternatively, you can use the `init` and `telinit` commands to shut down or reboot a system. As described earlier, **shutdown** mode is associated with runlevel 0, whereas reboot mode is associated with runlevel 6. Thus, to shut down or reboot a system, run the `telinit 0` or `telinit 6` command. Although the `telinit` command is nominally preferred for changing runlevels, the `init` command works equally well.

   NOTE

One other use for changing runlevels can bypass problems with the GUI. On Red Hat–type distributions, runlevel 5 is the default for logging into the GUI desktop. If the GUI has problems, it's still possible to log into a system at runlevel 3. To move to that runlevel, run the `telinit 3` command.

Properly Terminate a Process

The scripts in the /etc/init.d directory are designed to control processes. In general, such processes are run by daemons in the /usr/sbin directory. The scripts in the /etc/init.d directory provide a terrific convenience, because they support more than just the indiscriminate starting and stopping of a server process.

The options are listed at the bottom of each script in the /etc/init.d/ directory. Typical options are listed in Table 1.4.

Table 1.4 Command Options for /etc/init.d/ Scripts

/etc/init.d/ Script Option	Description
start	Starts the associated service.
stop	Stops the associated service.
reload	Reloads the associated configuration files without stopping or restarting a service. Can incorporate configuration changes without kicking off users.
restart	Stops and then restarts the associated service
force-reload	Restarts or reloads a service; the action is script specific.
status	Returns the current state of the associated service.

The proper termination of a process may require a couple of steps. First, responsible administrators warn current users that the process is about to stop. For example, users who are currently editing documents housed on a remote system deserve warning that a service is about to stop. One way you can warn users—without actually shutting down a system—is with the shutdown -k command described earlier. You can then terminate the process with the /etc/init.d/ *service* stop command, where *service* is the associated script in the /etc/init.d/ directory that actually controls the service.

Sometimes such terminations don't work. In that case, you may need to identify and then directly stop the process with the ps and kill commands. For more information, see Chapter 6, "Processes, Priorities, and Editing."

Several services can be controlled by specialized commands. For example, depending on the distribution, you can control the Apache service with the httpd, apachectl, or apache2ctl commands. The LPI Level 1 objectives no longer cover the configuration of the Apache Web browser.

Manage by Upstart

Although Upstart is not covered in the LPI objectives, it is designed as a "drop-in" replacement for the SysV init service, which includes the /etc/inittab configuration file. If you understand how Upstart works, you'll better understand how runlevels are managed on Linux. Because Upstart is not (yet) commonly used on Linux, this section is based on the Ubuntu configuration as of the Hardy Heron release.

NOTE

Even though some major distributions are moving from /etc/inittab to Upstart, the developers behind the LPI exams do not include Upstart in the latest exam objectives.

Upstart configuration files are stored in the /etc/event.d/ directory and have somewhat descriptive file names; for example, the control-alt-delete file drives system actions if the Ctrl, Alt, and Delete keys are pressed simultaneously.

The default runlevel is associated with the rc-default configuration file in this directory. As shown in Figure 1.6, the script looks for a command navigating to single user mode, from the kernel command line. If such a command does not exist, it looks for an existing /etc/inittab configuration file for the default runlevel. But on Ubuntu systems, that file does not exist either. So the default runlevel in that case is configured with the telinit 2 command, runlevel 2.

```
# rc - runlevel compatibility
#
# This task guesses what the "default runlevel" should be and starts the
# appropriate script.

start on stopped rcS

script
        runlevel --reboot || true

        if grep -q -w -- "-s\|single\|S" /proc/cmdline; then
            telinit S
        elif [ -r /etc/inittab ]; then
            RL="$(sed -n -e "/^id:[0-9]*:initdefault:/{s/^id://;s/:.*//;p}" /etc
/inittab || true)"
            if [ -n "$RL" ]; then
                telinit $RL
            else
                telinit 2
            fi
        else
            telinit 2
        fi
end script
"rc-default" [readonly] 23 lines, 485 characters
```

FIGURE 1.6 *Upstart and the default runlevel.*

Chapter Summary

The LPI exams are vendor neutral and include requirements associated with both Debian and Red Hat packages. This book uses the Ubuntu Hardy Heron and CentOS 5 releases to represent both sets of requirements.

Courtesy of HAL, the hardware detection capabilities of Linux are excellent. The capabilities of each hardware component are documented in various parts of the /sys and /proc directories. The /sys directory is mounted under a virtual file system known as sysfs. The udev system may assign device files to various components in the /dev directory. The dbus system enables communication between hardware as configured and the processes running within Linux. You can analyze these components with commands such as lsmod, lspci, lsusb, lshal, and lshw. You can manage drivers with commands such as insmod, rmmod, and modprobe.

The boot process starts with the BIOS and reads a pointer from the MBR of the first drive. That pointer reads the GRUB boot loader configuration file. The GRUB menu, which may be password protected, supports temporary editing of boot configuration commands. The selected kernel, when booted, starts hardware detection, loads the Linux kernel and initial RAM disk from the /boot directory, and loads the first process, known as init. This process can be reviewed in both the /var/log/dmesg file and through the dmesg command.

Services are organized by runlevels. Linux distributions share the same functionality for three runlevels: 0 (halt), 1 (single user mode), and 6 (reboot). The default runlevel varies by distribution type. Responsible administrators know how to manage services with minimal disruption to their users. They alert users before shutting down or rebooting a system. With the reload option, you can make configuration changes without kicking off users. Although some distributions are moving toward the Upstart system for runlevels, it is not yet part of the LPI requirements. Nevertheless, Upstart can be another way to learn about runlevels, because it is configured as a drop-in replacement for the current system.

Key Terms

- **Apache.** The most popular Web server software on the Internet.
- **BIOS.** The first Basic Input/Output System for a computer; includes a menu where you can collect and customize hardware data.
- **boot loader.** A transition between the BIOS and the operating system, normally located in the first 512 bytes of the first or second hard drive.
- **Canonical.** The corporate sponsor behind the Ubuntu releases for Linux.
- **CentOS.** The Community ENTerprise operating system, developed from Red Hat Enterprise Linux packages. This book uses the CentOS 5 release.
- **command-line interface.** The Linux command-line shell interface, as indicated by a $ prompt for regular users or a # prompt for the root administrative user.

- **dbus.** A system that enables IPC (interprocess communication), with a focus on desktop applications.

- **Debian.** A Linux distribution; also one of the major Linux package types. Ubuntu is developed from Debian packages.

- **dmesg.** The "kernel-ring buffer" includes boot events. Also refers to the /var/log/dmesg file, which includes events that change the kernel or related modules.

- **GRUB.** Short for the Grand Unified Boot Loader, it's the standard Linux boot loader configured in the /boot/grub/menu.1st file.

- **hald.** The hardware abstraction layer daemon (hald) maintains that database of hardware currently connected to the system.

- **Hardware Abstraction Layer (HAL).** The abstraction software that lies between the physical hardware and the operating system.

- **Hardy Heron.** As of this writing, the latest stable release of Ubuntu by Canonical with long-term support.

- **IEEE 1394.** A standard of the Institute of Electrical and Electronics Engineers, more commonly known by its trade names: FireWire and iLink.

- **init.** A command in the /sbin directory that can change runlevels; telinit is preferred for this purpose.

- **initial RAM disk.** A temporary filesystem that Linux uses during the boot process, before the actual top-level root filesystem is mounted.

- **insmod.** A command in the /sbin directory that inserts a specified module.

- **Linux Professional Institute (LPI).** The organization behind the LPIC-1 exams.

- **LPIC Level 1 (LPIC-1).** The exams developed by LPI to qualify junior-level Linux professionals.

- **lshal.** A command that includes a lot of information about most components connected to the internal system.

- **lshw.** A command similar to lshal, with a focus on internal system components.

- **lsmod.** A command that lists currently installed modules.

- **lspci.** A command that can reveal important details of hardware connected through the PCI (Peripheral Component Interconnect) bus.

- **lspcmcia.** A command that can reveal important details of hardware connected through a PC Card slot.

- **lsusb.** A command that can reveal important details of hardware connected through a USB (Universal Serial Bus) port.

- **MBR.** The Master Boot Record is the first sector, or 512 bytes of a hard drive.

- **modprobe.** A command in the /sbin directory that can insert or remove a specified module, with dependent modules.

◆ **PATA (Parallel Advanced Technology Attachment).** A standard common fc nal hard drives and CD/DVD drives on older PCs. A new acronym for the IL (Integrated Drive Electronics) interface, also known as ATA (Advanced Techn(Attachment) drives.

◆ **Power-On Self Test (POST).** POST tests for proper connections and checks connections to components such as RAM and internal cards. If there's a problem such as a loose connection, you may hear a beep.

◆ **/proc.** The /proc directory is a virtual filesystem, populated dynamically during the boot process.

◆ **process identifier (PID).** A number associated with a running Linux process.

◆ **Red Hat.** The company behind Red Hat Enterprise Linux 5. Its packages are released under open source licenses, which enable third parties such as CentOS to develop releases such as CentOS 5.

◆ **rmmod.** A command in the /sbin directory that removes a specified module.

◆ **runlevel.** A designation for starting or stopping a group of services.

◆ **Runlevel 0.** Known as the halt runlevel; associated with the /etc/rc0.d/ directory.

◆ **Runlevel 1.** Known as single user mode; associated with the /etc/rc1.d/ directory.

◆ **Runlevel 6.** Known as reboot mode; associated with the /etc/rc6.d/ directory.

◆ **SATA (Serial Advanced Technology Attachment).** A standard common for hard drives and CD/DVD drives on the latest PCs. It shares characteristics with SCSI disks. The first SATA drive on a system is normally assigned device file /dev/sda.

◆ **SCSI (Small Computer Systems Interface).** A standard common for hard drives on servers. It shares characteristics with SATA disks. The first SCSI drive on a system is normally assigned device file /dev/sda.

◆ **shutdown.** A command that can be used to shut down, reboot, or send a short message to users.

◆ **sysctl.** A command that reads kernel settings from /etc/sysctl.conf and writes them dynamically to the /proc directory.

◆ **sysfs.** The sysfs is the system filesystem, which is a virtual filesystem for the /sys directory, first implemented for Linux kernel 2.6.

◆ **System Architecture.** A high-level overview of the organization of Linux and how it works with hardware.

◆ **telinit.** A command in the /sbin directory that can change runlevels; similar to (and preferred over) init.

◆ **Ubuntu.** A Linux distribution developed by Canonical. This book uses the Hardy Heron release of Ubuntu.

◆ **udev.** The device manager for Linux operating systems associated with kernel version 2.6, which creates device files in the /dev directory to enable communication between the operating system and the hardware.

◆ **winmodems.** A telephone modem that uses Microsoft Windows driver libraries.

Review Questions

The number of review questions in this chapter and other chapters in this book is proportionate to each section's weight in the LPI objectives. Because this chapter covers items 101.1, 101.2, and 101.3, the total weight is 8; therefore, you'll see 16 questions in this section. You'll see multiple choice single answer, fill-in-the blank, and multiple choice multiple answer questions, as you'll encounter on the exam.

1. Which of the following is the daemon that maintains the current database of connected hardware?

    A. sysfs

    B. udev

    C. hald

    D. dbus

2. Which of the following files includes information on the local CPU?

    A. /sys/cpuinfo

    B. /dev/cpu0

    C. /proc/cpu0

    D. /proc/cpuinfo

3. The _____ command lists all currently loaded modules. Do not specify the full path to the command.

4. Which of the following commands installs the pcnet32 module with dependencies?

    A. modprobe -r pcnet32

    B. insmod pcnet32

    C. insmod -i pcnet32

    D. modprobe pcnet32

5. Which of the following sets of steps most closely represents the boot sequence?

    A. POST, GRUB, initial RAM disk, Kernel, init

    B. BIOS, GRUB, Kernel, initial RAM disk, Kernel

    C. POST, initial RAM disk, GRUB, Kernel, init

    D. BIOS, GRUB, init, initial RAM disk, Kernel

6. Enter the full path to the file with the kernel ring buffer.

    _____

7. In a GRUB menu stanza, what line is typically used to specify booting into single user
    mode?

    A. `root (0,0)`

    B. `kernel`

    C. `initrd`

    D. `grub>`

8. Which of the following files typically contains boot messages? Choose two.

    A. `/var/log/messages`

    B. `/var/log/grub`

    C. `/var/log/dmesg`

    D. `/var/log/kernel`

9. If the local system has two SATA hard drives, and you see `root (hd1,0)` in the
    GRUB menu, which of the following describes the location of the Kernel and initial
    RAM disk?

    A. The first drive, on the MBR

    B. The second drive, on the first partition

    C. The first drive, on the second partition

    D. The `/boot` directory

10. What is the full path to the file that specifies the default runlevel? Assume that
    Upstart is not installed.

    A. `/etc/init`

    B. `/boot/grub/menu.lst`

    C. `/etc/inittab`

    D. `/etc/default`

11. Which of the following runlevels corresponds to single user mode?

    A. 0

    B. 1

    C. 5

    D. 6

12. Which of the following shutdown commands does not actually halt or reboot a system? Assume you're either logged in as the root user or have otherwise acquired administrative privileges.

    A. `shutdown -r now`

    B. `shutdown -f -h +2 "Power Failure; System Shutting Down"`

    C. `shutdown -k 13:00 "This system is going down."`

    D. `shutdown -h now`

13. Enter the command that moves a system toward single user mode. Assume that the local account already has root user privileges, and don't use the full path to the command.

    _____

14. You've just edited the configuration file for the hypothetical bigbig service. Assume that you don't want to kick off currently connected users to implement the new configuration. Which of the following commands incorporates the new configuration file?

    A. `/etc/init.d/bigbig restart`

    B. `/etc/init.d/bigbig reload`

    C. `/etc/init.d/bigbig start`

    D. `/etc/init.d/bigbig force`

15. Which of the following commands does not reboot the system?

    A. `shutdown -r now`

    B. `reboot`

    C. `init 6`

    D. `telinit 0`

16. Which of the following commands is the preferred method to change runlevels? Choose two.

    A. `shutdown`

    B. `init`

    C. `telinit`

    D. `/etc/init.d/rc x`

Chapter 2

Configure a System for Linux

After completing this chapter, you will be able to

■ Configure mount points and partitions for Linux directories

■ Understand options for the boot manager

■ Identify and manage shared libraries

Introduction

This chapter is focused on several basic configuration options. You need to understand the standard purpose of certain Linux directories. When you also understand the variety of partitions and volumes, you can make better decisions on how to configure various Linux systems.

Two boot managers are listed in the LPI objectives: GRUB and **LILO**. Although these boot managers are acronyms, they're not normally spelled out, because terms like Grand Unified Bootloader and Linux Loader are irrelevant. What matters under the exam objectives is an understanding of boot loader locations, configuration files, and basic boot loader management skills.

In addition, shared libraries are common programs by various scripts and applications. As described in the exam objectives, you need to know how to trace the libraries that executable programs often depend on.

The relatively short length of this chapter reflects its relative weight in the LPI objectives. There is just as much (or little) emphasis on the topics in this chapter as there is in Chapter 10, "The GUI Desktop Environment."

 TIP

This chapter addresses three objectives in the LPI exam: 102.1 ("Design Hard Disk Layout"), 102.2 ("Install the Boot Manager"), and 102.3 ("Manage Shared Libraries").

Manage a Hard Disk

Before installing any Linux distribution on a production system, you need to know the functionality of the Linux directory tree, which is based on the FHS (Filesystem Hierarchy Standard). Understanding this standard can help you "tailor the design" of a Linux installation for different functions from Web servers to DNS services.

Once you understand the FHS, the next step is to configure partitions. You can configure FHS directories either directly on a partition, or on a hybrid device such as an LV (Logical Volume) or a **RAID** (Redundant Array of Independent Disks) array. One special case relates to the /boot directory. Although there are ways to make alternatives work, most Linux systems should not be configured to mount the /boot directory on anything but a regular partition.

TIP

It is possible to configure the /boot directory on a RAID array, but associated skills are beyond the scope of the LPIC-1 objectives.

Appropriate Directory Mount Points

This section assumes that you have a basic understanding of the FHS, the standard method for organizing files and directories on Linux. Different directories are reserved for different functions. In several cases, the directory name is at least somewhat descriptive. For example, the /home directory is used for directories for most regular users. The /boot directory contains files required during the boot process for the Linux operating system. The /dev directory includes device driver files.

Because this section examines directories that can serve as appropriate mount points, the focus is on those FHS directories that may be mounted separately. For a more complete discussion of the FHS, see Chapter 8, "File Permissions and More."

A **volume** is a generic term that can specify a partition, LV, or RAID array. A formatted volume is often referred to as a filesystem. The following directories are frequently mounted on separate filesystems:

- **/.** The top-level root directory is associated with its label in Linux, the single forward slash (/). By definition, the **top-level root directory (/)** is always mounted on its own filesystem. The space required depends in part on whether other directories are mounted on different filesystems. (The forward slash followed by the period is based on the standard format for this book. Do not confuse it with the symbol for the popular geek news site, http://slashdot.org.)
- **/boot.** The /boot directory contains the files required to boot the Linux operating system, including the **Linux kernel** and initial RAM disk.
- **/home.** The /home directory contains the home directories for all regular users. If you mount /home on a separate filesystem, you can upgrade the system upgrades with minimal changes to user files. Alternatively, you can expand the space available for users without affecting other parts of the operating system.
- **/opt.** The /opt directory is designed to contain files from third-party applications.
- **/srv.** The /srv directory is commonly used by network servers; it's particularly appropriate to mount this directory separately. Otherwise, files that users load on servers can easily overwhelm the space available to Linux.
- **/tmp.** The /tmp directory is a container for temporary files.
- **/var.** The /var directory is commonly used for logs and data caches. It's particularly appropriate to mount this directory separately. In some cases, network servers use /var subdirectories such as /var/ftp/pub, which can also be mounted separately.

Several other directories are designed for mounting of remote shares as well as removable storage devices such as media cards and CDs.

Any standard directory not included in the preceding list should not be mounted separately. Such directories generally include files that are essential to the basic functionality of the operating system. As such, these directories can and should remain as part of the top-level root directory (/) filesystem.

In brief, a filesystem on a disk is based on a format. The standard format for the most common Linux distributions is the third extended filesystem, also known by its acronym, **ext3**. (However, as of this writing, ext4 is being implemented for Fedora 11, which is beyond the scope of the new LPIC-1 objectives.) A filesystem also refers to mounted directories, whether they're mounted on a partition, LV, or RAID array.

Special care is required for the mounting of the /boot directory. Although there are workarounds, the /boot directory should generally be mounted on a regular partition. In other words, it can be difficult to configure a Linux boot loader to recognize a /boot directory configured on a software RAID array or an LV.

Tailored Mount Point Design

As noted in the LPIC objectives, you need to know how to "tailor the design" of mount points to the intended use of the system. Now that you know a bit about the FHS, you should understand appropriate mount points for different types of systems.

With the proliferation of virtual machines such as VMware, Xen, and KVM (Kernel-based Virtual Machine), there is no longer a reason to configure a server with more than one basic function.

For systems configured with the right mount points, upgrades are easier to handle. For example, I set up my laptop with the /home directory mounted on a separate partition, which makes it possible to upgrade the installed Linux distribution with minimal effect on my personal or work files. If my files become too big for my home directory, I can get a bigger hard drive and move those files to an appropriately configured volume on that drive. I can also back up my /home directory on a more regular basis, without including the rest of the Linux operating system in the backup.

Although I cover three general types of Linux systems in this section, the appropriate mount points for a system depend on the specific Linux distribution and service(s) configured on that system.

Basic Linux System

Newer Linux users configure basic Linux systems. They typically accept the defaults associated with an installation program. The more popular Linux distributions configure at least three partitions or volumes.

◆ **swap space.** Most Linux systems include a partition dedicated to swap space, typically twice the installed system RAM.

◆ **/boot.** Linux systems frequently configure a separate /boot partition.

◆ **/.** All other directories are configured in the same volume as the top-level root directory (/).

File Server

One common production use of Linux is as a file server. Files can be shared through a number of different services. A central /home directory is commonly configured on a central NFS (Network File Service) server. User home directories are often shared on a Samba server. Linux also supports different FTP (File Transfer Protocol) services.

Whichever server is selected, it can help to set up the shared directories on separate volumes. If users or administrators overload the volume on any of these services, it does not affect the basic operation of that system. For example, an overloaded /var/ftp/pub directory for an FTP server, when mounted separately, only prevents others from uploading to that server. The underlying Linux system can still boot and be otherwise managed in a regular fashion.

Web Server

It's an excellent idea to mount the directory associated with Web server files on a separate partition. You can back up files organized in this fashion on a more regular basis. If needed, you can then restore the Web server files to a newly installed Linux system.

However, besides databases, the space challenge associated with a Web server is based on log data. Whether logs include data from users or connection logs collected for marketing purposes, log data from Web servers has been known to add gigabytes of data—every day!

If the traffic spikes on a Web server, the logs can easily overload an improperly configured system. Logs for a Web server can be cited either in the main configuration file for the server or in supplementary configuration files commonly used for virtual servers. Depending on use, it may make sense to mount a directory such as /var/log/apache2 or the entire /var directory on a separate volume.

Hard Disk Options

Several options are available for hard disks, internal and external. Although there are variations, these options for hard disk media can be divided into five categories, based on how they are attached to and communicate with the system:

◆ **SATA.** Short for Serial Advanced Technology Attachment, it's the internal hard disk most commonly used on the latest PCs.

◆ **SCSI.** Short for Small Computer Systems Interface, it's the internal hard drive commonly used on servers. It shares characteristics with SATA disks, because such drives are attached in sequence, in serial fashion.

◆ **IEEE 1394.** A common option for external peripherals. IEEE 1394 is a standard of the Institute of Electrical and Electronics Engineers. It's also known by two trade names: FireWire and iLink.

◆ **USB.** Short for Universal Serial Bus, it's a common option for external peripherals, including storage media such as hard disks and solid state USB flash drives.

You can configure hard disks of all of these types on a Linux system. Depending on the BIOS (Basic Input/Output System) software embedded into the system, some or all of these devices can be detected during the boot process. However, those hard disks that can contain the /boot directory may be limited, as I explain in the following section.

Partitions, Logical Volumes, and RAID Arrays

This section describes the basic options for partitions, LVs, and RAID arrays. Partitions consist of dedicated sections of hard disks. LVs consist of selected reassignable portions of multiple partitions. Software RAID arrays, in the context of the Linux operating system, include two or more partitions configured for speed or redundancy.

TIP

Although it's good to know as much as possible about LVs and RAID arrays, configuration details for each of these systems are covered only in the objectives for the LPIC Level 2 exams.

Hard Disk Partitions

A hard disk, historically, was divided into cylinders, heads, and sectors. Partitions are normally configured in a fixed number of cylinders. With the advent of **LBA** (logical block addressing) and hard disks larger than 8GB, the cylinder/head/sector division is in many ways obsolete. However, because this organization is still used by many partition tools, LBA translates the cylinder/head/sector division into numbers that support larger hard drives.

A partition can be configured in part of a hard disk, or it can encompass the entire drive. There are three basic types of partitions:

◆ **Primary partition.** A hard disk can be configured with up to four primary partitions. Older systems would not boot Linux unless the partition with the /boot directory were configured in a primary partition.

◆ **Extended partition.** The last primary partition on a drive can be reassigned as an extended partition. It is designed as a container for logical partitions.

◆ **Logical partition.** The extended partition on a drive can be subdivided into distinct logical partitions.

Both primary and logical partitions can be configured as containers for Linux data. Once formatted, such partitions are commonly dedicated to specific directories.

Alternatively, primary and logical partitions can be configured as members of an LV or a RAID array.

 NOTE

For more information on creating and formatting partitions, see Chapter 7, "Manage and Maintain Filesystems."

Logical Volumes

An LV makes it easier to manage different filesystems. You can expand and contract LVs as needed. For example, if you configure the /home directory on an LV, and the company expands, it's relatively easy to add more disks and partitions—and then add that available space to the /home directory mounted on an LV. LVs are covered in the LPIC-2 objectives, but they are beyond the scope of the LPIC-1 exams.

Although not required, LVs run faster when they're configured from partitions on different physical hard disks. The basic components of an LV include a physical volume, a volume group, and a logical volume, as defined here:

- ◆ **Physical volume.** A physical volume is a hard disk partition (or RAID array) configured to the appropriate LV partition type.
- ◆ **Volume group.** A volume group includes the space assigned from one or more physical volumes.
- ◆ **Logical volume (LV).** An LV includes space from a volume group and is used as a mount point for a selected Linux directory.

A typical LV device file is /dev/mapper/VolGroup00-LogVol00. Although you may have seen a device file such as /dev/VolGroup00/LogVol00, the ls -l command shown in Figure 2.1 reveals that it's linked to the actual LV device file.

```
[michael@Fedora10vm ~]$ sudo ls -l /dev/VolGroup00
total 0
lrwxrwxrwx 1 root root 31 2008-12-16 12:20 LogVol00 -> /dev/mapper/VolGroup00-LogVol00
lrwxrwxrwx 1 root root 31 2008-12-16 12:20 LogVol01 -> /dev/mapper/VolGroup00-LogVol01
[michael@Fedora10vm ~]$
```

FIGURE 2.1 *Logical volume device files.*

RAID Arrays

Most references to RAID arrays are based on specialized hardware. RAID, as configured on a Linux operating system, is a software RAID array that requires no specialized hardware. Nevertheless, hardware RAID arrays are commonly used on Linux systems. Although RAID is covered in the LPIC-2 objectives, is is beyond the scope of the LPIC-1 exams.

Because software RAID arrays are based on partitions, the term "Redundant Array of Independent Disks" is a bit misleading. A software RAID array consists of two or more partitions. When properly configured, the components of a software RAID array come from different physical hard disks, from different controllers.

Software RAID components from different physical hard disks are required for redundancy. Otherwise, the failure of one physical hard disk can lead to the loss of data on the array.

The most efficient software RAID arrays are based on partitions from hard disks connected to different physical controllers. Different physical controllers reduce bottlenecks in data transmission, which makes it faster for a system to read and write to the array.

Although Linux software associated with RAID makes it possible to include multiple partitions from the same physical hard disk, that negates the benefits of RAID. In other words, the failure of one physical disk should not lead to the failure of a RAID array. If two partitions from the same physical disk are included in that array, the failure of that disk can lead to the loss of all data on that array.

Special Issues with the /boot Directory

On older systems, where LBA has not been enabled, the partition with the /boot directory must reside within the first 1,024 cylinders of one of the first two hard disks on a system. This problem rarely exists on systems built in this century.

Swap Space

On Linux, it is standard to have a dedicated area for swap space, which extends the effective volatile RAM (Random Access Memory) on a system. Although Microsoft systems typically configure swap space in a large file, most Linux systems set up swap space in a dedicated partition, formatted to its own Linux swap filesystem. Swap space can also be configured in an LV.

The amount of hard disk area required for a swap filesystem varies. The most common rule of thumb is to configure twice the amount of RAM as swap space. For example, a system with 2GB of RAM would be configured with a swap filesystem of 4GB of space.

However, because swap space serves as an overflow area for systems that require RAM, the need for swap space is often reduced on systems with large amounts of RAM. For example, the laptop that I'm using to write this book has 4GB of RAM, but the servers that I configure on it for test purposes work well with a swap partition of 2GB of RAM.

The Boot Manager

Two boot managers are commonly associated with current releases of the Linux operating system: GRUB and LILO. Although GRUB is the default for most Linux users, LILO is still commonly used in a few areas. For example, LILO is the only boot loader that works on Macintosh systems built on the Intel CPU.

A boot manager resides in the first 512 bytes of a hard disk. It's the area called by the BIOS when it looks to a hard disk to boot an operating system. This sector is known as the **Master Boot Record (MBR)**. Although the LILO configuration resides entirely in those 512 bytes, GRUB configures a pointer from that 512-byte sector to the actual configuration file in the /boot directory.

This section doesn't cover other boot loaders such as Microsoft's NTLDR, Microsoft's Boot Manager, or Avanquest's System Commander, even though each can be configured to boot Linux.

Backup Boot Options

The installation and configuration of any boot loader normally involves changes to the MBR of one or more hard disks. It's possible to back up the MBR. The following command backs up the MBR from the first PATA disk:

```
# dd if=/dev/hda of=backup.mbr bs=512 count=1
```

If a system ever becomes unbootable due to a bad MBR, you can restore that MBR from the noted file. There are numerous ways to boot a system damaged in this fashion; the preferred methods are based on a rescue disk or Live CD/DVD customized for your distribution.

Install, Configure, and Interact with GRUB

GRUB is more important in the LPI requirements than LILO. The LPIC-1 objectives specifically state that you need to know how to "install and configure a boot loader such as GRUB." That reflects the current usage of GRUB, which is used much more frequently than LILO on current Linux releases.

As discussed in Chapter 1, "System Architecture," the standard GRUB configuration file is /boot/grub/menu.lst. Some distributions, including those based on current Red Hat releases, configure this file (as well as /etc/grub.conf) as a soft link to the /boot/grub/grub.conf configuration file.

Install GRUB

If there's a different boot loader installed, you can use the `grub-install` command to implement GRUB by adding a pointer from the MBR of the specified hard disk. You'll need the device file of the hard disk with the `/boot` directory. Device files can be identified in the output to the `mount` command. For example, the following excerpt identifies device file `/dev/sda1` as the partition associated with the `/boot` directory.

```
/dev/sda2 on / type ext3 (rw,relatime,errors=remount-ro,commit=600)
/dev/sda1 on /boot type ext3 (rw,relatime,commit=600)
```

 NOTE

For more information on the `mount` command and filesystem formats, see Chapter 7.

But because the objective is to modify the MBR of a hard disk, the `grub-install` command should be targeted on the device file for that specific hard disk, `/dev/sda`. The following command

```
# grub-install /dev/sda
```

writes an appropriate link from the MBR to the GRUB configuration file. It scans different connected drives and writes to the MBR of an available hard drive, and a floppy drive, if one is configured.

Configure GRUB

To configure GRUB, open the `menu.1st` file available in the `/boot/grub/` directory. For a basic explanation of GRUB stanzas, see Chapter 1. The LPIC-1 administrator should know a couple of additional directives. First, the `default` directive specifies the default stanza booted from the GRUB menu. It's a bit tricky. For example, the following line specifies that the default stanza is the first stanza.

```
default=0
```

Some distributions omit the = for this GRUB directive; the following line specifies the default as the second stanza:

```
default 1
```

Current Linux systems may automatically boot the default stanza if the menu is not opened, usually in five seconds.

Next, many GRUB menus are password protected with a directive similar to the following, which specifies that the password is encrypted in MD5 format, based on the Message Digest 5 algorithm.

```
password --md5 $1$gLhU0/$aW78kHK
```

Interact with GRUB

Chapter 1 described basic interactions with the GRUB menu. If a system does not include a recovery mode in its GRUB menu, you can still boot that system into single user mode. For our purposes, that's equivalent to runlevel 1. When editing a stanza, add that runlevel to the end of the line that starts with kernel.

TIP

Other runlevels can start variations on rescue or recovery modes; in some cases, you can substitute emergency or s for 1 in the kernel command line.

Other options are available at the end of the GRUB kernel command line. For example, if there are problems detecting hardware based on ACPI (Advanced Configuration and Power Interface) standards, you can disable ACPI detection by adding the noacpi option to the end of the kernel command line. Some similar options are listed in Table 2.1.

Table 2.1   kernel Command-Line Options at the Boot Loader Menu

kernel Command Option	Description
noapic	Disables the Advanced Programmable Interrupt Controller, associated with the symmetric multiprocessing associated with multiple CPUs (or multiple CPU cores)
noapm	Disables the Advanced Power Management associated with older power management features
nodma	Disables Direct Memory Access channels
selinux=0	Disables Security Enhanced Linux; commonly used on Red Hat systems before Security Enhanced Linux is properly configured

You can use many of these options when booting from the LILO boot loader, as explained next. One source of additional options is an Ubuntu wiki at https://help.ubuntu.com/community/BootOptions.

Install and Interact with LILO

The major alternative to GRUB as a Linux boot loader is LILO. The standard LILO configuration file is /etc/lilo.conf. The location of this file is not relevant in a way, because it is written directly to the MBR of a target hard disk.

LILO is no longer in common use when Linux is installed on standard PCs, except for Macintoshes built on Intel-based systems. In fact, the lilo package isn't even available on most repositories associated with several Red Hat–based distributions. The developers of LILO maintain the associated package rather infrequently. As of this writing, the last revision to LILO was made in early 2007. For more information, see http://freshmeat.net/projects/lilo.

 NOTE

Several other architecture-specific boot loaders are available for Linux. The ELILO boot loader is short for the Extended Firmware Interface LILO boot loader, designed originally for Itanium CPUs. The OS/400 and YABOOT (Yet Another Bootloader) boot loaders are designed for IBM-based CPUs.

Install LILO

LILO can be installed in one of two ways. First, you can download it from the LILO home page just described. Second, if you're running a Debian or Ubuntu distribution, you can get it from standard repositories.

When installed, LILO can be configured with the **lilo** command. It takes the contents of the /etc/lilo.conf file and writes it to the MBR of the target hard disk.

LILO cannot boot from portable drives; if you need to write the LILO configuration file to anything but the first available hard disk, the -M switch can help. For example, the following command writes LILO to the second SCSI (or SATA) hard disk:

```
# lilo -M /dev/sdb
```

Interact with LILO

To interact with the current version of the LILO menu, press the Tab key within five seconds. It should provide access to a boot prompt, as shown:

```
Lin_2.6.24img0    Memory_Test+
boot:
```

If you want to boot into a different runlevel, type in the desired kernel image, followed by the runlevel. For example, the following command boots the noted kernel image in single user mode:

```
boot: Lin_2.6.24img0 single
```

Set Up Shared Libraries

Libraries are frequently used programs—functions and routines, shared by different applications. Because such programs are shared, the applications associated with all operating systems can stay relatively compact. Such programs are dynamically linked, called only as needed.

As suggested in the objectives, "Candidates should be able to determine the shared libraries that executable programs depend on and install them when necessary." To that end, you need to know the commands that point to library files, their standard locations, and the associated configuration files.

As you might guess, program libraries are normally stored somewhere in the /lib and /usr/lib directories. But these directories are not the only location for libraries, as you'll see in related configuration files.

Identify Required Library Files

Two commands can help identify library files. The **ldd** command displays the shared libraries associated with a specific program. It requires the full path to the program; for example, the commands shown in Figure 2.2 point to several program libraries associated with the ls command.

```
michael@UbuntuHH:~$ ldd /bin/ls
        linux-gate.so.1 =>  (0xb7fa2000)
        librt.so.1 => /lib/tls/i686/cmov/librt.so.1 (0xb7f85000)
        libselinux.so.1 => /lib/libselinux.so.1 (0xb7f6c000)
        libacl.so.1 => /lib/libacl.so.1 (0xb7f64000)
        libc.so.6 => /lib/tls/i686/cmov/libc.so.6 (0xb7e15000)
        libpthread.so.0 => /lib/tls/i686/cmov/libpthread.so.0 (0xb7dfd000)
        /lib/ld-linux.so.2 (0xb7fa3000)
        libdl.so.2 => /lib/tls/i686/cmov/libdl.so.2 (0xb7df9000)
        libattr.so.1 => /lib/libattr.so.1 (0xb7df5000)
michael@UbuntuHH:~$ ldd -u /bin/ls
Unused direct dependencies:

        /lib/tls/i686/cmov/librt.so.1
        /lib/libselinux.so.1
        /lib/libacl.so.1
michael@UbuntuHH:~$ []
```

FIGURE 2.2 *The ldd command points to libraries.*

The ldd -u command identifies unused dependencies and is a subset of the output to the ldd command. The output is from an Ubuntu system, where Security Enhanced Linux is not used. So it makes sense that the associated library, /lib/libselinux.so.1, is not used.

The **ldconfig** command reads and caches currently installed libraries. It finds libraries in standard locations such as the /lib directory. When run alone, this command caches library links in the /etc/ld.so.cache file. If you've just installed new libraries or have updated related configuration files in the /etc/ld.so.conf.d/ directory, the ldconfig command can ensure that cache file is up-to-date.

If you want to display the contents of the current cache from the noted file, watch out—it's big. To get a taste, run the following command:

```
# ldconfig -p
```

The output will likely display links from several hundred libraries to actual locations in the directory tree.

Library Configuration

The directories searched by the ldconfig command depend on the configuration in the /etc/ld.so.conf file, as well as the LD_LIBRARY_PATH directive, if that has been set. The configuration file typically includes a single directive, similar to this:

```
include /etc/ld.so.conf.d/*.conf
```

This includes all directives in *.conf files in the noted subdirectory. Although the files in this directory vary, their purpose is to point the system to library files in nonstandard directories.

Library File Directories

Many, perhaps most, active Linux library files are located in the /lib and /usr/lib directory trees. Although other groups of library files may exist in source code, such as that associated with the kernel, they are irrelevant to the discussion. However, additional directories are commonly configured in *.conf files in the /etc/ld.so.conf.d/ directory, as just discussed from the /etc/ld.so.conf file.

One example of such files is based on the installation of the MySQL service on CentOS 5, which is documented in the /etc/ld.so.conf.d/mysql-i386.conf file. That file points the system to the /usr/lib/mysql/ directory for related library files.

Once such configuration files are properly updated, the next execution of the ldconfig command ensures that the noted libraries are included in the associated cache file, /etc/lib.so.cache.

Chapter Summary

You can manage hard disks to accommodate Linux systems in many ways. Appropriate directory mount points can keep a system running even when certain volumes are overloaded with data. Typical mount points, other than the top-level root directory (/), include the /boot, /home, /opt, /srv, /tmp, and /var directories, in addition to included subdirectories. Such mount points can be configured on primary or logical partitions, either directly, or through a RAID array or LV.

On some older systems, the /boot directory should be configured on a separate partition within the first 1,024 cylinders of one of the first two system hard disks. Swap space is also configured on a separate volume, normally with twice the space of installed RAM.

The LPIC-1 requirements list two boot managers: GRUB and LILO. For GRUB, the `grub-install` command includes a pointer from the MBR to the `/boot/grub/menu.lst` file. For LILO, the `lilo` command installs the boot loader configuration from the `/etc/lilo.conf` file in the MBR. The MBR is located in the first block of a hard disk, in the first 512 bytes.

Program libraries are frequently shared by Linux commands. Most libraries are stored in the `/lib/` and `/usr/lib/` directories. Additional libraries can be specified in the `/etc/ld.so.conf` configuration file. The `ldd` command can identify the shared libraries associated with another Linux command. The `ldconfig` command can read and cache libraries, based on binary information stored in the `/etc/ld.so.cache` file.

Key Terms

- ◆ **/boot.** The `/boot` directory contains the files required to boot the Linux operating system.
- ◆ **ext3.** The standard format for the most common Linux distributions is the third extended filesystem, also known as ext3.
- ◆ **extended partition.** The last primary partition on a drive can be reassigned as an extended partition. It is designed as a container for partitions.
- ◆ **FHS.** Short for the Filesystem Hierarchy Standard, it's the standard organizational structure for files and directories on a Linux system.
- ◆ **grub-install.** The command that installs a pointer from the MBR to the GRUB configuration file, `/boot/grub/menu.lst`. It's located in the `/sbin` directory.
- ◆ **/home.** The `/home` directory contains the home directories for all regular users.
- ◆ **LBA (Logical Block Addressing).** It's the current method for specifying the location of data blocks on hard disks and similar storage devices.
- ◆ **ldconfig.** The `ldconfig` command reads and caches currently installed libraries. It finds libraries in standard locations such as the `/lib` directory; the command is located in the `/sbin` directory.
- ◆ **ldd.** The `ldd` command displays the shared libraries associated with a specific program or command. It requires the full path and is located in the `/sbin` directory.
- ◆ **lilo.** The command that installs the LILO boot loader as configured in `/etc/lilo.conf` in the MBR; located in the `/sbin` directory.
- ◆ **LILO.** Short for the Linux Loader, it's a legacy Linux boot loader still in use for systems such as Macs with Intel-based CPUs. It's configured in the `/etc/lilo.conf` file.
- ◆ **Linux kernel.** The Linux kernel is the core of the operating system.

◆ **logical partition.** The extended partition on a drive can be subdivided into distinct logical partitions.

◆ **LV.** Short for a Logical Volume; an LV includes space from a volume group and is used as a mount point for a selected Linux directory.

◆ **MBR (Master Boot Record).** Specifies the first sector, or 512 bytes, of a hard drive. It's used by GRUB and LILO to point to Linux boot options.

◆ **/opt.** The /opt directory is designed to contain files from third-party applications.

◆ **physical volume.** A physical volume is a hard disk partition (or RAID array) configured to the appropriate LV partition type.

◆ **primary partition.** A hard disk can be configured with up to four primary partitions.

◆ **RAID.** Short for Redundant Array of Independent Disks, it's implemented in Linux in the software, based on an array of partitions, not disks.

◆ **/srv.** The /srv directory is commonly assigned for use by network servers.

◆ **/tmp.** The /tmp directory is a container for temporary files.

◆ **top-level root directory (/).** This is always mounted on its own filesystem. The space required depends in part on whether other directories are mounted on different filesystems.

◆ **USB.** Short for Universal Serial Bus, it's a common option for external peripherals, including storage media such as hard disks and solid state USB flash drives.

◆ **/var.** The /var directory is commonly used for logs and data caches.

◆ **volume.** A generic term that can specify a partition, LV, or RAID array.

◆ **volume group.** A volume group includes the space assigned from one or more physical volumes.

Review Questions

The number of review questions in this chapter and other chapters in this book is proportionate to each section's weight in the LPI objectives. Because this chapter covers items 102.1, 102.2, and 102.3, the weight is 5; therefore, you'll see 10 questions in this section. You'll see multiple choice, fill-in-the blank, and multiple choice multiple option questions, as you'll encounter on the exam.

1. If you're configuring a network file server to share user files, enter the full path to an appropriate directory to mount separately.

   _____

2. For a system with a Core 2 Duo 2500MHz CPU, two 1TB hard disks, 2GB RAM, a 1GB USB key, and an external 2TB hard disk, which of the following represents the size of a typical swap partition?

   A. 2500MB

   B. 2000MB

   C. 4000MB

   D. 10000MB

3. Which of the following circumstances would not affect whether the /boot directory is mounted on a separate partition within the first 1,024 cylinders of a hard disk?

   A. An older system, designed before the year 2000

   B. LBA not being enabled

   C. A 4GB hard drive

   D. A virtual machine

4. Which of the following types of volumes may be suitable for mounting an appropriate Linux directory? Choose three.

   A. RAID array

   B. Volume group

   C. Logical volume

   D. Primary partition

5. To install the GRUB boot loader on the first SATA hard drive on a system, enter the command. Assume that you do not need to include sudo in the command or include the path.

   _____

6. Where is the MBR located on a hard disk?

   A. The last 512 bytes on the disk

   B. The first 512 bytes on the disk

   C. The first 512 blocks on the disk

   D. The first 1024 cylinders on the disk

7. If you're configuring the GRUB boot loader, which of the following files would you edit in a boot loader?

   A. /boot/grub.conf

   B. /boot/grub/menu.lst

   C. /boot/grub/grub.lst

   D. /etc/grub.conf

8. Which of the following commands installs the LILO boot loader from the `/etc/lilo.conf` configuration file, on the second SATA drive?

    A. `lilo -M /dev/sdb`

    B. `lilo-config /dev/sda`

    C. `lilo -M /dev/sda`

    D. `lilo-install /dev/sdb`

9. The _____ file specifies the configuration associated with shared libraries on the local system. Be sure to include the full path to the file.

10. Which of the following commands lists the shared libraries used by the `fdisk` command?

    A. `ldconfig /sbin/fdisk`

    B. `ldconfig -p /sbin/fdisk`

    C. `ldd -p /sbin/fdisk`

    D. `ldd /sbin/fdisk`

Chapter 3

Package
Management
Systems

After completing this chapter, you will be able to

- ■ Use the Debian Package Management System

- ■ Understand details of the `apt-*` commands

- ■ Use the Red Hat Package Management System

- ■ Understand details of the `yum` commands

Introduction

Linux developers distribute their software in packages. Originally, these packages were collected and distributed in compressed archives. But that was a time-intensive process, because archived packages of source code had to be compiled before they could be installed. It's a lot less time consuming to install a package from a binary archive.

The two major package management systems most commonly used today were developed originally for the Debian and Red Hat Linux distributions. They're currently used on a number of Linux distributions, including the Ubuntu Hardy Heron and CentOS 5 releases, which are the focus of this book. Such packages can normally be identified by their .deb and .rpm extensions. They're normally distributed in a precompiled binary format that is designed to simplify the installation process, and they can be installed with the **dpkg** and **rpm** commands.

Linux distributions often include hundreds or even thousands of packages. Many packages depend on others, such as applications that depend on program libraries. Such packages are frequently configured as dependent packages, known colloquially as **dependencies**. Such packages must normally be installed simultaneously. With thousands of available packages, dependencies can be difficult to monitor, which often leads to frustration. This frustration has led to the development of the **apt-*** and **yum** commands for package management because they automatically identify, find, download, and install dependent packages.

Many qualified candidates for the LPIC-1 credential may be experienced in either Red Hat or **Debian style-packaging**, but not both. If you're experienced with one packaging system, be patient with the descriptions in this chapter, because they're written for candidates who are not experienced with that system. If you're less experienced with one packaging system or another, it's especially important that you have an appropriate distribution available with which you can practice the commands described in this chapter.

TIP

This chapter addresses two objectives in the LPI exam: 102.4 ("Use Debian Package Management") and 102.5 ("Use RPM and YUM Package Management").

Debian Package Management Parameters

The Debian package management system works with the `dpkg` command. The command is versatile; it can be used to install, remove, or purge a package. It can also be used to list files, list installed packages, and identify the origin of installed files. And although that's just a start of what the `dpkg` command can do, it is limited by its inability to manage dependencies.

NOTE

Dependencies relate to target packages. When you install a package, it may not work properly unless other packages are installed. These other packages are known as dependencies.

Built into many Debian packages is a semiautomated configuration tool. In other words, when certain packages are installed, you are prompted to specify basic parameters for that package or associated service. If desired, such packages can be configured again, either through individual configuration files or with the **`dpkg-reconfigure`** command.

NOTE

Although Debian packages were developed for the Debian Linux distribution, they're also available on related popular distributions, including Ubuntu, Linspire, and Xandros.

The dpkg Command

As suggested by the exam objectives, you need to know how to "install, upgrade, and uninstall Debian binary packages." You'll learn how to perform these tasks in this section with the `dpkg` command.

TIP

When you learn a command, learn both uses of key switches. Although you may be used to a command like `dpkg -p` *pkgname*, don't be surprised to see an equivalent command such as `dpkg --print-avail` *pkgname*.

The best way to learn any command is to practice it on a test system. Because the `dpkg` command is rarely used alone, one way to find an appropriate package is to take advantage of a feature associated with the **apt** package management system. The `/var/cache/apt/archives/` directory normally includes packages downloaded from remote repositories.

As is true for much of this book, the following steps normally require a relatively high-speed Internet connection. I've only tested these commands on the Hardy Heron release of Ubuntu Linux. Some of the commands shown here are described in more detail later in this chapter. The following commands should work on other relatively independent Debian-style packages, on other Debian-based Linux distributions. However, these commands may not work on other distributions with the same Trivial File Transfer Protocol service package.

1. Install the Trivial File Transfer Protocol service with the following command; accept any warnings about dependent packages.

   ```
   # apt-get install tftpd-hpa
   ```

2. Uninstall the package with the following command:

   ```
   # dpkg -r tftpd-hpa
   ```

   If error messages are associated with dependencies, try a different server; removing the `samba` package worked for me.

3. Examine the associated configuration file, `/etc/default/tftpd-hpa`. Yes, the package had been removed, but the configuration files, based on the `-r` (which is the same as `--remove`) switch, are still there.

4. Try installing the package again. Because it has already been downloaded, it should be available in the aforementioned `/var/cache/apt/archives/` directory. If so, it should be installable with the following command:

   ```
   # dpkg -i /var/cache/apt/archives/tftpd-hpa*
   ```

5. Find out more about the package. Try the `-p` switch (lowercase), which displays the details about the given package. You'll see another method to display this information later in this chapter.

   ```
   # dpkg -p tftpd-hpa
   ```

6. Try purging the package. Note the use of the `-P` switch (uppercase), which is functionally equivalent to `--purge`:

   ```
   # dpkg -P tftpd-hpa
   ```

7. Check the same configuration file listed earlier. Is it there? It shouldn't be.

Now that you have some experience with the `dpkg` command, you should not be completely lost as you read Table 3.1, with `dpkg` command switches. Be aware that there's often more than one way to type in a command switch; for example, `-i` is functionally identical to `--install`. If an older version of the package was previously installed, this command upgrades that package.

Table 3.1 Important dpkg Command Switches

dpkg Command Switch	Function
-i (--install)	Installs the package specified. The full name of the package is required. (Wildcards can be used.)
-l (--list)	Lists installed packages; if a package name is included, notes the installation status of the noted package.
-L (--listfiles)	Lists the files from a specified package.
-P (--purge)	Uninstalls a package and removes associated configuration files.
-p (--print-avail)	Includes details about the specified package.
-r (--remove)	Uninstalls a package without removing or changing associated configuration files. It can help the administrator configure a package before putting it into service.
-S (--search)	Identifies the package associated with a specified file; the full path to the file must be used.

Practice the commands listed in Table 3.1. As described in the objectives, you do need to know how to "find packages containing specific files or libraries which may or may not be installed." For example, the following command identifies the passwd package as the one that includes the /etc/default/useradd file:

```
$ dpkg -S /etc/default/useradd
passwd: /etc/default/useradd
```

Try the dpkg -l command by itself. Note how it lists numerous packages. The ii in the left column indicates that the noted package is installed. If you add a package name to the command, the output is isolated to that package name.

Now try changing the switch; the first command shown in Figure 3.1 lists the status of the apt package.

```
michael@UbuntuHH:~/LPI-Level1v2/Ch03$ dpkg -l apt
Desired=Unknown/Install/Remove/Purge/Hold
| Status=Not/Installed/Config-f/Unpacked/Failed-cfg/Half-inst/t-aWait/T-pend
|/ Err?=(none)/Hold/Reinst-required/X=both-problems (Status,Err: uppercase=bad)
||/ Name           Version        Description
+++-===============-===============-========================================
ii  apt            0.7.9ubuntu17  Advanced front-end for dpkg
michael@UbuntuHH:~/LPI-Level1v2/Ch03$ dpkg -l postfix
Desired=Unknown/Install/Remove/Purge/Hold
| Status=Not/Installed/Config-f/Unpacked/Failed-cfg/Half-inst/t-aWait/T-pend
|/ Err?=(none)/Hold/Reinst-required/X=both-problems (Status,Err: uppercase=bad)
||/ Name           Version        Description
+++-===============-===============-========================================
un  postfix        <none>         (no description available)
michael@UbuntuHH:~/LPI-Level1v2/Ch03$ []
```

FIGURE 3.1 *The dpkg -l command can status a package.*

You might realize that the output meets several of the criteria listed in the objective line, which suggests that you need to know how to "obtain package information like version, content, dependencies, package integrity, and installation status (whether or not the package is installed)." Let's break this down.

The version number is clearly labeled in the output of the dpkg -l command. The content of a package is available with the dpkg -L *pkgname* command. You'll see how to find dependencies and confirm package integrity with the apt-* commands later in this chapter. Next, the installation status is shown in the figure.

The first two letters in the left column are associated with the Desired and Status lines. The ii in the output means that the cited apt package is installed, as intended. The un in the output for the postfix package means the database does not know what you want (u for unknown) and the current status is not installed. If a third letter exists in the left column, there's some sort of error.

Return to the previous exercise. Packages may not always be so easy to install. For example, the command shown in Figure 3.2 demonstrates what could happen when you try to install the Samba file server package.

```
michael@UbuntuHH:~$ sudo dpkg -i /var/cache/apt/archives/samba_3.0.28a-1ubuntu4.
7_i386.deb
(Reading database ... 165571 files and directories currently installed.)
Preparing to replace samba 3.0.28a-1ubuntu4.7 (using .../samba_3.0.28a-1ubuntu4.
7_i386.deb) ...
Unpacking replacement samba ...
dpkg: dependency problems prevent configuration of samba:
 samba depends on samba-common (= 3.0.28a-1ubuntu4.7); however:
  Version of samba-common on system is 3.0.28a-1ubuntu4.5.
dpkg: error processing samba (--install):
 dependency problems - leaving unconfigured
Errors were encountered while processing:
 samba
michael@UbuntuHH:~$ []
```

FIGURE 3.2 *Dependencies can be a problem.*

As shown in the figure, the Samba server package is not installed. You can force the issue, with a command like the following:

```
# dpkg --force-depends -i /var/cache/apt/archives/samba_*
```

However, this command entails risks. If you don't account for all dependencies, the package may not work as desired. Even worse, users who try to connect to the associated service may lose data.

Packages that are installed are stored in a local database, in the /var/lib/dpkg/ directory. Open the file named available from that directory in a text editor. You'll see a detailed description of installable packages.

Reconfigure a Package

Debian-style packages related to services often include options to configure that service. For example, the first time the Postfix e-mail server is installed on an Ubuntu system, you're prompted to answer a few configuration questions. Unless the package is purged, the `dpkg-reconfigure` command is required to go through the same sequence of prompts. The following command helps the administrator reconfigure the Postfix service:

```
# dpkg-reconfigure postfix
```

Changes made during this process are saved to an appropriate configuration file; in this case, it would be `/etc/postfix/main.cf`.

The Power of apt

Package management can be difficult. It was especially difficult before the development of the `apt-*` commands. When `dpkg` was all that was available for a Debian-style distribution, administrators had to either install all packages simultaneously with the same command or temporarily accept installed packages with unmet dependencies. When those second-level packages also have dependencies, the situation can become complex.

The power of the `apt-*` commands comes from its ability to include dependencies in the package installation or removal. When configured properly through its configuration file, **/etc/apt/sources.list**, the `apt-*` commands can also take advantage of package repositories, which are often mirrored in strategic locations around the world.

A good distribution configures the `apt` configuration file automatically. So on your Debian-style distribution (including Ubuntu), you should be able to immediately test the `apt` commands in this section.

Basic apt Commands

In this section, you'll examine the `apt-get`, `apt-cache`, and `apt-file` commands. The **apt-get** command is a versatile way to manage the status of a package on a system. The **apt-cache** command can tell you more about available packages. The **apt-file** command can help identify the package associated with desired files.

Other tools commonly used on Debian-based distributions such as `aptitude` and the **Synaptic Package Manager** are front ends to various `apt-*` commands. In other words, they're designed to provide prepackaged functionality, using intuitive interfaces.

The apt-get Command

The `apt-get` command by itself is not enough. It requires an action. The simplest actions associated with the `apt-get` command install and remove a specified package. If the package is already installed, the `install` option upgrades the noted package. If you want to remove the package along with associated configuration files, purge the package.

The apt-get command relies on a local package database in the /var/lib/apt/ directory. Before doing anything else with the apt-get command, make sure the local package database is up-to-date with the apt-get update command. Major apt-get options are summarized in Table 3.2.

Table 3.2 Important apt-get Command Options

apt-get Command Option	Function
autoclean	Clears out only obsolete packages from the local database in the /var/cache/apt/archives/ directory.
autoremove	Removes all packages still installed but no longer required by others.
clean	Clears out the local database of downloaded packages from the /var/cache/apt/archives/ directory.
dist-upgrade	Assumes the /etc/apt/sources.list file has been revised to point to the new release. Use only when upgrading between distribution releases.
dselect-upgrade	Installs updates and removes orphan packages.
install	Installs the package specified, with dependencies; normally, just the name of the package is required, which can be identified in the output from an appropriate apt-cache search command.
purge	Uninstalls a package and removes associated configuration files.
remove	Removes the specified package, with dependencies.
update	Updates the current local database of packages from repositories configured in the /etc/apt/sources.list file.
upgrade	Compares the date of locally installed packages with the latest available database, and upgrades packages when later versions are available.

For example, I use a Linux application frequently known as the GIMP (GNU Image Manipulation Program). To install it on my Ubuntu system, I run the following command:

```
apt-get install gimp
```

 NOTE

GNU is short for GNU's Not Unix. It's a recursive acronym common in Linux, and one way Linux devotees poke holes in the standard way of doing things.

If all dependent packages are already installed, the package associated with the GIMP is installed automatically. If there are dependent packages, they're listed with dependencies. The following message reads a current list of available packages. It takes data from each package with respect to dependencies, along with the current state of the system.

```
Reading package lists... Done
Building dependency tree
Reading state information... Done
```

Next, it reads the current state of the system. If orphan packages are currently installed, they are listed, with instructions for their removal:

```
The following packages were automatically installed and are no longer required:
  sendmail-base m4 sendmail-cf openbsd-inetd
Use 'apt-get autoremove' to remove them.
```

An "orphan package" is a dependency that is no longer required for a main package. For example, the output shown above suggests that the main sendmail e-mail server package is no longer installed. Therefore, the dependent sendmail-base and sendmail-cf packages are no longer needed.

Next, dependent packages are found. If additional packages are required for these dependent packages, they are also included in the list of packages to be installed:

```
The following extra packages will be installed:
  gimp gimp-data gimp-gnomevfs gimp-python gnome-games
```

The suggested and recommended packages that follow may add to the capabilities of the package. They are not included in the list of packages to be installed:

```
Suggested packages:
  gimp-data-extras gimp-help-en gimp-help libgimp-perl gnome-hearts
Recommended packages:
  gnome-games-extra-data python-gtkglext1 python-opengl
```

The packages to be installed are listed, along with the amount of disk space required. As an administrator, you need to confirm the download and installation of the noted packages:

```
The following NEW packages will be installed:
  gimp gimp-data gimp-gnomevfs gimp-python gnome-games ubuntu-desktop
0 upgraded, 6 newly installed, 0 to remove and 191 not upgraded.
Need to get 11.0MB/15.0MB of archives.
After this operation, 45.6MB of additional disk space will be used.
Do you want to continue [Y/n]?
```

Sometimes, you may see a message similar to the following:

```
WARNING: The following packages cannot be authenticated!
  libapt-pkg-perl libconfig-file-perl liblist-moreutils-perl menu apt-file
```

This message has several possible causes. First, make sure that the local database of packages is up-to-date with the `apt-get update` command. A momentary problem in the network may have affected a bit of one or more of the noted packages. In that case, rerunning the `apt-get install` command addresses the problem. Alternatively, authentication depends on digital signatures, normally associated with packages such as `ubuntu-keyring` or `debian-archive-keyring`. In that case, install the latest version of the appropriate keyring package before trying the previous installation command again. For more information on the related GPG (GNU Privacy Guard) signatures, see Chapter 15, "Security Administration."

Finally, in many cases, you may not know the name of the package to install. Fortunately, appropriate `apt-cache` commands can help identify the names of available packages.

The apt-cache Command

Although databases of available packages are stored locally in the `/var/lib/apt/` directory, it's best to search for such packages with the `apt-cache` command. It can help you identify the latest available version of a package. It can also search through package descriptions, which can help you identify related packages.

The simplest use of this package is with the `search` option. For example, the following command returns the names and brief descriptions of all packages with the term `gimp`:

```
$ apt-cache search gimp
```

If you want to find out more about a package, the `show` option is useful. Try it on the name of a package; for example, the following command

```
$ apt-cache show gimp
```

lists critical data about the package, including dependencies; packages that depend on the GIMP, also known as **reverse dependencies**; the size of the package; a description; the home page of package developers (when available); and more.

If you'd rather limit the search to dependencies to see what packages must be installed, in this case with the `gimp` package, run the following command:

```
$ apt-cache depends gimp
```

Pay attention to the long list of packages in the output. It includes dependencies, suggested and recommended packages that may add more features, conflicts, as well as related packages that may be replaced or upgraded.

Naturally, you can limit the search to reverse dependencies, packages that depend on the GIMP. Although these reverse dependencies are not themselves installed, the following command gives you a sense of those packages that use and therefore depend on the GIMP:

```
$ apt-cache rdepends gimp
```

The apt-file Command

The `apt-file` command is similar to `apt-cache` in a way, in that it keeps a database on the local system. To make sure that database is up-to-date, run the following command:

```
# apt-file update
```

It's a big database, including several hundred megabytes of compressed data in text format. Because it is a database of files linked to the thousands of packages available to a distribution, it can contain millions of lines. Therefore, it may take some time to create the database. And once the database is made available in the `/var/cache/apt/apt-file/` directory, it'll take some time to search the database. For example, if you're running the Hardy Heron release of Ubuntu and would like to know the location of available `inittab` files, run the following command:

```
# apt-file search inittab
```

The apt Configuration File

As suggested earlier, the `apt-*` commands don't work without the packages available on remote databases. Yes, the databases can be partially filled with information from distribution-based CD and DVD drives. But most physical media do not include the latest package updates.

Packages on Debian-based distributions are organized in repositories. Packages normally available from installation media are often organized in one repository. Different repositories are commonly configured for feature and security updates and may also be found in other categories.

Repositories are even used during the installation process. The default repositories that work during this process are documented in the `/etc/apt/sources.list` configuration file. Unfortunately, some of these repositories may be in remote locations. For example, the base repositories for Ubuntu systems in the United States of America are actually located in the United Kingdom, despite the URL shown here:

```
deb http://us.archive.ubuntu.com/ubuntu/ hardy main restricted
```

If you're interested in faster updates, you may want to change the URL to an appropriate mirror, as documented by the developers of your chosen distribution.

The preceding line of code points to repositories in the noted URL. The **deb** looks for binary packages; `hardy` is the code name for the release, which can be found in the `dists/` subdirectory of the URL; and `main` and `restricted` are the names of the actual repositories.

In contrast, examine this line from a typical Debian `/etc/apt/sources.list` configuration file:

```
deb-src http://http.us.debian.org/debian/ unstable main contrib non-free
```

The **deb-src** is used on source code packages, from repositories at the noted URL. `unstable` is linked to the current code name for the release, which can be found in the `dists/` subdirectory of the URL. The word `unstable` refers to packages currently being tested, which may not be suited for production systems. It's followed by `main`, `contrib`, and `non-free`, which are Debian repositories.

The aptitude Alternative

The `aptitude` command works in two ways. First, it can substitute for the `apt-get` and `apt-cache` commands previously described. Second, when run by itself, `aptitude` starts a low-level menu-driven utility that can be run from a text console. The commands available from the `aptitude` menu are front ends to the `apt-get` and `apt-cache` commands previously described.

Try out the `aptitude` command with the options described for the `apt-get` and `apt-cache` commands. The options described in Table 3.3 should be familiar, if you've paid attention to the chapter so far. There are subtle differences; for example, the `aptitude search` *term* command only searches for a given *term* based on package names.

Table 3.3 Important aptitude Command Switches

aptitude Command Option	Function
autoclean	Clears out obsolete packages from the local database in the /var/cache/apt/archives/ directory
clean	Clears out the local database of downloaded packages from the /var/cache/apt/archives/ directory
full-upgrade	Upgrades to the latest available version of all installed packages; some desirable packages may be removed, even if they're currently in use; contrast to safe-upgrade and apt-get install dist-upgrade
install	Installs the package specified, with dependencies; normally, just the name of the package is required, which can be identified in the output from an appropriate apt-cache search command
purge	Uninstalls a package and removes associated configuration files
remove	Removes the specified package, with dependencies
safe-upgrade	Installs updates and removes orphan packages
search	Searches configured repositories for packages that match a given search term
show	Displays detailed information on a specified package
update	Updates the current local database of packages from repositories configured in the /etc/apt/sources.list file
upgrade	Compares the date of locally installed packages with the latest available database and upgrades packages when later versions are available

As a tool, aptitude is menu driven, as shown in Figure 3.3. Shortcuts are listed in the second line. For example, to access the menu, press Ctrl+T; to quit, press q or Q.

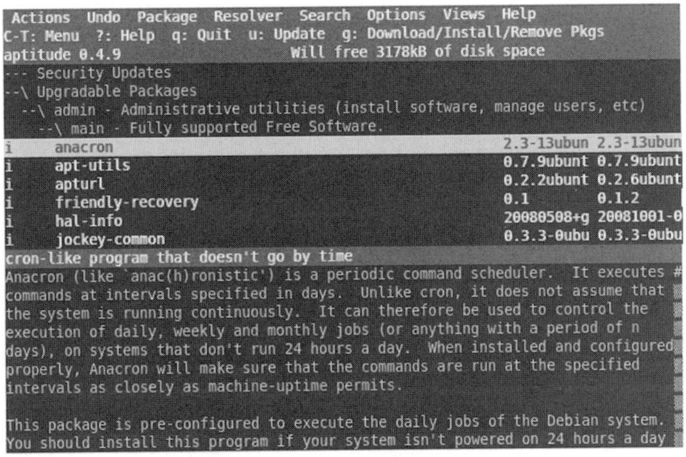

```
Actions  Undo  Package  Resolver  Search  Options  Views  Help
C-T: Menu  ?: Help  q: Quit  u: Update  g: Download/Install/Remove Pkgs
aptitude 0.4.9                    Will free 3178kB of disk space
--- Security Updates
--\ Upgradable Packages
  --\ admin - Administrative utilities (install software, manage users, etc)
    --\ main - Fully supported Free Software.
i    anacron                              2.3-13ubun  2.3-13ubun
i    apt-utils                            0.7.9ubunt  0.7.9ubunt
i    apturl                               0.2.2ubunt  0.2.6ubunt
i    friendly-recovery                    0.1         0.1.2
i    hal-info                             20080508+g  20081001-0
i    jockey-common                        0.3.3-0ubu  0.3.3-0ubu
cron-like program that doesn't go by time
Anacron (like `anac(h)ronistic') is a periodic command scheduler.  It executes #
commands at intervals specified in days.  Unlike cron, it does not assume that
the system is running continuously.  It can therefore be used to control the
execution of daily, weekly and monthly jobs (or anything with a period of n
days), on systems that don't run 24 hours a day.  When installed and configured
properly, Anacron will make sure that the commands are run at the specified
intervals as closely as machine-uptime permits.

This package is pre-configured to execute the daily jobs of the Debian system.
You should install this program if your system isn't powered on 24 hours a day
```

FIGURE 3.3 *The* aptitude *utility is menu driven.*

Red Hat Package Management Parameters

The Red Hat package management system works with the rpm command. The command is versatile; it can be used to install, upgrade, or remove a package. It can be used to list files, list installed packages, and identify the origin of installed files. And although that's just a start of what the rpm command can do, it is limited by its inability to manage dependencies.

In the following sections, you'll explore what you can do with the rpm command, how the rpm command works with kernels, and how you can convert Debian-style packages to **RPM** format, and vice versa.

The rpm Command

As with the dpkg command, the rpm command can be used to manage packages. RPM packages are fundamental to several distributions, including those released by Red Hat, Fedora, SUSE, Mandriva, and more.

As suggested by the exam objectives, you need to know how to "install, reinstall, upgrade, and remove" RPM packages. You'll learn how to perform these tasks in this section with the rpm command.

TIP

When you learn a command, learn both uses of key switches. Although you may be used to a command like `rpm -K pkgname`, don't be surprised to see an equivalent command such as `rpm --checksig pkgname`.

The best way to learn any command is to practice it on a test system. Because the `rpm` command is used much less frequently than it used to be, one way to find an appropriate package is to take advantage of a feature associated with the `yum` package management system. The `/var/cache/yum/updates/packages/` directory normally includes packages downloaded from remote repositories.

As is true for much of this book, the following steps normally require a relatively high-speed Internet connection. I've only tested these commands on the CentOS 5 distribution release. Some of the commands shown here are described in more detail later in this chapter. The following commands might work on other relatively independent **Red Hat–style packages**, on other Linux distributions that use RPM packages.

1. Download the Very Secure FTP service with the following command.

    ```
    # yumdownloader vsftpd
    ```

2. Now uninstall the package with the following command:

    ```
    # rpm -e vsftpd
    ```

    If there's an error message about `vsftpd` not being installed, that's acceptable.

3. Now try installing the package with the following `rpm` command. It should be available from the directory where you ran step 1. The `-i` switch installs the noted package.

    ```
    # rpm -i vsftpd-*
    ```

4. Find out more about the package. Try the `-q` switch, which identifies the package name with the version number. Then try the `-ql` switch, which displays all files from the given package.

    ```
    # rpm -q vsftpd
    # rpm -ql vsftpd
    ```

5. Next, install the package again, and try to upgrade it. Note the use of the `-U` switch, which is functionally equivalent to `--upgrade`. You should see an error message.

    ```
    # rpm -i vsftpd-*
    # rpm -U vsftpd-*
    ```

6. Remove (or back up) the configuration file associated with this service. For CentOS 5, the file is `/etc/vsftpd/vsftpd.conf`. For other distributions, it may be `/etc/vsftpd.conf`.

    ```
    # rm /etc/vsftpd/vsftpd.conf
    ```

7. Try installing the package again. Review the error message.
8. Then install the package with the `--replacepkgs` switch.

   `# rpm -i --replacepkgs vsftpd-*`
9. Does the configuration file reappear?
10. Remove the noted configuration file again. Then repeat the installation, substituting `--force` switch for `--replacepkgs`.

Now that you have some experience with the `rpm` command, you should not be completely lost as you read Table 3.4, with `rpm` command switches. Be aware that there's often more than one way to include a switch; for example, `-i` is functionally identical to `--install`. Some command switches require the full name of a package, including the `.rpm` extension. Other switches work with just the name of a package. More `rpm` command switches are described in the next section.

Table 3.4 Important rpm Command Switches

rpm Command Switch	Function
`-e` (`--erase`)	Uninstalls a package and removes associated configuration files.
`-F` (`--freshen`)	Upgrades the noted package; does not install the package if it isn't already installed. The full name of the package is required.
`-h` (`--hash`)	Prints hash marks to indicate the progress of an installation; normally used with the `-v` switch.
`-i` (`--install`)	Installs the package specified. The full name of the package is required, including version number and `.rpm` extension. (Wildcards can be used.)
`-K` (`--checksig`)	Verifies the signature of a package. The full name of the package is required, including version number and `.rpm` extension. (Wildcards can be used.)
`-U` (`--upgrade`)	Upgrades the noted package; installs the package if it isn't already installed. The full name of the package is required, including version number and `.rpm` extension.
`-v` (`--verbose`)	Includes additional messages; the `-vv` switch would include even more messages.
`-V` (`--verify`)	Verifies the installation status of a package, including whether files have been changed.

TIP

Linux commands are case sensitive, as are the answers you provide during the exam. If you see a question about upgrading a package and enter the `rpm -u` command, your answer would be wrong.

Practice the commands listed in Table 3.4. You might realize that the output meets several of the criteria listed in the objective line, which suggests that you need to know how to "obtain information on RPM packages such as version, status, dependencies, integrity, and signatures." This section includes commands that can help you verify the integrity and package signature associated with a package.

The `rpm` command (or even the `deb` command) must be used with care when applying it to packages related to the Linux kernel. If you find a new kernel package, it should always be installed, not upgraded.

Although the developers behind a distribution do their best to test new kernels to every conceivable situation, they can't test everything. And the kernel is at the core of the Linux operating system.

A new kernel that is installed and not upgraded will exist side by side with the original kernel. When installed, new kernels released by most distributions also exist side by side in the appropriate bootloader menu. If the new kernel does not work for whatever reason, the existing kernel can still be booted, without having to recover the system from a backup.

So if you update the kernel with the `rpm` command, be sure to install with the `-i` or `--install` switch. An upgrade with the `-U` or `--upgrade` switch would overwrite the existing working kernel.

Verify a Package Signature

One way to verify the signature of the noted `vsftpd` RPM package is with the following command (which assumes the package is in the local directory):

```
$ rpm -K vsftpd-*
vsftpd-2.0.5-12.el5.i386.rpm: (sha1) dsa sha1 md5 gpg OK
```

Note the variety of symbols after the name of the package. The `-K` switch, equivalent to `--checksig`, verifies the signatures described. More information is available with the `-Kvv` switch, as shown in Figure 3.4.

Note how the output includes the location of various public encryption keys, including SHA1 (Secure Hash Algorithm 1), DSA (Digital Signature Algorithm), MD5 (Message Digest 5), and GPG (GNU Privacy Guard).

```
[michael@CentOS5-LPI yum]$ rpm -Kvv vsftpd-2.0.5-12.el5.i386.rpm
D: Expected size:       140505 = lead(96)+sigs(344)+pad(0)+data(140065)
D:   Actual size:       140505
D: opening  db index       /var/lib/rpm/Packages rdonly mode=0x0
D: locked   db index       /var/lib/rpm/Packages
D: opening  db index       /var/lib/rpm/Pubkeys rdonly mode=0x0
D:   read h#    774 Header sanity check: OK
D: ========== DSA pubkey id a8a447dc e8562897 (h#774)
vsftpd-2.0.5-12.el5.i386.rpm:
    Header V3 DSA signature: OK, key ID e8562897
    Header SHA1 digest: OK (96cc41ef580520cf93bc29bee9ea648d501eba74)
    MD5 digest: OK (a9450f6b10a8284fefb67daf9ede15d3)
    V3 DSA signature: OK, key ID e8562897
D: closed   db index       /var/lib/rpm/Pubkeys
D: closed   db index       /var/lib/rpm/Packages
D: May free Score board((nil))
[michael@CentOS5-LPI yum]$ []
```

FIGURE 3.4 *You can learn a lot in verbose mode.*

Verify Package Contents

You can also verify the status of individual files from an installed package. With information from the rpm -V command, you can determine how files have changed relative to their original status in the package. Assuming the vsftpd package is installed, and if there's no output from the following command

```
$ rpm -V vsftpd
```

I might be sure that there have been no changes since the noted package had been installed. But there's doubt when I see the following output:

```
..?..... c /etc/vsftpd/ftpusers
..?..... c /etc/vsftpd/user_list
..?..... c /etc/vsftpd/vsftpd.conf
```

Each of the dots in the left column may be replaced by a failure code, for any changes that have been made. The question mark (?) specifies a test that could not be performed. Failure codes from left to right are listed in Table 3.5. The last five entries are not failure codes but mutually exclusive options for the last character position that identify the purpose of the file.

Table 3.5 Codes Associated with rpm -V

rpm -V Failure Code	Description
5	Mismatched MD5 checksum
S	Change in file size
L	Mismatched link path
T	Different file modification time
D	Changed device file
U	Different user owner

Table 3.5 Continued

rpm -V Failure Code	Description
G	Different group owner
c	Configuration file
d	Documentation file
g	Ghost file
l	License file
r	Readme file

Queries and More with rpm

The rpm -q pkgname command, which returns the current version number of the package, may seem simple. For example, take a look at the following command, which returns the currently installed version of the Samba file server:

```
$ rpm -q samba
samba-3.0.28-1.el5_2.1
```

This assumes that the Samba file server package is currently installed. If you want to try out another version of this query, run the rpm -qa command, which lists all currently installed packages. But that just scratches the surface of what you can do with the rpm --query command. (In this case, -q is synonymous to --query.) Review other options in Table 3.6.

Table 3.6 Important rpm --query Options

rpm Query Commands	Purpose
-q pkgname	Returns the version number of the noted pkgname
-qa	Displays the version number of all installed packages
-qc pkgname	Extracts the name of configuration files from the noted pkgname
-qd pkgname	Lists all documentation files contained in the noted pkgname
-qf /path/to/file	Determines the package owner of the /path/to/file file
-qi pkgname	Returns a full description for the noted pkgname
-ql pkgname	Lists all files contained in the noted pkgname
-qR pkgname	Specifies all dependencies of the noted pkgname

On any exam, be aware that you might see different options for the same switch. For example, the following two commands are functionality identical:

```
$ rpm -qa
$ rpm --query --all
```

I included only the single letter switches in the table to avoid overcrowding. To review in the context of the LPI objectives, from the information in this section, you should now know how to obtain information on RPM packages such as version, status, dependencies.

Conversions with rpm2cpio and alien

This section focuses on two related commands that convert RPM packages to different formats. The rpm2cpio command can extract a cpio archive from an RPM package, associated with a different archive format. The alien command can convert from Debian to RPM package formats (and vice versa). Generally, alien is available only on Debian-based distributions.

NOTE

The latest LPI objectives no longer specifically include a reference to the alien command. However, do not be surprised to see a question on the topic, because the objectives are careful to note that they specify only "a partial list."

The rpm2cpio Command

The rpm2cpio command converts a given RPM package into a text stream. In other words, the information from this command should be directed to a file; otherwise, the output appears directly on the command line screen, and it looks like gibberish.

NOTE

This section uses command "redirection" and "pipe" concepts, which are described in more detail in Chapter 5, "Command Filters and Pipes."

The rpm2cpio command often works hand in hand with the cpio command. For example, the following command redirects the noted RPM to the vsftpd.cpio file:

```
$ rpm2cpio vsftpd-* > vsftpd.cpio
```

Take a look at the contents of the file with the following command, and note the list of files within. These are the files packaged in the RPM.

```
$ less vsftpd.cpio
```

You can review the same list of files with the following command, which pipes the archive stream to the cpio command, with the list (-t) switch.

```
$ rpm2cpio vsftpd-* | cpio -t
```

Now take the archive just created, and extract the files with the cpio command. The following command extracts (-i) the noted file in verbose mode (-v), creating directories as needed (-d).

```
$ cpio -ivd < vsftpd.cpio
```

If you've run this command in the local home directory, the directories will be created as sub-directories of the local home directory. If you want these files written to locations appropriate for the package, the command has to be run from the top-level root directory (/).

The alien Command

Use the alien command with care. Most Linux packages have a whole raft of dependencies. Assume that you want to install a package that exists only for the Ubuntu distribution on a CentOS 5 system. You would then use the alien command to convert that package for use on that CentOS release. There's a risk, because the converted package may not check for appropriate dependencies. Even if all dependencies are satisfied, other features of the target release may prevent proper operation. For example, an FTP server built for Ubuntu does not consider the Security Enhanced Linux features built into Fedora Linux releases.

 NOTE

The same caution applies when mixing packages between distributions with the same packaging system. For example, RPM packages built for SUSE Linux may not work on Red Hat systems; Debian packages built for Ubuntu may not work on Debian Linux systems.

With all that in mind, the alien command is fairly simple. If you have an RPM package and want to convert it for use on a Debian-based distribution, just run the following command:

```
# alien --to-deb package.rpm
```

To reverse the process, just run the following command:

```
# alien --to-rpm package.deb
```

The Power of yum

The yum command was developed to address dependency issues. In other words, when installing or removing packages with the yum command, dependent packages are automatically installed or removed as needed.

Originally developed for the Yellow Dog Linux distribution, yum has been adapted by Red Hat for its distributions. Some changes were made, so the command as currently used is known as the Yellowdog Updater, Modified, which is the genesis of the yum command name.

Although the yum command is similar to the apt-* commands, the default versions of yum commands always gather information from configured repositories. Because yum doesn't normally rely on a local cache, cited packages are always up-to-date.

In contrast, administrators have to run a command like apt-get update before installing a new package to ensure they download the latest version of that package.

 NOTE

Some Linux developers have ported the apt-* commands for Red Hat–based distributions. Their popularity has waned as fewer developers have created mirrors customized for use with apt-* commands.

Basic yum Commands

When current Red Hat-based distributions are installed, they come with a default configuration which connects to valid repositories of current and updated packages. Therefore, you should be able to use the yum commands immediately, without modifying any related configuration files. Of course, this assumes that networking to the Internet is active from the local system.

Start with a big picture. Try the yum list command. As shown in Figure 3.5, it loads a couple of plug-ins and then lists available packages.

 NOTE

In standard written English, "plug-in" is hyphenated. However, as shown in the figure, Linux does not always follow proper English.

```
Loading "fastestmirror" plugin
Loading "priorities" plugin
Loading mirror speeds from cached hostfile
 * base: mirrors.liquidweb.com
 * updates: mirrors.bluehost.com
 * addons: linux.mirrors.es.net
 * extras: mirrors.versaweb.com
0 packages excluded due to repository priority protections
Installed Packages
GConf2.i386                        2.14.0-9.el5            installed
ImageMagick.i386                   6.2.8.0-4.el5_1.1       installed
MAKEDEV.i386                       3.23-1.2                installed
NetworkManager.i386                1:0.6.4-8.el5           installed
NetworkManager-glib.i386           1:0.6.4-8.el5           installed
NetworkManager-gnome.i386          1:0.6.4-8.el5           installed
ORBit2.i386                        2.14.3-4.el5            installed
PyQt.i386                          3.16-4                  installed
PyXML.i386                         0.8.4-4                 installed
SDL.i386                           1.2.10-8.el5            installed
SysVinit.i386                      2.86-14                 installed
a2ps.i386                          4.13b-57.2.el5          installed
acl.i386                           2.2.39-3.el5            installed
acpid.i386                         1.0.4-5                 installed
alacarte.noarch                    0.10.0-1.fc6            installed
alchemist.i386                     1.0.36-2.el5            installed
--More--
```

FIGURE 3.5 *The yum list command displays all available packages.*

The fastest mirror plug-in looks through a list of mirrors and determines the repository with the optimal mirror. Each mirror has identical copies of the same repositories. The `priorities` plug-in sets an order of precedence for different repositories. Generally, repositories created by developers of a distribution are considered first, over repositories created by third parties. For example, if CentOS were to incorporate a package for the `apt-*` commands into its base repositories, the `priorities` plug-in would give it precedence over a similar package from a third party.

Then the URL to the selected mirrors is listed for each repository. As shown in Figure 3.5, four repositories are configured, as defined in the configuration files in the next section.

Installed packages are listed first, with architecture in the left column. The middle column specifies the version number. The right column lists whether the package is installed, or the source repository.

I describe several other useful yum command switches in Table 3.7.

The commands described in Table 3.7 are just the beginning. Run the yum | more command. The following output lists all yum command options:

```
usage: yum [options] < grouplist, localinstall, groupinfo, localupdate,
resolvedep, erase, deplist, groupremove, makecache, upgrade, provides,
shell, install, whatprovides, groupinstall, update, repolist, groupupdate,
info, search, check-update, list, remove, clean, grouperase >
```

There is one other related command listed in the objectives: **yumdownloader.** It downloads RPM packages from configured repositories and is a fairly straightforward command; just include the package name, and it'll download a copy of the specified RPM package into the local directory. You tested this earlier in this chapter with the yumdownloader vsftpd command. More is possible; with the --resolve switch, the download includes dependencies.

Table 3.7 Important yum Command Switches

yum Command Switch	Function
list	Lists installed and available packages from configured repositories.
check-update	Compares installed RPMs against those in configured repositories to collect a list of packages available to update.
install *pkgname*	Installs the noted package, with dependencies. If the package is installed and an update is available, the package is updated.
remove *pkgname*	Uninstalls the noted package, with dependencies.

The yum Configuration Files

The yum configuration is based on the /etc/yum.conf file. Other configuration files may be and are often referenced from this file. So let's examine the default version of this file on my CentOS 5 system; the active directives from this file are described in Table 3.8.

Table 3.8 Directives from /etc/yum.conf

yum Configuration Directive	Description
cachedir	Specifies the directory with cached information from remote repositories
keepcache	Determines whether the cache of headers is stored after each yum command
debuglevel	Sets the logging message level
logfile	Specifies the file where yum log messages are written
pkgpolicy	Determines a priority between packages, if they exist on multiple repositories
distroverpkg	Specifies the distribution code
tolerant	Continues whether there's an error (or not)
exactarch	Limits access to one specific architecture
obsoletes	Supports checks of obsolete packages
gpgcheck	Performs a GPG key signature check
plugins	Enables plug-ins via the /etc/yum/pluginconf.d/ directory

Although the last lines in the yum.conf file are commented out, they still indicate the default configuration, which incorporates settings from files in the /etc/yum.repos.d/ directory. The CentOS-Base.repo file from the CentOS 5 release includes stanzas linked to four different repositories, as shown in Figure 3.6.

```
[base]
name=CentOS-$releasever - Base
mirrorlist=http://mirrorlist.centos.org/?release=$releasever&arch=$basearch&repo=os
#baseurl=http://mirror.centos.org/centos/$releasever/os/$basearch/
gpgcheck=1
gpgkey=http://mirror.centos.org/centos/RPM-GPG-KEY-CentOS-5

#released updates
[updates]
name=CentOS-$releasever - Updates
mirrorlist=http://mirrorlist.centos.org/?release=$releasever&arch=$basearch&repo=updates
#baseurl=http://mirror.centos.org/centos/$releasever/updates/$basearch/
gpgcheck=1
gpgkey=http://mirror.centos.org/centos/RPM-GPG-KEY-CentOS-5

#packages used/produced in the build but not released
[addons]
name=CentOS-$releasever - Addons
mirrorlist=http://mirrorlist.centos.org/?release=$releasever&arch=$basearch&repo=addons
#baseurl=http://mirror.centos.org/centos/$releasever/addons/$basearch/
gpgcheck=1
gpgkey=http://mirror.centos.org/centos/RPM-GPG-KEY-CentOS-5

#additional packages that may be useful
[extras]
name=CentOS-$releasever - Extras
mirrorlist=http://mirrorlist.centos.org/?release=$releasever&arch=$basearch&repo=extras
#baseurl=http://mirror.centos.org/centos/$releasever/extras/$basearch/
gpgcheck=1
gpgkey=http://mirror.centos.org/centos/RPM-GPG-KEY-CentOS-5

#additional packages that extend functionality of existing packages
[centosplus]
name=CentOS-$releasever - Plus
mirrorlist=http://mirrorlist.centos.org/?release=$releasever&arch=$basearch&repo=centosplus
#baseurl=http://mirror.centos.org/centos/$releasever/centosplus/$basearch/
gpgcheck=1
enabled=0
gpgkey=http://mirror.centos.org/centos/RPM-GPG-KEY-CentOS-5

(END)
```

FIGURE 3.6 *Repositories are configured in an /etc/yum.repos.d/ file.*

Note the five different stanzas, as named in brackets. The first stanza, which starts with [base], includes a link to base installation files. The standard directives from this file are described in Table 3.9.

The mirrorlist line in each stanza requires some explanation. For example, with the [base] repository, you'll see the following line:

mirrorlist=http://mirrorlist.centos.org/?release=$releasever&arch=$basearch&repo=os

The release version is substituted for $releasever, and architecture is substituted for $basearch. The URL shown here points to a specific file, with other URLs, a list of mirrors. Each time the yum command is run, it evaluates each of these repositories for optimal access.

mirrorlist=http://mirrorlist.centos.org/?release=5.2&arch=i386&repo=os

Plug-ins as cited in the /etc/yum/pluginconf.d/ directory are enabled through Python-based configuration scripts in the /usr/lib/yum-plugins/ directory.

Table 3.9 Directives from /etc/yum.conf

Repository Configuration Directive	Description
[base]	Specifies basic installation files
[updates]	Points to updates to basic installation files
[addons]	Includes unreleased additional packages
[extras]	Specifies a repository of additional packages
[centosplus]	Associated with basic installation files
name	Names the repository
$releasever	Notes the release version, available from /etc/redhat-release
$basearch	Specifies the CPU architecture
gpgcheck	Performs a GPG key signature check
gpgkey	Specifies the location of the GPG signature key
enabled	Enables or disables access to the noted repository

Third-Party Repositories

Third-party repositories are commonly available from a number of sources. Packages in such repositories are popular but are frequently not supported by vendors such as Red Hat. Several third-party repositories are working on a common standard; for more information, see http://www.rpmrepo.org. One element shared by such repositories is their use of configuration files in the /etc/yum.repos.d/ directory.

Chapter Summary

In this chapter you focused on the package management systems associated with the two major types of Linux packaging systems, originally developed for the Debian and Red Hat Linux distributions. You can control these packaging systems with the dpkg and rpm commands. These commands can be used to install and remove packages, as well as list files, identify the package associated with a specific file, and list installed packages.

Dependencies are a common problem with both package systems, which has led to the development of the apt-* and yum commands. The apt-* commands are associated with Debian-style distributions including Ubuntu; the yum command is associated with Red Hat–style distributions including SUSE. Both sets of commands can install and remove packages and dependencies.

Key Terms

◆ **apt.** A package management system for repository management on Debian-style distributions such as Ubuntu.

◆ **apt-*.** A reference to several commands most commonly used for repository management on Debian-style distributions such as Ubuntu.

◆ **apt-cache.** A command that searches for package information from downloaded and cached repository data.

◆ **apt-file.** A command that searches for files from downloaded cached repository data.

◆ **apt-get.** A command that can install, remove, or purge specified packages, with dependencies.

◆ **aptitude.** A front end to the apt-* commands; also opens a menu-driven package management tool.

◆ **deb.** A term for binary Debian-style packages in /etc/apt/sources.list; also the extension for Debian-style package files.

◆ **Debian-style packaging.** The package management system associated with Debian and allied distributions such as Ubuntu.

◆ **deb-src.** A term for source code Debian-style packages in /etc/apt/sources.list.

◆ **dependencies.** Packages that are required when another is being installed or removed. Often multiple dependencies are included in an installation (or removal).

◆ **dpkg.** A command that installs or removes specified Debian-style packages. Does not include dependencies.

◆ **dpkg-reconfigure.** A command used for packages where manual configuration is enabled.

◆ **/etc/apt/sources.list.** The configuration file that points Debian-based distributions, including Ubuntu, to appropriate repositories.

◆ **/etc/yum.conf.** The configuration file that points Red Hat-based distributions, including CentOS, to appropriate repositories.

◆ **Red Hat–style packaging.** The package management system associated with Red Hat and allied distributions such as Fedora.

◆ **reverse dependencies.** Packages that satisfy the requirements of another that is being installed or removed. *Also see* dependencies.

◆ **rpm.** A command that installs or removes specified Red Hat–style packages. Does not include dependencies; also the extension for Red Hat–style package files.

◆ **RPM.** A reference to the Red Hat Package Management type.

◆ **Synaptic Package Manager.** A graphical front end to the apt-* commands.

◆ **yum.** A command that can install, remove, or purge specified packages, with dependencies; it can also search for package information from downloaded and cached repository data.

◆ **yumdownloader.** A command that can download specified RPM packages.

Review Questions

The number of review questions in this chapter and other chapters in this book is proportionate to each section's weight in the LPI objectives. Because this chapter covers items 102.4 and 102.5, the weight is 6; therefore, you'll see 12 questions in this section. You'll see multiple choice single answer, fill-in-the blank, and multiple choice, multiple answer questions, as you'll encounter on the exam.

1. Which of the following commands uninstalls and removes the associated configuration files for the Postfix e-mail service?

    A. `apt-get remove postfix`

    B. `dpkg -r postfix`

    C. `aptitude remove postfix`

    D. `dpkg -P postfix`

2. Which of the following commands identifies the package that owns the `/path/to/file` file?

    A. `apt-file search /path/to/file`

    B. `dpkg -S /path/to/file`

    C. `dpkg -qf /path/to/file`

    D. `apt-cache search /path/to/file`

3. If you want to learn more about the package named `bigpkg`, which of the following commands includes the description? Choose two.

    A. `apt-file show bigpkg`

    B. `apt-get show bigpkg`

    C. `apt-cache show bigpkg`

    D. `aptitude show bigpkg`

4. Which of the following commands identifies the dependencies required for the package named `bigpkg`?

    A. `apt-file depends bigpkg`

    B. `apt-get depends bigpkg`

    C. `apt-cache depends bigpkg`

    D. `aptitude depends bigpkg`

5. The _____ command can help identify a file from an uninstalled Debian-style package. Do not include the full path to the command. Do include the switch.

6. Which of the following files includes URLs for the repositories associated with the apt-* commands?
   - **A.** /etc/sources/apt.list
   - **B.** /etc/sources.list
   - **C.** /etc/apt/apt.list
   - **D.** /etc/apt/sources.list

7. Which of the following commands uninstalls the bigpkg package?
   - **A.** rpm -e bigpkg
   - **B.** rpm -u bigpkg
   - **C.** rpm -r bigpkg
   - **D.** rpm -p bigpkg

8. The _____ command verifies the status of files from the bigpkg RPM package.

9. Which of the following commands lists all installed RPM packages? Choose two.
   - **A.** rpm -ql
   - **B.** yum list
   - **C.** rpm -qa
   - **D.** yum -qa

10. Which of the following is the main configuration file for the yum command?
    - **A.** /etc/yum.conf
    - **B.** /etc/yum/yum.conf
    - **C.** /etc/yum.repos.d/yum.conf
    - **D.** /etc/yum/yum-updatesd.conf

11. Enter the command that downloads a desired RPM package. Do not include the full path.

    _____

12. If there is an unmet dependency that you want to supersede, which of the following switches would you include with the rpm command?
    - **A.** --depends
    - **B.** --nodeps
    - **C.** --force-depends
    - **D.** --nd

Chapter 4

Command Lines and Files

After completing this chapter, you will be able to

- Work with the bash shell

- Manage the bash environment

- Manage files and directories

- Understand archives and globbing

Introduction

The heart of Linux is in the **command-line interface (CLI)**, a text interface for typed commands. Although Linux does include excellent options for a graphical user interface (GUI), over 90% of the LPIC-1 exams are focused on the CLI. The LPI exams are intended to be practical tests, and administrative functionality can be found at the CLI.

In this chapter, you'll focus on two basic topics: the command-line **shell** and basic file management. A shell provides the interface between users and an operating system. The default command-line shell for most Linux distributions is bash, which is an acronym for the Bourne Again Shell. It's known recursively as the **bash shell**. An understanding of how to manage the bash shell environment can help the prospective Linux administrator use the command line more efficiently.

Of course, the shell is just the beginning. The command line is focused on files and directories. This chapter will help you understand how to create, remove, find, and manage files and directories with a variety of commands.

TIP

This chapter addresses two objectives in the LPI exam: 103.1 ("Work on the Command Line") and 103.3 ("Perform Basic File Management").

The Structure of the Shell

The shell is the command-line interpreter, and the default for most Linux distributions, as well as the LPIC-1 exams, is the bash shell. To that end, this section describes how you can interact with bash by changing the environment, by taking advantage of the **PATH**, and by using the command-line history.

Of course, the shell is not useful without some basic shell commands, which you'll also explore in this section.

TIP

Although several other shells are commonly used in Linux, bash is the only shell cited in the LPIC-1 objectives. However, many users, especially on Ubuntu systems, are configured with a default dash shell, which is the Debian-Almquist shell.

A bash Shell Environment

Users can implement any installed shell of their choice. Some major distributions specify shells other than bash as defaults for regular users. The default shell is based on the user entry in the authentication database. When implemented locally, that database starts with the /etc/passwd configuration file. The important bit from the entry for my account is in the last column, delineated by colons:

```
michael:x:1000:1000:Michael Jang,,,:/home/michael:/bin/bash
```

In other words, when I log into my system from a command-line console, I'm greeted by a command-line prompt, with the bash shell as the command-line interpreter.

The settings associated with the shell are configured through system-wide and user-specific configuration files. There are several common files in the latest distributions, starting with **/etc/profile**. The commands in /etc/profile are executed whenever a new login shell is started. Depending on the configuration, /etc/profile may call a system-wide bash configuration file such as **/etc/bash.bashrc**.

However, the system-wide configuration files are called only when a user logs into a system. Before that user gets a CLI, user-specific bash configuration files are also invoked. Such files are hidden in individual user home directories. For example, my user-specific configuration files are stored in the /home/michael directory, in the **.bashrc** configuration file.

Because there is some overlap between this topic and LPIC-1 Objective 105.1, some of the explanations in this section may seem incomplete. For more information on many of these topics, see Chapter 9, "Shells, Scripting, and Data Management."

NOTE

Hidden files in Linux start with a dot. To review the hidden files in the current directory, run the ls -a command.

When a user moves from a different shell to bash, which can be done with the bash command, the .bashrc and **.bash_profile** files, if they exist in that user's home directory, are executed.

Whenever a user logs out of a system, the commands in the `.bash_logout` file are run. Yes, users can configure these hidden files in their own home directories to better fit their needs. Several commands are associated with the bash shell and related environment, as follows.

bash

The `bash` command invokes another instance of the bash shell, in another CLI. It is also run whenever a user logs into a system. When run by a user, it's most commonly invoked to change from a different shell such as dash.

env

Every process includes **environment variables**, parameters such as a username, a home directory, and a command-line shell. Environment variables carry the same value from shell to shell. But the LPIC-1 objectives are limited to bash, and the bash shell uses environment variables as shell variables.

Current environment variables can be listed with the **env** command. One view is shown in Figure 4.1, which I explain partially in Table 4.1.

```
michael@ubuntuHHserver:~$ env
TERM=xterm
SHELL=/bin/bash
XDG_SESSION_COOKIE=82d92151e5ded2d7ed0dd4c548d92640-1229536518.662651-1987656958
SSH_CLIENT=192.168.0.8 46285 22
SSH_TTY=/dev/pts/0
USER=michael
LS_COLORS=no=00:fi=00:di=01;34:ln=01;36:pi=40;33:so=01;35:do=01;35:bd=40;33;01:c
d=40;33;01:or=40;31;01:su=37;41:sg=30;43:tw=30;42:ow=34;42:st=37;44:ex=01;32:*.t
ar=01;31:*.tgz=01;31:*.svgz=01;31:*.arj=01;31:*.taz=01;31:*.lzh=01;31:*.lzma=01;
31:*.zip=01;31:*.z=01;31:*.Z=01;31:*.dz=01;31:*.gz=01;31:*.bz2=01;31:*.bz=01;31:
*.tbz2=01;31:*.tz=01;31:*.deb=01;31:*.rpm=01;31:*.jar=01;31:*.rar=01;31:*.ace=01
;31:*.zoo=01;31:*.cpio=01;31:*.7z=01;31:*.rz=01;31:*.jpg=01;35:*.jpeg=01;35:*.gi
f=01;35:*.bmp=01;35:*.pbm=01;35:*.pgm=01;35:*.ppm=01;35:*.tga=01;35:*.xbm=01;35:
*.xpm=01;35:*.tif=01;35:*.tiff=01;35:*.png=01;35:*.svg=01;35:*.mng=01;35:*.pcx=0
1;35:*.mov=01;35:*.mpg=01;35:*.mpeg=01;35:*.m2v=01;35:*.mkv=01;35:*.ogm=01;35:*.
mp4=01;35:*.m4v=01;35:*.mp4v=01;35:*.vob=01;35:*.qt=01;35:*.nuv=01;35:*.wmv=01;3
5:*.asf=01;35:*.rm=01;35:*.rmvb=01;35:*.flc=01;35:*.avi=01;35:*.fli=01;35:*.gl=0
1;35:*.dl=01;35:*.xcf=01;35:*.xwd=01;35:*.yuv=01;35:*.aac=00;36:*.au=00;36:*.fla
c=00;36:*.mid=00;36:*.midi=00;36:*.mka=00;36:*.mp3=00;36:*.mpc=00;36:*.ogg=00;36
:*.ra=00;36:*.wav=00;36:
MAIL=/var/mail/michael
PATH=/home/michael/bin:/usr/local/sbin:/usr/local/bin:/usr/sbin:/usr/bin:/sbin:/
bin:/usr/games
PWD=/home/michael
LANG=en_US.UTF-8
HISTCONTROL=ignoreboth
SHLVL=1
HOME=/home/michael
LOGNAME=michael
SSH_CONNECTION=192.168.0.8 46285 192.168.0.50 22
LESSOPEN=| /usr/bin/lesspipe %s
DISPLAY=localhost:10.0
LESSCLOSE=/usr/bin/lesspipe %s %s
_=/usr/bin/env
michael@ubuntuHHserver:~$
```

FIGURE 4.1 *User environment variables.*

Table 4.1 Selected Environment Variables

Variable	Description
SHELL	Default shell for the user
USERNAME	Login name for the current user
PATH	See the section, "Commands and the PATH"
PWD	Current directory; also known as the print working directory
HOME	Home directory for the current user

As environmental settings are variables, you can review them with the help of the echo command. For example, to find the current value of the HOME environment variable, include the $ with the variable, as shown with the following command:

```
$ echo $HOME
```

export to Set an Environment Variable

It's fairly easy to add to the current list of environment variables. The **export** command is the key to the process. As just suggested, environment variables are typically capitalized. So if you wanted to set ABC as an environment variable with a value of alphabet, you could run the following two commands, which sets a value for and then implements the environment variable.

```
$ ABC=alphabet
$ export ABC
```

Now you can verify the new environment variable with the following command:

```
$ echo $ABC
```

 NOTE

The set command is frequently used in scripts to set an environment variable for other shells. For example, under the C shell, the set ABC=alphabet command may be used to set the noted variable.

unset

To cancel a set environment variable, use the **unset** command. For the ABC variable, the following command unassigns the previous value of that variable.

```
$ unset ABC
```

Dots and Directories

One important character at the Linux command line is the **dot (.)**, which represents the current directory. Although most commands refer to the local directory, the dot can be useful for executable commands.

If you've configured a script such as databasejob in a local directory, it can't normally run directly, even if executable permissions are properly set. From the local directory, one way to execute the noted script is with the following command:

```
$ ./databasejob
```

The dot indicates the local directory, and the forward slash specifies files in that directory.

A dot in front of a file indicates a hidden file. As described in the "Create and Manage Files and Directories" section, hidden files are included when commands to copy or move files include a dot.

There are dots, and there are **double dot**s (..). A double dot specifies the next higher level directory. For example, when I'm in my home directory (/home/michael), the ls .. command leads to the following output, which specifies the directories within the /home directory.

```
dickens donna katie ftp michael nancy randy
```

Commands and the PATH

When running a command, you could type in the /usr/kerberos/bin/kinit command to get a Kerberos encryption ticket, but that's going through a lot of different directories. Long typing sequences often lead to errors. That is one reason why the PATH variable was implemented on Linux. It is an environment variable that specifies default directories searched for a typed-in command. It normally includes some standard directories suitable for regular and administrative users.

But first you need to understand a couple of definitions:

◆ **Relative path.** A directory defined relative to the current directory. For example, the ls Desktop/ command means different things depending on the current directory. If run in the /home/michael directory, it lists files in the /home/michael/Desktop directory.

◆ **Absolute path.** A directory defined absolutely, based on the top-level root directory (/). For example, the ls /home/michael/Desktop/ command defines the full path to the target subdirectory.

The PATH defines the directories where the shell looks when you type in a command. To review its current value, run the echo $PATH command. For example, it reveals the following on my CentOS-5 system:

```
/usr/kerberos/bin:/usr/local/bin:/bin:/usr/bin:/home/michael/bin
```

In other words, I do not need to type in the full path for commands in any of the noted directories. For example, to execute the `who` command, with the given PATH, I could type in either of the following commands:

```
$ /usr/bin/who
$ who
```

Some administrators prefer to log in with the root account based on the extended PATH for that account, which supports direct access to a wider variety of commands.

```
/usr/kerberos/sbin:/usr/kerberos/bin:/usr/local/sbin:/usr/local/bin:/sbin:
/bin:/usr/sbin:/usr/bin:/root/bin
```

But as a regular user, you can still execute commands not included in the PATH. On many Red Hat–based distributions, the /sbin directory is not in the PATH for regular users. But you can still review the current network configuration using the full path with commands such as this:

```
$ /sbin/ifconfig
```

The previous section described how you can execute a command in the local directory. That workaround can be avoided if you add the dot (.) to the PATH. But that option is strongly discouraged, because it makes it easier for a cracker to run malicious commands if he breaks into your system.

 NOTE

In the Linux world, a hacker is a good person who just wants to create better software. Because that varies with the more common definition for "hacker," knowledgeable Linux users define a cracker as someone who wants to break into your system.

For more information on changing the PATH, see Chapter 9.

Command Completion

Command completion features make life easier for anyone working from the command line at the bash shell. It's a shell characteristic that fills in or provides options for partially typed in commands. At the command-line prompt, press the Tab key twice. You'll see output similar to the following, which specifies the number of available commands in PATH directories.

```
Display all 1885 possibilities? (y or n)
```

Of course, most users would not want to scan so many options. However, if you're uncertain about spelling, command completion can help. At the command line for my CentOS 5 system, it's easy to review most available system configuration tools. Just type in `system-` and press the Tab key twice, as shown in Figure 4.2.

```
[michael@CentOS5-LPI ~]$ system-
system-cdinstall-helper        system-config-nfs
system-config-authentication   system-config-printer
system-config-date             system-config-rootpassword
system-config-display          system-config-securitylevel
system-config-httpd            system-config-securitylevel-tui
system-config-kdump            system-config-services
system-config-keyboard         system-config-soundcard
system-config-language         system-config-time
system-config-lvm              system-config-users
system-config-network          system-control-network
system-config-network-cmd      system-install-packages
[michael@CentOS5-LPI ~]$ system-█
```

FIGURE 4.2 *The advantage of command completion.*

If you want to narrow the options further, just add some letters. In CentOS 5, if you type system-config-s and then press the Tab key twice, you'll see fewer options for commands.

Basic Shell Commands

Several basic shell commands are listed in the LPIC Level 1 objectives. There is no common theme with these particular commands. The commands are **pwd**, **man**, **uname**, and **exec**.

pwd

The pwd command is also an acronym, based on the UNIX heritage on teletype machines. It returns the current directory, known as the print working directory.

man

The man command is used to access any number of command manuals, known colloquially as man pages. It's straightforward, because all you need to do is cite the command in question. For example, the following command displays the manual for the man command:

```
$ man man
```

You can navigate through the page with standard keyboard buttons, such as the up and down arrow as well as the PageUp and PageDown keys. When you're finished, press q. To search through the page, commands associated with the vi editor can help; for more information, see Chapter 6, "Processes, Priorities, and Editing."

If you want to search through available commands, the -k switch can help. For example, to find a list of commands that relate to Linux archives, run the following command:

```
$ man -k archive
```

 TIP

The man -k command is equivalent to the **apropos** command. The man -f command is equivalent to the **whatis** command.

Review the output. It actually searches through a list of all commands and manual page titles. In this case, it returns a list of all commands with "archive" in either the command or the title. In many cases, you'll also notice more than one man page available for some commands. For example, the following command reveals four different manuals associated with the sync command:

```
$ man -f sync
sync    (1)   - flush filesystem buffers
sync    (2)   - commit buffer cache to disk
sync    (3p)  - schedule filesystem updates
sync    (8)   - synchronize data on disk with memory
```

If you ran the man sync command, it would display the first man page, from the first manual section. If you want to display the man page for the last sync command on the list, run the following command:

```
$ man 8 sync
```

Alternatively, you could display all four man pages in sequence, with the following command:

```
$ man -a sync
```

You may need to know the different basic sections associated with man pages, as listed in Table 4.2.

Table 4.2 Man Page Sections

Section	Description
1	Executable programs and shell commands
2	System calls
3	Library calls
4	Special files
5	File formats and conventions
6	Games
7	Miscellaneous
8	System administration commands
9	Kernel routines

Although there are additional sections of man pages, they go beyond the scope of the LPIC Level 1 requirements.

uname

The uname command includes system information associated with the architecture and kernel. To review all basic information, run the uname -a command, which returns the following on my CentOS-5 system:

```
Linux CentOS5-LPI 2.6.18-92.1.18.el5 #1 SMP Wed Nov 12 09:30:27 EST 2008 i686 athlon i386
GNU/Linux
```

In order, this output includes the name of the kernel, the hostname of the system, the kernel version, the release date and type of kernel, the machine hardware name, the processor type, the hardware platform, and the operating system.

Each of these items can be individually specified with other switches, as specified in Table 4.3.

Table 4.3 uname Command Switches

Switch	Description
-a	All uname options
-i	Hardware platform
-m	Machine hardware name
-n	Hostname
-o	Operating system name
-p	Processor
-r	Kernel release
-s	Kernel name
-v	Kernel version

exec Runs Apart from a Shell

The exec command, as cited in the LPIC-1 objectives, is the command that can override a current shell. The command cited with the command is run, and then the object shell process is stopped. It is different from the program system call of the same name.

The exec command is also used as a switch. For example, the rm command is limited in the numbers of files that it can delete in any one command. If you ever run into this limitation, the exec command switch can help.

During a test, I set up a camera that takes one picture every second. Each picture is uploaded to my server. That's nearly 100,000 files every day. If I tried to delete all these files with the rm command, it would lead to an error message. Alternatively, the following command finds all files in the local directory, with file names that start with `camera1`. Once those files are found, the `-exec` command switch removes all of those files.

```
$ find . -name 'camera1*' -exec rm {} \;
```

For more information on the pipe and redirection characters in the noted command, see Chapter 5, "Command Filters and Pipes."

Basic Command History

The bash shell keeps a record of recently executed commands, known as the command history. The history for each user is stored in the hidden `.bash_history` file, in that user's home directory. The length of this file, which corresponds to the number of stored commands, is based on the **HISTSIZE** variable. One way to find that limit is with the following command:

```
$ echo $HISTSIZE
```

However, the history of previous commands is also accessible with the **history** command, with output shown in Figure 4.3. You may note a difference between the output of the `history` command and the contents of the `.bash_history` file.

```
476  man -k test
477  man man
478  man -k pax
479  man man
480  man ls
481  man -k ls
482  man -k shells
483  man -k man
484  man man
485  man man
486  man uname
487  uname -a
488  man uname
489  uname -a
490  uname -p
491  uname -i
492  uname -s
493  man uname
494  uname -v
495  uname -i
496  man uname
497  vi .bash_history
498  history
michael@UbuntuHH:~$ []
```

FIGURE 4.3 *A history of previous commands.*

The difference includes the commands run during the current shell session. Such commands aren't written to the `.bash_history` file until you log out of that session. One way to view your command history is based on the commands run during the current session, appended to the contents of the `.bash_history` file.

To review previous commands, use the up and down arrows. Each time the up arrow is pressed from the command line, you're taken back one command in the history. When you run the history command, you'll see numbers associated with each command. So that leads to three ways to use the history of previous commands:

First, you could just press the up arrow as many times as needed to find the command previously executed. Once seen in the command line, just press Enter to execute that command again.

Second, you could use the command number. For example, based on the list shown in Figure 4.3, the following command executes the uname -a command:

```
$ !489
```

Third, you could use the first letter (or more) of the command. Based on the command history shown in the figure, the following command opens the .bash_history file in the vi editor:

```
$ !v
```

If there's more than one command in the history that starts with a v, you can specify more letters of the desired command. Otherwise, bash runs the most recently run command that starts with a v.

Basic File Management

Candidates should be able to use the basic Linux commands to manage files and directories. With the tens of thousands of files available, search commands are an important part of the administrative process. To help manage the available files, archives can manage group of files as well as facilitate backups. Globbing is the Linux term for file wildcards, which go beyond simple asterisks.

 TIP

Understand the switches associated with file management commands. Because administrators use commands with switches, they are commonly fair game on associated exams.

Linux Wildcards and Globbing

Wildcards in Linux go beyond the standard asterisk (*). Although the concept in Linux is known as **globbing**, individual wildcards are known as globs. Several wildcards are available, as described in Table 4.4.

Table 4.4 Linux Globs (Wildcards)

Glob	Description
*	Matches zero or more characters; *at would match at, cat, 1at, and so on
?	Matches one character; ?at would match cat, 1at, and so on
[ab]	Matches characters within the brackets; [ab]at would match aat and bat
[!a-x]	Matches all but the noted range of characters; [!a-x]at would match yat and zat

These globs can be combined. For example, if I were to run the ls ?at* command, I'd see file names such as cat, bat, tatters, and tate. But such globs may be tempered; for example, if I ran the ls ?at*. command, the only file names that would show up in the output would end with the dot.

In addition, there is one character that, strictly speaking, is not a glob. The exclamation point (!), known as a "bang" in Linux, means "everything but." Globs and characters such as the exclamation point (!) have other meanings and are therefore known as metacharacters.

NOTE

To use a glob character in a file name or search term, you need to use the backslash (\) to "escape" the meaning of the glob. For example, one way to search for an asterisk (*) within the /etc/shadow configuration file is with the grep * /etc/shadow command.

Create and Manage Files and Directories

The nitty-gritty of the command line comes through the management of files. In Linux, a directory is just a special kind of file that happens to contain other files. In this section, you'll see how to list existing files, as well as how to create, copy, move, and delete files and directories. But first, it can help to identify the types of files available and the way Linux wildcard options operate.

file Lists File Types

In general, Linux files do not have extensions. There is no certainty associated with file extensions; for example, a .doc file may not be a document, and a .pdf file may not even conform to the portable document format created by Adobe Systems.

The **file** command can help you identify the kinds of files in a directory. For example, the command shown in Figure 4.4 shows the types of files in the Desktop/ subdirectory.

```
michael@ubuntuHHserver:~$ file Desktop/*
Desktop/broadcom_bcm94301mp_314016.exe:  MS-DOS executable PE  for MS Windows
(GUI) Intel 80386 32-bit, UPX compressed
Desktop/claim2.pdf:                      PDF document, version 1.4
Desktop/dhcpd.conf:                      ASCII English text
Desktop/jeos.iso:                        ISO 9660 CD-ROM filesystem data UDF f
ilesystem data (unknown version, id 'NSR01') 'CDROM                         ' (
bootable)
Desktop/jre-6u6-linux-i586.bin:          POSIX shell script text executable
Desktop/testdisk.log:                    ASCII text
Desktop/vmwarereg.txt:                   ASCII text
Desktop/VMware-server-1.0.7-108231.tar.gz: gzip compressed data, from Unix, last
 modified: Sat Aug  2 00:18:03 2008
Desktop/vmware-server-distrib:           directory
Desktop/wagthedog.odt:                   data
Desktop/xyz:                             directory
michael@ubuntuHHserver:~$ []
```

FIGURE 4.4 *Identify file types.*

touch Sets File Times and Creates a New Empty File

You can use the **touch** command to create empty files. However, it was originally developed to change the time stamp on a file. Empty files can be useful; for example, some services may not be able to create data or log files. In that case, a command like the following can help:

```
$ sudo touch /var/log/abc
```

However, if you're just changing the time stamp for the file, the -a, -m, or -t switches can help:

♦ **-a.** Change the access time of a file

♦ **-m.** Change the modification time of a file

♦ **-t.** Specify a different time in YYMMDDhhmm format, associated with the two-digit year, month, day, hour, and minute

NOTE

The dot (.) in the bulleted list after the command switch is not included in that switch. For example, while the touch -a xyz command changes the access time of file xyz, the touch -a. xyz command is meaningless. In the bulleted list, the dot in the bulleted list is simply a publishing convention.

ls for List

The **ls** command lists files—and much more. With the right switches, ls can identify file characteristics such as size, ownership, permissions, types, inodes, and modification times. Run by itself, it reveals just the names of all nonhidden files in the local directory. One command I use frequently is the ls -lhtr command, which lists all files in the local directory, in a long listing (-l) format, with sizes in a more easily readable format (-h), based on their last modification times (-t), in reverse (-r) chronological order. It lists the newest files last.

Details from the output are especially useful in specifying and changing file permissions and ownership. Other important ls command switches are listed in Table 4.5.

Table 4.5 Important `ls` Command Switches

Switch	Description
-a	All files in the list
-F	File type character at the end of a name; / specifies a directory, * specifies an executable file, @ specifies a soft link
-g	Long listing format, just with the group (not user) owner
-i	Inode number of a file
-l	Long listing format
-n	Long listing format, substituting the user and group ID numbers for the user and group names
-o	Long listing format, just with the user (not group) owner
-r	Reverse order
-t	Modification time

Try the `ls` command with each of these switches. Then try combining some of these switches in a single command. Observe what happens.

cp for Copy

As suggested by the LPIC-1 objectives, you need to know how to use the **cp** command to copy files and directories: one by one—and recursively, in a way that applies the same changes to subdirectories. The simplest version of the `cp` command copies the contents of one file to another. For example, the following command copies the contents of `file1` and writes it to `file2`.

```
$ cp file1 file2
```

If `file2` already exists, the contents are overwritten. Although directories are just special types of files, copying a directory requires a bit more information. In fact, the `-a` switch enables the copying of directories, along with files and included subdirectories.

The following command is a bit different, because it copies `file1` to the `/home/michael/Desktop` directory. If a `file1` already exists in that directory, it is overwritten.

```
$ cp file1 /home/michael/Desktop/
```

However, some systems are configured to prevent automatic overwriting of an existing file; in that case, you may get a warning message similar to the following:

```
cp: overwrite `file1'?
```

You could just confirm the overwrite by entering y at the prompt. That's not a big deal for a single file, especially if it helps prevent the overwriting of an important configuration file.

However, if you're copying directories with hundreds or even thousands of files, typing y every time is not practical. The -f switch would overwrite the file, without the noted prompt.

> **NOTE**
>
> The -f switch does not override an `alias cp='cp -i'`; aliases are described in Chapter 9.

One possible problem associated with file copying is that the file in the copied location has a different modification time relative to the original file. Such changes can affect the ability of some backup programs to preserve the latest versions of key files. You can use the -p switch to preserve the modification time of a file.

Of course, you can use the cp command to back up directories and more. To back up my home directory to the /backups/ directory, it's not enough to run a command like

```
$ cp /home/michael/. /backups/
```

because it does not copy subdirectories without the right switches. So this command doesn't copy files. The -r or -R switches copy all files and subdirectories recursively. In other words, if subdirectories have their own subdirectories, the files therein are also copied. The dot, as described earlier, is the preface for hidden file names. So one way to copy all files and directories is with a command like this:

```
$ cp -r /home/michael/. /backups/
```

But the -r switch isn't necessarily the best way. In many cases, the -a switch is a better option, because it combines the effect of -r's recursive copying, -p's preservation of modification times, as well as the -d switch, which preserves links. These cp command switches are summarized in Table 4.6.

Table 4.6 Important cp **Command Switches**

Switch	Description
-a	Archive; combines the effect of -d, -p, and -r
-d	Preserves links
-f	Forces an overwrite
-i	Prompts before overwriting a file
-p	Preserves ownership, mode, last revision time
-r, -R	Applies the command recursively
-v	Sets verbose mode

mv for Move

You also need to know how to use the **mv** command to change the location of files and directories one by one—and recursively, in a way that applies the same changes to subdirectories. The simplest version of the mv command takes the contents of one file, erases that file, and copies the contents to a second specified file. For example, the following command copies the contents of file1, writes it to file2, and deletes file1:

```
$ mv file1 file2
```

If file2 already exists, the contents are overwritten.

The moving of directories is a bit easier with the mv command, because subdirectories along with associated files are automatically moved when applying the mv command to a directory. File modification times are also preserved, along with applicable linked files. In other words, when applied to a directory, the mv command doesn't need a switch to work recursively. Although it is similar to the cp command, mv shares only three of the same switches described in Table 4.6: -f, -i, and -v.

rm for Remove

Because the **rm** command is fraught with danger, it's important to know how to use it properly. Mistakes could be disastrous for any Linux system, especially when the rm command is applied recursively, in a way that applies the same changes to subdirectories. The simplest version of this command removes a list of files cited at the command line. For example, the following command deletes both file1 and file2:

```
$ rm file1 file2
```

But because there is no "undelete" option at the Linux command line, you really should be sure about what you're deleting. You can apply the rm command recursively to files and directories. All you need is the -r switch. For example, the following command removes the /backups/test directory as well as subdirectories:

```
# rm -r /backups/test
```

But the success of this command is highly dependent on your typing skills. For example, if you accidentally include a space between the /backups and the /test directories, the rm -r command would first delete the /backups directory and all subdirectories, and then it would try to delete the /test directory.

Not only would that command delete anything else stored in the /backups directory (perhaps your backups), but it would delete a /test directory, if it existed. But it could get worse. If you accidentally included a space between the first slash and the rest of the expression, the command would first delete everything in the top-level root directory (/) and then recursively delete everything in all subdirectories—your entire Linux system.

CAUTION

Be careful when using the rm -r command; mistakes can easily lead to the deletion of the entire local Linux system.

Although there are similarities to the cp command, rm shares only four of the same switches described in Table 4.6: -f, -i, -r, and -v.

Create and Remove Directories with mkdir and rmdir

The **mkdir** and **rmdir** commands are straightforward. They create and remove directories. For example, the following commands, run in the /home/michael directory, create the /home/michael/Downloads and /backup directories:

```
$ mkdir Downloads
$ mkdir /backup
```

If you're unsure about the current directory, run the pwd command described earlier.

More can be done with the mkdir command. If you want to create a whole group of new sub-directories, and the /path directory doesn't currently exist, the -p switch can help. The following command creates the /path directory, the /path/to subdirectory, as well as the /path/to/life subdirectory, another level down in the directory tree:

```
$ mkdir -p /path/to/life
```

The process can be reversed with the following command, also using the same -p switch:

```
$ rmdir -p /path/to/life
```

The error message that appears is trivial. The rmdir command works only if a directory is already empty, so there is less risk of losing actual data.

The permissions associated with a newly created directory are associated with concepts described in Chapter 8. Suffice to say for this section that you can specify nondefault permissions for directories you create. For example, the following command, with the -m switch, would limit read but not execute access to the owner of the noted new directory:

```
$ mkdir -m 711 test
```

However, users other than the owner of the test directory would have execute permissions on files within that directory. See Chapter 8 for more information how to interpret permission numbers such as 711, in the discussion on the chmod command.

Basic File Searches with find

With the many thousands of files included in a Linux system, tools are necessary to help search for those files. The `find` command performs searches based on the file name and related characteristics in real time. In other words, the `find` command doesn't rely on a separate database.

One example of the `find` command searches for all files with the `.conf` extension. Although there's no requirement as such, most Linux configuration files include this extension. The following command starts the search in the top-level root directory (/):

```
$ find / -name "*.conf"
```

If this command is run without administrative privileges, errors will appear based on the lack of read permissions in a number of directories.

More on the `find` command, along with the related `locate` command, is described in Chapter 8. This section describes how you can use the `find` command to identify the full path to files based on their types, sizes, and last modification times.

 NOTE

For more detailed searches, including within readable files, learn more about the Tracker daemon; one source is https://wiki.ubuntu.com/Tracker. Although this is an Ubuntu page, it's also descriptive on how Tracker is used on Fedora systems.

Use find to Identify a File Based on Type

Several different file types are available on a Linux system, as described in Table 4.7. After the desired file type is identified, you can use the `find -type` command, with an appropriate file type and term to start the search for the desired file.

Table 4.7 Important Linux File Types

Type	Description
b	Block; often associated with storage devices
c	Character; often associated with terminals
d	Directory
p	Named pipe
f	Regular file
l	Symbolically linked file

For example, the following command looks for block device files that start with sd.

```
$ find / -name "sd*" -type b
```

Depending on the distribution, this command may work only for the administrative root user. On my laptop, it reveals files such as /dev/sda1, /dev/sda2, and so on. If you're familiar with partition device files as described in Chapter 1, "System Architecture," you'll recognize these files as partition devices.

Use find to Identify a File Based on Size

What happens if you've downloaded or copied an ISO file associated with a Live DVD? Those files can reach into the gigabytes. If you forget the location of the file, it could occupy a lot of space, which you may need for other purposes. That's where the -size switch can help the find command identify such files.

 NOTE

ISO is not an acronym, but a reference to standards of the International Organization for Standardization. In this context, it's a reference to the type of file that is used to "burn" CDs and DVDs, based on ISO 9660. It's also a standard for Linux filesystems mounted from such media.

Because most ISO files have .iso extensions, the following command starts its search for such files in the top-level root directory. It returns the full path to those files larger than 500MB.

```
# find / -name "*.iso" -size +500M
```

This command works fully only for the administrative root user; the associated prompt at the bash shell is the hash mark (#). For more information on root administrative access, see Chapter 15, "Security Administration."

Use find to Identify a File Based on Time

The find command can identify three different characteristics associated with a file, based on the last access time, the last time the file was changed, and the last time the file was modified. These characteristics are associated with the following switches to the find command:

- ◆ -atime. Time when the file was last accessed
- ◆ -ctime. Time when the file, and associated characteristics, was last changed
- ◆ -mtime. Time when the file contents were last modified

The access time, associated with the -atime switch, is relatively straightforward; when you read a file, you access it, and no changes are required to specify that access time. The change time, associated with the -ctime switch, specifies when the file was last modified—even if the modifications were limited to the ownership or permissions associated with the file. The modification time, associated with the -mtime switch, is associated with the last time the file contents were modified.

Time for each switch is specified in days. For example, the following command identifies *.conf files in the /etc/ directory that were last modified at least two days ago:

```
$ find /etc/ -name "*.conf" -mtime 1
```

Yes, the -mtime 1 setting specifies files that were modified more than two days ago. In contrast, the -mtime 2 setting would specify files that were modified more than three days ago.

Different File Archives

Several file-archiving commands are available to Linux. Linux archives are based on commands originally used to back up systems to tape drives, and are thus known as the tape archive command, tar. Other related commands collect, compress, and uncompress files. This section covers the **cpio, dd, gzip, gunzip, bzip2, bunzip2**, and **tar** commands.

File Archives with the cpio Command

The cpio command can archive a group of files. The simplest way to employ cpio is to use it to process a list of files. For example, the following command takes the contents of the current directory, excluding hidden files, and archives it in the test.cpio file:

```
$ ls | cpio -o > test.cpio
```

Just be sure that there's sufficient room on the volume with the test.cpio file, because the size of the file is a bit bigger than the files on the local directory.

One drawback to the cpio command is that it doesn't handle subdirectories recursively. In other words, because files in local subdirectories are not listed with the ls command, those files are not included in the archive created with the cpio command. But it's still quite useful, because it can take list input from other sources. For example, if you use the find command to identify all local RPM files, the following command would pipe that output to a cpio-based archive:

```
# find / -name '*.rpm' | cpio -o > rpmarchive.cpio
```

 NOTE

For more information on the pipe (|) and redirection arrows (>, <), see Chapter 5.

Other major switches for the `cpio` command are listed in Table 4.8.

Table 4.8 cpio Command Switches

Switch	Description
-A	Append to an existing archive
-F	Specify a file name for an archive; can substitute for a forward redirection arrow (>)
-i	Extract from an existing archive
-o	Create an archive from an input list of files
-u	Replace all files in an existing archive
-v	Specify verbose mode

Disk Dumps with dd

The disk dump command, `dd`, creates disk images. Although you could apply it to files, it is perhaps most commonly used as a backup tool to create images of sectors, partitions, or entire hard disks.

One method you can use to back up an image of a partition is based on the device file. For example, if your /home directory is mounted on /dev/sda5, the following command would back up that device file in the /backups directory

```
# dd if=/dev/sda5 of=/backups/homedir.img
```

which is presumably mounted on a hard disk with sufficient space. You could then test the result with the following command, which should mount the disk image on the /test directory:

```
# mount /backups/homedir.img /test
```

You can also write images to partitions. If you need to restore from the noted backup, and a partition of the appropriate size (or larger) is available, the process can essentially be reversed. The following command restores the image on the first logical partition on the second SCSI (or SATA) hard drive:

```
# dd if=/backups/homedir.img of=/dev/sdb5
```

Another common practice is to use the `dd` command to back up the MBR (Master Boot Record) of a hard disk, in case of problems with a boot loader, as discussed in Chapter 2, "Configure a System for Linux." To restore the boot loader to the first PATA drive, you could run the following command:

```
# dd if=backup.mbr of=/dev/hda
```

NOTE

One useful variant on dd is the dd_rescue command, which is designed to rescue crashed partitions. It saved my data once after my laptop hard disk was about to crash. Yes, the disk was still under warranty, but that was not as important as my data.

Compression and Uncompression with gzip and gunzip

The gzip and gunzip commands compress and uncompress a given file, based on the LZ77 (Lempel-Ziv) data compression algorithm. Whereas the gzip command adds a .gz extension to indicate a compressed file, the gunzip command removes the noted extension by default. Several important switches for both commands are shown in Table 4.9.

Table 4.9 gzip and gunzip Command Switches

Switch	Description
-d	Uncompress; applies only to the gzip command
-f	Force compression or uncompression
-r	Compress or uncompress, recursively
-v	Specify verbose mode

Compression and Decompression with bzip2 and bunzip2

The bzip2 and bunzip2 commands compress and decompress a given file, based on the Burrows-Wheeler block sorting text compression algorithm, with Huffman coding. Whereas the bzip2 command adds a .bz2 extension to indicate a compressed file, the bunzip2 command removes the noted extension by default. Several important switches for both commands are shown in Table 4.10.

Table 4.10 bzip2 and bunzip2 Command Switches

Switch	Description
-d	Uncompress; applies only to the bzip2 command
-f	Force compression or uncompression
-r	Compress or uncompress, recursively
-v	Specify verbose mode
-z	Compress; applies to the bunzip2 command

Archives and Compression with tar

The tar command is used to collect a group of selected files into a single file archive. With the right switch, it can compress (or decompress) that archive in the same formats used by the gzip and bzip2 commands. One unusual bit about the tar command is that the dash is not required when one or more single-letter switches are used.

A common use of the tar command is to decompress the kernel source code, which you may download from the home page of the Linux kernel development team, http://kernel.org. Kernel source code archives are made available in both compressed formats, which correspond to the following files for version 2.6.27.10:

```
linux-2.6.27.10.tar.bz2
linux-2.6.27.10.tar.gz
```

 NOTE

Archived files created with the tar command are known as tarballs.

Normally, source code tarball archives such as those listed above are copied or moved to the /usr/src/ directory and then decompressed and unarchived with the appropriate one of the following commands:

```
# tar xjvf linux-2.6.27.10.tar.bz2
# tar xzvf linux-2.6.27.10.tar.gz
```

In other words, the tar command extracts (x) from the archive, using either the bzip2 (j) or gzip (z)-based compression algorithm, in verbose mode (v), from the file cited (f). Obviously, if you don't want to watch the file names fly by on the screen, you can leave out the verbose (v) switch.

But was it necessary to move these archives to the /usr/src/ directory prior to extraction? You can check out the contents of the archive with the tf switch, which applies the --list switch to the given file. Output similar to the following indicates that archives are extracted directly as a subdirectory:

```
linux-source-2.6.27/
linux-source-2.6.27/COPYING
linux-source-2.6.27/CREDITS
linux-source-2.6.27/Documentation/
```

If you downloaded this tarball to your home directory and extracted it there, the files would be written to a local linux-source-2.6.27 subdirectory. If you're familiar with the process of compiling the source code for the Linux kernel, you'll know that such files must be located in the /usr/src/ directory. But such details are beyond the scope of the LPIC-1 objectives.

Finally, to create an archive of the /home directory, you could run the following command:

```
# tar cjvf /tmp/home.tar.gz /home
```

But the first message that appears indicates that the leading slash is being removed, which means that the archive is being saved through the relative path. For example, if you restore the archive from the /tmp directory, the archive is written to the /tmp/home directory, which isn't the desired location. Several important switches for the tar command are shown in Table 4.11. Note the inclusion of the single-word equivalents to the letter switches; you could see either the word or letter switches for many commands on the LPIC-1 exams.

Table 4.11 tar Command Switches

Switch	Description
-c	Create an archive (--create)
-d	List the differences between tar archives (--diff, --compare)
-f	Use the following file name for the archive (--file); otherwise, the command will freeze while looking for standard input
-j	Compress (or uncompress) files in bzip2 format (--bzip2)
-k	Avoid overwriting existing files in an archive (--keep-old-files)
-r	Append files to an existing archive (--append)
-t	List files in an existing tar archive (--list)
-u	Update an existing tar archive (--update)
-v	Specify verbose mode (--verbose)
-z	Compress (or uncompress) in gzip format (--gzip or --gunzip)

Chapter Summary

To pass the LPIC-1 exams, you need to know how to administer Linux from the bash shell. What you can do from bash depends on environment variables. The PATH makes it easier to run commands without using the absolute path; the dot should never be included in the PATH.

Command completion makes it easier to type in longer commands. Basic shell commands described in this chapter include pwd, man, uname, exec, and history.

Globbing provides the fine-grained wildcard options that help the administrator manage the tens of thousands of files on a system. Associated file management commands covered in this chapter include file, touch, ls, cp, mv, rm, mkdir, rmdir, and find.

Archives can help manage files in groups and can be used for backups. Commands that can help create and manage archives include cpio, dd, gzip, gunzip, bzip2, bunzip2, and tar.

Key Terms

◆ **absolute path.** A directory defined absolutely, based on the top-level root directory (/).

◆ **apropos.** A command used to search manual page names and descriptions.

◆ **-atime.** A find command switch, which specifies the time the file was last accessed.

◆ **.bash_history.** The user-specific file with a list of previously executed commands.

◆ **.bash_logout.** The user-specific configuration file executed when a user exits the shell.

◆ **.bash_profile.** The user-specific file for shell and environment variables.

◆ **bash shell.** The Bourne Again Shell, or the default Linux command-line interface shell.

◆ **.bashrc.** The user-specific configuration file for the bash shell, in user home directories.

◆ **bunzip2.** A command that uncompresses a file based on the Burrows-Wheeler block sorting text compression algorithm, with Huffman coding.

◆ **bzip2.** A command that compresses a file based on the Burrows-Wheeler block sorting text compression algorithm, with Huffman coding.

◆ **command completion.** A shell characteristic that fills in or provides options for partially typed in commands.

◆ **command-line interface (CLI).** A text interface for typed commands.

◆ **cp.** A command that copies files.

◆ **cpio.** A command that takes listed files as input and processes them for archiving.

◆ **-ctime.** A find command switch that specifies the time when the file and associated characteristics were last changed.

◆ **dd.** A command that takes and processes the contents of a file or disk device, often used for backups.

◆ **dot.** A symbol (.) that refers to the current directory.

◆ **double dot.** A symbol (..) that refers to the next higher directory.

◆ **env.** A command that lists current environment variables.

◆ **environment variable.** Every process includes a set of environment variables, such as HISTORY, HOME, and SHELL.

◆ **/etc/bash.bashrc.** The system-wide profile file for the bash shell; may also be /etc/bashrc.

◆ **/etc/profile.** The system-wide profile file for the bash shell.

◆ **exec.** A command that overrides the current shell to execute another command.

◆ **export.** A command that adds a variable to the current list of environment variables.

◆ **file.** A command that lists file types.

◆ **find.** A command that finds files, which may be based on a search term or other file characteristic such as size.

◆ **globbing.** The Linux concept associated with wildcards, which include *, ?, and custom square brackets. The singular of globbing is glob.

◆ **gunzip.** A command that uncompresses a file using the LZ77 (Lempel-Ziv) data compression algorithm.

◆ **gzip.** A command that compresses a file using the LZ77 (Lempel-Ziv) data compression algorithm.

◆ **history.** A command that lists recently run commands, based on the HISTSIZE variable.

◆ **HISTSIZE.** An environment variable that specifies the size of the command history.

◆ **HOME.** An environment variable that specifies the home directory for the current user.

◆ **ls.** A command that lists files.

◆ **man.** A command used to open command manuals, known as man pages; the man -k command is equivalent to the aproprs command; the man -f command is equivalent to the whatis command.

◆ **mkdir.** A command that creates a directory.

◆ **-mtime.** A find command switch that specifies time when the file content was last modified.

◆ **mv.** A command that moves files.

◆ **PATH.** An environment variable that specifies default directories searched for a typed-in command.

◆ **pwd.** A command that returns the current directory; also an acronym for the print working directory.

◆ **PWD.** An environment variable that specifies the current directory.

◆ **relative path.** A directory defined relative to the current directory.

◆ **rm.** A command that deletes files.

◆ **rmdir.** A command that deletes a directory.

◆ **shell.** An interface between users and an operating system; bash is the default Linux command-line interface shell.

◆ **SHELL.** An environment variable that specifies the default shell.

◆ **tar.** A command that is used to collect a group of selected files into a single file archive.

◆ **touch.** A command that creates empty files and modifies time stamps.

◆ **uname.** A command that removes a variable from the current list of environment variables.

◆ **unset.** A command that includes system information associated with the architecture and kernel.

◆ **USERNAME.** An environment variable that specifies the login name for the current user.

◆ **whatis.** A command that displays the description associated with a manual page.

Review Questions

The number of review questions in this chapter and other chapters in this book is proportionate to each section's weight in the LPI objectives. Because this chapter covers items 103.1 and 103.3, the weight is 8; therefore, you'll see 16 questions in this section. You'll see multiple choice, fill-in-the blank, and multiple option questions, as you'll encounter on the exam. A multiple option question has more than one correct answer.

1. Which of the following files does not affect the bash shell environment for all users? Choose two.

   A. /etc/profile

   B. /etc/bashrc

   C. /etc/protocols

   D. /etc/termcap

2. To customize the bash shell for only your account, enter just the file name to be modified in your home directory.

   _____

3. Which of the following commands returns the value of the HOME variable?

   A. echo $HOME

   B. env HOME

   C. echo HOME

   D. env $HOME

4. If you've opened a bash shell command-line interface in the GNOME desktop environment, and you are interested in the commands that start with gnome-, what can you do after typing in gnome- to identify those commands in your PATH?

   A. Add an asterisk (*) and press the Tab key.

   B. Press the Tab key twice.

   C. Add a question mark (?) and press the Tab key.

   D. List the commands with the ls gnome-* command.

5. Which of the following commands corresponds to the `apropos` command?
   A. `whatis -k`
   B. `man -k`
   C. `whatis -f`
   D. `man -f`

6. Which of the following commands lists the most available system information related to the architecture and kernel?
   A. `uname -p`
   B. `uname -r`
   C. `uname -a`
   D. `uname -v`

7. Which of the following variables includes the number of commands in the local command history?
   A. `HISTSIZE`
   B. `HIST`
   C. `HISTORY`
   D. `COMMAND`

8. If you don't know the full path to the current directory, enter the command that identifies it. Do not include the full path to the command.

   _____

9. Which of the following files is included in the output to the `ls number[!1-3]` command?
   A. `number1`
   B. `number3`
   C. `number13`
   D. `number4`

10. Which of the following commands lists hidden and regular files in the local directory, based on the modification time?
   A. `ls -a`
   B. `ls -la`
   C. `ls -at`
   D. `ls -t`

11. If you're copying files and subdirectories from an existing directory, which of the following switches works with the cp command, preserving links and ownership?

    A. -a

    B. -c

    C. -d

    D. -r

12. Enter the single command that creates the /united/states/of/america/ directory? Assume that none of the directories currently exists. Do not include the full path to the command.

    _____

13. Assume that you have appropriate permissions. If you want to identify all files on the local system that start with the letter l, and you want to be sure the file is a regular file, enter the remainder of this command: find / -name _____

14. Which of the following commands can be used to back up the contents of a volume, based on its device file?

    A. if

    B. tar

    C. dd

    D. cp

15. Which of the following commands can compress a file using the LZ77 (Lempel-Ziv) data compression algorithm?

    A. gunzip

    B. bzip2

    C. gzip -d

    D. gzip

16. Which of the following command switches for the tar command can be used to specify a compression algorithm? Choose two.

    A. c

    B. x

    C. j

    D. z

Chapter 5

Command Filters and Pipes

After completing this chapter, you will be able to

■ Redirect text streams to process data

■ Apply filters to text streams

■ Search through and manipulate text files

Introduction

The essence of Linux is in its text files. Properly managed, text files can be searched, filtered, and redirected as if they were databases. And, in fact, you can use many of the commands described in this chapter to manage and manipulate text-based databases.

The way data is streamed, piped, and redirected from a file makes such database manipulation possible. Such data flows can then be processed and filtered. Alternatively, data flows from text files can be searched using a variety of commands and expressions.

TIP

This chapter addresses three objectives in the LPI exam: 103.2 ("Process Text Streams Using Filters"), 103.4 ("Use Streams, Pipes, and Redirects"), and 103.7 ("Search Text Files Using Regular Expressions").

Text Files as a Stream

Standard input, standard output, and **standard error** are text streams at the command-line interface. You can create commands that pipe different text streams from one command to another. If necessary, you can pipe text streams in multiple directions, with commands applied periodically.

To administer Linux, you need to understand these text streams, as well as how to redirect and process them to files and commands. Redirected text streams in files can be saved for later analysis and processing. If you already have a plan to process a text stream, you can send that data directly to other commands for processing.

Standard Input, Output, and Error Concepts

The output of a regular command is sent to the text console. That's standard output (`stdout`). Linux (and UNIX) systems include two other data streams: standard input (`stdin`) and standard error (`stderr`). Colloquially, data goes in, data comes out, and errors are sent in a third direction. (But that's not quite true, because `stderr`, like `stdout`, also gets sent to the console.)

> **NOTE**
>
> To keep the explanations clear, I avoid the use of the `stdin`, `stdout`, and `stderr` acronyms in this section. However, you do need to know these acronyms for the exam and to communicate properly with other Linux experts.

Standard Output

Standard output is what's normally seen at the command line when a command is executed. Standard output is normally sent to the terminal. In the "Data Redirection" section, you'll see how to redirect standard output with the regular right arrow (>).

Standard Input

Standard input is what you type as data for a program. There are three basic ways to send standard input to a command or program:

◆ **When prompted.** Some programs prompt for standard input, such as y or n to confirm downloads.

◆ **When redirected from a file.** Some programs can take the contents of a file as standard input.

◆ **When redirected from standard output.** Standard output can be piped (|) as standard input to another program, as described shortly.

Standard Error

Like standard output, standard error messages are sent to the terminal console. In the "Data Redirection" section, you'll see how to redirect standard error with a slightly modified right arrow (2>).

An example of standard error is the following output from restarting the Network File System server as shown. The bolded code specifies standard error messages, which you'll see redirected into a different file in the next section.

```
$ sudo /etc/init.d/nfs-kernel-server restart

[sudo] password for michael:
 * Stopping NFS kernel daemon                      [ OK ]
 * Unexporting directories for NFS kernel daemon... [ OK ]
 * Exporting directories for NFS kernel daemon...
exportfs: /etc/exports [1]: Neither 'subtree_check' or 'no_subtree_check' specified for
export "192.168.0.0/255.255.255.0:/home/michael/Desktop".
  Assuming default behaviour ('no_subtree_check').
  NOTE: this default has changed since nfs-utils version 1.0.x
```

NOTE

One annoyance for those sensitive to grammar and spelling is the variety of dialects used in Linux. For example, "behaviour" in the aforementioned code output is a British English spelling, which suggests that at least some of the developers of NFS use British English.

Data Redirection

As implied by the title, you do not have to accept the defaults for sending standard output or standard error to the terminal. In addition, data redirection can help redirect the contents of a file, or standard output from a command, as standard input to another command or program.

Data redirection is made possible with the help of redirection arrows (**>**, **2>**, **>>**, **<**), the pipe character (**|**), as well as the **tee** and **xargs** commands. The tee command provides intermediate output; the xargs command can be used to help other commands that do not take standard input.

Redirection Arrows

This section describes six basic redirection arrows, which can direct the data coming into or out of a program or command.

- ◆ The single backward redirection arrow (**<**) takes the contents from one file as standard input to a command or program. For example, if you have a databasefile in the /usr/bin/local directory, with data for a program named databaseapp, the following command feeds the data to the application:

  ```
  $ /usr/local/bin/databasepp < databasefile
  ```

- ◆ The single forward redirection arrow (**>**) sends standard output to a file. For example, the following command sends the standard output from the noted command to the file named nfsrestart:

  ```
  # /etc/init.d/nfs-kernel-server restart > nfsrestart
  ```

  Be aware: if the nfsrestart file already exists, the contents of that file are overwritten by the command as shown. The single forward redirection arrow can also be written as **1>**.

- ◆ The double forward redirection arrow (**>>**) appends standard output to the end of a file. For example, the following command appends the standard output from the noted command to the end of the file named nfsrestart:

  ```
  # /etc/init.d/nfs-kernel-server restart >> nfsrestart
  ```

  In other words, the existing contents of nfsrestart are still there; the added information from the command as shown is added to the end of the file. The double forward redirection arrow can also be written as **1>>**.

◆ The error redirection arrow sends error messages from a command to a noted file. For example, the following command sends the standard output from the noted command to the file named nfserror:

```
# /etc/init.d/nfs-kernel-server restart 2> nfserror
```

Be aware: if the nfserror file already exists, the contents of that file are overwritten by the command as shown.

◆ The double-forward error redirection arrow appends error messages from a command to a noted file. For example, the following command appends the standard error from the noted command to the end of the file named nfserror:

```
# /etc/init.d/nfs-kernel-server restart 2>> nfsrestart
```

In other words, the existing contents of nfserror are still there; the added information from the command as shown is added to the end of the file.

◆ Both standard output and standard errors can be sent to one file with either of the following commands:

```
# /etc/init.d/nfs-kernel-server restart &> nfsdata
# /etc/init.d/nfs-kernel-server restart > nfsdata 2>&1
```

These options can be combined. For example, the following command sends regular messages to nfsrestart and errors to nfserror:

```
# /etc/init.d/nfs-kernel-server restart >nfsrestart 2> nfserror
```

A Pipe Redirects Output as Input

Redirection arrows work if you want to save output to a file. That file can then be used as input to another program or command. For example, if you want to find the number of regular files in the local directory, you can run the following two commands

```
$ ls > filenumber
$ wc -l < filenumber
60
```

which happen to show 60 nonhidden files in the local directory. Some may realize that the same basic information as the second command is available from the wc -l filenumber command; however, that leads to the following output:

```
60 filenumber
```

The command that you would enter in answer to an exam question may vary. You can combine the commands shown, courtesy of the pipe character (|), which looks like two short vertical lines on a keyboard atop each other. On a U.S. keyboard, it's the uppercase character on the same key as the backslash (\).

The following combines the first two commands in this section:

```
$ ls | wc -l
```

The output of the ls command is taken as standard input to the wc -l command. The effect is as if the redirection arrow was used; that's confirmed by the output:

60

In other words, the pipe (|) combines the effect of both the forward (>) and backward (<) redirection arrows.

Read between Pipes with tee

You can use the tee command with pipes to display output on the console at the same time data is being redirected to a different file or command. For example, you can modify the NFS service command used earlier in this section as follows:

```
# /etc/init.d/nfs-kernel-server restart | tee nfsrestart
```

This command sends standard output both to the console and to the nfsrestart file. If you'd rather append standard output to the end of the file, use the tee -a command.

Apply a Command to a Data Stream with xargs

The xargs command supports piping to other commands that otherwise could not handle standard input from other commands. But what does that really mean?

If you want to delete a large group of files, the standard input and output concepts might lead you to believe that the following command would delete those files:

```
$ ls *.png | rm
```

The first part of the command lists all files with the .png extension. However, piping the output to the rm command leads to the following error message:

```
rm: missing operand
Try `rm --help' for more information.
```

The rm command can't handle standard input piped from another command. The xargs command can take that standard input. It's just as suggested by the title of its man page: "Build and execute command lines from standard input." The command run as follows successfully deletes all *.png files from the local directory:

```
$ ls *.png | xargs rm
```

Text Stream Management

To make Linux work best, you need to know how to manage text streams. Text files are in essence a database of information to be managed and manipulated. The database of text files can be read, managed, formatted, and more. As suggested by the LPIC-1 requirements, you need to know how to "send text files and output streams through text utility filters to modify the output using standard UNIX commands found in the GNU textutils package."

However, there is no GNU textutils package installed on at least the selected distributions. The components of the former textutils package are now part of the coreutils package.

With these commands, you'll learn how to apply filters to text streams.

CAUTION

This chapter uses generic configuration files such as /etc/passwd to illustrate the use of different commands. Back up any such files before making changes. Do not write changes to the noted configuration files unless you understand what you're doing.

Text File Contents as a Database

There are two ways to think of databases with text files. There are databases of text files, and databases of the contents of the text files. Commands like **cat, head, tail, more,** and **less** read the contents of a file in different ways. In contrast, commands like **wc, fmt, expand, unexpand, nl,** and **tr** can measure and manipulate the contents of individual files.

NOTE

Command switches normally require a space between the switch and parameter. For example, the head -n 2 /etc/passwd command lists the first two lines in the /etc/passwd file. However, a space is not always required for such commands; in this case, head -n2 /etc/passwd works equally well.

Reading with cat

Although the cat command is short for concatenate, it's normally used to display the contents of a text file on a screen. For example, the cat /etc/passwd command displays the contents of the basic local user authentication database. However, if multiple files are listed with the command, they are shown on the terminal in sequence as if they were one file; thus, they are concatenated. To see this for yourself, run the following command:

```
$ cat /etc/passwd /etc/group
```

You should try out some of the switches listed in the associated man page. For example, both the -b and -n switches include line numbers in the output. The difference is that the -b switch does not include empty lines. Several interesting switches for cat are listed in Table 5.1.

Table 5.1 cat Command Switches

Switch	Description
-b	Number all nonblank output lines
-E	Add a "$" at the end of each line; can help identify empty spaces (which can cause syntax errors in some services)
-n	Number all output lines
-T	Substitute ^I for tab characters

Tops and Bottoms of Files with head and tail

The head and tail commands are in some ways opposite ends of the same coin. When applied to a text file, the head command lists the first 10 lines of that file. The tail command lists the last 10 lines of the target file. In both cases, you can use the -c switch to specify a number of bytes to display; for example, the following command displays the first 100 bytes of the /etc/passwd configuration file:

```
$ head -c 100 /etc/passwd
```

But many users prefer to specify a number of lines, which is possible with the -n switch. For example, the following command lists the last 20 lines in the /etc/group configuration file:

```
$ tail -n 20 /etc/group
```

If you're monitoring a log file, the tail -f command may be useful. For example, the following command monitors the main system log file for new messages:

```
# tail -f /var/log/messages
```

As configured, the command lists the last 10 lines from /var/log/messages; however, as new log messages are sent to this file, they are shown in the console. To exit from this monitoring mode, press Ctrl+C. These switches are summarized in Table 5.2.

Table 5.2 head and tail Command Switches

Switch	Description
-c *bytes*	Specify the number of bytes of a file to display
-n *lines*	Specify the number of lines of a file to display
-f	Keep a file open, waiting for input; requires a Ctrl+C to exit

Pagers with more and less

The more and less commands aren't quite opposite ends of the same coin. When applied to a text file, both commands start at the beginning of a text file and display enough of that file to fill the screen. As an example, try the following command:

```
$ more /etc/passwd
```

Press the spacebar. You'll see a second screen of user information. To return to the command line, press the spacebar as many times as needed to get to the end of the file, or press q.

Although the spacebar works just as well when using the less command, the q or ZZ command exits from the pager. Both the more and less commands are pagers, because they display text files one page at a time.

One advantage of the less command is that it supports additional scrolling options, including the up and down arrows, as well as the PageUp and PageDown keys.

The second advantage is search support; when you access a text file with the less command, try typing 10z. You'll see the screen advance 10 lines. Finally, it supports searches in the same way as can be done with the vi editor, as discussed in Chapter 6, "Processes, Priorities, and Editing." For example, after running the /etc/passwd command, the /michael command searches for my name in the user authentication database.

File Statistics with wc

Although the wc command is short for word count, it can also identify the number of lines and characters in a file. It's fairly straightforward; for example, the following three commands identify the number of lines, words, and characters in the /etc/passwd file, respectively:

```
$ wc -l /etc/passwd
$ wc -w /etc/passwd
$ wc -c /etc/passwd
```

These options are summarized in Table 5.3.

Table 5.3 wc Command Switches

Switch	Description
-c	Identify the number of characters in a file
-l	Specify the number of lines of a file to display
-w	Keep a file open, waiting for input; requires a Ctrl+C to exit

Format the Output with fmt

The fmt command is known as the "simple optimal text formatter." It can help set up a text file for printing. It removes "newline" characters and sets up a paragraph within specified line lengths. For example, if the introduction to this chapter were written in a text editor, it might appear as shown in the output to the cat intro command, as you can see in Figure 5.1.

```
[michael@CentOS5-LPI ~]$ cat intro
The essence of Linux is in its text files. Properly managed, text files can be s
earched, filtered, and redirected as if they were databases. And in fact, you ca
n use many of the commands described in this chapter to manage and manipulate te
xt-based databases.
The way data is streamed, piped, and redirected from a file makes such database
manipulation possible. Such data flows can then be processed and filtered. Alter
natively, they can also be searched using a variety of commands and expressions.
[michael@CentOS5-LPI ~]$
[michael@CentOS5-LPI ~]$ fmt -w50 intro
The essence of Linux is in its text
files. Properly managed, text files can be
searched, filtered, and redirected as if they
were databases. And in fact, you can use many
of the commands described in this chapter to
manage and manipulate text-based databases.
The way data is streamed, piped, and redirected
from a file makes such database manipulation
possible. Such data flows can then be processed
and filtered. Alternatively, they can also
be searched using a variety of commands and
expressions.
[michael@CentOS5-LPI ~]$ []
```

FIGURE 5.1 *An introduction ready for formatting.*

If the fmt command were applied as shown in Figure 5.1, it would

- Remove newline (carriage return) characters; the transition between the first and second paragraphs in the introduction would be eliminated. If you wanted to retain the different paragraphs, you'd have to set up two newline characters between paragraphs by pressing the Enter key twice.
- Format the paragraph with a 50-character line limit, as specified by the -w50 switch. (Without the switch, the default is a 75-character line limit.)

The fmt command may not be appropriate for configuration files. When applied to a configuration file such as /etc/passwd, it eliminates line breaks between authentication information for each user. Interesting switches for the fmt command are summarized in Table 5.4.

Table 5.4 fmt Command Switches

Switch	Description
-c	Retain indentations in the first two lines
-u	Set up one space between words, two spaces between sentences; however, this does not work with regular sentences in a paragraph
-w*num*	Specify a number of characters for each line format (a space is not required between -w and *num*)

Substitute Spaces for Tabs with expand

For the purpose of this section, I've set up a file named `numbers` with the following line, with tabs at the start of the line and between each number:

    1   2   3   4

The `expand` command shown here replaces each tab character with eight spaces, which can be implemented with the following command. The command writes the result to the `expandednumbers` file. Try this command for yourself, and check the result in a text editor.

```
$ expand numbers > expandednumbers
```

The `expand` command can substitute a different number of spaces; for example, the following command substitutes 11 spaces:

```
$ expand -t11 numbers > expandednumbers
```

There's one more variation on the `expand` command. The following command retains a tab at the beginning of each line in a file, while replacing all other tabs with spaces:

```
$ expand -i numbers > expandednumbers
```

Substitute Tabs for Spaces with unexpand

The `unexpand` command isn't quite the antidote to the `expand` command. For example, the following command substitutes tabs for only the first eight consecutive spaces in a line:

```
$ unexpand expandednumbers > detabbednumbers
```

If you want to substitute tabs for all incidences of eight consecutive spaces in the `expandednumbers` file, run the following command:

```
$ unexpand -a expandednumbers > detabbednumbers
```

Alternatively, the following command substitutes tabs for each incidence of four consecutive spaces in the expanded numbers file:

```
$ unexpand -t4 expandednumbers > detabbednumbers
```

In each case, the result is written to the `detabbednumbers` file. Yes, you can substitute the file names of your choice.

Add Line Numbers with nl

The `nl` command can help format a page of data with line numbers. For example, the following command adds line numbers to each entry of the `/etc/passwd` configuration file:

```
$ nl /etc/passwd
```

However, the `nl` command doesn't normally add line numbers to blank lines, unless specified with the `-b a` switch. For example, the following command adds lines to the empty spaces in the main Samba configuration file:

```
$ nl -b a /etc/samba/smb.conf
```

There is one more switch of interest, which uses a search term to identify the lines to be numbered. For example, the following command numbers only those lines with the term home in them. There's no space between the p and home in this command; it's one case where a space between p and home would change the result.

```
$ nl -b phome /etc/samba/smb.conf
```

Process and Translate Characters with tr

The `tr` command takes the input of a text stream, selects certain characters, and processes changes in the output. Just to illustrate, try the following command:

```
$ cat /etc/passwd | tr a-c 0-2
```

Although the output may appear to be gobbledygook, it actually substitutes the range of numbers for the noted range of characters. If you had access to my system, you'd see that the original version of /etc/passwd includes the following output for my user account:

```
michael:x:1000:1000:Michael Jang,,,:/home/michael:/bin/bash
```

If you were then to apply the preceding command as shown, it would change my user account line to

```
mi2h0el:x:1000:1000:Mi2h0el J0ng,,,:/home/mi2h0el:/1in/10sh
```

In other words, it would change every instance of the lowercase letter a to the number 0, change every instance of the lowercase letter b to the number 1, and change every instance of the lowercase letter c to the number 2. The same types of changes are made to the contents of every other line in /etc/passwd.

An equivalent command uses the left redirection arrow (<) to feed the /etc/passwd file (or the file of your choice) as input to the specified `tr` command:

```
$ tr a-c 0-2 < /etc/passwd
```

Try it out for yourself. You should see the same output from both commands. To verify, run the following commands in sequence:

```
$ cat /etc/passwd | tr a-c 0-2 > trans1
$ tr a-c 0-2 < /etc/passwd > trans2
$ diff trans1 trans2
```

The first two commands write the text stream from the previous commands to the trans1 and trans2 files. Any output from the `diff` command specifies a difference between the two files noted. So if you run the commands correctly, you should not see output to the noted `diff` command.

In a different twist, you can use the `tr` command to specify characters to delete. To that end, the following command would delete the lowercase a, b, and c from the text stream associated with the `/etc/passwd` file:

```
$ cat /etc/passwd | tr -d a-c
```

For the previously noted user authentication line, that command would lead to the following output:

```
mihel:x:1000:1000:Mihel Jng,,,:/home/mihel:/in/sh
```

The `tr` command is, in a sense, a filter, a command that takes components of a text file and creates output based on filtering parameters of your choice.

Text Utility Filters

Several utility filters can help you format text files in useful ways. Commands like **cut, paste**, and **join** are useful ways to process text files as databases. The **sort** and **uniq** commands can help rearrange text file databases. The **pr, split**, and **od** commands can process text files into different formats. Finally, the **sed** utility is an important way to make global changes to configuration files.

Create Data Excerpts with cut

The `cut` command is designed to isolate specific columns. Earlier in this chapter, you applied the expand and unexpand commands on a simple file named `numbers` with four columns. I add more information to this file, which now looks like this:

```
    1       2       3       4
    9       10      11      12
```

There's a tab in front of and between each column of numbers. Now try applying the following `cut` command, which lists the information in the first column:

```
$ cut -c1 numbers
```

Do you see empty output? Good. Now try the command again with the first 12 columns. The following is the output when the fourth column is specified:

```
2
1
```

Only the first column digit is specified. That's a misleading result from the database, which is why text databases have delimiters, such as a comma or colon.

Comma-based delimiters are common in database files; spreadsheet programs can write their files to comma-delimited databases. For the purpose of this section, I downloaded a .csv file from the U.S. Census and then ran the following command:

```
$ cut -d, -f 10 NST-EST2008-alldata.csv  | less
```

It specifies the comma (,) as the delimiter and lists out the tenth column, piped to the less command for easy scrolling.

Alternatively, files such as /etc/passwd provide a database with columns separated by colons. For example, the following command lists the users from this file, which are shown in the first column:

```
$ cut -d: -f1 /etc/passwd
```

These cut command switches are summarized in Table 5.5.

Table 5.5 cut Command Switches

Switch	Description
-c	Specify a character column
-d	Identify a delimiter between columns
-f	Note the column to cut and display on the screen

Divide a File with split

The split command can take the contents of a file and separate them into different but smaller files based on a specified number of rows. For example, if I were to take the aforementioned census data and apply the following command

```
$ split -5 NST-EST2008-alldata.csv census_
```

it would take the first five lines of the data from the noted .csv file and write them to the census_aa file. It would then take the next five lines of data and write them to the census_ab file, and so on until the original census file is completely read.

The file can then be recombined elsewhere with the double redirection arrow (>>). In this particular case, the last file is census_am, so the following command would re-create the contents of the noted .csv file:

```
$ cat census_a? >> census.csv
```

Combine Columns with paste or join

The paste and join commands are similar but not identical ways to combine columns from different files. The join command assumes that the two files in question have a common consecutive numeric list. If a number in one list is out of order, the join command stops at that point.

The join command by itself assumes the common index is in the first column. If it's in a different column, the -j switch can help. For example, the following command looks to the second column for the common numeric list:

```
$ join -j2 user1 account1
```

In contrast, the paste command is somewhat more flexible. It does not require a common numeric index in each file; it assumes a one-to-one correlation between files. For example, take a file named piece1 with the following lines:

```
the
is
the
closet
```

And then take a file named piece2 with the following lines:

```
treasure
in
basement
```

You could then combine the files with the following command:

```
$ paste piece1 piece2
```

As an exercise, create both files in a text editor. Run the paste command yourself. Where is the treasure?

If you prefer to add a delimiter, the -d switch can help; the following command would add a comma between the words in each row:

```
$ paste -d, piece1 piece2
```

Reorder a File with sort

One of the basic advantages of a database is the ability to sort it by the system of your choice. The sort command takes the start of each line and rearranges the lines in alphabetical or numeric order. For example, the following command arranges the local authentication database by the alphabetic order of usernames:

```
$ sort /etc/passwd
```

The -r switch reverses the order, from z through a or 9 through 0. The way the sort command works on numbers is based on the first digit. If I have a list of data numbered 1 through 10, the sort command would prioritize the lines in the following order: 1, 10, 2, 3, 4, 5, 6, 7, 8, and 9.

Filter Out Duplicates with uniq

For the purpose of this section, assume a less experienced administrator has made a mistake with the /etc/passwd file. It now includes duplicates of user michael's account information. Here's an excerpt:

```
haldaemon:x:111:123:Hardware abstraction layer,,,:/var/run/hald:/bin/false
michael:x:1000:1000:Michael Jang,,,:/home/michael:/bin/bash
michael:x:1000:1000:Michael Jang,,,:/home/michael:/bin/bash
statd:x:112:65534::/var/lib/nfs:/bin/false
```

The duplicate user entries can lead to trouble the next time user michael tries to log in. And you're not sure about other possible duplicate entries made by the less experienced colleague. If the duplicate entries are consecutive, the following command would eliminate those duplicates:

```
$ uniq /etc/passwd
```

If you're satisfied with the result, the output could be redirected to a local file such as /tmp/passwd for inspection before you write the result to the actual /etc/passwd configuration file.

If you'd just rather list those lines that are duplicates of a previous line, the following command will display them:

```
$ uniq -d /etc/passwd
```

The uniq command finds duplicate lines only if they run consecutively. As such, it may be useful to run the sort command first; when the sort command is applied to a file, duplicate lines are grouped. So if there are three, nonconsecutive instances of my user account line in the /etc/passwd configuration file, the following command sorts the database before filtering out the duplicate lines with the uniq command:

```
$ sort /etc/passwd | uniq
```

Format for Printing with pr

You can use the pr command to format a text file for printing. When run by itself, this command takes a text file and sets up pages with a header every 56 lines. Five lines are added for both the header and footer of each page, which leads to 66 lines in a standard printout.

For example, if you run the pr smb.conf command, you may see the following header with the first couple of lines at the beginning of the file:

```
2008-09-07 03:23                    smb.conf                        Page 1
     1  #
     2  # Sample configuration file for the Samba suite for Debian GNU/Linux.
```

Several switches are available that can modify the appearance in the output, and thus how it would appear in a printed page. Some of the more interesting switches are listed in Table 5.6.

Table 5.6 pr Command Switches

Switch	Description
-c	Include control characters in the output; for example, ^L is a form feed character
-d	Format the output in double space
-f	Add a form feed character to keep pages separate in the output
-h *HEADER*	Replace the file name with a header of your choice
-l *Num*	Format each page with the specified number of lines
-t	Leave out the header

Convert File Text to Another Format with od

Regular decimal numbers have digits that range from 0 through 9; this is also known as the base 10 numeral system. Computers communicate with binary numbers, 0 and 1, which is known as base 2. In contrast, some programs are configured to process data in **octal** (base 8) or even **hexadecimal** (base 16) format.

That's where the od command comes in, because it can covert text to octal or hexadecimal format. Apply it to a text file and examine the output. You'll see a bunch of numbers that look like this:

```
0000000 067562 072157 074072 030072 030072 071072 067557 035164
```

Each digit is in octal format, with numbers between 0 and 7. If it were in decimal format, the numbers 8 and 9 would appear. To convert the /etc/passwd file to octal format, run the following command:

```
$ od /etc/passwd
```

Now try converting it to ASCII format. Output similar to Figure 5.2 should appear. You may recognize the first few lines as the ASCII representation of the first few lines of a standard /etc/passwd configuration file.

```
0000000  r  o  o  t  :  x  :  0  :  0  :  r  o  o  t  :
0000020  /  r  o  o  t  :  /  b  i  n  /  b  a  s  h  \n
0000040  d  a  e  m  o  n  :  x  :  1  :  1  :  d  a  e
0000060  m  o  n  :  /  u  s  r  /  s  b  i  n  :  /  b
0000100  i  n  /  s  h  \n  b  i  n  :  x  :  2  :  2  :
0000120  b  i  n  :  /  b  i  n  :  /  b  i  n  /  s  h
0000140  \n  s  y  s  :  x  :  3  :  3  :  s  y  s  :  /
0000160  d  e  v  :  /  b  i  n  /  s  h  \n  s  y  n  c
0000200  :  x  :  4  :  6  5  5  3  4  :  s  y  n  c  :
0000220  /  b  i  n  :  /  b  i  n  /  s  y  n  c  \n  g
0000240  a  m  e  s  :  x  :  5  :  6  0  :  g  a  m  e
0000260  s  :  /  u  s  r  /  g  a  m  e  s  :  /  b  i
0000300  n  /  s  h  \n  m  a  n  :  x  :  6  :  1  2  :
0000320  m  a  n  :  /  v  a  r  /  c  a  c  h  e  /  m
0000340  a  n  :  /  b  i  n  /  s  h  \n  l  p  :  x  :
0000360  7  :  7  :  l  p  :  /  v  a  r  /  s  p  o  o
0000400  l  /  l  p  d  :  /  b  i  n  /  s  h  \n  m  a
0000420  i  l  :  x  :  8  :  8  :  m  a  i  l  :  /  v
0000440  a  r  /  m  a  i  l  :  /  b  i  n  /  s  h  \n
0000460  n  e  w  s  :  x  :  9  :  9  :  n  e  w  s  :
0000500  /  v  a  r  /  s  p  o  o  l  /  n  e  w  s  :
0000520  /  b  i  n  /  s  h  \n  u  u  c  p  :  x  :  1
0000540  0  :  1  0  :  u  u  c  p  :  /  v  a  r  /  s
:█
```

FIGURE 5.2 *The od command can specify ASCII characters.*

Finally, try converting the same file to hexadecimal format with the following command, and observe the result:

```
$ od -t x /etc/passwd
```

Because hexadecimal numbers are counted 0, 1, 2, 3, 4, 5, 6, 7, 8, 9, a, b, c, d, e, and f, the numbers shown in the output will fall into the noted range.

Rework the Text Stream with sed

One of the most powerful text database management tools is the sed command, known as the stream editor. It's sufficiently complex that it's covered in two sections, under both LPIC-1 objectives 103.2 and 103.7.

I use sed frequently to change the default servers associated with remote updates. For example, when I install Ubuntu on a new system, the /etc/apt/sources.list configuration file is configured to find updates from servers at http://us.archive.ubuntu.com. But that leads to slower updates, because such servers are actually located in the United Kingdom (while I live on the west coast of the United States).

I like to change the /etc/apt/sources.list file to look for updates from a server closer to me. I could change these URLs by hand, but I would have to do that over a dozen times in each file, and that process is prone to error. So I like to use the sed command to change all desired URLs—in two commands:

```
$ sed 's/us.archive.ubuntu.com/mirrors.kernel.org/g' /etc/apt/sources.list > sources.list
$ sudo cp sources.list /etc/apt/sources.list
```

The advantage of the two commands is that you can stop and inspect the sources.list configuration file in the local directory before making the change permanent in the /etc/apt/sources.list configuration file.

However, I could also change the file in place, courtesy of the `-i` switch. Because files in the `/etc/apt/` directory require administrative privileges, I could substitute the following for the preceding two commands:

```
$ sed -i 's/us.archive.ubuntu.com/mirrors.kernel.org/g' /etc/apt/sources.list
```

Now analyze the command as shown. The `'s/us.archive.ubuntu.com/mirrors.kernel.org/g'` portion substitutes (s) in place of `us.archive.ubuntu.com`, the term `mirrors.kernel.org`. The substitution is made globally (g). The changes are applied and written to every line in the `/etc/apt/sources.list` file.

Without the g, if there were a second instance of `us.archive.ubuntu.com` on one or more lines, it would not be replaced.

For more information on Linux update systems, see Chapter 3, "Package Management Systems."

Search through Text Files

Now that you know how to manipulate text files in different ways, you can take advantage of the results with different types of search commands. These search commands are commonly used to search within existing text files, as well as text streams output from many of the commands discussed in this chapter. Examples that include related commands are included in this section.

But to use search terms effectively, you need to understand the variety of regular expressions used in Linux. Some expressions such as Linux globs are discussed in Chapter 4, "Command Lines and Files."

Text Substitution and Regular Expressions

The **sed** command is the stream editor. Earlier in this chapter, you learned how to use the `sed` command to modify multiple expressions in a file. This section explores additional features of `sed`. But to use even the `sed` command effectively, you need to know more about **regular expressions**. As suggested in the LPIC-1 objectives, they relate to those described with the `man 7 regex` command.

A Review of Regular Expressions

Regular expressions in Linux go beyond the globs and wildcards discussed in Chapter 4. In fact, if you need to search for terms used as Linux globs in a file, one important regular expression is the backslash (\), because it escapes the meaning of a character.

For example, the following command, as a glob, uses all files in the local directory as search terms for the main Samba configuration file:

```
$ grep * /etc/samba/smb.conf
```

But if you wanted to search for asterisks (*) in that file, you would need to "escape" the meaning of the search term, which is possible with the backslash, as shown here:

```
$ grep \* /etc/samba/smb.conf
```

Backslashes also escape the meaning of a space; for example, if I've mounted the remote My Documents directory from my wife's computer on the /wife directory, I could list the files on that directory with the following command:

```
$ ls /wife/My\ Documents
```

Yes, the same search is possible with the use of quotes, a different regular expression.

```
$ ls "/wife/My Documents"
```

Chapter 4 described the use of the $ with environment variables. For example, whereas the echo HOME command returns the term HOME, the echo $HOME command returns a value of the current user's home directory.

Three types of quotes are used in Linux commands: the single quote ('), the double quote ("), and the back quote (`). The way they affect a command depends on the contents of that command. The behavior described here assumes the use of the default bash shell. To summarize:

- ◆ **Single quote.** Variables or commands within single quotes are not processed.
- ◆ **Double quote.** Variables within double quotes are processed, but commands are not.
- ◆ **Back quote.** Variables within the quotes are processed, and then any commands within the quotes are run.

Review the following examples, which use all three types of quotes. For the purpose of these examples, assume that you've run OS=Linux. The date command returns the current date and time. Try the first command, without quotes, and review the result:

```
$ echo The operating system installed on date is $OS
The operating system installed on date is Linux
```

Now enclose the expression in single quotes and see how the OS variable and date are both not interpreted:

```
$ echo 'The operating system installed on date is $OS'
The operating system installed on date is $OS
```

Next, try double quotes around the expression; as happened without quotes, the OS variable is interpreted:

```
$ echo "The operating system installed on date is $OS"
The operating system installed on date is Linux
```

Try enclosing the expression in back quotes and see how it looks at the first word as a command. If the first word were a command, the shell would try to interpret the second word as a command switch.

```
$ echo `The operating system installed on date is $OS`
-bash: The: command not found
```

When you need a set of back quotes, use them carefully to ensure they enclose the command in question. Try it out within the double-quoted expression:

```
$ echo "The operating system installed on `date` is $OS"
The operating system installed on Wed Apr 3 15:07:17 PST 2009 is Linux
```

You can configure mixed quote characters in different contexts. For example, directives in the sendmail e-mail server configuration macro file commonly include expressions that start with a back quote and end with a single quote.

Important regular expressions are summarized in Table 5.7.

Table 5.7 Important Regular Expressions

Expression	Description
&	An ampersand after a command runs that command in the background and returns control to the shell prompt.
'	Single quote; variables and commands within single quotes are not processed.
"	Double quote; variables within double quotes are processed; commands are not.
`	Back quote; variables and commands within back quotes are processed.
\	A backslash escapes the meaning of an expression, including a space.
{}	Matching braces enclose functions.
[]	Matching brackets specify a range.
()	Matching parentheses specify options.
$	A $ specifies a variable; may also specify the last character in a search.
!	An exclamation point is known in Linux as a "bang," which negates the intent of a range.
#!	The #! is known as a "she-bang" character, configured at the start of a script with the shell, such as #!/bin/bash.
~	A tilde (~) represents the home directory of the current user.
^	A carat (^) commonly specifies the start of a line, especially in a search.

Stream a Substitution with sed

The abilities of the stream editor command, sed, go beyond simple substitutions in configuration files. Earlier, you saw how I use the sed command to customize a configuration file. In this section, you'll learn more about the capabilities of sed.

To break down the sed command, review the following syntax:

```
$ sed -switch 'action/term/replacement/flag' file
```

In other words, the sed command uses a *switch* to process the term in single quotes. The *action* is what is to be done; the *term* is what is searched for in the *file*; and the *replacement* term substitutes for the search term, as modified by the *flag*.

There are just a few commonly used switches for sed. For example, if you have a couple of substitutions to run in sequence, the following command processes those substitutions, in order:

```
$ sed -e 's/mirrors.cat.pdx.edu/mirrors.kernel.org/' \
-e 's/mirrors.kernel.org/mirrors/' /etc/apt/sources.list
```

NOTE

The backslash is used in some commands to "escape" the meaning of a carriage return. If you see a backslash between commands that appear on two lines, the command is read by the shell as if it were on one line.

If you have more than a couple of substitutions, you may want to set them up in a text file. You can then run all those substitutions in sequence. The following command runs the substitutions stored in the *subst* file on the sources.txt file:

```
$ sed -f subst sources.txt
```

Four actions are commonly used in a sed expression: d, s, g, and y. These actions delete (d), substitute (s), and translate (y) text streams from a file. The g action applies the command to all instances of the search term in the target file. The following command omits the tenth line of the noted file:

```
$ sed '10d' sources.list
```

In contrast, the following command omits the third through tenth lines of that file:

```
$ sed '3,10d' sources.list
```

The s action substitutes, as shown in previously described sed commands.

Kids have had fun creating codes, based on substituting certain alphanumeric digits for others. The following command substitutes the numbers 1, 2, and 3 respectively for the lowercase letters a, b, and c:

```
$ sed 'y/abc/123/' sources.list
```

Every Kind of grep

The `grep` command searches within files based on a pattern. The LPIC-1 objectives list three different variations on this command: **grep**, **egrep**, and **fgrep**. The egrep and fgrep commands are functionally equivalent to the `grep -E` and `grep -F` commands and are discussed separately in this section.

Search through a File with grep

The `grep` command supports basic searches within a text file. When a search term is found, the entire line from the searched file is listed. For example, if you used `grep` to search for my username in the `/etc/passwd` file, as shown, you'd see the following result:

```
$ grep Michael /etc/passwd
michael:x:1000:1000:Michael Jang,,,:/home/michael:/bin/bash
```

One interesting variation is the `-v` switch, which inverts the meaning of a search. For example, the following command returns a list of all users from `/etc/passwd` without reference to the `sh` term, which usually includes all users who do not have a standard default shell.

```
$ grep -v sh /etc/passwd
```

You can combine the `grep` command with others to make them more powerful. Generally, other commands are piped to `grep`, using standard output as a search database. For example, the following command searches for files with the term `test` within the local directory:

```
$ ls | grep test
bigtest
test
test.doc
```

The output demonstrates that the search term works as if asterisked wildcards were added to the beginning and end of the term.

If you're searching for a term that starts with a dash, such as `-abc`, the following command would not work, because it assumes that you're trying to use the `grep` command switches, `-a`, `-b`, and `-c`. So the command looks for appropriate input, does not search for `-abc`, and can be stopped by pressing Ctrl+C.

```
$ grep -abc text.file
```

Even a backslash does not escape the meaning of the dash for this particular command. The right way to search for a term that starts with a dash is with the `-e` switch:

```
$ grep -e -abc text.file
```

One more interesting pair of switches is `-l` and `-L`. For example, the first of these commands searches all local files and lists those with the noted search term. The second command returns the opposite list:

```
$ grep -l term *
$ grep -L term *
```

Several other important switches are described in Table 5.8.

Table 5.8 Interesting grep Switch Options

Switch	Description
-e	Supports searches with terms that start with a dash (-)
-i	Disables case sensitivity in a search
-l	Lists files with a search term match
-L	Lists files without a search term match
-v	Inverts the intent of a search

The grep command is commonly used with a variety of regular expressions described earlier in this chapter. For example, the following command searches for the files f04-01.tif, f04-02.tif, f04-03.tif, f04-11.tif, f04-12.tif, and f04-13.tif in the output to the noted ls command:

```
$ ls LPI-Level1v2/Ch04 | grep f04-[0-1][1-3].tif
```

If you want to search using a wildcard or other regular expression, you'll generally need to escape the intent of the wildcard. For example, the following command searches the /etc/test file for asterisks:

```
$ grep \* /etc/test
```

Without the backslash, the command searches using the name of every file in the local directory.

Use Multiple Search Terms with egrep

The egrep command is equivalent to the grep -E command. It supports choices in a search, using regular expressions. For example, the following command returns all users with the /bin/bash or /bin/dash default shells in their user authentication lines.

```
$ egrep '/bin/[bd]ash' /etc/passwd
```

Search Using Globs with fgrep

The fgrep command is equivalent to the grep -F command. It's used to search through a group of files based on one search term. For example, the following command searches for the 127.0.0.1 search term in all noted configuration files:

```
$ fgrep 127.0.0.1 /etc/*.conf
```

Chapter Summary

Text files are streams of data, ready for mining with a variety of Linux text commands. These streams of data can be classified as standard input, standard output, and standard error. These data streams can be redirected with a variety of arrows, including >, >>, 2>, 2>>, and <. The pipe (|) is commonly used to redirect standard output from one command as standard input to a second command. The tee command can provide intermediate output; the xargs command can be used for those commands that cannot otherwise handle standard input.

Text streams can be managed with commands from the coreutils package, which is a variation on the GNU textutils package listed in the LPIC-1 objectives. Related commands include cat, head, tail, more, less, wc, fmt, expand, unexpand, nl, and tr. The best way to learn these commands is to try them for yourself, as discussed in the chapter.

With a basic understanding of regular expressions—from quotes through brackets—you can use commands like sed, grep, egrep, and fgrep to search through and substitute for text files. You can apply the same commands to text streams created from other commands.

Key Terms

- **&.** An ampersand after a command runs that command in the background and returns control to the shell prompt.
- **\.** A backslash escapes the meaning of an expression, including a space.
- **<.** Redirection arrow for stdin; data from a file for a command or program.
- **>.** Redirection arrow for stdout; overwrites an existing file; also may be written as 1>.
- **2>.** Redirection arrow for stderr; overwrites an existing file.
- **2>>.** Redirection arrow for stderr; appends to an existing file.
- **>>.** Redirection arrow for stdout; appends to an existing file.
- **{}.** Matching braces enclose functions.
- **[].** Matching brackets specify a range.
- **().** Matching parentheses enclose options.
- **'.** Single quote; variables or commands within single quotes are not processed.
- **".** Double quote; variables within double quotes are processed, but commands are not.
- **`.** Back quote; variables within the quotes are processed, and then any commands within the quotes are run.
- **^.** Specifies the start of a line, especially in a search.
- **$.** Specifies a variable; may also specify the last character in a search.
- **!.** An exclamation point is known in Linux as a "bang," which negates the intent of a range.

◆ **#!.** Known as a "she-bang" character, configured at the start of a script with the shell, such as #!/bin/bash.

◆ **cat.** Command that reads specified files to stdout, normally the console.

◆ **cut.** Command that extracts column-based character excerpts.

◆ **egrep.** Equivalent to grep -E; supports choices in a search, using regular expressions.

◆ **expand.** Command that substitutes spaces (8 by default) for tabs from a text file.

◆ **fgrep.** Equivalent to grep -F; supports searches through a series of files.

◆ **fmt.** Command that reworks input from a text file in paragraph format.

◆ **grep.** Command that supports searches within a text file.

◆ **head.** Command that outputs the first few lines of a file (10 lines by default).

◆ **hexadecimal.** Reference to the base 16 numbering system, 0, 1, 2, 3, 4, 5, 6, 7, 8, 9, a, b, c, d, and e.

◆ **join.** Command that joins two files based on a common index, such as line numbers.

◆ **less.** Command that supports searches and scrolling through the contents of a given file.

◆ **more.** Command that pages through the contents of a given file.

◆ **nl.** Command that adds line numbers to a text file.

◆ **octal.** Reference to the base 8 numbering system, 0, 1, 2, 3, 4, 5, 6, and 7.

◆ **od.** Command that converts the contents of a file to octal or hexadecimal format.

◆ **paste.** Command that joins the columns of two specified files.

◆ **pr.** Command that formats a text file for printing, with page numbers.

◆ **regular expressions.** Include wildcards, brackets, quotes, and related symbols.

◆ **sed.** Command that supports the manipulation of data streams; also known as the stream editor.

◆ **sort.** Command that reorders lines from a file in alphanumeric order.

◆ **split.** Command that divides a file into equal-sized files, normally by number of lines.

◆ **standard error.** Known as stderr; error messages from a program; may be processed with the 2> redirection arrow.

◆ **standard input.** Known as stdin; input to a program or command.

◆ **standard output.** Known as stdout; output from a command or program normally sent to the console.

◆ **stderr.** Also known as standard error.

◆ **stdin.** Also known as standard input.

◆ **stdout.** Also known as standard output.

◆ **tail.** Command that outputs the last few lines of a file (10 lines by default); the tail -f command monitors new messages to a log file.

◆ **tee.** Command that provides intermediate output between the stdout from one command or program and the stdin to a second command or program.

◆ **tr.** Command that translates one range of alphanumeric characters in a text file to a second specified range.

◆ **unexpand.** Command that substitutes tabs for spaces (8 by default) from a text file.

◆ **uniq.** Command that omits consecutive duplicate lines.

◆ **wc.** Command that allows a line, word, or character count of a given file.

◆ **xargs.** Supports stdin to commands that otherwise are not equipped to handle it.

Review Questions

The number of review questions in this chapter and other chapters in this book is proportionate to each section's weight in the LPI objectives. Because this chapter covers items 103.2, 103.4, and 103.7, the weight is 9; therefore, you'll see 18 questions in this section. You'll see multiple choice single answer, fill-in-the blank, and multiple choice multiple answer questions, as you'll encounter on the exam.

In addition, by the very nature of the topic, few questions can cover item 103.4 alone; they require the use of other commands in this chapter.

1. Which of the following data redirection arrows overwrites the text file with standard error?

   A. >

   B. >>

   C. 2>

   D. 2>>

2. Which of the following commands redirects the output of the ls command for processing by the script named program?

   A. ls > program

   B. ls | program

   C. ls >> program

   D. ls | tee program

3. Enter the command that lists the last 14 lines in a local file named bigshot. Do not specify the full path to the command. _____

4. Enter the command that redirects error messages from the /etc/init.d/good script to the local gooderror file. _____

5. Which of the following commands returns the number of files in the local directory?

   A. ls | wc -l

   B. wc -l < ls

   C. ls wc -l

   D. wc -l | ls

6. Which of the following commands supports paging through a file and search tools?

   A. pr

   B. cat

   C. more

   D. less

7. Which of the following commands adds numbers to the /etc/passwd file and writes the result to the passwdnumber file in the local directory?

   A. set nu | /etc/passwd > passwdnumber

   B. nl /etc/passwd > passwdnumber

   C. nl /etc/passwd | passwdnumber

   D. nl /etc/passwd 2> passwdnumber

8. Which of the following commands can combine columns from different files? Choose two.

   A. paste

   B. add

   C. join

   D. column

9. Which of the following Linux commands can help set up a written page for printing? Choose two.

   A. tr

   B. pr

   C. fmt

   D. nl

10. Enter the command that substitutes tabs for every four spaces in a file named tabby. Do not include the path to the command. _____

11. Which of the following statements best describes what happens in the output to the
    `cat /etc/passwd | tr -d a` command?

    A. All instances of the letter d in the `/etc/passwd` file are translated to the letter a.

    B. All instances of the letter a in the `/etc/passwd` file are translated to the letter d.

    C. All instances of the letter d in the `/etc/passwd` file are deleted in the output.

    D. All instances of the letter a in the `/etc/passwd` file are deleted in the output.

12. Which of the following commands breaks out the second column from a comma-
    delimited list named `/etc/census`?

    A. `$ cut -d: -f0 /etc/census`

    B. `$ cut -d: -f1 /etc/census`

    C. `$ cut -d, -f2 /etc/census`

    D. `$ cut -d, -f1 /etc/census`

13. Which of the following commands reorders the lines from a text file in alphabetical
    order?

    A. `order`

    B. `sort`

    C. `nl`

    D. `list`

14. Enter the command that substitutes the word `Linux` for `Solaris` from a file named
    `UnixOS`. Focus on the output, and don't enter that output to the `UnixOS` file. Also,
    don't use the full path to the command. _____

15. Which of the following commands support searches in multiple files? Choose two.

    A. `grep -F`

    B. `egrep`

    C. `fgrep`

    D. `grep -f`

16. Which of the following commands eliminates duplicate lines from the `/etc/config`
    file?

    A. `uniq /etc/config`

    B. `dup /etc/config`

    C. `diff /etc/config`

    D. `sort /etc/config`

17. Review the following line. Which of the following numbering systems does it represent? And what is the associated command?

```
642f 6369 656b 736e 3a32 622f 6e69 642f
```

   A. Binary: od -t 2

   B. Octal: od

   C. Decimal: od -x

   D. Hexadecimal: od -t x

18. Which of the following commands searches the output of the main log file for lines that start with Aug?

   A. grep ^Aug /var/log/messages

   B. grep ~Aug /var/log/messages

   C. grep !Aug /var/log/messages

   D. grep Aug /var/log/messages

Chapter 6

Processes, Priorities, and Editing

After completing this chapter, you will be able to

- Work with text files using the vi editor

- Manage running processes

- Make processes work the way you want

Introduction

Because the essence of Linux is in the text files, capable Linux users know how to edit text files. Although editing is intuitive with graphical tools, such tools are not always available. The LPIC-1 objectives therefore require basic knowledge of a console text editor, vi.

When administering a Linux system, you need to know how to manage and reprioritize processes. To that end, this chapter describes the command-line tools available to create, monitor, and kill a process, as well as how to make one process more important on the local system. Although this is in some ways one topic, it's split into two topics in this chapter to reflect the organization of the LPIC objectives.

TIP

This chapter addresses three objectives in the LPI exam: 103.5 ("Create, Monitor, and Kill Processes"), 103.6 ("Modify Process Execution Priorities"), and 103.8 ("Perform Basic File Editing Operations Using vi").

The vi Text Editor

There are a variety of text editors available for Linux, including ed, emacs, pico, joe, nano, and **vi**. All can be used in some form from the command-line console. At least one of these editors is available when booting a Linux system from rescue media. It would be unreasonable to test all of these editors in any depth. The LPIC-1 objectives focus on vi. It's a reasonable choice, because the rescue media for the releases of some older distributions supported access only to vi.

As suggested by the objectives, you need to know how to edit text files using the vi editor. To that end, this section describes how you can navigate a file through vi and operate in different vi modes. You'll also see how to use vi to insert, edit, delete, copy, and find text.

Strictly speaking, the standard version of the vi editor available in current Linux distributions is the **vim editor**, which is the "improved" version of vi. The differences are not relevant for this book.

In this section, you'll test the vi editor on the /etc/passwd configuration file.

Basic Operation

The simplest way to open the vi editor is with the vi command. When run with the name of an existing text file, it opens that file for editing. For the purpose of this section, log in as a regular user and open the main password configuration file with the following command:

```
$ vi /etc/passwd
```

Because regular users do not have write access to the /etc/passwd file, changes should not be allowed. However, it's prudent to back up this file before making changes. One way to copy this file to your home directory from within the editor is with the following command:

```
:!cp /etc/passwd ~/passwd
```

The colon and exclamation point (:!) utilizes execute mode, which runs commands from the local directory. The command as shown copies the /etc/passwd file from the standard location to the passwd file in your home directory, as indicated by the tilde (~).

If you need to get out of the vi editor at this time, enter :q!, to exit without changes. But this chapter continues with an exploration of what you can do with vi.

Speaking of modes, three are associated with the vi editor:

◆ **Command mode.** The default when starting the vi editor, where navigational and editing commands are run within the editor on the file.

◆ **Insert mode.** The mode where text and lines can be added to a file. To return to command mode, press the Esc key.

◆ **Execute mode.** The option that executes commands from within the editor; requires a :! before the command.

Now you'll see how to search through, navigate within, and insert text into a file.

Searches within vi

One of the powers of the vi editor is the ability to search for text. The tools are the forward slash (/) and the question mark (?). When these symbols are followed by the search term, the vi editor searches for the term in question. Spaces are allowed; for example, the following command starts from the current position of the cursor and searches forward in the text for my name:

```
/Michael Jang
```

If found, the first instance of the search term is highlighted. To search for the next instance of the search term, press n. Once the search reaches the end of the page, the search starts over, with the following message at the bottom of the screen:

```
search hit BOTTOM, continuing at TOP
```

A question mark enables a reverse search. For example, the following command starts the search at the current position of the cursor and looks up toward the beginning of the file for my name:

```
?Michael Jang
```

Navigation through vi

Most users navigate through text editors with the arrow keys on a keyboard. However, vi dates back to a time before arrow keys were included on a keyboard. So when you open a file in vi, the h, j, k, and 1 keys are used as arrow keys to navigate through a file. These key options are explicitly listed in the LPIC-1 objectives, so they're fair game on the exam. Try it out for yourself, and confirm the entries in Table 6.1.

Table 6.1 vi Arrow Keys

Command	Equivalent Arrow
h	Left arrow
j	Down arrow
k	Up arrow
1	Right arrow

Two other useful navigation commands are G and gg. Whereas the G command moves to the end of a file, the gg (or 1G) command moves to the start of the file. Either command can be prefaced by the line number; in other words, the 10G and 10gg commands both move to the tenth line in a file.

Insert Text Via vi

It's easy to start insert mode in the vi editor. The i, o, and a commands open the file. Try them one at a time by typing in a few letters. To leave insert mode, press the Esc key. You can undo the last change with the u command. These insert mode options and more are listed in Table 6.2. Note the difference in the upper- and lowercase versions of each command.

Table 6.2 vi Insert Mode Commands

Command	Description
a	Start insert mode at the next character position
A	Start insert mode at the end of the current line
i	Start insert mode at the current character position
I	Start insert mode at the beginning of the current line
o	Open a line below the current line and start insert mode
O	Open a line above the current line and start insert mode
cw	Delete the current word and start insert mode in its place
cc	Delete the current line and start insert mode in its place

More vi Commands

This book just scratches the surface of available vi commands. But that's as far as you need to go, because the certification is just Level 1. You can learn about the other commands listed in the LPIC-1 objectives in this section.

The c and d Commands

Although the **c** and **d** commands refer to "change" and "delete," they require additional explanation, because they don't work by themselves. A second letter added to the command may result in an action; for example, the **dd** command deletes the current line. The 2dd command deletes the current line plus the one below.

These commands also work with an action; for example, the c and d commands, followed by the down arrow (or the j key), delete the current line along with the line below. The difference is that a command such as cj deletes the noted two lines and enters insert mode.

Open the /etc/passwd configuration file in the vi editor and try out the c and d commands with the following steps:

1. Log into a standard account.
2. Back up the /etc/passwd file with the cp /etc/passwd ~/passwd command.
3. Run the vi /etc/passwd command to open the noted file in the vi editor.
4. Scroll down the file a few lines with the down arrow.
5. Try the c2j command. Note how it deletes three lines: the current line plus the two lines below. Then it enters insert mode.
6. Press Esc to exit insert mode.

7. Use the **u** command to undo changes, and press k to move up a line.

8. Try the c2 command followed by the down arrow. Did the same changes appear?

9. Press Esc to exit insert mode, and press u to undo changes.

10. Try the d3k command. It deletes four lines: the current line plus the three lines above. You can substitute the down arrow for the k in the command.

11. Press u to undo changes.

12. Try the d3l command. It deletes the current character with the two characters to the right.

13. Type :q! to exit the vi editor, which quits without saving changes.

Yanks, Puts, and the Register

The **y** command works in a similar fashion to the c and d commands. But instead of deleting a line, it "yanks" one or more lines and places it into a register, a buffer that can be used to paste the lines of your choice.

To yank a copy of the current line, the **yy** command works. You can then copy that line as desired. Just move the cursor to the line before where you want the line copied, and press p.

To yank two lines, type y1. It yanks the current line, plus one more, depending on the next action. If you type y1k, or y1 followed by the up arrow, the current line, plus the one above, is placed into the register. Alternatively, the 2yy command yanks the current line plus the one below into the register.

The dd command deletes the current line and places it into the register. If you want to move the current line, move the cursor to the line before the desired location.

If you want to delete two lines and place them into the register, the 2dd command would serve the purpose. The two deleted lines are then ready to be put with the **p** command in the location of your choice.

In contrast, the x command deletes the current character. When you then use the **p** command, it places that character after the current cursor position.

If you want to delete two characters and place them into the register, the 2x command would serve the purpose. The two deleted characters are then ready to be put—after the current cursor position—with the p command.

Exit from vi

Several commands are available to exit from the vi text editor. These commands can be combined; for example, I often use the :wq command to write changes to a file and exit from the vi editor. Exit command options for the vi editor are listed in Table 6.3. Pay attention to the difference when a command includes the exclamation point (!).

Table 6.3 vi Exit Commands

Command	Equivalent Arrow
ZZ	Write and exit; equivalent to :wq
:w	Writes changes to a file; does not overwrite read-only files
:w!	Writes changes to a file, overwriting even read-only files (if directory permissions allow it)
:q	Exits from a file; it works only if no changes have been made
:q!	Exits from a file, discarding any changes that have been made
:e	Restart editing of a file
:e!	Restart editing of a file, discarding any changes that have been made

Other variations are possible; for example, to write changes to a file named differentfile, you could enter the following command:

```
:w differentfile
```

Priority Management

Linux sets its own priorities with different processes, which may not meet your needs. Therefore, you need to know how to review the processes currently running, as well as how to change which processes get first crack at the resources of the local system. To that end, this section describes the **ps**, **top**, **nice**, and **renice** commands.

Linux process priorities are counterintuitive. These priorities, also known as **nice numbers**, range from -20 to 19. A nice number is also known as a scheduling priority. The process with first crack at your resources has a nice number of -20; the process at the low end of the totem pole has a nice number of 19. Default priorities are generally set to 0, unless started with the nice command, which sets a default nice number of 10.

A List of Running Processes

The ps command lists currently running processes. If run by itself, it lists processes running in the current console. Naturally, that list is normally pretty short; here's an example of output from a current console:

```
   PID TTY          TIME CMD
 12333 pts/2     00:00:00 bash
 13238 pts/2     00:00:00 ps
```

Two processes are shown: the bash shell associated with the current console and the ps command run to show this output. The PID is the process identifier, the number associated with the current process. The TTY is the current terminal; the acronym is based on the historical teletype terminal. The TIME specifies how long the current process has been running. The CMD specifies the command that started the process.

With the right switches, the ps command can show a lot more about currently running processes, beyond the current terminal, and for the entire system. Several significant ps command switches are shown in Table 6.4.

Table 6.4 ps Command Switches

Switch	Option
-a	Lists currently running processes in a terminal, not including the console shell process
a	Lists currently running processes accessible to the current user
-C *cmd*	Identifies a process by command name
-e	Selects all processes
-f	Includes output in full format
f	Includes processes with parent processes in a tree format
-l	Formats output in a long listing format
l	Formats output in a long listing format, with process information from other terminals
-U *user*	Specifies processes owned by *user*
u	Specifies the user owner of each process
x	Includes processes not running in a terminal, such as daemons and services

As you read the table, try out some of the switches on your own system. Be aware that the effect of ps command switches often differs when used with and without a dash. Refer to this table later in this chapter for further discussion on ps command output.

Try the pstree command. As shown in Figure 6.1, it includes a list of processes in a tree format. As you can see, init is the first process, and other processes in branches are "child" processes.

```
init-+-NetworkManager---{NetworkManager}
     |-NetworkManagerD
     |-acpid
     |-apache2-+-apache2
     |          `-3*[apache2---26*[{apache2}]]
     |-atd
     |-avahi-daemon---avahi-daemon
     |-battstat-applet
     |-bonobo-activati---{bonobo-activati}
     |-console-kit-dae---61*[{console-kit-dae}]
     |-cpufreq-applet
     |-cron
     |-cupsd---ipp
     |-2*[dbus-daemon]
     |-dd
     |-dhcdbd
     |-evolution-alarm---{evolution-alarm}
     |-evolution-data----2*[{evolution-data-}]
     |-evolution-excha---{evolution-excha}
     |-freshclam
     |-gconfd-2
     |-gdm---gdm-+-Xorg
     |            `-gnome-session-+-evolution---3*[{evolution}]
--More--
```

FIGURE 6.1 *A tree of processes.*

The full list of processes is available with the following command:

$ ps alx

The list is long, and it is suitable for processing as a database. For example, to isolate daemon processes related to the Apache Web server, the ps alx | grep apach command works as shown in Figure 6.2. (The name of the Apache Web server daemon on Red Hat–based systems including CentOS 5 is httpd.)

```
michael@UbuntuHH:~$ ps axl | grep apach
1     0  6678     1  20   0  10476  2576 -      Ss    ?      0:00 /usr/sbin/a
pache2 -k start
5    33  6679  6678  20   0  10248  1784 -      S     ?      0:00 /usr/sbin/a
pache2 -k start
5    33  6684  6678  20   0 231812  2404 -      Sl    ?      0:00 /usr/sbin/a
pache2 -k start
5    33  6689  6678  20   0 231812  2408 -      Sl    ?      0:00 /usr/sbin/a
pache2 -k start
5    33  6694  6678  20   0 231812  2408 -      Sl    ?      0:00 /usr/sbin/a
pache2 -k start
0  1000 17971  7413  20   0   3008   780 -      S+    pts/1  0:00 grep apach
michael@UbuntuHH:~$ ▮
```

FIGURE 6.2 *Isolating processes related to a server.*

Perhaps the key items in the output are in the second, third, fourth, and final columns. They list the UID (user ID) owner of the process, the **PID** (process identifier), the **PPID** (parent PID), and the command that started the process (the parent). For information on the NI column, read the description of the nice command later in this chapter.

The UID can be identified in the third column of the /etc/passwd configuration file. If you want to kill a process, you need the PID. If the command you use to try to kill a process doesn't work, you may try to kill the parent of the process, as identified by the PPID. Commands associated with killing a process are described in the "Process Management" section.

Processes in top

The top command can help you identify those processes that may be overwhelming the local system. For example, the output shown in Figure 6.3 is what this book refers to as the top task browser, which illustrates what happens when I open too many Firefox browser windows.

```
top - 14:21:21 up  3:16,  4 users,  load average: 1.23, 0.49, 0.23
Tasks: 159 total,   3 running, 156 sleeping,   0 stopped,   0 zombie
Cpu(s): 69.9%us,  2.8%sy,  0.0%ni, 26.8%id,  0.0%wa,  0.3%hi,  0.2%si,  0.0%st
Mem:   3366876k total,  2209040k used,  1157836k free,    39888k buffers
Swap:  1959888k total,        0k used,  1959888k free,  1410080k cached

  PID USER      PR  NI  VIRT  RES  SHR S %CPU %MEM    TIME+  COMMAND
 7292 michael   20   0  547m 265m  29m R  117  8.1  8:28.32 firefox
18732 michael   20   0 31424  15m 8164 S    7  0.5  0:00.20 screenshot
 6485 root      20   0  427m  68m  13m S    6  2.1  2:29.56 Xorg
 7284 michael   20   0 21300  12m 7924 S    3  0.4  0:22.48 metacity
 7285 michael   20   0 45756  25m  13m S    2  0.8  0:15.44 gnome-panel
 7307 michael   20   0 35344  18m  10m S    1  0.6  0:38.80 python
 7271 michael   20   0 15208 2708 1812 S    1  0.1  0:09.16 gnome-screensav
 7293 michael   20   0 62468  19m  10m R    1  0.6  0:06.36 gnome-terminal
 7974 michael   20   0 23920 6108 4996 S    1  0.2  0:37.44 vmware-remotemk
17123 michael   20   0  125m  55m  31m S    1  1.7  0:16.40 ld-linux.so.2
 7672 michael   20   0  222m  89m  54m S    0  2.7  1:53.05 soffice.bin
17725 michael   20   0 93056  36m  13m S    0  1.1  0:04.80 gimp-2.4
    1 root      20   0  2844 1688  544 S    0  0.1  0:02.46 init
    2 root      15  -5     0    0    0 S    0  0.0  0:00.00 kthreadd
    3 root      RT  -5     0    0    0 S    0  0.0  0:00.02 migration/0
    4 root      15  -5     0    0    0 S    0  0.0  0:00.94 ksoftirqd/0
    5 root      RT  -5     0    0    0 S    0  0.0  0:00.00 watchdog/0
```

FIGURE 6.3 *The top command identifies a process overload.*

As shown in the top task browser, the process that is using the most resources is firefox, which is using more than 100% of current CPU capacity. Although the Firefox browser sometimes still works under these circumstances, response is slow. If Firefox locks up, I can use this information to kill the firefox process, as described in the "Process Management" section.

But for now, just observe the details of the top task browser. It includes information on RAM (as specified by the Mem label) and swap space usage. Processes are prioritized by their CPU and RAM use.

If a process isn't showing up in the top task browser, you may want to reprioritize it, as described in the next section. To quit from the browser and return to a command-line prompt, press q.

Making nice and renice

Normally, you'll never need to change the priority associated with a process. Priorities are dynamically changed by the kernel to share resources fairly. But there are times when you'll want to raise or lower the priority of a program's process.

To this end, you can start processes with a certain priority with the nice command. If the process is already started, you can reprioritize such processes with the renice command. To review, the nice number of a process can range from -20 (highest) to 19 (lowest).

Start a Process with nice

If a system is slow, normal troubleshooting commands may get stuck in whatever problems might be slowing down the system. That's a good time to use the nice command; for example, you may need to use the nice command to start the top task browser.

Regular users can set a priority of 0 or lower; in other words, you do not need superuser privileges to run either of the following commands:

```
$ nice -0 top
$ nice -19 top
```

Be aware: these commands are easy to misunderstand. The -19 sets a priority of positive 19, which, as just described, is the lowest possible value.

But if a system is running slowly, neither of these commands would help. The following command would set a higher priority of -10:

```
# nice --10 top
```

If the double-dash leading to a negative is too confusing, you could run top with the following equivalent command:

```
# nice -n -10 top
```

Now that you've started the top task browser, watch as the top command is shown in the list. From the following excerpt, the value of the NI column (nice) for the top command is set to -10.

```
PID   USER    PR  NI  VIRT  RES  SHR S %CPU %MEM   TIME+    COMMAND
27352 root    10 -10  2308 1144 856 R   1  0.0   0:00.20  top
```

Reprioritize a Process with renice

Visualize two basic scenarios. First, assume that the top task browser isn't running as it should. In that case, you'd want to give that command a higher priority. Second, assume that some database program is taking up all local resources, and you need to run some other programs on that system.

To address the first scenario, you could use the renice command to give the top task browser a lower nice number, thus giving it a higher priority. Because the process is already running, you'll need the PID. As shown in the previous section, this particular PID is 27352. The following command would change its nice number to -15:

```
# renice -15 27352
```

Administrative privileges are required, because the priority is being raised from -10 to -15. The output lists the old and new nice number for the process:

```
27352: old priority -10, new priority -15
```

Now for the second scenario. Database programs may be scripts that run other programs. In that case, the process in question is part of the script, which you may need to review. In any case, if the program is using too many local resources, it should show up atop the top task browser. In that case, identify the PID and review the number in the NI column. For example, if the PID is 1111 and the NI column is listed as 0, you could lower the priority of that program to a nice number of 10 with the following command:

```
# renice 10 1111
```

Because the priority of the noted process is being lowered, administrative privileges are not required on all Linux distributions.

Process Management

Now that you know more about processes and priorities, you're ready to review the tools associated with process management. The LPIC-1 objectives suggest that you need to understand several tasks and commands, which are divided in this section into three categories.

The tools associated with current processes and system status provide a baseline. Individual processes can then be managed in the foreground or background. Additional tools are available to stop a job or keep it running. These are the tools associated with basic process management.

Current Processes and System Status

Anyone who administers a Linux system needs to understand the basic tools associated with the current status of the local system. These tools include the ps, top, **free**, and **uptime** commands. These tools can help you monitor active processes. With the right switches, they can also help you focus on the right processes.

uptime

The uptime command can provide basic operational information on the current system. When the command is run, you'll see output similar to the following.

```
09:26:28 up 19 days, 19 min,  4 users,  load average: 0.00, 0.03, 0.00
```

From this data, you can see that the current time is 9:26 a.m., and the system has been running for 19 days and 19 minutes. Four users are currently logged into the system. The load average numbers are based on data from 1, 5, and 15 minutes ago. If the value were 1.00, a single CPU system would be fully loaded.

free

The free command displays the current status of system memory, based on detected RAM and configured swap space. The default output shown next is in KB. In other words, the system shown here has 256MB of RAM and 512MB of swap space. Although a little free space is available in RAM, about 64MB of swap space is in use. The numbers aren't precise, but they reflect how this particular system was configured.

```
$ free
                total      used      free    shared   buffers    cached
Mem:           255592    207256     48336         0      2752     96136
-/+ buffers/cache:       108368    147224
Swap:          524280     63776    460504
```

Several free command switches of interest are included in Table 6.5.

Table 6.5 free Command Switches

Switch	Option
-b	Leads to output in bytes
-g	Creates output in GB
-k	Sets up output in KB, the default
-m	Leads to output in MB
-t	Includes a total, based on RAM and swap space
-s *n*	Reruns the same command every *n* seconds

For more detailed information, see the /proc/meminfo file, which dynamically adjusts with changes to memory status information. Some information is currently buffered and cached in local RAM.

top

The top command was briefly covered earlier in this chapter. Review the output again, from Figure 6.3. You should now recognize the information in the upper part of the top task browser as the same information available from the uptime and free commands. It can be customized to monitor and sort active processes in different ways.

First, the top command can be started with different switches. By default, the top task browser is refreshed every three seconds. The following command starts the browser to refresh every two seconds. (The dash is not required.)

```
$ top -d 2
```

Alternatively, once you're in the top task browser, press d. You'll be prompted from within the browser as follows, which indicates a current refresh interval of 2.0 seconds:

```
Change delay from 2.0 to:
```

Just type in the desired refresh interval in seconds at the noted prompt, and the change will be reflected immediately. Now try pressing r. Note how the sort changes by PID. If you want to isolate just a few processes, press n. The following prompt appears in the top task browser window:

```
Maximum tasks = 0, change to (0 is unlimited):
```

Now let's go a bit further. In the top task browser, press b to highlight processes with heavy loads. From the top task browser output on my system shown in Figure 6.4, it appears that the vmware-vmx services are using a lot of CPU and memory.

```
top - 12:22:46 up 19 days, 20:15,  0 users,  load average: 0.55, 0.47, 0.36
Tasks: 137 total,   6 running, 131 sleeping,   0 stopped,   0 zombie
Cpu(s):  3.3%us, 14.0%sy,  0.0%ni, 82.3%id,  0.0%wa,  0.0%hi,  0.3%si,  0.0%st
Mem:   2029520k total,  1975088k used,    54432k free,   239348k buffers
Swap:   987988k total,     1276k used,   986712k free,  1277836k cached

  PID USER      PR  NI  VIRT  RES  SHR S %CPU %MEM    TIME+  COMMAND
18143 michael   10 -10  378m 286m 278m R  7.7 14.5  1886:07 vmware-vmx
15903 michael   10 -10  415m 291m 277m R  3.0 14.7 340:38.82 vmware-vmx
24669 michael   10 -10  370m 277m 270m R  2.3 14.0 698:22.64 vmware-vmx
18160 michael    0 -20     0    0    0 R  0.7  0.0 128:40.61 vmware-rtc
24556 root      20   0 18500  15m 4280 S  0.3  0.8  43:58.37 vmware-serverd
    1 root      20   0  4184 1112  660 S  0.0  0.1   0:01.20 init
    2 root      15  -5     0    0    0 S  0.0  0.0   0:00.02 kthreadd
    3 root      RT  -5     0    0    0 S  0.0  0.0   0:00.00 migration/0
    4 root      15  -5     0    0    0 S  0.0  0.0   1:28.05 ksoftirqd/0
    5 root      RT  -5     0    0    0 S  0.0  0.0   0:01.46 watchdog/0
    6 root      15  -5     0    0    0 S  0.0  0.0   0:38.95 events/0
    7 root      15  -5     0    0    0 S  0.0  0.0   0:00.01 khelper
   39 root      15  -5     0    0    0 S  0.0  0.0   0:13.16 kblockd/0
   42 root      15  -5     0    0    0 S  0.0  0.0   0:00.00 kacpid
   43 root      15  -5     0    0    0 S  0.0  0.0   0:00.00 kacpi_notify
  134 root      15  -5     0    0    0 S  0.0  0.0   0:00.00 kseriod
  180 root      15  -5     0    0    0 S  0.0  0.0   0:54.17 kswapd0
```

FIGURE 6.4 *The top task browser highlights loaded processes.*

Now you'll see how to change the nice number associated with a process from within the top task browser. Press r; the following prompt appears in the upper part of the browser:

```
PID to renice:
```

The PID is listed in the left column. So if you want to change the process associated with PID 15903 (and it's active), you'll see the following prompt:

```
Renice PID 15903 to value:
```

As a regular user, you're allowed to lower the priority of a process. To raise the priority of a process through the top task browser, you have to start that browser with administrative privileges.

As discussed earlier in this chapter, priority numbers are counterintuitive, because the highest-priority process has a nice value of -20; the lowest priority process has a value of 19.

ps

More information is available from the ps command, beyond what was discussed earlier in this chapter. The PID is available from the ps command, which can then be used to kill or reprioritize a process. For more information on the command switches listed in this section, see Table 6.4.

The ps command exhibits different behavior for some switches with and without a dash. As an example, try the ps a and ps -a commands. See a difference? Whereas the ps -a command includes processes for the current user, the ps a command includes terminals. As shown in Figure 6.5, these particular terminals include the X window, as depicted by process 5096.

```
michael@ubuntuHHserver:~$ ps -a
  PID TTY          TIME CMD
 6137 tty1     00:00:00 bash
 6163 tty1     00:00:00 su
 6165 tty1     00:00:00 bash
 6179 tty2     00:00:00 bash
25498 pts/2    00:00:00 ps
michael@ubuntuHHserver:~$ ps a
  PID TTY      STAT   TIME COMMAND
 4447 tty4     Ss+    0:00 /sbin/getty 38400 tty4
 4448 tty5     Ss+    0:00 /sbin/getty 38400 tty5
 4452 tty2     Ss     0:00 /bin/login --
 4453 tty3     Ss+    0:00 /sbin/getty 38400 tty3
 4455 tty6     Ss+    0:00 /sbin/getty 38400 tty6
 5906 tty7     Ss+   51:57 /usr/bin/X :0 -br -audit 0 -auth /var/lib/gdm/:0.Xaut
 6120 tty1     Ss     0:00 /bin/login --
 6137 tty1     S      0:00 -bash
 6163 tty1     S      0:00 su
 6165 tty1     S+     0:00 bash
 6179 tty2     S+     0:00 -bash
12842 pts/0    Ss+    0:00 -bash
20321 pts/2    Rs     0:00 -bash
25511 pts/2    R+     0:00 ps a
michael@ubuntuHHserver:~$ []
```

FIGURE 6.5 *The ps command can include or omit terminals.*

Compare the output from Figure 6.5 to the difference between the ps l and ps -l commands. The ps -l command is essentially the same as the ps command, except the output is in a long listing format. In contrast, ps l command output includes information on all open terminals.

Contrast Figure 6.5 with the output to the ps x command. Although terminal console processes are not included in the output, open applications *are* included. In many cases, these applications are open in a GUI and have not been opened directly from a terminal.

Now try the ps u command. You'll see active processes associated with the current user account. And if you're paying attention, you'll see similarities with the output from the ps l command. The ps u command includes resource usage of a process—specifically what each listed process is using of the local RAM and CPU. In contrast, the ps l command specifies PID and PPID numbers, useful to identify processes that need to be killed or have their nice numbers changed.

When combining switches, the l and the u cannot be used together.

Next, put the a and u switches together. The ps au command includes terminal information for all users, typically a standard user account, along with the root administrative account. Contrast this to the output of the ps al command, and note how the difference between the ps u and ps l commands is retained in the output. For an example of both ps au and ps al commands, see Figure 6.6.

TIP

Be aware that ps command switches can be combined in reverse order; for example, ps al is the same command as ps la.

```
michael@ubuntuHHserver:~$ ps au
USER       PID %CPU %MEM    VSZ   RSS TTY      STAT START   TIME COMMAND
root      4447  0.0  0.0   3864   584 tty4     Ss+  2008    0:00 /sbin/getty 384
root      4448  0.0  0.0   3864   588 tty5     Ss+  2008    0:00 /sbin/getty 384
root      4452  0.0  0.0  45700  1296 tty2     Ss   2008    0:00 /bin/login --
root      4453  0.0  0.0   3864   584 tty3     Ss+  2008    0:00 /sbin/getty 384
root      4455  0.0  0.0   3864   584 tty6     Ss+  2008    0:00 /sbin/getty 384
root      5906  0.1  0.9  86688 19072 tty7     Ss+  2008   51:59 /usr/bin/X :0 -
root      6120  0.0  0.0  45700  1300 tty1     Ss   2008    0:00 /bin/login --
michael   6137  0.0  0.1  20816  3748 tty1     S    2008    0:00 -bash
root      6163  0.0  0.0  32480  1300 tty1     S    2008    0:00 su
root      6165  0.0  0.1  18876  2056 tty1     S+   2008    0:00 bash
michael   6179  0.0  0.1  20816  3744 tty2     S+   2008    0:00 -bash
michael  20321  0.0  0.1  20816  3748 pts/2    Rs   08:53   0:00 -bash
michael  28229  0.0  0.0  15064  1088 pts/2    R+   13:34   0:00 ps au
michael@ubuntuHHserver:~$ ps al
F   UID   PID  PPID PRI  NI    VSZ   RSS WCHAN  STAT TTY       TIME COMMAND
0     0  4447     1  20   0   3864   584 -      Ss+  tty4      0:00 /sbin/getty
0     0  4448     1  20   0   3864   588 -      Ss+  tty5      0:00 /sbin/getty
4     0  4452     1  20   0  45700  1296 wait   Ss   tty2      0:00 /bin/login
0     0  4453     1  20   0   3864   584 -      Ss+  tty3      0:00 /sbin/getty
0     0  4455     1  20   0   3864   584 -      Ss+  tty6      0:00 /sbin/getty
4     0  5906  5901  20   0  86688 19072 -      Ss+  tty7     51:59 /usr/bin/X
4     0  6120     1  20   0  45700  1300 wait   Ss   tty1      0:00 /bin/login
4  1000  6137  6120  20   0  20816  3748 wait   S    tty1      0:00 -bash
4     0  6163  6137  20   0  32480  1300 wait   S    tty1      0:00 su
0     0  6165  6163  20   0  18876  2056 -      S+   tty1      0:00 bash
4  1000  6179  4452  20   0  20816  3744 -      S+   tty2      0:00 -bash
0  1000 20321 20320  20   0  20816  3748 -      Rs   pts/2     0:00 -bash
0  1000 28236 20321  20   0   6644   872 -      R+   pts/2     0:00 ps al
michael@ubuntuHHserver:~$ 
```

FIGURE 6.6 *The ps command can include processes with active users.*

In both cases, two active users are shown. The output to the ps au command identifies these users by name: root and michael. The output to the ps al command identifies these users by UID: 0 and 1000. If you checked my /etc/passwd file, you could confirm that these UID numbers correspond to usernames root and michael.

Finally, add an x; try the ps aux and ps alx commands. Both commands provide a complete list of currently running processes.

Foreground and Background Processes

You can run processes in the background. For example, if you're working with a system using the rescue disks associated with some distributions, you'll have only one terminal console available. If you run a process that takes some time, you'll normally have to wait until that process is finished. But it isn't necessary to wait. To that end, this section uses one example to demonstrate the use of the ampersand (**&**), along with the **bg**, **fg**, and **jobs** commands. You can get a similar result by starting a job with the **nohup** command.

Try the sleep 1000 command. It'll either run for 1,000 seconds, or you can stop it with the Ctrl+C or Ctrl+Z key combinations. The **Ctrl+C** combination stops the command completely; in contrast, the **Ctrl+Z** combination suspends the currently running program. This section also explains how to restore such suspended programs.

The Ampersand (&)

If you want to retain access to the command-line interface while running a command such as sleep 1000, add the & to the end of it.

The sleep command is just an example that anyone with a Linux system can use for the purpose of this chapter. (And I hope this section doesn't put you to sleep!) A more practical example might be a command that restores a backup from a remote location.

Now try the noted sleep command, with the &:

```
$ sleep 1000 &
```

Press Enter, and you should be taken back to a command-line interface. This particular job is still running, which you can confirm with the jobs command.

The jobs Command

You can use the jobs command to list programs that are either running in the background or have been suspended.

```
$ jobs
[1]+  Running          sleep 1000 &
[2]+  Running          somethingelse &
[3]+  Stopped          sleep 2000
```

In this case, there are multiple jobs in the background. The second job is associated with the somethingelse program; the third job was suspended either by an error or by a user pressing Ctrl+C while the program was running.

If you need to know the PID associated with a suspended or background job, run the following command:

```
$ jobs -p
```

The bg and fg Commands for Background and Foreground Jobs

The bg command can allow a job to run in the background, with the command-line prompt available for other purposes. In contrast, the fg command brings a job from the background and supersedes the current command-line prompt.

The bg command confirms that jobs are in the background:

```
$ bg
-bash: bg: job 3 already in background
```

However, to confirm that jobs 1 and 2 are still running in the background, you need to specify the job number with the bg 1 or bg 2 commands.

If you want to bring the job back into the foreground, the fg command works, repeating the command in progress, brought out of the background:

```
$ fg
sleep 1000
```

If there's more than one job running simultaneously, you should include the job number.

But what if you forgot to add an & at the end of a command? You could stop the command by pressing Ctrl+C and start it all over again. Alternatively, you could suspend the command by pressing Ctrl+Z while the job is running. For the purpose of this example, run the sleep 3000 command and then press Ctrl+Z. Note the following output to the jobs command:

```
[1]   Running        sleep 1000 &
[2]-  Running        somethingelse &
[3]-  Running        sleep 2000 &
[4]+  Stopped        sleep 3000
```

The sleep 3000 command isn't currently running. To make it run in the background, run the following command:

```
$ bg 4
```

If there's only one currently stopped job, as shown in the output to the jobs command, the job number is not required. Confirm the result by running the jobs command again.

Alternatively, you can specify jobs by name, using either the fg or bg commands. For example, the following command is equivalent to fg 6, because it restores the noted job to the foreground:

```
$ fg "sleep 3000"
```

TIP

A job that is running in the background continues to run after the user who started the job has logged out of that terminal.

It's helpful to be able to set up a job that survives a user logout. If you're just about to leave for the day and need to start a program that may run for hours, start the job, make sure it's working, and then press Ctrl+Z to suspend that job, followed by bg to get that job running in that background. You can leave for the day secure in the knowledge that the job will keep running as long as the system is up.

There are two alternatives to set up a job to keep running after you log out. First, you can set up a job on a regular or scheduled basis, using the cron and at daemons described in Chapter 11, "Administrative Tasks." Second, you can start a job with the nohup command.

No Stop with nohup

The nohup command works as a preface to a second command. To see how it works, take the following steps, which demonstrate what happens when you start a process with nohup and then log out of that system. To see the full capabilities of this command, you should have at least two regular user accounts on the target system:

1. Open a virtual console. If you're in a GUI, you can do so by pressing Ctrl+Alt+F1. (You can substitute F2 through F6 for F1.)
2. Log into that console. If you're already logged into a different console (including the GUI), use a different user account.
3. Run the nohup sleep 120 & command.
4. Type logout to exit from the local virtual console.
5. Log into the same console with a different account. It's acceptable if that account is already logged into the GUI; just make sure it's different from the account used in step 2.
6. Run the ps u -C sleep command. If you run this command within two minutes of executing step 3, the output should reflect the user who ran the original sleep 120 command.

Any output is sent to the local nohup.out file; but in this case, there's no output from the sleep command.

Kill a Process

Sometimes a process just takes over the local system. It slows down other programs to the point that they're essentially unusable. At that point you may need to kill a process. One example described earlier, associated with the Firefox Web browser, was shown in the top task browser display from Figure 6.3.

At that point, one option is to kill the associated process. When done properly, the current Linux session is fully operational. Options to this end include the **kill** and **killall** commands. A third option is to kill the process directly from the top task browser.

Kill a Process from the top Task Browser

Processes can be managed from the top task browser. You saw how processes can be reprioritized by changing its "nice" number earlier in this chapter. Based on the scenario associated with Figure 6.3, assume you've logged in as user michael. In that case, you can start the "kill" of the firefox process by pressing k.

The following prompt appears in the top task browser:

```
PID to kill:
```

At that point, all you need to do is type in the PID of the target process. (If you want to cancel, just press Enter.) Based on Figure 6.3, that PID was 7292. Type in the target PID number, and you'll be prompted to confirm the kill:

```
kill PID 7292 with signal [15]:
```

Just press Enter at that point. If your account has permissions to do so (and the process isn't having other problems), the process is then killed. (If you want to abort the "kill," enter 0 at the prompt shown previously.)

The ability to kill a process is one reason why Linux systems can run continuously for months or even years at a time.

The kill Command

The **kill** command is generally used to kill a process. If the process is cooperative, the **kill** command is simple. All you need is the PID of the process in question. Although you could identify the PID from the top task browser as just described, another method is to use the **ps axl** command, which identifies all running processes with associated PID numbers.

For example, you can identify the PID and PPID numbers from the output to the following command:

```
$ ps axl | grep firefox
0  1000 31279    1  20   0 279452 143488 -  Sl  ?   7:17 /usr/lib/firefox-3.0.1/firefox
```

The firefox process is shown in the /usr/lib/firefox-3.0.1/ directory. The first few columns tell me that the owner of the process is user michael (who has a UID of 1000 in the /etc/passwd file), the PID is 31279, and the PPID is 1.

> **TIP**
>
> Don't kill any process with a PID of 1. That's the process associated with the init daemon, the parent process of all other processes. In fact, if the local Linux system is running properly, any attempt to kill it should fail, even from the root administrative account.

Now, after all of these gymnastics, here's the simple kill command, which should stop the Firefox Web browser:

```
$ kill 31279
```

This assumes that the user running the command is UID 1000; otherwise, this command will be rejected because the user wouldn't have permissions as such. The default signal sent by the kill command is 15, also known as TERM, which I interpret as short for "terminate that process!"

For a full list of available kill signals, run the kill -l command (that's the letter l, not the number 1). Other actions are available with the kill command; some of the more important options are described in Table 6.6.

Table 6.6 Major kill Signal Options

Switch	Option
-1	Kill and restart the service; equivalent to -HUP
-9	Kill the process in a way that orphan processes may remain; equivalent to -KILL
-15	Kill the process normally; equivalent to -TERM

If all else fails, Linux should respond to the kill -9 *PID* command. If that command fails to kill a process, there are other issues beyond the scope of this certification.

The killall Command

There are times when you don't want to bother with a PID number. For example, the Apache Web browser starts multiple processes to better accommodate multiple connections. The related processes on my CentOS 5 system are illustrated in Figure 6.7.

```
michael@UbuntuHH:~$ ps u -C apache2
USER       PID %CPU %MEM    VSZ   RSS TTY    STAT START   TIME COMMAND
root      2840  0.0  0.0  10476  2576 ?      Ss   18:07   0:00 /usr/sbin/apache2 -k
www-data  2841  0.0  0.0  10248  1784 ?      S    18:07   0:00 /usr/sbin/apache2 -k
www-data  2844  0.0  0.0 231812  2404 ?      Sl   18:07   0:00 /usr/sbin/apache2 -k
www-data  2847  0.0  0.0 231812  2408 ?      Sl   18:07   0:00 /usr/sbin/apache2 -k
www-data  2851  0.0  0.0 231812  2408 ?      Sl   18:07   0:00 /usr/sbin/apache2 -k
michael@UbuntuHH:~$ []
```

FIGURE 6.7 *Multiple instances of one process.*

And this is just the default for Apache; many Web services set up more Apache processes. You could kill each of these processes, one by one, based on the PID. Alternatively, you could kill all the processes simultaneously with the killall command. In this particular case, the appropriate command is

```
# killall apache2
```

Chapter Summary

This chapter is focused in two areas: the vi editor and process administration. It addresses three of the LPIC-1 objectives: 103.5 ("Create, Monitor, and Kill Processes"), 103.6 ("Modify Process Execution Priorities"), and 103.8 ("Perform Basic File Editing Operations Using vi").

Whereas the selection of the vi editor is arbitrary, a knowledge of at least one console-based text editor is important for every serious Linux user. The vi command skills described in this chapter correspond to its three modes: command, insert, and execute. Review the vi-specific commands noted in the Key Terms. Because they are listed in the LPIC objectives, they are fair game for the exam.

When administering a Linux system, you need to know when a process may be overwhelming that system. That's where priority management tools such as the top and ps commands can help. You can reprioritize processes based on their nice number using the nice and renice commands.

Priority and process management are in many ways one topic. The LPIC objectives include some of the same commands under both topics. Process management tools go a bit further, because they include tools that enable you to move jobs to the background or foreground or even to kill those jobs when appropriate.

Key Terms

◆ **&.** An ampersand after a command runs that command in the background and returns control to the shell prompt.

◆ **a (vi).** The a command in the vi editor enters insert mode, after the character associated with the current position of the cursor.

- **bg.** The bg command activates a suspended process in the background.
- **c (vi).** The c command (change) in the vi editor by itself is not complete; for example, the cc command deletes the current line and enters insert mode; the cw command deletes the current word and enters insert mode.
- **command mode (vi).** In the command mode of the vi editor, you can run navigational and editing commands.
- **Ctrl+C.** When you run the Ctrl+C command combination in the command-line interface while a program is running, it stops that program.
- **Ctrl+Z.** When you run the Ctrl+Z command combination in the command-line interface while a program is running, it suspends that program; you can then continue that program with the bg command.
- **d (vi).** The d command in the vi editor by itself is not complete; for example, the dd command deletes the current line; the dw command deletes the current word.
- **dd (vi).** The dd command in the vi editor deletes the current line; the 2dd command deletes the current line plus the next line below.
- **:e! (vi).** The :e! command in the vi editor drops any changes and keeps the editor open.
- **execute mode (vi).** When you're in the execute mode of the vi editor, regular shell commands can be run with the :! preface.
- **fg.** The fg command brings a background process to the foreground, possibly superseding the current command line.
- **free.** A command that displays the status of free and used memory in RAM and swap space.
- **h (vi).** The h command in the vi editor moves to the left one character, equivalent to the left arrow key.
- **i (vi).** The i command in the vi editor enters insert mode.
- **insert mode (vi).** When in the insert mode of the vi editor, text and lines can be added to a file.
- **j (vi).** The j command in the vi editor moves down one line, equivalent to the down arrow key.
- **jobs.** The jobs command returns the number of a job in the background.
- **k (vi).** The k command in the vi editor moves up one line, equivalent to the up arrow key.
- **l (vi).** The l command in the vi editor moves to the right one character, equivalent to the right arrow key.
- **nice.** The nice command prefaces another command with a selected nice number, also known as a scheduling priority. The nice command sets a nice number of 10 by default.

◆ **nice number**. A nice number is also known as a scheduling priority. It ranges from -20 to 19 and is counterintuitive, because a process with a nice number of -20 has the highest priority on a system.

◆ **nohup.** The nohup command prefaces another command and can be used to keep a process running even after the user who ran the command logs out of the system.

◆ **o (vi).** The o command in the vi editor enters insert mode, opening the line below the current position of the cursor.

◆ **p (vi).** The p command in the vi editor takes the contents of the register (buffer) and pastes it based on the current position of the cursor.

◆ **PID.** Short for process identifier, the number associated with a running process. A PID may be revealed from the top task browser or the ps command.

◆ **PPID.** Short for parent process identifier, the number associated with the ancestor of a running process. A PPID may be revealed using the ps command with certain switches.

◆ **ps.** A command that creates a configurable snapshot of current processes.

◆ **:q! (qi).** The :q! command in the vi editor exits from the editor; the ! in the command exits without saving changes.

◆ **renice.** The renice command alters the nice number associated with a currently running process, normally based on that process's PID.

◆ **top.** A command that takes load data from currently running processes and displays them in the top task browser.

◆ **u (vi).** The u command in the vi editor in command mode undoes the most recent change.

◆ **uptime.** A command that displays current system uptime, logged in users, and load averages over the past 1, 5, and 15 minutes.

◆ **vi.** A text editor that works from command-line consoles.

◆ **vim editor.** The vi, Improved editor, which is the current implementation of vi on most Linux systems.

◆ **:w! (vi).** The :w! command in the vi editor writes changes; the ! in the command supersedes read-only mode for the file, assuming the user owns the file.

◆ **y (vi).** The y command in the vi editor by itself is not complete. For example, the yy command copies the current line into the register (buffer); it is associated with the p command. Alternatively, the y1j command copies the current line and the line below into the register.

◆ **yy (vi).** The yy command copies the current line into the register (buffer); it is associated with the p command. The 3yy command yanks the current line plus the two below it into the buffer.

◆ **ZZ (vi).** The ZZ command in the vi editor writes changes and exits from the editor.

Review Questions

The number of review questions in this chapter and other chapters in this book is proportionate to each section's weight in the LPI objectives. Because this chapter covers items 103.5, 103.6, and 103.8, the weight is 9; therefore, you'll see 18 questions in this section. You'll see multiple choice single answer, fill-in-the blank, and multiple choice multiple answer questions, as you'll encounter on the exam.

1. While in the vi editor, which of the following commands writes and exits from a file? Choose two.

   A. :wx

   B. ZZ

   C. :wq

   D. :w!

2. In the vi editor, which of the following commands moves to edit mode, adding a line directly above the position of the cursor?

   A. A

   B. a

   C. O

   D. o

3. Which of the following vi commands is functionally equivalent to the down arrow key?

   A. h

   B. j

   C. k

   D. l

4. In the vi editor, enter the command that searches backward in a file for the term passwd. _____

5. In the vi editor, which of the following commands lists files from the current directory?

   A. :!ls

   B. !ls

   C. ?ls

   D. /ls

6. In the vi editor, which of the following commands deletes the current and the next line from the current file?

   A. dd2

   B. 2dd

   C. d2

   D. 2d

7. Ignoring the potential risks, enter the command that sets PID 25 to the highest possible priority. _____

8. When running the renice 100 command on PID 100, which of the following is the new priority of that PID?

   A. 100

   B. 10

   C. 19

   D. −20

9. When the top command is running, you see a process that's taking over 100% of the local CPU. Which of the following commands prompts for the PID to stop that process?

   A. k

   B. s

   C. p

   D. q

10. Which of the following commands is the simplest way to isolate the running processes (if any) associated with the hypothetical xyz service?

    A. ps a | grep xyz

    B. ps x | grep xyz

    C. ps ax | grep xyz

    D. ps axl | grep xyz

11. Which of the following actions or commands places a currently running job in the background?

    A. Press Ctrl+Z.

    B. Run the bg command.

    C. Add an & after the command.

    D. Identify the process by running the top command, and then type bg.

12. Which of the following commands displays the amount of time that the current system has been active? Choose two.

    A. uptime

    B. top

    C. active

    D. load

13. If there are multiple instances of the samba process running, which of the following commands would end all of those processes?

    A. kill -9 samba

    B. killall samba

    C. kill -1 samba

    D. kill -HUP samba

14. Enter the command you can use to start a long-running process so that it keeps running after you log out. Do not include the path to the command.

    _____

15. Which of the following actions can be run from the top command? Choose two.

    A. Killing a process by its PID.

    B. Measure the free space on the hard drive.

    C. A process can be given a lower priority.

    D. New processes can be started.

16. Which of the following statements describes what happens when you run the local dataprocess script with the nohup ./dataprocess & command?

    A. The dataprocess script is restarted.

    B. The dataprocess script is run in the background.

    C. The dataproces script is started for the first time.

    D. The dataprocess script is stopped.

17. Which of the following commands lists just the current processes running in the background?

    A. bg

    B. jobs

    C. ps aux

    D. top

18. Enter the switch or character that runs a process while immediately returning access to the command-line prompt. _____

Chapter 7

Manage and Maintain Filesystems

After completing this chapter, you will be able to

- Create partitions and format filesystems on those partitions

- Monitor and maintain the integrity of a filesystem

- Control the conditions for mounting and unmounting a filesystem

Introduction

In this chapter, you'll learn about the management of filesystems, starting with the creation of partitions with the `fdisk` command utility. The chapter continues with a guide to the `mkfs` formatting tools for regular and swap partitions.

You'll learn the basics of filesystem integrity. Various commands are available to verify the integrity of a filesystem, monitor available resources, and repair relatively simple problems.

A filesystem isn't useful for files until it's mounted. That's why this chapter also examines how filesystems are mounted based on the `/etc/fstab` configuration file, how filesystems can be made mountable by regular users, as well as basic commands for mounting and unmounting a properly configured filesystem.

TIP

This chapter addresses three objectives in the LPI exam: 104.1 ("Create Partitions and Filesystems"), 104.2 ("Maintain the Integrity of Filesystems"), and 104.3 ("Control Mounting and Unmounting of Filesystems").

Create and Configure a Partition

In this section, you'll see how to set up a partition to the filesystem formats described in the LPIC-1 objectives. To this end, you'll use the `fdisk` command utility to find configured partitions. You'll also see how to create new partitions suitable for Linux files as well as swap space. But an unformatted partition can't store files. To that end, you'll also sample a variety of commands that set up a partition for different filesystem formats.

Configure Partitions with fdisk

Although multiple partition management tools are available for Linux, the `fdisk` command utility is the one specified in the LPIC-1 objectives. It's the current tool with the most history, and its popularity remains strong. `fdisk` is also commonly available on rescue media, which increases its importance.

Nevertheless, other excellent tools are available for Linux. Perhaps most prominent is `parted`, an open source tool developed by the Free Software Foundation for Linux. GUI-based tools have been developed from `parted`.

In the following sections, you'll see how to use `fdisk` to find configured partitions, and you'll create three types of partitions: a regular Linux partition, a non-Linux partition, and a partition suitable for swap space.

Find Configured Partitions

The command that displays existing configured partitions is simple:

```
# fdisk -l
```

If you don't see output, make sure you have administrative permissions. Through the Fedora 10 release, Red Hat–style distributions (including CentOS 5) did not include utilities from the /sbin or /usr/sbin directories in the PATH for normal users. That's one reason why it helps to log in as an administrative user. You should see output similar to Figure 7.1, which lists partitions on all detected hardware devices.

```
michael@UbuntuHH:~$ sudo fdisk -l
[sudo] password for michael:

Disk /dev/sda: 160.0 GB, 160041885696 bytes
255 heads, 63 sectors/track, 19457 cylinders
Units = cylinders of 16065 * 512 = 8225280 bytes
Disk identifier: 0xe686f016

   Device Boot      Start         End      Blocks   Id  System
/dev/sda1               1          26      208813+   6  FAT16
/dev/sda2     *        27        3851    30724312+   7  HPFS/NTFS
/dev/sda3            3852        3864      104422+  83  Linux
/dev/sda4            3865       19457   125250772+   f  W95 Ext'd (LBA)
/dev/sda5            3865        5858    16016773+  83  Linux
/dev/sda6            5859        9945    32828796    b  W95 FAT32
/dev/sda7            9946       10189     1959898+  82  Linux swap / Solaris
/dev/sda8           10190       11406     9775521   83  Linux
/dev/sda9           11407       11419      104391   83  Linux
/dev/sda10          11420       12694    10241406   83  Linux
/dev/sda11          12695       15264    20643493+  83  Linux
/dev/sda12          15265       19457    33680241   83  Linux

Disk /dev/mmcblk0: 1023 MB, 1023934464 bytes
32 heads, 63 sectors/track, 992 cylinders
Units = cylinders of 2016 * 512 = 1032192 bytes
Disk identifier: 0x00000000

       Device Boot      Start         End      Blocks   Id  System
/dev/mmcblk0p1              1         992      999813+   6  FAT16
michael@UbuntuHH:~$ 
```

FIGURE 7.1 *Detected partitions.*

In this case, there are 12 partitions on a single SATA drive. Make note of what appears to be a second hard drive. It's actually an SD (Secure Digital) card. The information identifies several bits of data:

◆ The device file, such as /dev/sda1.

◆ Whether the device is bootable. In this case, the only "bootable" device is /dev/sda2, which accommodates a "dual-boot" with a Microsoft Windows system. Surprisingly, there is no requirement to make the partition with the /boot directory bootable under `fdisk`.

◆ The start and end cylinder of each partition.

◆ The number of blocks associated with each partition.

◆ The partition ID, which will become clearer shortly when you see how to create a non-Linux partition.

◆ The associated partition system. Filesystem formats such as ext3 require a compatible partition system such as Linux.

Pay particular attention to the number of cylinders. It's the easiest way to check for free space if you want to create a new partition. In both cases, there are no free cylinders, so for the purpose of this chapter, I've set up a virtual machine with an extra hard disk.

Explore a Hard Disk with fdisk

Before creating a new partition with fdisk, it's important to know what it can do. It's best if you've set up an empty hard disk for this purpose, because changes made through fdisk can lead to the loss of all data on that hard drive.

Assume that you've set up a second SATA or SCSI drive on a local system. On a CentOS 5 system, it might appear in the output to the fdisk -l command as follows:

```
Disk /dev/sda: 5368 MB, 5368709120 bytes
255 heads, 63 sectors/track, 652 cylinders
Units = cylinders of 16065 * 512 = 8225280 bytes
   Device Boot      Start        End      Blocks   Id  System
/dev/sda1   *           1         13      104391   83  Linux
/dev/sda2              14        652    5132767+   8e  Linux LVM

Disk /dev/sdb: 1073 MB, 1073741824 bytes
255 heads, 63 sectors/track, 130 cylinders
Units = cylinders of 16065 * 512 = 8225280 bytes

Disk /dev/sdb doesn't contain a valid partition table
```

This output tells me that the first SATA or SCSI drive on this system is full, as indicated by the cylinders occupied by the first two partitions. Furthermore, the second SATA or SCSI drive on this system, labeled /dev/sdb, has no current partitions. So open this drive with the fdisk /dev/sdb command:

If your test system has a different empty device, substitute accordingly. You should see the following fdisk prompt:

```
Command (m for help):
```

Run the m command to see other available fdisk commands. The options described in Table 7.1 relate to the LPIC-1 objective for configuring disk partitions.

TIP

You can exit from the fdisk utility at any time with the q or w commands. The q command exits without saving changes; the w command writes changes to disk.

Table 7.1 fdisk Commands

Command	Description
a	Toggles the bootable flag on a specified partition; at least one partition must be bootable, but it doesn't have to be the partition with the /boot directory
d	Deletes a specified partition by its number
l	Lists known partition types
m	Displays available fdisk commands
n	Configures a new partition; you'll be prompted for additional information
p	Lists the current partition table
q	Exits fdisk without saving changes
t	Changes the system ID of a specific partition to a type listed with the l command
w	Writes changes to disk; after this command is run, changes are irrevocable

Press p to print the current partition table. If this is a new hard disk, the partition table will be empty, and the output will appear similar to the following:

```
Disk /dev/sdb: 1073 MB, 1073741824 bytes
255 heads, 63 sectors/track, 130 cylinders
Units = cylinders of 16065 * 512 = 8225280 bytes

   Device Boot      Start         End      Blocks   Id  System

Command (m for help):
```

For the purpose of this subsection, exit from fdisk without saving changes with the q command.

Create a New Regular Partition

In this section, you'll see how to create a regular partition on a CentOS 5 system with the fdisk utility. As a regular partition, it will be able to accommodate standard Linux filesystems as soon as it is formatted.

To create the new regular partition, take the following steps:

1. Check the status of configured partitions. Run the following command and identify a partition with the following command:

   ```
   # fdisk -l
   ```

2. Check free space on an existing hard disk. If you see output such as the following, do not be concerned. It is a typical message associated with a newly installed hard drive.

   ```
   Disk /dev/sdb doesn't contain a valid partition table
   ```

3. Open the disk with free space with the fdisk utility. If that disk is the second SATA or SCSI drive, that command would be as follows:

   ```
   # fdisk /dev/sdb
   ```

4. If the disk has not been configured before, you'll see the following warning, which really applies whenever a partition is configured:

   ```
   Building a new DOS disklabel. Changes will remain in memory only,
   until you decide to write them. After that, of course, the previous
   content won't be recoverable.
   ```

5. Now enter n to start the process of creating a new partition. Under the noted circumstances, you'll see the following options:

   ```
   Command action
      e   extended
      p   primary partition (1-4)
   ```

   If an extended partition has been created, the options displayed will include an option to create a logical partition. In this case, enter the p command.

6. You'll be prompted to enter a partition number, with a range of available partition numbers. In the following case, make it the first partition by entering the number 1.

   ```
   Partition number (1-4): 1
   ```

7. You're prompted to enter the start of the desired partition, based on available cylinders, similar to the following. For the purpose of this exercise, accept the default entry of 1 to start the partition at the first cylinder.

   ```
   First cylinder (1-130, default 1): 1
   ```

8. You're prompted to enter the last cylinder as shown. You can also enter the desired size of the partition in bytes, kilobytes, or megabytes. Enter 500MB as follows (and don't forget the plus sign):

   ```
   Last cylinder or +size or +sizeM or +sizeK (1-130, default 130): +500M
   ```

9. Confirm the change by displaying the partition table with the p command.

10. If you're satisfied with the changes, write them to the disk with the w command.

11. Pay attention to the output messages. The syncing output message confirms that the new partition is ready to be formatted.

12. Rerun step 1 to confirm the new partition. Note that the Linux in the system column, associated with the new partition, indicates it's ready as a standard Linux partition.

NOTE

The standard Linux filesystem type is suitable for the different Linux filesystem formats described in this chapter, including ext2, ext3, `reiserfs`, and `xfs`.

Create a Non-Linux Partition

Now that you've seen how to create a regular Linux partition using the `fdisk` utility, it's time to take another step and show you how to create a non-Linux partition. Many of the steps are the same. Once the new partition is created after step 8 of the previous exercise, you can set up a new partition as a non-Linux partition.

To do so from the `fdisk` prompt, run the t command. Specify the number of the partition that you want to set up as a non-Linux partition. You'll see the following prompt:

```
Hex code (type L to list codes):
```

Enter the L command to see available partition types that can be configured through `fdisk`, as shown in Figure 7.2.

```
 0  Empty           1e  Hidden W95 FAT1 80  Old Minix        be  Solaris boot
 1  FAT12           24  NEC DOS         81  Minix / old Lin  bf  Solaris
 2  XENIX root      39  Plan 9          82  Linux swap / So  c1  DRDOS/sec (FAT-
 3  XENIX usr       3c  PartitionMagic  83  Linux            c4  DRDOS/sec (FAT-
 4  FAT16 <32M      40  Venix 80286     84  OS/2 hidden C:   c6  DRDOS/sec (FAT-
 5  Extended        41  PPC PReP Boot   85  Linux extended   c7  Syrinx
 6  FAT16           42  SFS             86  NTFS volume set  da  Non-FS data
 7  HPFS/NTFS       4d  QNX4.x          87  NTFS volume set  db  CP/M / CTOS / .
 8  AIX             4e  QNX4.x 2nd part 88  Linux plaintext  de  Dell Utility
 9  AIX bootable    4f  QNX4.x 3rd part 8e  Linux LVM        df  BootIt
 a  OS/2 Boot Manag 50  OnTrack DM      93  Amoeba           e1  DOS access
 b  W95 FAT32       51  OnTrack DM6 Aux 94  Amoeba BBT       e3  DOS R/O
 c  W95 FAT32 (LBA) 52  CP/M            9f  BSD/OS           e4  SpeedStor
 e  W95 FAT16 (LBA) 53  OnTrack DM6 Aux a0  IBM Thinkpad hi  eb  BeOS fs
 f  W95 Ext'd (LBA) 54  OnTrackDM6      a5  FreeBSD          ee  EFI GPT
10  OPUS            55  EZ-Drive        a6  OpenBSD          ef  EFI (FAT-12/16/
11  Hidden FAT12    56  Golden Bow      a7  NeXTSTEP         f0  Linux/PA-RISC b
12  Compaq diagnost 5c  Priam Edisk     a8  Darwin UFS       f1  SpeedStor
14  Hidden FAT16 <3 61  SpeedStor       a9  NetBSD           f4  SpeedStor
16  Hidden FAT16    63  GNU HURD or Sys ab  Darwin boot      f2  DOS secondary
17  Hidden HPFS/NTF 64  Novell Netware  b7  BSDI fs          fd  Linux raid auto
18  AST SmartSleep  65  Novell Netware  b8  BSDI swap        fe  LANstep
1b  Hidden W95 FAT3 70  DiskSecure Mult bb  Boot Wizard hid  ff  BBT
1c  Hidden W95 FAT3 75  PC/IX
Hex code (type L to list codes): []
```

FIGURE 7.2 *Partition types in* `fdisk`.

The variety of available partition types is incredible! But just a few partition types are commonly used, as described in Table 7.2. Type 83, a standard Linux partition, is the default. There are variations on certain file formats, such as the four different FAT32 partition types, beyond the scope of the LPIC-1 exams.

Table 7.2 Major fdisk Partition Types

Code	Description
b	W95 FAT32, associated with older Microsoft 32-bit filesystem partitions, originally developed for Microsoft Windows 95
c	W95 FAT32 (LBA), associated with older Microsoft 32-bit filesystem partitions, with LBA (logical block addressing)
6	FAT16, associated with older Microsoft partitions as large as 2GB
7	HPFS/NTFS, associated with current Microsoft file formats
82	Linux swap, suitable for swap space partitions
83	Standard Linux partition type, suitable for several different formats (default)
85	Linux extended
8e	Linux LVM, suitable for logical volumes
fd	Linux raid auto, suitable for configuration in RAID arrays

In other words, to create a non-Linux partition, you'll take many of the same steps as creating a regular Linux partition. The fdisk utility supports changes to the desired partition type. To follow along with the "Format the Filesystem" section, create a W95 FAT32 partition, using code b.

Any changes made to a partition type are just the first step; the partition must still be formatted with the appropriate command.

Create a Linux Partition for Swap Space

The steps required to create a partition for swap space are similar to those required to create a non-Linux partition. To set up a partition for swap space, configure it as type 82, Linux swap. If you need guidance, reread the previous section.

Once you've created a new partition for a regular Linux filesystem, for Linux swap space, and for a non-Linux partition, run the p command from the fdisk prompt. The output should resemble the following. In this case, the /dev/sdb2 partition is ready to be configured as swap space.

```
   Device Boot      Start         End      Blocks   Id  System
/dev/sdb1              1          62      497983+  83  Linux
/dev/sdb2             63          87      200812+  82  Linux swap / Solaris
/dev/sdb3             88         112      200812+   b  W95 FAT32
```

When you're satisfied with the changes, run the w command to write the partitions to the newly configured hard disk.

Format the Filesystem

In this section, you'll format three partitions to the filesystems described in the LPIC-1 objectives. The standard format command for this purpose is mkfs, which normally formats the partition to a standard Linux filesystem. But courtesy of command completion, you can review available mkfs commands. Type in /sbin/mkfs and press the Tab key twice. You should see output similar to the following:

```
mkfs           mkfs.ext2    mkfs.msdos    mkfs.xfs
mkfs.cramfs  mkfs.ext3    mkfs.vfat
```

If you don't see the **mkfs.xfs** or **mkfs.reiserfs** commands in the output, install the xfsprogs and reiserfsprogs package on the local system. These commands configure Linux partitions to the XFS and ReiserFS filesystems. The XFS filesystem is a 64-bit format developed by Silicon Graphics to support extra large files on their high-end workstations. The ReiserFS filesystem is designed for journaling. For convenience, these formats are described by their command switches, xfs and reiserfs.

 NOTE

The LPIC-1 objectives specify coverage of version 3 of the ReiserFS filesystem. In other words, ReiserFS version 4 (as well as the ext4 filesystem implemented on Fedora 11) is not yet covered.

Because the LPIC-1 objectives cover both the xfs and reiserfs filesystem formats, you need to know something about the associated format commands. Table 7.3 describes applicable filesystem formats. See the "Support for the XFS and ReiserFS Filesystems" sidebar for more information on installing appropriate packages.

Table 7.3 Linux Filesystem Formats

Format	Description
ext2	Second extended filesystem, no journaling; old default on many Linux systems
ext3	Third extended filesystem, with journaling; the default on many Linux systems
ext4	Fourth extended filesystem, with journaling; first major implementation on Fedora 11
reiserfs	General-purpose journaling filesystem; version 3 is current as of this writing
swap	General format designed for Linux swap partitions
vfat	Linux filesystem designed to be compatible with Microsoft FAT16 and FAT32 filesystems; can be read by both Linux and Microsoft operating systems
xfs	64-bit journaling filesystem developed by Silicon Graphics; well suited for larger files

SUPPORT FOR THE XFS AND REISERFS FILESYSTEMS

Red Hat has chosen to omit support for the XFS and ReiserFS filesystems in its Red Hat Enterprise Linux 5 (RHEL5) release. It believes that the ext3 and the upcoming ext4 filesystems provide sufficient support for journaling and larger files. CentOS 5, as a rebuild of RHEL5, reflects this lack of support for XFS and ReiserFS. To add that support, you have to install or customize a nonstandard Linux kernel.

If you're using CentOS 5, you can still install associated filesystem format commands to study for the LPIC-1 exams. On the CentOS 5 distribution, plan to install the xfsprogs and reiserfs-utils packages for access to the mkfs.reiserfs and mkfs.xfs commands.

To install these packages, you need to activate the CentOS 5 Plus repositories, available in the /etc/yum.repos.d/CentOS-Base.repo file. In that file, you have to change the value of the enabled directive in the [centosplus] stanza shown here from 0 to 1.

```
[centosplus]
name=CentOS-$releasever - Plus
mirrorlist=http://mirrorlist.centos.org/?release=$releasever&arch=
$basearch&repo=centosplus
#baseurl=http://mirror.centos.org/centos/$releasever/centosplus/
$basearch/
gpgcheck=1
enabled=1
gpgkey=http://mirror.centos.org/centos/RPM-GPG-KEY-CentOS-5
```

You should then be able to install the noted packages with the following command:

```
# yum install reiserfs-utils xfsprogs
```

In contrast, the Ubuntu distribution includes the equivalent of these packages (xfsprogs and reiserfsprogs) in its main repositories, so similar gymnastics are not required. If the mkfs.reiserfs and mkfs.xfs commands are not yet available, you can install them with the following command:

```
# apt-get install reiserfsprogs xfsprogs
```

Once you've installed the right packages, the format commands are simple. Assuming that you're applying the command to the /dev/sdb1 partition, the following commands format it to the ext2, ext3, reiserfs, and xfs filesystems:

```
# mkfs.ext2 /dev/sdb1
# mkfs.ext3 /dev/sdb1
# mkfs.reiserfs /dev/sdb1
# mkfs.xfs /dev/sdb1
```

To format a partition such as /dev/sdb2 for swap space, run the following command:

```
# mkswap /dev/sdb2
```

Finally, to format a partition to the vfat filesystem, run the **mkfs.vfat** command on a filesystem configured to an appropriate partition type via fdisk. Earlier in this chapter, you created a /dev/sdb3 partition for this purpose and therefore can format that partition with the following command:

```
# mkfs.vfat /dev/sdb3
```

These commands are not unique; equivalent options are described in Table 7.4.

Table 7.4 Linux Filesystem Format Command Equivalents

Command 1	Command 2	Command 3
mkfs.ext2	mkfs -t ext2	mke2fs
mkfs.ext3	mkfs -t ext3	mke2fs -j
mkfs.reiserfs	mkfs -t reiserfs	mkreiserfs
mkfs.xfs	mkfs -t xfs	
mkfs.vfat	mkfs -t vfat	mkdosfs -F 32

Manage Filesystem Integrity

Anyone with expertise in Linux needs to know how to maintain its filesystems. Such skills are fundamental to keeping data secure. To that end, you'll learn how to verify that a filesystem is fully operational, how to check a system against size and file limits, as well as how to perform basic filesystem repair operations. This section covers associated commands, including du, df, fsck, e2fsck, mke2fs, debugfs, dumpe2fs, tune2fs, xfs_check, xfs_info, and xfs_metadump.

Monitor a Partition

Proactive Linux users know how to monitor the status of every partition on their systems. In other words, they use commands like df to monitor free space and available **inodes**. The du command can identify the file space used on a specific directory.

But first you need to understand that an inode represents every data structure on a Linux system. Every file requires an inode. You can set up only so many files on a partition, as based on the maximum number of inodes on that partition.

Although the commands described in this section also apply to logical volumes and RAID arrays, the LPIC-1 objectives are primarily focused on partitions.

Capacity Reports with df

You can use the df command to measure the capacity of currently mounted filesystems. As shown from the following excerpt, the output lists the total amount of memory in 1KB blocks, the amount used, and the remaining amount available, all in kilobytes.

```
$ df
Filesystem          1K blocks      Used Available Use% Mounted on
/dev/sda2            7753868    5585260   1777828  76% /
/dev/sda1              93307      25476     63014  29% /boot
```

Of course, the output can be configured in different units of capacity; for example, the df -m command displays output in megabytes. One less commonly used option is df -i, which lists the relative availability of inodes on each filesystem. Compare this excerpt with the one listed earlier:

```
$ df -i
Filesystem          Inodes   IUsed    IFree IUse% Mounted on
/dev/sda2           489600  140077   349523   29% /
/dev/sda1            24096      53    24043    1% /boot
```

Note the different usage levels on the top-level root directory (/) /dev/sda2 filesystem. Although 76% of the space of the filesystem is currently in use, 29% of the inodes are in use on that same filesystem. This suggests the filesystem is being occupied by several large files. For example, an .iso file download of a Linux distribution DVD may take several gigabytes of space while occupying only one inode.

If you see an opposite discrepancy, the local system might be filled with a lot of small files. Alternatively, there might be a problem with corruption. When you delete a file, the inode should also be freed. File corruption can affect this process, but such corruption can be addressed with the fsck command described later in this chapter.

Some of the more important df command switches are listed in Table 7.5.

Table 7.5 Command Switches for df

Switch	Output Description
.	Current filesystem only
-h	Human-readable format
-i	Inodes
-k	Kilobytes
-m	Megabytes

Directory Space Reports with du

The du command is focused on the space used by files in a directory. Output includes the space taken by each regular and hidden file and directory. However, output is limited, because it does not include the names of files in subdirectories.

For example, Figure 7.3 displays the output of the du command from one of my local directories.

```
224     ./.gstreamer-0.10
8       ./.redhat/esc
32      ./.redhat
48      ./.metacity/sessions
56      ./.metacity
12      ./.elinks
32      ./.nautilus/metafiles
48      ./.nautilus
16      ./.local/share/icons
24      ./.local/share/desktop-directories
16      ./.local/share/applications/wine/Programs
24      ./.local/share/applications/wine
32      ./.local/share/applications
80      ./.local/share
88      ./.local
16      ./.config/menus/applications-merged
24      ./.config/menus
32      ./.config
8       ./.mozilla/extensions
8       ./.mozilla/plugins
24      ./.mozilla
43216   .
[michael@CentOS5-LPI ~]$ ▮
```

FIGURE 7.3 *du command output.*

Although the output includes the hidden .local/ directory and subdirectories, it does not include files in those subdirectories.

The du command can be focused on specific file types. For example, the following command run on my server identifies each .iso file in the noted directory, along with its size in kilobytes. (My user is the owner of the /isofiles directory.)

```
$ du /isofiles/*.iso
```

Although the du command does not measure inodes, it can display output in other size formats, using the same switches shown in Table 7.5 (except the -i).

Putting the fsck on a Partition

If you boot a Linux system fairly frequently, you may have noticed occasional delays during the boot process. If you're running an informative Linux distribution, you may have seen a message similar to the following:

```
/dev/sda2 has been mounted 30 times without being checked, check forced
```

At that point, the boot process stops, and the fsck command (one pronunciation is "fisk") is run on the noted partition to check and repair the associated filesystem. Be especially careful when running the fsck command by itself, because it tries to check and repair every filesystem listed in the /etc/fstab configuration file.

If you try the fsck command on a regular mounted partition, you'll see the following message:

```
# fsck /dev/sda10
fsck 1.40.8 (13-Mar-2008)
e2fsck 1.40.8 (13-Mar-2008)
/dev/sda10 is mounted.

WARNING!!!  Running e2fsck on a mounted filesystem may cause
SEVERE filesystem damage.

Do you really want to continue (y/n)? no
```

Take the warning seriously. Running the fsck command on a mounted filesystem can destroy your data. You should always type n at the noted prompt, which causes the word "no" to appear; then fsck aborts and returns to the command-line prompt. Furthermore, note the e2fsck command in the message; the command detects the ext2 or ext3 filesystem and applies the e2fsck command.

Next, the following command suggests what fsck would do to each filesystem listed in the /etc/fstab configuration file, with selected excerpts from my output:

```
# fsck -N
[/sbin/fsck.ext3 (1) -- /] fsck.ext3 /dev/sda10
[/sbin/fsck.vfat (1) -- /media/sda6] fsck.vfat /dev/sda6

[/sbin/fsck.reiserfs (1) -- /SuSE] fsck.reiserfs /dev/sdb1
[/sbin/fsck.xfs (1) -- /mnt] fsck.xfs /dev/sdc1
[/sbin/fsck.ext2 (1) -- /boot] fsck.ext2 /dev/sda9
```

The output tells me that the fsck command uses the information from /etc/fstab to identify the filesystem check that would be run. The fsck command, when run on an ext2 or ext3 formatted partition, checks that partition in five different areas:

- ◆ Inodes, disk blocks, and file sizes
- ◆ Directory structure, starting with the top-level root directory (/)

◆ Directory connectivity with subdirectories

◆ Reference counts, which relate to lost files

◆ Group summary information

The fsck command is commonly used to address corruption issues, such as the inode problems described earlier. Normally, if problems are detected, you're prompted to confirm changes. But some systems can have hundreds of problems or more. In that case, consider the fsck -y command, which automatically accepts changes. Several significant fsck command switches are described in Table 7.6.

Table 7.6 Command Switches for fsck

Switch	Output Description
-b	Use a nonstandard superblock as specified
-c	Check for bad blocks
-f	Force the filesystem check
-p	Repair filesystems without prompting; -y is generally safer
-t	Specify the filesystem type to be checked
-V	Include verbose output; unlike other commands, verbose output requires a capital -V
-y	Confirms changes; equivalent to -a for ext2, ext3, and vfat filesystems

Generally, if you run the fsck command, it should be run only on unmounted filesystems to minimize the risk of data loss. For more information, see "Mount and Unmount a Filesystem," later in this chapter. But the fsck command works with filesystem-specific commands as described in Table 7.7.

Table 7.7 Linux Filesystem Check Command Equivalents

Command 1	Command 2	Command 3
fsck -t ext2	fsck.ext2	e2fsck
fsck -t ext3	fsck.ext3	e2fsck
fsck -t reiserfs	fsck.reiserfs	reiserfsck
fsck -t xfs	fsck.xfs	xfs_check
fsck -t vfat	fsck.vfat	dosfsck

If the filesystem is not specified with the -t switch, fsck searches for an existing setting in the /etc/fstab configuration file. Remember, before testing fsck on a filesystem, make sure to unmount it.

Once you've unmounted a filesystem, see what happens when the fsck command is run on unmounted filesystems of several different types. First, look at the output of a check on an ext2 filesystem:

```
# fsck -V /dev/sda1
fsck 1.40.8 (13-Mar-2008)
[/sbin/fsck.ext2 (1) -- /boot] fsck.ext2 /dev/sda1
e2fsck 1.40.8 (13-Mar-2008)
/dev/sda1: clean, 53/24096 files, 24411/96356 blocks
```

The fsck command as shown first checks /etc/fstab for the configured format for this partition. Based on the format, it runs the fsck.ext2 command, which is really another name for the e2fsck command.

> **NOTE**
>
> Try the ls -i command to find the inode number of the /sbin/fsck.ext2, /sbin/fsck.ext3, and /sbin/e2fsck files. You should find the same number for all three files. In other words, these files are three different names for the same command.

When applied to an ext3 formatted partition, the fsck -V command leads to almost identical output. The only difference is the substitution of fsck.ext3 for fsck.ext2. No mention is made of the status of ext3 as a journaling filesystem.

When applied to a reiserfs formatted partition, the fsck -V command leads to a request for confirmation; ReiserFS is also a journaling filesystem.

For xfs-formatted partitions, the fsck command doesn't check or repair the filesystem. This functionality is split into two commands—**xfs_check** and **xfs_repair**—which work as their names suggest.

Finally, the fsck command, when applied to a vfat-formatted partition, uses the fsck.vfat command, which is another name for the dosfsck command.

As suggested by some of the messages, the fsck command can also be used to maintain filesystems by repairing common problems. But maintenance and repairs can go further.

Filesystem Maintenance and Repair

The LPIC-1 objectives include references to several other filesystem maintenance tools, mostly focused on the ext2 and ext3 filesystems. These tools include the **dumpe2fs**, **debugfs**, and `tune2fs` commands. These commands do not work when run on other filesystems. However, additional commands serve some of the same functionality for other filesystems.

Dumping Filesystem Information with dumpe2fs

As suggested by the name, the `dumpe2fs` command dumps filesystem information for volumes configured to the `ext2` and `ext3` formats. In other words, it doesn't provide information on other filesystem formats. As with other "dumps" in operating systems, the output includes a lot of information.

Test `dumpe2fs` on a partition formatted to `ext2` and `ext3`. Note some of the differences. One way to avoid being overwhelmed by the output is to pipe it to the `less` command; for example, the following command pipes information about partition `/dev/sda9` to `less`:

```
# dumpe2fs /dev/sda9 | less
```

Some important bits from the output are described in Table 7.8, listed in the order in which they appear. The importance of some of this information won't become clear until the discussion on "The /etc/fstab Configuration File" later in this chapter.

Table 7.8 Output Information from dumpe2fs

Item	Description
Filesystem volume name	`LABEL` on Red Hat systems in `/etc/fstab`
Filesystem UUID	Universal Unique Identifier on Ubuntu systems in `/etc/fstab`
Filesystem features	If journaling is enabled, `has_journal` is shown here
Mount count	Number of times this filesystem has been mounted since the last `fsck`
Maximum mount count	Number of times this filesystem may be mounted before the `fsck` command is automatically applied to it
Backup superblock	Alternate superblock to use with the `e2fsck` command if a problem arises

Debugging Filesystems with debugfs

The `debugfs` command works only on `ext2`- and `ext3`-formatted filesystems. It's an interactive filesystem debugger, which doesn't make changes unless you open it with the `-w` switch to write changes.

This command opens a `debugfs:` prompt that can help you interactively work with a filesystem. Even outside of write mode, it can reveal a lot about the selected filesystem. For this purpose, it's best to make sure there's a ready backup of the filesystem in question.

Normally this book describes steps you should take and practice. Although I've tested the debugfs command on the partition with the /boot directory, I can't recommend that you run debugfs on that partition. If you were to accidentally delete a key file from that partition, recovery would be time consuming even if a backup were available.

To show you how the debugfs command works, I've set up a virtual machine with a snapshot. If something goes wrong with the snapshot, it's relatively easy to restore. Snapshot methods vary by virtual machines and should be the subject of their own book.

Fortunately, there's no evidence that the LPIC-1 objectives go beyond the *basic* capabilities of the debugfs command. To illustrate these capabilities, I've run the following commands:

1. I copy the /etc/passwd file to the /boot directory.
2. I unmount and remount the /boot directory partition with the following commands:

```
# umount /boot
# mount /dev/sda1 /boot
```

3. I run the following command to open the /dev/sda1 partition, which contains the /boot directory, in write mode. The debugfs: prompt should appear.

```
# debugfs -w /dev/sda1
debugfs 1.39 (29-May-2006)
debugfs:
```

4. At the prompt, I run the help command, and then I press the spacebar twice to scroll through available commands.
5. I then run the ls command, which lists files in the local directory, based on their inode numbers. I confirm the existence of the passwd file in the local directory.
6. I read the contents of the local passwd file with the cat passwd command.
7. I delete the file with the rm passwd command.
8. I see the file that's been deleted with the lsdel command. In my case, the output appears as follows:

```
debugfs:  lsdel
 Inode  Owner  Mode    Size    Blocks   Time deleted
    19      0 100644    680    1/    1 Sun Jan 11 23:51:13 2009
1 deleted inodes found.
```

9. I restore the deleted file based on its inode number, with the following command, and yes, the angle brackets are required.

```
debugfs: undel <19> group
```

10. I exit from the debugfs: prompt with the q command and confirm that the passwd file still exists in the /boot directory.
11. To keep my /boot directory clean, I delete the passwd file from that directory.

Tuning Parameters with `tune2fs`

The `tune2fs` command can be used to adjust parameters on filesystems configured with the `ext2` and `ext3` formats. Although it's most commonly used to add or delete a journal from a filesystem, it can also be used to change parameters listed in the output to the aforementioned `dumpe2fs` command.

To add a journal to an unmounted filesystem such as `/dev/sdb1`, run the following command:

```
# tune2fs -j /dev/sdb1
```

The change will be implemented the next time the filesystem is mounted. To make sure the change is implemented the next time the system boots, you should edit the `/etc/fstab` configuration file as discussed shortly. One way to ensure the command works is with the `dumpe2fs` command described earlier; the following command confirms the changes on a local Ubuntu system, with the *has_journal* setting:

```
# dumpe2fs /dev/sda9 | grep features
```

```
dumpe2fs 1.40.8 (13-Mar-2008)
Filesystem features:      has_journal resize_inode dir_index filetype needs_recovery
sparse_super
```

Some distributions automatically configure the `ext3` filesystem for all partitions. But that's not always appropriate for small partitions, because the space requirements of a journaling filesystem may crowd out other data. If that situation applies, you can disable the journal on the noted filesystem with the following command:

```
# tune2fs -O ^has_journal /dev/sdb1
```

Note the carat (^), which disables a feature. In other words, you could also enable journaling with the following command:

```
# tune2fs -O has_journal /dev/sdb1
```

Because they were built exclusively for journaling, there is no corresponding command to disable this feature in the `reiserfs` or `xfs` filesystems.

Maintenance Commands for Other Filesystems

Two other commands are explicitly listed in the LPIC-1 objectives: `xfs_repair` and `xfs_info`. These are two of many commands related to the `xfs` filesystem; most are in the `/usr/sbin/` directory and start with `xfs_`. Because the focus of the LPIC-1 objectives is clearly on the `ext2` and `ext3` filesystems, just be sure to understand the purpose of these commands:

◆ The `xfs_repair` command is used to repair `xfs` formatted filesystems. For more information, apply the command to a filesystem previously formatted to `xfs` as follows, and read over the results.

```
# xfs_repair -v /dev/sdc1
```

◆ The `xfs_info` command works only on a mounted `xfs` filesystem. To test this command on a filesystem device such as `/dev/sdc1`, make sure to format that filesystem, and then mount it on a temporary directory.

◆ The `xfs_metadump` command can be used to copy debugging data to a file.

◆ The `debugreiserfs` command includes some of the same information available from the `dumpe2fs` command, including journaling information.

Mount and Unmount a Filesystem

The mounting and unmounting of a filesystem is a fundamental skill for expert Linux administrators. Mounting is configured during the boot process with the `/etc/fstab` configuration file. It works with commands like **mount** and **umount**. (And if you think `umount` is misspelled, read this section carefully.)

The mounting of certain filesystems is normally automated; for example, when external media such as CDs/DVDs or SD cards are inserted, Linux configurations often mount them automatically. Although the use of `mount` and `umount` commands is normally limited to administrative users, regular users can be allowed access to the filesystems of your choice.

The /etc/fstab Configuration File

In Chapter 2, "Configure a System for Linux," you read about appropriate directories to mount as separate filesystems. Selected directories are documented and configured during the boot process in the `/etc/fstab` configuration file. Each line in this file works with a different filesystem. Changes such as the addition of journaling or quotas require changes in this file to make sure they're implemented the next time Linux boots on this system.

Although Linux distributions handle `/etc/fstab` in different ways, the differences can better help you understand the intricacies of this file. Two examples are displayed in Figure 7.4; the first is from an Ubuntu Hardy Heron release, the second from a CentOS 5 release.

Each active line in these files configures how the local system mounts a filesystem during the boot process. As with most Linux scripts and configuration files, lines that start with a hash mark (#) are comments. The lines shown in these files actually demonstrate three ways to configure a mounted filesystem:

◆ **UUID.** If a Universally Unique Identifier is used, it can be matched to a partition or volume by an administrative user with the `blkid` command.

◆ **Device files.** Files like `/dev/sda1` represent partition devices; files like `/dev/VolGroup00/LogVol00` represent logical volumes.

◆ **LABEL.** Labels like `/boot` can also be matched to a partition or volume by an administrative user with the `blkid` command.

```
michael@ubuntuhardy3:~$ cat /etc/fstab
# /etc/fstab: static file system information.
#
# <file system> <mount point>    <type>  <options>      <dump>  <pass>
proc             /proc            proc    defaults        0       0
# /dev/mapper/ubuntuhardyrc-root
UUID=cf5a7a09-9412-44aa-b34b-fb812e4f4c63 /              ext3    relatime,errors=remount-ro 0      1
# /dev/sdb1
UUID=2d25405a-121c-4ec4-82e1-31c1e5849e7d /boot          ext3    relatime        0       2
# /dev/sdb2
/dev/sdb2                              /home    ext3    relatime        0       2
#UUID=1a3a11bc-d7b3-4bad-ae6a-5ba1e30499e8 /home  ext3    relatime        0       2
# /dev/mapper/ubuntuhardyrc-swap_1
UUID=f235dc12-9189-45b5-9057-699b89f5c390 none           swap    sw              0       0
# /dev/sdb3
UUID=489102d1-244c-46b2-9316-89e68a7945b8 none           swap    sw              0       0
/dev/scd0        /media/cdrom0   udf,iso9660 user,noauto,exec,utf8 0       0
/dev/fd0         /media/floppy0  auto    rw,user,noauto,exec,utf8 0       0
michael@ubuntuhardy3:~$ cat fstab
/dev/VolGroup00/LogVol00 /              ext3    defaults        1 1
LABEL=/boot              /boot          ext2    defaults        1 2
tmpfs                    /dev/shm       tmpfs   defaults        0 0
devpts                   /dev/pts       devpts  gid=5,mode=620  0 0
sysfs                    /sys           sysfs   defaults        0 0
proc                     /proc          proc    defaults        0 0
/dev/VolGroup00/LogVol01 swap           swap    defaults        0 0
michael@ubuntuhardy3:~$ █
```

FIGURE 7.4 *Two examples of* /etc/fstab.

Where device files aren't used in /etc/fstab, they can also be matched with their UUIDs or LABELs in the output to the dumpe2fs command.

The commented line with angled bracket entries suggests there are six columns of information for each filesystem in the /etc/fstab file. The columns are described from left to right in Table 7.9.

Table 7.9 Description, by Column, of /etc/fstab

Column	Description
<file system>	The device to be mounted; may be a partition or volume; if it's a UUID or LABEL, that represents a partition or volume
<mount point>	The directory where the filesystem is to be mounted.
<type>	The filesystem format, such as ext2, ext3, xfs, reiserfs, or vfat
<options>	Number of times this filesystem has been mounted since the last fsck
<dump>	Boolean 0 or 1; if 1, files are automatically saved during the shutdown process
<pass>	Based on the order for filesystem checks during the boot process; the top-level root directory (/) is set to 1; other local systems are set to 2; removable filesystems such as CD/DVD drives are set to 0

Various settings are available for the <options> column, which require further explanation. Several mount options are listed in Table 7.10. Be aware that opposites like async and sync and user and nouser are available, which go beyond those options listed in the table. For more options, run the man mount command.

Table 7.10 Mount Option Settings Specified in /etc/fstab

Option	Description
acl	For access control lists on a filesystem
async	Data may be read and written at different times, asynchronously, which speeds data transfer but may lead to a higher risk of data loss
auto	Setting that mounts the filesystem during the boot process
defaults	A combination of async, auto, dev, exec, nouser, rw, and suid; defaults are implicit
dev	For a virtual filesystem with device files in the /dev directory
errors	To specify actions or behavior if an error occurs
exec	Supports the execution of compiled programs
grpquota	For quotas of space and inodes, configurable by group
nouser	Access limited to administrative users
relatime	For file updates
ro	Read-only
rw	Read-write
suid	For superuser ID permissions; see Chapter 8, "File Permissions and More"
sw	For swap filesystems
usrquota	For quotas of space and inodes, configurable by user
utf8	For conversions of 16-bit unicode characters, normally on CD/DVD drives
user	Regular users allowed to mount and unmount the filesystem

Modify /etc/fstab

Expert Linux users should know how to customize /etc/fstab as needed. For example, if journaling has been enabled on the /home directory filesystem shown in Figure 7.4, you'll want to make sure the filesystem format type is ext3 and not ext2. Of course, the reverse is true if journaling has just been disabled.

Based on the /home directory filesystem shown, the following changes would enable journaling, user and group quotas, as well as access control lists.

```
/dev/sdb2    /home    ext3    relatime,usrquota,grpquota,acl    0    2
```

You can implement such changes in several ways. The simplest to explain is to reboot Linux. However, that would kick off any currently connected users.

A second option is to change runlevels, to move to single user mode (runlevel 1) and then back to the default runlevel (2, 3, or 5, depending on the distribution and configuration). But that, too, would kick off any currently connected users.

A third option is to unmount and then remount the filesystem in question. As will be explained shortly in the section on mount and umount, the following commands would unmount and then remount the system as noted:

```
# umount /home
# mount /home
```

Once again, this is simple to explain, but it would kick off any currently connected users. Such users may quite possibly lose data.

In contrast, the safest way to implement changes is with the mount command, using the -o remount switch described shortly.

Users and Mounting External Media

Appropriate settings in the /etc/fstab configuration file vary, especially if the filesystem is associated with external media such as a CD/DVD drive. Other settings are required to support access by regular users. The following option from an Ubuntu /etc/fstab configuration file serves both purposes:

```
/dev/scd0    /media/cdrom0  udf,iso9660 user,noauto,exec,utf8  0 0
```

Of course, variations occur frequently depending on media; depending on local hardware, options such as /dev/hdc or /dev/cdrom may be shown in place of /dev/sdc0. Given the hardware detection capabilities of Linux, these options should be considered if the noted /dev file actually exists.

The user setting in the options column supports mount access by regular users. Filesystems without this setting can only be mounted and unmounted by users who have administrative privileges. The privilege extends to related commands; for example, regular users would be able to use the **eject** command, which would unmount a CD/DVD drive before sending a signal to open that drive.

The `noauto` setting means that installed media are not mounted during the boot process. Access to the related filesystem requires the use of the `mount` command, or active automount options in the GNOME Desktop Environment. Although GNOME automounts is standard behavior on some recent distributions, that bit is not part of the LPIC-1 objectives.

mount Commands

The `mount` and `umount` commands mount and unmount selected filesystems. Normally, filesystems are mounted with a command in the following format:

```
# mount -switch /dev/sda1 /directory
```

The `mount` command works with appropriate switches, which will seem familiar if you know the `/etc/fstab` configuration file. For example, assume you've just formatted a new partition, `/dev/sdc1`, to the ext3 format. You can set it up with that format—with user quota, group quota, and ACL options—with the following command:

```
# mount -t ext3 -o usrquota,grpquota,acl /dev/sdc1 /mnt
```

To confirm the result, run the `mount` command. The following output verifies the desired settings:

```
/dev/sdc1 on /mnt type ext3 (rw,usrquota,grpquota,acl)
```

Two other ways to confirm changes to mounted directories are through the following two files:

```
/etc/mtab
/proc/mounts
```

To go further, if you're making a change to an existing, mounted filesystem such as `/dev/sdb2` on the `/home` directory, the following command implements the noted changes, without requiring anyone to log off or reboot:

```
# mount -t ext3 -o remount,usrquota,grpquota,acl /dev/sdb2 /home
```

Once a system is configured in `/etc/fstab`, less information is required for the `mount` command. If you've configured the target filesystem in `/etc/fstab` and accept current settings in that file, all you need is the `mount` command and either the device file or mount directory. In other words, either of the following commands would work equally well:

```
# mount /dev/sdb2
# mount /home
```

Unmounting the filesystem is easier, as long as you remember how to spell the command. All that's required is either the directory or the device. In other words, either of the following commands would work equally well:

```
# umount /dev/sdb2
# umount /home
```

If you're running these commands from the /home directory tree, you may need to include the -l switch; in other words, the command would be umount -l /home. Sometimes you need to force the issue, such as when a remote NFS (Network File System) server gets disconnected.

```
# umount -f /home
```

During the boot process, the mount -a command can implement everything not already mounted from the /etc/fstab configuration file. Some of the switches that work for both the mount and umount commands are described in Table 7.11.

Table 7.11 Command Switches for mount and umount

Switch	Description
-a	Mount all filesystems as configured in /etc/fstab
-f	Force an unmounting of a target filesystem
-o	Mount with options, in comma-separated format, such as those configured in /etc/fstab
-r	Mount the given filesystem in read-only mode
-t	Mount with the noted filesystem format
-w	Mount the given filesystem in read-write mode

Chapter Summary

This chapter focused on several aspects of filesystem management. You learned to prepare a regular Linux system and a different kind of partition with the fdisk utility, and you learned to format them to the desired filesystem with commands like mkfs and mkswap. Several commands are closely related to and may be called by the mkfs command, including mke2fs, mkreiserfs, and mkdosfs. Filesystem-specific variations on mkfs include mkfs.ext2, mkfs.ext3, mkfs.reiserfs, mkfs.xfs, and mkfs.vfat.

Once a filesystem is created, expert Linux users should know how to monitor and maintain it. Simple commands such as df and du can help monitor free disk space and inodes. Related filesystem check and maintenance commands include fsck, e2fsck, mke2fs, debugfs, dumpe2fs, tune2fs, xfs_check, xfs_info, xfs_repair, and xfs_metadump.

Linux users with administrative privileges can mount and unmount configured filesystems. Those filesystems already configured in the /etc/fstab configuration file are mostly mounted automatically during the boot process. The mount command uses parameters in this file. Filesystems with removable media are frequently configured for mounting and unmounting by regular users.

Key Terms

- ◆ **acl.** Specifies access control lists on a filesystem; for use with /etc/fstab or the mount command.

- ◆ **async.** Supports data reads and writes at different times, asynchronously; for use with /etc/fstab or the mount command.

- ◆ **auto.** Setting that mounts the filesystem during the boot process; for use with /etc/fstab or the mount command.

- ◆ **blkid.** A command that lists UUIDs and LABELs associated with block devices such as partitions.

- ◆ **debugfs.** A command that can help debug volumes formatted to the ext2 or ext3 filesystem.

- ◆ **defaults.** A combination of async, auto, dev, exec, nouser, rw, suid. Defaults are implicit; for use with /etc/fstab or the mount command.

- ◆ **dev.** For a virtual filesystem with device files in the /dev directory; for use with /etc/fstab or the mount command.

- ◆ **df.** A command that can measure the usage of a filesystem in bytes or inodes.

- ◆ **dosfsck.** A command that can help check and repair a filesystem based on MS-DOS.

- ◆ **du.** A command that can estimate the disk usage of a directory.

- ◆ **dumpe2fs.** A command that dumps filesystem information configured to the ext2 or ext3 formats.

- ◆ **e2fsck.** A command that is used to check and possibly repair a volume formatted to the ext2 or ext3 filesystem.

- ◆ **errors.** A setting that specifies actions or behavior if an error occurs; for use with /etc/fstab or the mount command.

- ◆ **/etc/fstab.** A configuration file associated with filesystems to be mounted during the boot process and more.

- ◆ **exec.** A setting that supports the execution of compiled programs; for use with /etc/fstab or the mount command.

◆ **ext2.** An older Linux filesystem format, without journaling.

◆ **fsck.** A command that can check and repair primarily Linux filesystems.

◆ **fsck.ext2.** A command that can check and repair Linux ext2-formatted filesystems.

◆ **fsck.ext3.** A command that can check and repair Linux ext3-formatted filesystems.

◆ **fsck.reiserfs.** A command that can check and repair Linux reiserfs-formatted filesystems.

◆ **fsck.vfat.** A command that can check and repair older Microsoft FAT16- or FAT32-formatted filesystems.

◆ **fsck.xfs.** A command that can check and repair Linux xfs-formatted filesystems.

◆ **grpquota.** A setting for quotas of space and inodes, configurable by group; for use with /etc/fstab or the mount command.

◆ **inodes.** Every filesystem includes a limited number of inodes, data structures on a filesystem. You can allocate each inode to a file or directory.

◆ **mkfs.** A command that formats a given filesystem device.

◆ **mke2fs.** A command that formats a given device to the ext2 or ext3 filesystem.

◆ **mkfs.ext2.** A command that formats a given device to the ext2 filesystem.

◆ **mkfs.ext3.** A command that formats a given device to the ext3 filesystem.

◆ **mkfs.reiserfs.** A command that formats a given device to the reiserfs filesystem.

◆ **mkfs.vfat.** A command that formats a given device to the vfat filesystem.

◆ **mkfs.xfs.** A command that formats a given device to the xfs filesystem.

◆ **mount.** A command that mounts a formatted filesystem device on a directory.

◆ **nouser.** A setting that limits mount access to administrative users; for use with /etc/fstab or the mount command.

◆ **reiserfs.** Setting for a ReiserFS-formatted filesystem.

◆ **relatime.** Specialized setting for file updates; for use with /etc/fstab or the mount command.

◆ **ro.** Read-only; for use with /etc/fstab or the mount command.

◆ **rw.** Read-write; for use with /etc/fstab or the mount command.

◆ **suid.** For superuser ID permissions; for use with /etc/fstab or the mount command. See Chapter 8.

◆ **sw.** For swap filesystems; for use with /etc/fstab or the mount command.

◆ **swap.** Setting for a Linux swap partition filesystem format; for use with /etc/fstab or the mount command.

◆ **tune2fs.** A command that can change the status of a journal on a filesystem.

◆ **umount.** A command that can unmount a filesystem device from a directory.

◆ **user.** Regular users allowed to mount and unmount the filesystem; for use with `/etc/fstab` or the `mount` command.

◆ **usrquota.** For quotas of space and inodes, configurable by user; for use with `/etc/fstab` or the `mount` command.

◆ **utf8.** For conversions of 16-bit unicode characters, normally on CD/DVD drives; for use with `/etc/fstab` or the `mount` command.

◆ **vfat.** Setting for a FAT16- or FAT32-formatted filesystem.

◆ **xfs.** Setting for an `xfs`-formatted filesystem.

◆ **xfs_check.** A command that can check the status on an `xfs`-formatted filesystem.

◆ **xfs_info.** A command that can provide more info on a current `xfs`-formatted filesystem.

◆ **xfs_metadump.** A command that can copy `xfs` filesystem metadata to a file for backup purposes.

◆ **xfs_repair.** A command that can repair problems on an `xfs`-formatted filesystem.

Review Questions

The number of review questions in this chapter and other chapters in this book is proportionate to each section's weight in the LPI objectives. Because this chapter covers items 104.1, 104.2, and 104.3, their collective weight is 7; therefore, you'll see 14 questions in this section. You'll see multiple choice single answer, fill-in-the blank, and multiple choice multiple answer questions, as you'll encounter on the exam.

1. Which of the following commands is equivalent to the `mke2fs -j` command?

   A. `mkfs -t ext3`

   B. `mkfs`

   C. `mkfs -t ext2`

   D. `mkswap`

2. Enter the command that lists existing partitions on the local system. Do not include the path to the command, and assume that the current account has administrative privileges. _____

3. Which of the following file formats does not support journaling?

   A. `ext3`

   B. `xfs`

   C. `vfat`

   D. `reiserfs`

4. Enter the command that converts an ext2-formatted /dev/hda2 partition to a journaling filesystem. Do not include the path to the command, and assume that the current account has administrative privileges. _____

5. Which of the following commands can you use to check and repair a filesystem? Choose two.

   A. e2fsck

   B. mkfs

   C. debug2fs

   D. fdisk

6. A Linux system boots into single user mode because of problems with the partition with the top-level root directory (/). Which of the following commands should you apply to that partition?

   A. mkfs

   B. tune2fs -j

   C. fsck

   D. df

7. Enter the command that lists the status of inodes on mounted partitions. The full path to the command is not required. _____

8. When you create a partition with fdisk, which of the following filesystem types will work with the xfs filesystem? All the answers are associated with fdisk partition–type codes.

   A. xfs

   B. Linux

   C. SGI

   D. Linux xfs

9. Which of the following settings in the /etc/fstab configuration file allows a regular user to mount a filesystem?

   A. relatime

   B. user

   C. auto

   D. defaults

10. Enter the command that unmounts a system that may still have active connections. The full path to the command is not required. _____

11. If you see just the relatime setting in an /etc/fstab line for a particular filesystem, which of the following settings also apply? Choose two.

   A. rw

   B. ro

   C. user

   D. nouser

12. Which of the following actions or commands is the quickest way to implement the changes to a filesystem associated with the /home directory once its settings in the /etc/fstab file have been changed? Assume these commands are being run with administrative privileges.

   A. mount /home

   B. mount -o remount /home

   C. umount /home; mount /home

   D. mount -a

13. Enter the typical directory associated with an automatically mounted DVD disk inserted into its drive and detected by the local Linux system.

_____

14. Which of the following lines represents a valid line in the /etc/fstab configuration file, mounted from the remote system at server.example.org?

   A. /dev/sda10   /home   ext3   relatime,usrquota,acl

   B. server.example.org:/home   /home   ext3   relatime,usrquota,acl

   C. /home   server.example.org:/home   ext3   relatime,usrquota

   D. server.example.org:/home   /home   ext3   relatime,usrquota,xfs

Chapter 8

File Permissions and More

After completing this chapter, you will be able to

■ Configure disk quotas

■ Manage file permissions and ownership

■ Work with hard and symbolically linked files

■ Work with system files and searches

Introduction

Because Linux is a multiuser operating system, Linux administration requires that you manage files through permissions and more. Quotas can regulate the number of files and space available to individual users. The permissions associated with files depend on and can be regulated by user and group ownership. Hard and soft file links are frequently used for easy access by users and standard scripts. Finally, file databases, based on the FHS (Filesystem Hierarchy Standard), make it easier to find desired files and commands.

For anyone with expertise at the command line, the topics in this chapter should be straightforward. However, this chapter assumes knowledge of users and groups covered in Chapter 11, "Administrative Tasks." Special methods to control files, such as advanced control lists, Security Enhanced Linux, and AppArmor, are covered in more advanced LPIC exams.

TIP

This chapter addresses four objectives in the LPI exam: 104.4 ("Manage Disk Quotas"), 104.5 ("Manage File Permissions and Ownership"), 104.6 ("Create and Change Hard and Symbolic Links"), and 104.7 ("Find System Files and Place Files in the Correct Location").

Quota Configuration

Quotas can regulate users and groups in two ways. First, they can limit the amount of space available to users and groups. Second, they can limit the number of files available to users and groups.

Quotas work on filesystems mounted with appropriate quota settings. After quotas are activated for the filesystem, you need to set them up for users and groups before they actually limit available resources. Once they're configured, you also need to know how to get regular quota usage reports. But don't get overworked in this section, because quotas have a weight of 1 in the LPIC-1 objectives.

Configure a Filesystem for Quotas

Although quotas are normally enabled in the Linux kernel, quota configuration still requires additional commands. On our selected distributions (Ubuntu Hardy Heron and CentOS 5), such commands are part of the **quota** package and may be installed with the appropriate command, as described in Chapter 3, "Package Management Systems."

One common option is to configure quotas on a /home directory filesystem, when it's mounted on a separate partition or volume. In that case, you can enable user and group quotas in the /etc/fstab configuration file with the usrquota and grpquota options, respectively. Here's one sample excerpt from the /etc/fstab file on one of my systems:

```
/dev/sda11    /home    ext3    relatime,usrquota,grpquota    0    2
```

When the quotas are configured, you can reboot or activate the changes immediately with the following command:

```
# mount -o remount /home
```

Before proceeding, it's best to make sure that quotas are turned off with the following command:

```
# quotaoff /home
```

Then you can create basic quota configuration files with the following **quotacheck** command, where the -c scans the filesystem, the -u scans for user quotas, the -g scans for group quotas, and the -m remounts the noted filesystem.

```
# quotacheck -cugm /home
```

This command creates the **aquota.user** and **aquota.group** configuration files in the noted filesystem, in this case, /home. Next, you can activate the ability to configure user and group quotas with the following command:

```
# quotaon /home
```

User Quotas

To configure quotas for selected users, use the **edquota** command. For example, to create quotas of disk space or inodes for user katie, open the configuration with the following command (the -u stands for user):

```
# edquota -u katie
```

Depending on the distribution, the command may open a user-specific quota configuration file in the vi or nano editors. The vi editor was discussed in Chapter 6, "Processes, Priorities, and Editing." Quotas in the nano editor are shown in Figure 8.1. The limits of 0 that are shown in the figure are the default, which is no limit.

```
GNU nano 2.0.7              File: /tmp//EdP.arpngFd

Disk quotas for user katie (uid 1006):
  Filesystem                  blocks      soft      hard    inodes      soft      hard
  /dev/sda11                      16         0         0         5         0         0




^G Get Help    ^O WriteOut    ^R Read File   ^Y Prev Page   ^K Cut Text    ^C Cur Pos
^X Exit        ^J Justify     ^W Where Is    ^V Next Page   ^U UnCut Text  ^T To Spell
```

FIGURE 8.1 *Configure quotas for a user.*

After the filesystem, the next three columns relate to the amount of space for the user. The final three columns relate to the number of inodes for the user. The columns are described from left to right in Table 8.1.

Table 8.1 Quota Configuration Columns

Column	Information
filesystem	Partition or volume device being regulated
blocks	Amount of space in current use, in kilobyte (KB) blocks
soft	Soft limit in blocks
hard	Hard limit in blocks
inodes	Number of inodes in current use
soft	Soft limit in inodes
hard	Hard limit in inodes

If you're satisfied with the quota for one user, you can apply that same quota to other users. For example, the following command copies the current quota settings configured for user katie to users dickens and bub, where the -u stands for user, and the -p sets the first user in the list as the "prototype" for the other users.

```
# edquota -up katie dickens bub
```

If there's a grace period, the **soft limit** acts as an alarm, and the **hard limit** serves as an absolute limit. For example, if there's a soft limit of 100 inodes, the user is warned when more than 100 files, owned by that user, exist in the noted filesystem. The user is not allowed to exceed the (presumably larger) hard limit during the grace period.

Although you can customize quotas by user, grace periods are constant over a filesystem. To modify a grace period, run the edquota -t command. The default grace period is seven days.

Group Quotas

You can configure group quotas using the same principles and basic commands as user quotas. The differences are small; for example, to edit a group quota, use the `edquota -g` *groupname* command. To edit group grace periods, run the `edquota -gt` *groupname* command.

Quota Reports

Quota reports are available by user and filesystem. Regular users can check their own quotas with the `quota` command. Administrative users can check quotas for all users for a specific filesystem with the `repquota` command. For example, the following command takes all local users and checks their quota status, by blocks and inodes, in a format similar to that shown in Figure 8.1.

```
# repquota /dev/sda11
```

Of course, this assumes that `/dev/sda11` is configured for quotas, as described in this section.

Manage File Permissions and Ownership

Basic Linux file permissions determine whether a user, members of a group, and other users can read, write, and execute a file.

Now break that down. There are three basic file permissions: read, write, and execute. Permissions can vary depending on the user and group owners of a file. Special user access mode permissions exist that can extend the rights to use a file outside the owner or group.

NOTE

The permission concepts addressed by the LPIC-1 objectives are relatively basic. More sophisticated file permission schemes, such as access control lists, are part of the LPIC-3 objectives.

Basic File Permissions

The current permissions on a Linux file are shown in the output to the `ls -l` command. Take a look at the permissions associated with the `ls` command, as shown:

```
$ ls -l /bin/ls
-rwxr-xr-x 1 root root 92376 2008-04-03 23:42 /bin/ls
```

The permissions and file type are shown in the far left column. Note the 10 characters in that column, which are explained in Table 8.2. Except for the first character position, the use of a dash (-) means that the permission is not included. Some descriptions are explained further in the sections "The SUID Bit," "The SGID Bit," and "The Sticky Bit," later in this chapter.

Table 8.2 File Permission Column Characters

Character Position	Description
1	File type: - is a regular file, d is a directory, l is a linked file
2	Read permission for the file owner
3	Write permission for the file owner
4	Execute permission for the file owner; may also indicate SUID (Super User ID) permissions
5	Read permission for the group owner
6	Write permission for the group owner
7	Execute permission for the group owner; may also indicate SGID (Super Group ID) permissions
8	Read permission for other users
9	Write permission for other users
10	Execute permission for other users; may also indicate sticky bit permissions

File Permission Numeric Values

File permissions as shown in the output to the ls -l command can be translated to a numeric value, also known as the **octal mode**. You'll see shortly how these values are useful when modifying permissions with the **chmod** command.

Take the file permissions just shown for the ls command in the /bin directory. Leave the first character aside. Octal mode file permissions are based on the permissions for the user owner, the group owner, and all other users. As shown in Table 8.2, user owner permissions are based on character positions 2, 3, and 4; group owner permissions are based on character positions 5, 6, and 7; permissions for all other users are based on character positions 8, 9, and 10.

With this in mind, permissions are given numeric values, as shown in Table 8.3.

Table 8.3 Numeric Value of Permissions

Permission	Value
r (read)	4
w (write)	2
x (execute)	1

Now review the permissions in the output to the `ls -l /bin/ls` command. Because the user owner has read (4), write (2), and execute (1) permissions, these values are added (4 + 2 + 1); the user owner octal permission for the `/bin/ls` command is 7. The group owner has read and execute permissions; that group's octal permission has a value of 5. The octal permission for all other users is the same as that for the group owner: 5.

To derive the full octal permissions, these permissions are listed together. In other words, the octal permission for the `/bin/ls` command is 755.

As suggested in Table 8.2, there are also special permissions available for files, which would be included in the fourth numeric column. The numeric value of these special permissions is listed in Table 8.4. These special permissions are explained in the next section.

Table 8.4 Numeric Value of Special Permissions

Permission	Description	Value
SUID	Super User ID	4
SGID	Super Group ID	2
Sticky Bit	Retain other user permissions	1

To put this all together, assume you're told that a file named `canine` has octal permissions of 5765. Break it down.

The first number is the special permissions column and, based on Table 8.4, it can only result from 4+1. In other words, the `canine` file has SUID and sticky bit special permissions.

The second number is the user owner permissions column. Based on Table 8.3, that can only result from 4+2+1. In other words, the user owner of the `canine` file has read, write, and execute permissions on that file.

The third number is the group owner permissions column. You should now be able to see that members of the group who own the `canine` file have read (4) and write (2) permissions.

The fourth number is the permissions column for all other users. You should now be able to see that all other users' `canine` files have read (4) and execute (1) permissions.

User Access Modes and More

In this section, you'll see how to implement permissions on different files with the `chmod` command. But you should also be aware that available permissions go beyond read, write, and execute. Three user access modes are available for standard files: **SUID (Super User ID)** permissions, also known as the SUID bit; **SGID (Super Group ID)** permissions, also known as the SGID bit; and the so-called **sticky bit**, normally used on directories.

As suggested by their names, these bits are associated with different kinds of users. To implement them with the chmod command, you need to know the symbols associated with the user owner, group owner, and other users, as listed in Table 8.5.

Table 8.5 Symbols and Ownership

User Category	Symbol
User owner	u
Group owner	g
Other users	o
All users	a

Now with users and permissions in mind, you can learn how to activate the SUID, SGID, and sticky bits, with or without different read, write, and execute permissions.

The SUID Bit

When the SUID bit is set, it supports access by regular users to administrative tools. For example, look at the permissions associated with the /usr/bin/passwd file:

```
$ ls -l /usr/bin/passwd
-rwsr-xr-x 1 root root 29104 2008-04-02 18:08 /usr/bin/passwd
```

The s in place of the executable permission for the user owner allows a user to change his own password. Sure, the executable bit is also available for other users. But without the SUID bit, a regular user can't change even his own password in the local authentication database.

The following commands present two ways to set the SUID bit on a hypothetical ~/bin/abc file. If you're the file owner, you can set the SUID bit without administrative access. The u+s sets (+) the SUID bit (s) for the user owner (u) of the file.

```
$ chmod u+s ~/bin/abc
$ chmod 4755 ~/bin/abc
```

The second command also sets regular 755 permissions. The 4 in front of the 755 sets the SUID bit.

The SGID Bit

When the SGID bit is set, it supports access by regular users in a group to each other's files. For example, users who are members of a group named project can have access to common files in a directory, such as /home/project, as long as it's owned by the project group and the

SGID bit is set on that directory. Examine the permissions associated with this particular version of this directory:

```
$ ls -ld /home/project/
drwxrws--- 2 nobody project 4096 2009-01-15 06:52 /home/project/
```

The s in place of the executable permission for the group owner allows members of the project group full permissions to the files in this directory. So when members of this group copy files to this directory, they retain ownership of files in this directory:

```
$ ls -l /home/project/
total 8
-rw-r--r-- 1 donna   project 2107 2009-01-15 06:57 auth
-rw-r--r-- 1 michael project 1599 2009-01-15 06:57 ubuntutest.txt
```

Other members of the project group can also read these files and write other files to the /home/project directory.

The following commands present two ways to set the SGID bit on a /home/project directory. The g+s sets (+) the SGID bit (s) for the group owner (g) of the file.

```
# chmod g+s /home/project
# chmod 2750 /home/project
```

The second command also sets 750 permissions. That means users who aren't members of the project group won't have access, which can help keep project data confidential. The 2 in front of the 750 sets the SGID bit.

The Sticky Bit

The sticky bit is normally set only on directories in Linux. As such, it supports access by all users to each other's files. The standard example of a Linux directory with the sticky bit is the /tmp directory, as shown by its permissions:

```
$ ls -ld /tmp/
drwxrwxrwt 23 root root 4096 2009-01-15 07:10 /tmp/
```

The t in place of the executable permission for other users supports a limited amount of sharing. It retains the user and group owners for files copied to that directory. As such, other users are allowed to copy files in this directory, but they're not allowed to overwrite or delete such files.

The following commands present two ways to set the sticky bit on a /home/shared directory. The o+t sets (+) the sticky bit (t) for all the other users (o).

```
# chmod o+t /home/shared
# chmod 1777 /home/shared
```

The second command also sets 777 permissions. Without the sticky bit, any user would have full read, write, and execute permissions on files in the /home/shared directory. With the sticky bit, user access is limited, as just described. The 1 in front of the 777 sets the sticky bit.

Default Files and the umask

Default permissions for a new file are driven by the current value of **umask**. The value varies by distribution and may also vary between regular and administrative users; run the umask command to see the current value.

When a new directory is created, the value of umask cancels out full permissions for all users. For example, the default umask on a CentOS 5 system is 002. So when you create a directory on that system, it automatically gets 775 permissions, as shown in this excerpt from ls -l command output.

```
$ ls -l
drwxrwxr-x 2 michael michael    4096 Jan 14 20:06 abcd
```

 NOTE

The actual output to the umask command in CentOS 5 is 0002, which implies its use for the SUID, SGID, and sticky bits. In reality, that first 0 does not apply, at least to current Linux distributions.

However, Linux does not support default executable permissions for new regular files. That makes it more difficult for crackers who have broken into a system to plant programs for malicious purposes. So, based on a umask value of 002, a new file gets everything but the executable permissions.

```
-rw-rw-r-- 1 michael michael       0 Jan 14 20:09 xyz
```

Changing Permissions

You can use the chmod command to change permissions on one or more files. It's a straightforward command. All you need is the desired octal permissions for a file. For example, to set up read, write, and execute permissions for all users on the bigfile file, run the following command:

```
# chmod 666 bigfile
```

 NOTE

Although this section does repeat concepts from the "User Access Modes and More" section, I'm a believer in repetition when learning new concepts.

You can do more with the chmod command. To change permissions on all files in subdirectories, recursively, use the -R switch. For example, if you want to set all files and subdirectories in the LPIbook directory to 755 permissions, run the following command:

```
# chmod -R 755 LPIbook/
```

 NOTE

Linux directories aren't functional without at least executable permissions. Read permissions are required to read files on a directory; write permissions are required to create or write files to a directory.

As described earlier, you can change more than just read, write, and execute permissions on a file or directory. To recap, the following commands set the SUID bit on a file and the SGID bit and sticky bit on a directory:

```
# chmod u+s /usr/bin/abc
# chmod g+s /home/project
# chmod o+t /shared
```

You can express these options numerically; the following commands are equivalent, except they also set 755 octal permissions on the noted file or directory:

```
# chmod 4755 /usr/bin/abc
# chmod 2755 /home/project
# chmod 1755 /shared
```

But you don't need numbers to set up permissions on a file or directory. Perhaps all you need to do is activate or deactivate read, write, or execute permissions for the user owner, group owner, or everyone else. You've already seen the following command, which activates the SUID bit on a file.

```
# chmod u+s /usr/bin/abc
```

Similarly, the following commands activate the read, write, and execute bits on the same file, for the user owner of that file:

```
# chmod u+r /usr/bin/abc
# chmod u+w /usr/bin/abc
# chmod u+x /usr/bin/abc
```

The following command combines the effects of the previous four commands:

```
# chmod u+rwxs /usr/bin/abc
```

If the abc file already has one of these permissions, it isn't canceled out. Canceling a permission is just as straightforward; the following command removes write permissions from the noted file:

```
# chmod u-w /usr/bin/abc
```

Based on Table 8.3, similar changes can be made to the group owner and all other users. For example, the following commands add write permissions for the group owner and all other users, respectively:

```
# chmod g+w /usr/bin/abc
# chmod o+w /usr/bin/abc
```

Here's one more example. The following command would remove write permissions for all users. As per Table 8.3, the a applies to the user owner, group owner, and all other users.

```
# chmod a-w /usr/bin/abc
```

Basic File Ownership

The permissions just described apply to the user owner and group owner of a file or directory. You also need to know how to change these user and group owners. But first, users and groups are documented in the local authentication database, in the /etc/passwd and /etc/group configuration files described in Chapter 11. Unless the local system is connected to a networked database such as NIS (Network Information Service) or LDAP (Lightweight Directory Access Protocol), only users and groups documented in the noted files are eligible to be user owners and group owners of a file.

Now you'll examine the two commands that can be used to change the user and group owner of a file (or directory): **chown** and **chgrp**.

Change User Ownership with chown

The chown command is a straightforward command that is designed to change the user owner of a file or directory. If you want to create a /home/project directory and set up a user named projmgr as the owner of the directory, you would run the following command:

```
# chown projmgr /home/project
```

If there are subdirectories in /home/project, you can apply the ownership changes recursively with the -R switch, which would result in the following command:

```
# chown -R projmgr /home/project
```

Of course, when the chown command is applied to a user such as projmgr, that user has to be in the authentication database, specifically in the /etc/passwd configuration file.

Change Group Ownership with chgrp or chown

The chgrp command is a straightforward command that is designed to change the group owner of a file or directory. If you want to create a /home/project directory and set up a group named project as the group owner of the directory, you would run the following command:

```
# chgrp project /home/project
```

If there are subdirectories in /home/project, you can apply the ownership changes recursively with the -R switch, which would result in the following command:

```
# chgrp -R project /home/project
```

Of course, when you apply the chgrp command to a user such as projmgr, that user has to be in the authentication database, specifically in the /etc/group configuration file.

You can also use the chown command to change the user owner and group owner of a file or directory simultaneously. The following command makes the user owner projmgr and the group owner project:

```
# chown projmgr.project /home/project
```

You can substitute a colon (:) for the dot (.) in the command.

Create and Change Hard and Symbolic Links

Linked file names are two pointers to the same file. They can exist in separate directories, which can make it easier to find or access the file. When you open a link or the original copy of a file, you're accessing the same data, from the same location on the storage medium. Changes made either to the original file or the link can be accessed from either file name.

In contrast, a copy of a file exists in a different location on the storage medium. In this section, you'll examine the difference between a hard-linked and a soft-linked file, learn how to create such links, and discover how such links can facilitate system administration. Of course, you'll also create soft and hard links with the **ln** command.

Hard Links

A **hard link** is a second pointer to the same data. The following command creates a hard link between the Samba configuration file in its normal location and the current user's home directory:

```
# ln /etc/samba/smb.conf ~
```

To verify the hard link, run the `ls -i` command on both files. If you run that command on my system, you can verify that both file names have the same inode number.

```
$ ls -i samba.conf
462146 samba.conf
$ ls -i /etc/samba/smb.conf
462146 /etc/samba/smb.conf
```

An inode number is a pointer to a location on a storage medium, such as a hard disk partition. Because both file names have the same inode number, they both access the same information. In contrast, if you copy a file, the copy will have a different inode number than the original version of that file.

Here's one bit unique to hard links: If you delete one hard-linked file name, the same data can still be opened from the second file name. However, hard links can't be created on separate volumes. For example, if the /home directory were mounted on a separate partition, the `ln` command shown earlier wouldn't work. That's where soft links can help.

Soft Links

In contrast to a hard link, a **soft link** is a pointer to a file name in its original location. If the original file is deleted, the data from that file is lost, and the soft link no longer points to anything. To demonstrate how that works, create a soft link on your system. Run the following command to create a soft link (with the `-s` switch) from a `passwdlink` file on the current user's home directory to the /etc/passwd configuration file:

```
# ln -s /etc/passwd ~/passwdlink
```

Next, review the permissions of the soft-linked file with the following command. (The output assumes that `michael` is the current user.)

```
$ ls -l ~/passwdlink
lrwxrwxrwx 1 root root 11 Jan 15 16:08 /home/michael/passwdlink -> /etc/passwd
```

The first letter in the left column, `l`, specifies the soft link. The `rwxrwxrwx` in that column just passes along the decision on permissions to the original file. It does not by itself provide such permissions to a user. The arrow in the right side of the output specifies the linked file.

One common example of soft links on Red Hat–based systems such as CentOS 5 is the GRUB boot loader configuration file. Two soft links are included to the actual configuration file, /etc/grub/grub.conf. Check it out for yourself with the following commands:

```
$ ls -l /boot/grub/menu.lst
$ ls -l /etc/grub.conf
```

The first soft-linked file name specifies the name of the GRUB configuration file on other distributions, including Ubuntu. The second link helps organize files in the directory most closely associated with configuration files, /etc.

Find and Manage System Files

This section is focused on LPIC-1 objective 104.7, which could easily be split into two or three separate topics. The FHS is the baseline structure of directories on current Linux systems. You can find files on a Linux system with commands such as find and locate. The locate command depends on a database configured through the /etc/updatedb.conf configuration file. Finally, commands such as **whereis, which,** and **type** can identify more information about a command, such as its location and any existing aliases.

The Filesystem Hierarchy Standard

The FHS documents the standard Linux directory structure. Although it serves as the baseline directory structure, current Linux distributions don't completely follow the FHS. Some FHS directories are suitable for mounting on separate volumes or partitions. These directories are discussed in more detail in Chapter 2, "Configure a System for Linux."

As you should already know, every Linux distribution starts with the top-level root directory (/). Every other Linux directory is a subdirectory. Basic directories in the FHS are documented in Table 8.6.

Table 8.6 Directories of the Filesystem Hierarchy Standard

Directory	Description
/	The top-level root directory
/bin	Basic command-line utilities such as ls, cp, and rm
/boot	For Linux boot files, including the kernel
/dev	Device files primarily for storage hardware and terminals
/etc	Configuration files
/home	Home directories for all users (except root)
/lib	Program libraries
/media	Standard mount point for removable media
/mnt	Legacy mount point for removable media
/opt	Common directory for third-party applications
/proc	Current kernel process values, such as hardware ports; a virtual filesystem
/root	Home directory for the root administrative user
/sbin	Administrative commands

Table 8.6 Continued

Directory	Description
/srv	A directory commonly used for servers
/tmp	A directory for temporary files; normally configured with the sticky bit
/usr	Commands and libraries commonly available to most users
/var	Variable data, including log files and print spools

Several FHS directories are virtual filesystems; in other words, they're created during the boot process. The files in these directories are not normally stored in media such as hard drives. Because the last official revision to the FHS was released in 2004, it is not up-to-date with the latest Linux developments. For example, on many distributions, the /sys directory is replacing the functionality of /proc as a virtual filesystem.

File Location Databases and Commands

Two commands are used to locate individual files: find and locate. The find command is more accurate because it searches for files in real time. However, the locate command is faster because it uses a database normally refreshed only once per day.

The find Command

The find command is designed to search through the desired directory tree for one or more files. It can search based on file name, user, permissions, and more. One simple example searches for the Desktop file, starting with the top-level root directory (/).

```
$ find / -name Desktop
```

But if you use the find command to search through directories you don't have permissions for, this command returns a number of Permission denied messages. So, for a regular user, this command makes more sense when it's set up to start searching from your home directory:

```
$ find ~ -name Desktop
```

Although Linux is generally case sensitive, the -iname switch makes for a case-insensitive search.

Of course, as an administrator, you may be asked to help other users find files. As such, you'll want to be able to identify files by username. The following command looks for all files owned by user donna:

```
$ find / -user donna
```

You could run a more general search, such as for all files owned by a specific group, by the GID number:

```
$ find / -gid 50000
```

If you want to learn something about the activity on the local system, the `-atime` switch, which looks for files based on their last access time, can help. The way it works is a bit odd; for example, the following command lists files in my `/home` directory that were last accessed two days ago.

```
$ find /home/michael -atime 1
```

The output is pretty specific; it doesn't include either files changed in the past day or files changed over three days ago.

Other specialty searches can be configured. For example, if you want to search for all files with the sticky bit enabled, the `-perm` switch can help. You can also use `-perm` with the octal-formatted permissions described earlier:

```
$ find / -perm /o+t
```

A variety of `find` command switches are listed in Table 8.7. These switches provide just a taste of the capabilities of the command; for example, there is a `-mindepth` switch that is functionally similar to the `-maxdepth` switch.

Table 8.7 Switches for the find Command

Switch	Description
`-atime` *n*	Find files last accessed *n*+1 days ago
`-ctime` *n*	Find files with a last status change of *n*+1 days ago
`-gid` *n*	Find files that belong to a group owner with a GID of *n*
`-maxdepth` *n*	Search *n* levels of subdirectories
`-mount`	Refrain from searching directories on other filesystems
`-mtime` *n*	Find files last modified *n*+1 days ago
`-name` *term*	Find files that match the search term
`-perm` */permission*	Identify files that match the specified permission
`-size` *n*	Identify files larger than *n* blocks; can substitute other sizes such as 100M for 100MB
`-type` *n*	Identify files of a given type, such as l for link and d for directory
`-user` *n*	Find files owned by user *n*, a user in `/etc/passwd`

The Updateable File Database

The locate command is faster. It works like a search term for the grep command, as asterisk (*) wildcards before and after the search term are assumed. Unlike the find command, locate searches through a previously created database in the /var/lib/mlocate/mlocate.db file.

The following command searches the local system for any files with LPI in its name. If I forget the files that I've created for this book, this command can help me find them again:

```
$ locate LPI
```

Linux systems are normally configured to update this database daily, as configured in the /etc/cron.daily/ directory. For more information on the working of these cron scripts, see Chapter 11. If you want to update the database immediately, run the updatedb command. The command can only be run with administrative privileges, because the ownership and permissions on the /var/lib/mlocate/mlocate.db file are limited to administrative users.

In any case, the file database is updated per the configuration defined in the /etc/updatedb.conf configuration file. Although the details of this file vary by distribution, it contains directories and filesystems that are not to be included in the database.

Command Location Files

Three other commands are listed in the LPIC-1 objectives, related to finding more information about commands. The type command can identify existing aliases that may affect how the command is executed. The which command identifies the full path to a command and any existing aliases. Finally, the whereis command finds the full path to the binary and man page to a command.

Identify the Path and Alias with which and type

Try the type command with the ls and passwd commands, as shown:

```
$ type ls
ls is aliased to `ls --color=auto'
$ type passwd
passwd is /usr/bin/passwd
```

If an alias exists, it's revealed by the type command. For more information on aliases, see Chapter 9, "Shells, Scripting, and Data Management." Otherwise, the type command just reveals the full path to the command.

To find both the alias and the full path to a command, try the type -a or which commands:

```
$ which ls
ls is aliased to `ls --color=auto'
ls is /bin/ls
```

Locate More on a Command with whereis

The whereis command identifies more about a command, including the binary and associated man page. Examine the following output:

```
$ whereis -u system-config-users
system-config-users: /usr/bin/system-config-users /usr/share/system-config-users
/usr/share/man/man8/system-config-users.8.gz
```

The output identifies three things:

- ◆ The full path to the command
- ◆ The full path to the associated command binary, if it exists
- ◆ The full path to the associated man page for the command

Chapter Summary

In this chapter, you examined quotas, which can be configured to regulate the amount of space and number of files available by user and group. The quota package must be installed, the target filesystem must be configured, and then target users and groups can be regulated.

Another way to regulate users and groups is through ownership and permissions. Linux permissions go beyond read, write, and execute for user owners, group owners, and all other users. They incorporate the use of the SUID bit, the SGID bit, and the sticky bit. You can regulate such permissions with the chmod command using numeric or symbolic options. You can change user and group owners with the chown and chgrp commands.

Hard and symbolic links can be created with the ln command. A hard link is a second file name that points to the same location on a volume. Hard-linked files have the same inode number. A soft link can exist on different volumes, but the soft link points to the original file.

System files and more are configured in different directories per the FHS. Other directories are subdirectories of the top-level root directory (/). Searches through the FHS are facilitated with the find and locate commands. Although the find command is versatile, the locate command works with an existing database of files. Commands such as type, which, and whereis can help identify more information on other commands.

Key Terms

- ◆ **aquota.group.** File associated with configured group quotas.
- ◆ **aquota.user.** File associated with configured user quotas.
- ◆ **chgrp.** Command that changes the group owner of a file.
- ◆ **chmod.** Command that can change the permissions on a file.
- ◆ **chown.** Command that changes the user owner of a file.

- **edquota.** Command that can edit user and group quotas.
- **hard limit.** Reference to basic quota limits.
- **hard link.** Two file names pointing to the same location on a volume. Hard-linked files have the same inode number; created with the `ln` command.
- **ln.** Command that can create a hard- or a soft-linked file.
- **locate.** Command that searches through an `mlocate.db` database in the `/var/lib/mlocate/` directory.
- **octal mode.** The numeric value of file permissions for users, groups, and other users.
- **quota.** Command that checks the current status of quotas; also the package with quota configuration commands.
- **quotacheck.** Command that can activate quotas on a filesystem; can be used to create the `aquota.user` and `aquota.group` files.
- **SGID (Super Group ID).** Permission that allows other users the same access as the group owner of a file.
- **soft limit.** Quota limits during a grace period.
- **soft link.** A file name that points to an actual file; a soft link can exist on a different volume and is created by the `ln -s` command.
- **sticky bit.** Permission on a directory that does not change ownership of files copied to that directory.
- **SUID (Super User ID).** Permission that allows other users the same access as the user owner of a file.
- **type.** Command that can reveal aliases and the full path to a command.
- **umask.** Command that specifies mask bits for permissions.
- **whereis.** Command that can locate the full path to a command, associated binary file, and associated man page.
- **which.** Command that reveals aliases and the full path to a command.

Review Questions

The number of review questions in this chapter and other chapters in this book is proportionate to each section's weight in the LPI objectives. Because this chapter covers items 104.4, 104.5, 104.6 and 104.7, the weight is 8; therefore, you'll see 16 questions in this section. You'll see multiple choice single answer, fill-in-the-blank, and multiple choice multiple answer questions, as you'll encounter on the exam.

1. Enter the setting that configures group quotas for a desired filesystem; it can be used with the `mount` command or added to the `/etc/fstab` configuration file.

2. Which of the following commands can be used to customize quotas for a user?

   A. quota

   B. usrquota

   C. edquota

   D. quotacheck

3. You've run the `ls -l file` command and see `-rwsrwsr-x` permissions. Which of the following permissions apply? Choose two.

   A. SUID bit

   B. SGID bit

   C. Sticky bit

   D. Write permissions for other users

4. Which of the following commands can you use to change the permissions on a file?

   A. chusr

   B. chown

   C. chgrp

   D. chmod

5. Assume that your account is the owner of a file named `big` in the local directory. Enter the command that activates the SGID bit on the file. _____

6. If you set 4765 permissions on a file, which of the following permissions are not active?

   A. The SGID bit

   B. Write permissions for the user owner

   C. Read permissions for all other users

   D. Write permissions for the group owner

7. Which of the following commands change the user and group owner of the file named `smart` to `supervisor` and `engineers`?

   A. chown supervisor smart

   B. chgrp engineer smart

   C. chown engineer.supervisor smart

   D. chown supervisor:engineer smart

8. Which of the following commands activates execute permissions for all users on the file named `bigscript`?

   A. `chmod o+x bigscript`

   B. `chmod g+x bigscript`

   C. `chmod a+x bigscript`

   D. `chmod u+x bigscript`

9. Enter the command that creates a hard link from the `/etc/httpd/conf/httpd.conf` file to a file named `apache` in the local directory. Assume that the local directory is on the same volume or partition as the `/etc` directory.

   _____

10. Which of the following commands, when run on `file1` and `file2`, can confirm whether they are hard linked?

    A. `ln -i`

    B. `ls -i`

    C. `ln -l`

    D. `ls -l`

11. Which of the following symbols in the output to the `ls -l` command indicates whether a file is a soft link?

    A. `s`

    B. `l`

    C. `f`

    D. `-`

12. Which of the following commands creates a soft link?

    A. `ln -s`

    B. `ls -s`

    C. `ln -i`

    D. `ls -i`

13. Which of the following commands includes information about a target man page?

    A. `type`

    B. `which`

    C. `whereis`

    D. `locate`

14. Enter the full path to the directory primarily used for configuration files.

_____

15. Which of the following commands identifies all files owned by user engineer? Assume that the account already has administrative privileges.

   A. `find / -uid engineer`

   B. `find / -user engineer`

   C. `locate -uid engineer`

   D. `locate -user engineer`

16. Which of the following commands updates the current database of files for the `locate` command?

   A. `updatedb`

   B. `locate -U`

   C. `find / -update`

   D. `mlocate`

PART

II

LPI Exam 102

Chapter 9

Shells, Scripting, and Data Management

After completing this chapter, you will be able to

■ Manage the environment for a shell

■ Create simple shell scripts

■ Work with basic SQL commands

Introduction

As this book starts coverage of LPI exam 102, this chapter focuses on the topics associated with LPIC-1 objective 105. In this chapter, you'll see how the bash shell environment works for users and how to customize it with environment variables, **functions**, and **aliases**. This sets the stage for shell scripts, because a better understanding of the shell environment can help you write better scripts.

This chapter also moves a bit beyond the normal purview of the Linux operating system, to basic **SQL** (structured query language) commands. You'll learn about the SQL commands used to manipulate elements of a database. It's a basic overview, befitting its relatively small weight on the exam.

 TIP

This chapter addresses three objectives in the LPI exam: 105.1 ("Customize and Use the Shell Environment"), 105.2 ("Customize or Write Simple Scripts"), and 105.3 ("SQL Data Management").

Manage the Shell Environment

A shell provides a command-line interface between the user and the operating system. Linux power users like you should know how to customize shells for user needs, based on global and individual configuration files.

To understand what you can customize, you need to understand what the shell can do. As a command-line interface, the shell provides the framework for the operation of other programs and utilities, many of which are discussed throughout the book. Shell commands can be combined in scripts, as discussed later in this chapter in the "Write Simple Shell Scripts" section.

In some ways, this section is a continuation of Chapter 4's section titled "The Structure of the Shell." However, the LPIC-1 objectives are limited to the bash shell; therefore, for the purpose of this book, environment variables are shell variables.

Shell Shortcuts

Several options from the LPIC-1 objectives make it easier to work at the command line. Directories can be added to the PATH. New environment variables can be set and exported. Aliases and functions can be configured for frequently used commands.

Add a Directory to the PATH

PATH has value because it supports shortcuts to commands, as well as a search order between different directories. When you type in a command like ls, it isn't normally run from the current directory. The bash shell uses the value of PATH to identify the directories where it should search for the ls command. For example, on a CentOS 5 system, the echo $PATH command in my home directory leads to the following output:

```
/usr/kerberos/bin:/usr/local/bin:/bin:/usr/bin:/home/michael/bin:
```

In other words, with the given value of PATH, the bash shell first searches the /usr/kerberos/bin directory for the ls command. If it's not found in that directory, the shell then searches the /usr/local/bin directory, and so on.

Despite the presence of the PATH variable, all commands can be run based on their full path. If installed, you can run the fortune command by typing in the full path, /usr/games/fortune or /usr/bin/fortune, or possibly something else, depending on the distribution. But if these directories are in the PATH, you don't need to type in the full path to the command.

But what if you want to add a directory that is not currently in the value of PATH? One method is shown in the hidden .bash_profile configuration file, in every user's home directory. The following excerpt from a Ubuntu Hardy Heron home directory checks for the existence of a ~/bin directory, a subdirectory of that user's home directory.

```
if [ -d ~/bin ] ; then
    PATH=~/bin:"${PATH}"
fi
```

> **NOTE**
>
> For more information on if command construct options in scripts, see Table 9.1 later in this chapter.

If you want to add additional directories, the CentOS 5 version of the .bash_profile file can be instructive, with the following directive:

```
PATH=$PATH:$HOME/bin
export PATH
```

You can add more directories to the value of PATH in a similar fashion. For example, power users who want to configure CentOS 5 from the command line may want to add directories such as /sbin and /usr/sbin to the path in a similar fashion. One method would be to add the following line to the .bash_profile file, as shown in bold:

```
PATH=$PATH:$HOME/bin
PATH=$PATH:/sbin:/usr/sbin
export PATH
```

To implement such changes for all users, review the "Skeleton and User Files" section later in this chapter.

New Environment Variables

Environment variables can go further than what you see in the output to the env command. For more information, see Chapter 4, "Command Lines and Files," which also describes how you can add (or delete) an environment variable using the export and unset commands.

In practice, environment variables are frequently used for administrative purposes. For example, the following commands create, confirm, and set an administrative environment variable:

```
$ ADMIN=/usr/local/sbin:/usr/sbin:/sbin
$ echo $ADMIN
/usr/local/sbin:/usr/sbin:/sbin
$ export ADMIN
```

Then every user who wants easier access to administrative tools can include the following directive in their .bash_profile file:

```
$PATH=$PATH:$ADMIN
```

However, the next time a user logs in, that's not enough. The ADMIN variable has to be set. One way to do so is to configure it for all users in a universal file. The appropriate file for this purpose, at least as listed in the LPIC-1 objectives, is /etc/profile, as you'll see shortly.

Of course, you can add the ADMIN variable directly to /etc/profile. Shortly, in the "Write Simple Shell Scripts" section, you'll see how to do the same thing in a more elegant fashion.

Create and Configure an Alias

Aliases can make life easier at the command-line interface. For example, take the following (slightly) complex command from Chapter 4, which searches for all files with the .iso extension greater than 500MB:

```
$ find / -name "*.iso" -size +500M
```

I make this command a bit more generic, so it starts the search in a local directory. It works as long as my user account has read and execute permissions on the directory:

```
$ find . -name "*.iso" -size +500M
```

Now I create an alias from this command, as follows:

```
$ alias findiso='find / -name "*.iso" -size +500M'
```

The next time I run the `findiso` command alias, it runs the noted command. Obviously, such command aliases can be as complex as needed. However, to make sure this alias is available the next time I connect to this system, I add this same line to the hidden `.bashrc` file in my home directory. To confirm, I log into a new terminal and check the output to the `alias` command:

```
$ alias
alias findiso='find . -name "*.iso" -size +500M'
alias l.='ls -d .* --color=tty'
alias ll='ls -l --color=tty'
alias ls='ls --color=tty'
alias vi='vim'
alias which='alias | /usr/bin/which --tty-only --read-alias --show-dot --show-tilde'
```

Then I see other aliases currently active for my account. If I want to apply this as an alias for all users, I add the `alias` directive shown here to the `/etc/bashrc` file (or `/etc/bash.bashrc` on Ubuntu distributions).

Create and Configure a Function

A function is similar to an alias; however, functions can be incorporated into scripts. The best way to understand a function is to create one. For example, the following command sets up a simple function named `topp ( )`:

```
$ topp ( ) { ps; top; }
```

Note the format; `topp ( )` is the function, and the commands in brackets { } are executed by the function. The semicolon is required to end each command expression included in the function. Once it's created, try the `topp` command. Note how it runs the `ps` and `top` commands, in order.

The following comment in the CentOS 5 version of the `.bashrc` configuration file suggests that it's the right location for user-specific functions and aliases.

```
# User specific aliases and functions
```

In other words, you can place functions that should apply to all users in the `/etc/bashrc` configuration file (or the `/etc/bash.bashrc` configuration file for Ubuntu-based distributions).

Take another step and create a file with a function. The following example with multiple functions is from the standard Linux Documentation Project introduction to bash programming, available online at http://tldp.org/HOWTO/Bash-Prog-Intro-HOWTO.html.

```
#!/bin/bash
    function quit {
        exit
    }
```

```
function e {
    echo $1
}
e Hello
e World
quit
```

To see how it works, take the following steps:

1. Open a text file named `func`.
2. Copy the directives as shown to the `func` file.
3. Make the file executable with the following command:
   `$ chmod u+x func`
4. Execute the newly created `func` script with the following command, where the dot (`.`) represents the current directory. It's necessary because the current directory is not in the `PATH`.
   `$ ./func`

Now that you've seen the output, it should be easier to understand the function. The first directive (`#!/bin/bash`) specifies that the directives that follow are interpreted by the bash shell.

NOTE

Most directives in scripts that start with a pound sign (#) are comments that are not interpreted by Linux or any shell. However, scripts often start with a directive such as `#!/bin/bash`, which specifies the shell that interprets the commands following in the script. In that one case, the line that starts with a # is not a comment.

The first stanza creates a `quit` function, which runs the `exit` command. If you entered the same lines at a bash shell prompt, the `quit` function would log out of that shell console.

The second stanza creates an e function, which runs the `echo $1` command. That directive applies the `echo` command to the first expression that follows, as expressed by the `$1`.

So the last three commands, in order, apply the `echo` command to the word `Hello`, apply the `echo` command to the word `World`, and then run the `exit` command to leave the function.

CAUTION

Do not include the current directory in the `PATH` variable, especially as represented by the dot (`.`), because that can enable damage from crackers who have broken into your system.

Profiles in bash

As noted in the LPIC-1 objectives, several files affect user profiles for the bash shell. The main global configuration file for the bash shell is /etc/profile. That file refers to others in the **/etc/profile.d** directory, as well as a bash shell–specific global file such as /etc/bashrc or /etc/bash.bashrc.

Each of these files can be supplemented by hidden files in user home directories. For example, if a ~/.**profile** file exists, it supplements settings in /etc/profile. Other related user-specific bash configuration files are ~/.bash_profile, ~/.**bash_login**, ~/.profile, ~/.bashrc, and ~/.bash_logout. To review, the tilde (~) is the generic symbol for a user's home directory, and the dot (.) in front of the file name specifies a hidden file.

TIP

When a user logs in, the bash shell typically runs the directives in one of the following files, in order: .bash_profile, .bash_login, or .profile. In other words, if all three files exist, only the directives in .bash_profile are run.

/etc/profile, /etc/profile.d/, and ~/.profile

The bash shell runs based on global profiles configured in the /etc directory and user profiles configured in hidden files in each user's home directory. Because the CentOS 5 version of this file is more detailed than the one included with Ubuntu Hardy Heron, I focus on the CentOS 5 version here.

First, the following stanza creates a function named pathmunge, which will be used shortly. It evaluates directories that follow for inclusion in a user's value of PATH.

```
pathmunge () {
        if ! echo $PATH | /bin/egrep -q "(^|:)$1($|:)" ; then
          if [ "$2" = "after" ] ; then
             PATH=$PATH:$1
          else
             PATH=$1:$PATH
          fi
        fi
}
```

The next stanza uses the pathmunge function to add the following directories to the value of PATH for the user with an ID of 0, the root administrative user.

```
if [ "$EUID" = "0" ]; then
        pathmunge /sbin
        pathmunge /usr/sbin
        pathmunge /usr/local/sbin
fi
```

For a given user ID, based on that user's UID number, the USER, LOGNAME, and MAIL environment variables are assigned based at least indirectly on that number.

```
if [ -x /usr/bin/id ]; then
        USER="`id -un`"
        LOGNAME=$USER
        MAIL="/var/spool/mail/$USER"
fi
```

The following directives set three other environment variables:

```
HOSTNAME=`/bin/hostname`
HISTSIZE=1000
if [ -z "$INPUTRC" -a ! -f "$HOME/.inputrc" ]; then
    INPUTRC=/etc/inputrc
fi
```

Unless there's an .inputrc file in a user's home directory and no current value of INPUTRC, that
variable is set to /etc/inputrc.

The variables set in this script are set for all users with the following directive:

```
export PATH USER LOGNAME MAIL HOSTNAME HISTSIZE INPUTRC
```

If you set other variables in /etc/profile, you should add those variables to this list. As suggested by both versions of /etc/profile, other global settings can be configured with files in
the /etc/profile.d directory.

User-specific profile options can be set in each user's home directory, in the hidden .profile
file.

/etc/bashrc, /etc/bash.bashrc, and ~/.bashrc

For more bash shell settings, the /etc/profile configuration file typically refers to the
/etc/bashrc or /etc/bash.bashrc configuration files. Although the file names differ, the
intent is the same. Systemwide functions and aliases belong in the global version of that file.
Additional settings for individual users may be found in the hidden .bashrc file in each user's
home directory.

Details of directives that actually go in each of these files vary by distribution. As described earlier in this chapter, you saw how a function and alias can be added to one user's .bashrc file.
If you prefer, you can add global aliases to the /etc/bashrc or /etc/bash.bashrc configuration file.

Other User-Specific bash Configuration Files

User-specific configuration files are typically hidden with a dot (.) in front and are located in each user's home directory. The user-specific bash configuration files not already covered include .bash_profile, .bash_login, and .bash_logout. As suggested in the previous Tip, only the first available file among .bash_profile, .bash_login, and .profile is run when a user logs into the bash shell.

For both selected distributions, the .bash_profile file is partially a placeholder. It refers to the .bashrc file for more information, but it is also used to modify the value of PATH for that user. The .bash_login and .profile files are rarely used.

Finally, to repeat information from Chapter 4, directives in the .bash_logout file are run. The default version of this file just clears the screen. Alternatively, you could add more directives to this file, such as notifying the administrator when a user logs out of a system.

Skeleton and User Files

When a user is created, a skeleton of files is added to that user's home directory, based on the current contents of the **/etc/skel** directory. At first glance on Red Hat–based distributions such as CentOS 5, you might think this directory is empty, because standard bash files are hidden files. But the ls -a /etc/skel command reveals the hidden files in this directory.

But files in this directory do not have to be hidden. In fact, it's an excellent location to include other desirable files for new users, such as scripts or even corporate policies. The Ubuntu Hardy Heron version of this directory includes a soft link from the Examples/ subdirectory to the /usr/share/example-content directory.

It's all right that the files and directories in the /etc/skel directory are owned by the root administrative user. When a new user account is created, the files from the /etc/skel directory are copied, and the ownership is converted to that of the new user.

Environment Variables and Aliases

The objectives associated with this chapter are somewhat repetitive to those described in Chapter 4. They include references to the env, export, **set**, and unset commands. The way these commands work varies by shell, so it's important to remember that the default shell for Linux and the LPI exams is the bash shell.

The env command lists current environment variables. Once an environment variable is assigned, as shown in the CentOS 5 version of the /etc/profile configuration file, it can be exported. The set command suggested in the objectives is not required in the bash shell. The following directive sets a hypothetical FLOWERS variable to paperwhites

```
FLOWERS=paperwhites
```

and is then set as an environment variable with the export command as follows:

```
export FLOWERS
```

As shown in both versions of the /etc/profile file, the unset command is used to clear a variable. For example, the i variable is set in this file with the following directive:

```
for i in /etc/profile.d/*.sh ; do
```

When the associated stanza is complete, the following directive unsets the variable, potentially for later use in the file:

```
unset i
```

Existing environment variables in the shell are revealed by the env command. Such variables can also be disabled with the unset command. For example, the MAIL variable is normally set for command-line mail applications, as you can see with the following command:

```
$ env | grep MAIL
```

It does not affect GUI e-mail applications, such as Evolution or Thunderbird. So if you don't use a command line e-mail application, you can safely run the following command:

```
$ unset MAIL
```

You can confirm the change by running the previous env | grep MAIL command again.

Write Simple Shell Scripts

No administrator or even power user should have to type in a bunch of commands to maintain her system—more than once. Such is the role of the simple shell script, a group of commands configured in a file, executed either on demand or on some preconfigured schedule.

One way to learn about scripts is to review those already created for Linux. You've already seen some examples earlier in this chapter as they relate to the configuration of the bash shell. In this section, you'll explore the ins and outs of these scripts in detail. You can then modify existing scripts and even start writing your own scripts to simplify various administrative tasks.

Review and Customize Existing Scripts

In this section, you'll examine and learn from some existing scripts on a typical Linux system. This includes some of the scripts described earlier in this chapter as they relate to the bash shell. But first, examine a simple excerpt from the /etc/crontab configuration file, which includes several basic environment variables:

```
SHELL=/bin/bash
PATH=/sbin:/bin:/usr/sbin:/usr/bin
MAILTO=root
HOME=/
```

These variables are straightforward, because they assign the bash shell to interpret the commands that follow and create a PATH. The MAILTO variable mails notification of events to the root administrative user (who is associated with the LPIC-1 objective for "conditional mailing to the superuser") and sets the top-level root directory (/) as the HOME directory variable.

TIP

The #!/bin/sh directive at the beginning of most scripts refers to the bash shell. However, on Ubuntu distributions, it actually refers to a different shell known as dash, the Debian-Almquist shell. Fortunately, for the purpose of this book and the LPI exams, you can assume that the dash shell is essentially the same as the bash shell.

The existence of these variables in the shell script confirms that the command-line shell environment variables described in the first part of the chapter don't apply to scripts on the system.

NOTE

For more information on how the crontab and related at daemons work, see Chapter 11, "Administrative Tasks."

The files in the directories listed in /etc/crontab include a number of additional scripts. Once you're comfortable with the scripts in this chapter, analyze them. It will help you learn more about bash shell scripts.

Command Constructs

In this section, you'll examine various command constructs typically found in scripts, at least as specified in the LPIC-1 objectives. Several constructs configure the conditions for a loop stanza, a group of commands that are executed as long as the conditions are met. Because they are components of parts of a script in a conditional or a loop, they are known as command constructs. You may find such conditionals and loops with the **for**, **while**, **seq**, **do**, **test**, **read**, and **if** constructs.

TIP

Pay attention to the start and end of stanzas in a script. For example, an if conditional always ends with a **fi**; a do loop always ends with a **done**. An if conditional often also includes a **then** and possibly an **else** option for additional commands. The combination is also known as an if/else command construct.

This section includes some user-created scripts, which should be created with a text editor such as vi. Once saved, you'll need to make the script executable before running it. For example, if you create a script named test1, make it executable, and then run the script with the following two commands

```
$ chmod u+x test1
$ ./test1
```

the execute command assumes that the test1 script is located in the current directory. Administrative permissions aren't required, as long as you create the script, use commands accessible to your account, and execute it as the same user. As the owner of the script file, your account has the necessary rights to change the permissions on the file.

A for Command

First, look at a simple for command construct:

```
for n in 1 2
do
    echo "hello world #$n"
done
```

This for command construct sets the variable n and executes additional command constructs between the do and done directives. To test it for yourself, save these directives in a text file. For the purpose of this section, call the file loop1. Then, to execute the file, make it executable and then run it with the following two commands:

```
$ chmod u+x loop1
$ ./loop1
```

The output is also fairly simple:

```
hello world #1
hello world #2
```

The echo command was run twice. This corresponds to the first for directive, which specified the numbers 1 and 2. These numbers were substituted for the variable n, in the echo command as shown. Now that you've seen how the for command works, proceed to the next section, and see how it works with an if conditional.

An if Conditional with a for Command

The /etc/profile file from both selected distributions includes the following stanza, which executes each file in the /etc/profile.d directory.

```
for i in /etc/profile.d/*.sh ; do
    if [ -r "$i" ]; then
        . $i
    fi
    done
unset i
```

If all this seems confusing, examine these lines one by one. The first line is just a slightly more elaborate version of the for command construct shown previously. In this case, the variable is i, and instead of numbers, there are file names in the /etc/profile.d directory with the .sh extension.

The if conditional looks at each of these files and includes them if they have read permission, as specified by the -r. In other words, the contents of all files in the /etc/profile.d directory, if they have read permissions and the .sh extension, are included in the /etc/profile file as global parameters for all users who log in using the bash shell.

Finally, the i variable is disabled with the unset i command, to free it for use in other stanzas later in the configuration file. Even though the rest of the file is empty, it's an excellent practice, just in case you or a colleague need to add stanzas to a script at a later date.

Test Operators

One reason that scripts may seem confusing is the language within brackets, especially those associated with conditional statements. As you review different scripts, Table 9.1 may help decipher some of the language. Generally, the output from a test operator is either true or false. For example, if the /etc/passwd file exists (-e), the if conditional is true, and the constructs between the if and fi are executed.

```
if [ -e /etc/passwd ]; then
    construct1
    construct2
fi
```

Be aware, the bang (!) is commonly used to negate the effect of an operator. For example, to apply a stanza to anything but a certain IP address, you might specify the following if conditional:

```
if [ $addr != 192.168.0.1 ]; then
```

Table 9.1 Script Test Operators

Operator	Description
-b	Is the file a block file?
-d	Is the file a directory?
-e	Does the file exist?
-eq	Are the values noted equal; an equal to operator, also known as =?
-f	Is the file a regular file?
-ge	Is the variable noted greater than or equal to; a greater than or equal to operator, also known as >=?
-lt	Is the variable noted less than; a less than operator, also known as <?
-le	Is the variable noted less than or equal to; a less than or equal to operator; also known as <=?
-ne	Are the values noted not equal; a not equal to operator, also known as !=?
-r	Does the file have read permission?
-w	Does the file have write permission?
-x	Does the file have execute permission?
-z	Is there a value to the expression?
||	Is the previous expression false?
&&	Is the previous expression true?

The test Command

The easiest way to understand the operators from Table 9.1 is with the test command. The examples shown here are taken from the Ubuntu version of the /etc/cron.daily/quota script. If desired, you can install this file from the Ubuntu build of the quota package. The comments are straightforward, too. The test -x command checks for the existence of an executable /usr/sbin/warnquota file. If true, the exit 0 command is associated with success.

```
# check if quota package is available
test -x /usr/sbin/warnquota || exit 0
```

The next stanza checks if the /etc/default/quota file exists as a regular file. If successful, the exit 0 command is associated with success, and the directives within that file are included in this script.

```
# check if warnquota run is configured
test -f /etc/default/quota || exit 0
. /etc/default/quota
```

A while Loop

Now that you have more information, it should be easier to understand a slightly more complex script. For example, the following script sets up the bash shell, sets the variable n to 1, and creates the while loop, which executes as long as n is less than or equal to 10. For the purpose of this section, save the file as script1.

```
#!/bin/sh
n=1
while [ $n -le 10 ]
do
  echo "hello world #$n"
  n=`expr $n + 1`
done
unset n
```

When the script1 script is made executable and then run, the commands within the loop print out hello world #1 through hello world #10. The n variable is incremented, courtesy of the n=`expr $n +1` directive. When n=10, the condition in the while directive is no longer met, the n variable is unset, and the script is complete.

The read Gets Input

Take the script1 previously created for the while loop. Change the n=1 directive to

```
read n
```

When the script is executed, it looks for input from the command line. In other words, it looks for input. When I enter the number 9, as shown, the script takes it as the initial value of n and lists the noted hello world 9 and hello world 10 output.

```
~$ ./script1
9
hello world #9
hello world #10
```

A seq Command

Perhaps the simplest way to explain the seq command is through the for loop described earlier. The following is the functional equivalent of the previous loop:

```
for n in `seq 2`
do
    echo "hello world #$n"
done
```

As before, the for command sets the variable n, and executes the command(s) between the do and done directives. It works as the `seq 2` command sets n to 1, runs the commands in the do loop, sets n to 2, and runs the commands in the do loop again.

Command Substitution

Command substitution in a script works like a function. A couple of examples are available in the Ubuntu Hardy Heron version of the /etc/bash.bashrc configuration file. The following example applies only when the dchroot feature is used on Ubuntu and other Debian-based distributions. (While the dchroot feature may also be replaced by the schroot command in the future, such differences are not the point of the LPIC-1 exams.) First, it checks (-z) for a current value of debian_chroot. If there's also (&&) an existing /etc/debian_chroot file with read (-r) permissions, the debian_chroot variable is given the current value of the contents of the /etc/debian_chroot file.

```
# set variable identifying the chroot you work in (used in the prompt below)
if [ -z "$debian_chroot" ] && [ -r /etc/debian_chroot ]; then
    debian_chroot=$(cat /etc/debian_chroot)
fi
```

In this case, the command substitution works like an alias; on the command line, this would be functionally equivalent to the following command:

```
$ alias debian_chroot = 'cat /etc/debian_chroot'
```

The example that follows is slightly different. It configures the command-line prompt as the PS1 command, based on the newly created debian_chroot command.

```
# set a fancy prompt (non-color, overwrite the one in /etc/profile)
PS1='${debian_chroot:+($debian_chroot)}\u@\h:\w\$
```

The remaining elements specify the username (u@), the hostname (h:), and the current directory (w), followed by the standard command-line prompt ($).

Use Basic SQL Commands

Relational databases on modern operating systems are frequently organized using SQL (Structured Query Language) commands. Two major SQL systems for Linux include MySQL and PostgreSQL. Whichever system you prefer, the basic commands and queries listed in the LPIC-1 objectives apply.

This section may seem odd especially to newer Linux users, because it goes beyond the Linux operating system. The people behind the LPI exams believe that a basic knowledge of SQL is a fundamental job skill even for Linux power users. If you're unfamiliar with SQL, this section focuses on the functionality of the basic commands listed in the LPIC-1 objectives.

In any case, SQL has a weight of 2 in the LPIC-1 objectives, which means you can expect to see an average of 2 SQL-related questions out of 60 on the LPI 102 exam. Because the passing score for LPIC-1 exams is approximately 50%, even expert users who are clueless about SQL have an excellent chance of qualifying for the LPIC-1 certification.

However, as such, a full explanation of SQL would require a book full of information. Given its weight on the LPIC-1 exams, I describe SQL concepts in the briefest of terms. For more information, see *PHP 6/MySQL Programming for the Absolute Beginner* (2008), published by Course Technology.

 NOTE

The format of SQL commands and variables differs from Linux. SQL commands such as INSERT are generally in uppercase; SQL variable names such as address_book are in lowercase.

Elementary SQL Concepts

SQL is a language that can help manage relational databases. Each database includes different categories of data. For example, an address book may have information such as people's names, e-mail addresses, phone numbers, physical street addresses, and zip codes. One example is shown in Table 9.2.

For the purpose of this database, each column is associated with a single-word variable. You can assign variables such as name, e-mail_address, phone_number, street_address, and zip_code. Of course, the database table gets its own single-word name, such as address_book.

When you add information to any database, an **INSERT** command expects information for every element of that database. An **UPDATE** command can revise the information associated with each person. A **DELETE** command can remove entire entries from a database. The **SELECT** command can search through existing databases, with the help of additional commands. Finally, the right SQL queries can search through multiple databases.

Table 9.2 Sample Database Table

Name	E-Mail Address	Phone Number	Street Address	Zip Code	Grade
Amy Albert	amy@example.com	111-1111	123 Main	00001	99
Bob Ball	bob@example.net	222-2222	456 Broad	00001	100
John Bull	john@example.org	333-3333	789 Fifth	99998	89
John Doe	john@example.zzz	444-4444	123 Port	99999	78

The SQL INSERT Command

A typical INSERT command adds information to a given database, based on the database name and data to be added. For example, the following command adds an entry based on each column in the database:

```
INSERT INTO address_book (name, e-mail_address, phone_number, street_address, zip_code, grade) VALUES ('Eddie East', 'eddie@example.com', '555-5555', '456 77th', '00001', '85');
```

This command adds an entry to the address_book, based on the variables as shown, from name to grade. Every variable shown must have a data entry. If you don't have the zip code for a new entry, leave out the zip_code variable from the INSERT statement. All SQL commands end with the semicolon (;).

The SQL DELETE Command

Although the opposite of insert is delete, the SQL INSERT and DELETE commands aren't formatted in the same way, because a deletion needs some way to specify which line(s) is to be deleted. For example, the following command deletes the entry associated with zip code 99999:

```
DELETE FROM address_book WHERE zip_code = '99999';
```

This command searches the address_book database, in the zip_code column, for an entry of 99999. If found, that entry is deleted. If more than one entry has that zip code, those entries are also deleted.

Multiple filters can be used. For example, with the previous INSERT command, there are three address book entries with a zip code of 00001. If you want to delete an entry with the 222-2222 phone number, the command becomes this:

```
DELETE FROM address_book WHERE zip_code = '99999' AND phone_number = '222-2222';
```

Of course, you can just specify the name, but this example provides a feel for the flexibility of the DELETE command.

The SQL UPDATE Command

Sometimes data changes. For example, people in an address book may move. One option is to use the DELETE command to delete and then use the INSERT command to insert new information for such data. But it is often simpler to change current data with the UPDATE command. For example, from Table 9.2, if user John Bull changed his e-mail address to bull@example.org, you could update the database with the following command:

```
UPDATE address_book SET e-mail_address = 'bull@example.org' WHERE e-mail_address =
'john@example.org';
```

This command takes the database named address_book and sets a new value for e-mail_address of bull@example.org, based on a previous entry of john@example.org.

SQL SELECT and Subselect Searches

Databases can be searched. The root SQL search command is SELECT. When searching a database, you can use the **FROM** command to specify the name of the database. You can use the **WHERE** command to specify the database column and search value.

You can choose a specific column of a database with a command like this:

```
SELECT zip_code FROM address_book;
```

You can then go further and specify a zip code value in the address book with the WHERE command:

```
SELECT zip_code FROM address_book WHERE zip_code = '99999';
```

The command can be simplified; substituting an asterisk for the first zip_code variable as shown here brings the entire database into the search:

```
SELECT * FROM address_book WHERE zip_code = '99999';
```

A subselect goes further, with a second search parameter. For example, the following also searches for users where the grade is at least 80:

```
SELECT * FROM address_book WHERE zip_code = '99999' AND grade >= 80;
```

SQL SELECT Database ORDER BY

Databases can be organized with the help of the SELECT command. When coupled with an **ORDER BY** command, a database can be reorganized in alphabetical order, based on the specified column. For example, the following command reorganizes the database specified in Table 9.2 by e-mail address:

```
SELECT * FROM address_book ORDER BY e-mail_address;
```

You can reconfigure the database in reverse alphabetical order just by adding the DESC command to the end of the command line:

```
SELECT * FROM address_book ORDER BY e-mail_address DESC;
```

SQL SELECT Database GROUP BY

Databases often are organized by common elements. For example, companies may organize address books by zip code. A mailing that is organized by zip code may qualify for a lower postal rate. So if you want to organize the database from Table 9.2 by zip code, you can run the following command:

```
SELECT * FROM address_book GROUP BY zip_code;
```

SQL Join Queries

Databases can get complex. One level of complexity is associated with additional data categories. For example, assume that separate databases of grades are kept for different semesters. Call the databases fall_semester and spring_semester.

A search of the two databases also starts with the SQL SELECT command. First, however, the databases may be aliased:

```
FROM fall_semester AS fs NATURAL JOIN spring_semester AS ss
```

With these aliases, you can set up the SELECT command to read from the grade column in both databases:

```
SELECT fs.grade, ss.grade
```

The search needs a parameter, such as this:

```
WHERE grade >=80
```

Of course, these queries are not coherent unless they're put together:

```
SELECT fs.grade, ss.grade
FROM fall_semester AS fs NATURAL JOIN spring_semester AS ss
WHERE grade >=80;
```

Chapter Summary

Experienced Linux users need to know how to manage the shell environment. The default shell for Linux is bash. Bash interprets a command based on the value of PATH, aliases, and functions. These variables are defined globally in the /etc/profile, /etc/bashrc, or /etc/bash.bashrc configuration file. Files for new users are generally hidden and stored in the /etc/skel directory.

Power users need to know how to manage and create scripts. One way to learn how scripts work is to analyze existing scripts such as /etc/crontab and related scripts in directories such as /etc/cron.daily. Scripts include various command tests such as for, while, seq, do, test, read, and if. Some scripts use command substitution similar to functions.

This chapter also covers the use of several basic SQL commands. Entries can be added and removed with the INSERT and DELETE commands or revised with the UPDATE command. Searches are possible with the SELECT command, whereas the FROM command specifies the database and the WHERE command specifies the search parameter. Databases can be reordered with **GROUP BY** and ORDER BY commands. Queries can be applied to multiple databases given appropriate aliases.

Key Terms

- **alias.** A command that represents others; you can identify current aliases such as alias ls='ls --color=auto' with the alias command.
- **.bash_login.** A configuration file in user home directories run when users log in, unless superseded by the .bash_profile file.
- **command substitution.** A feature of a script, similar to a function or a shell alias.
- **DELETE.** A SQL command that can delete a database entry based on a specified datapoint.
- **do.** A script command that starts a loop; the end of a do loop is specified with the done command.
- **done.** A script command that ends a loop; the start of a done loop is specified with the do command.
- **else.** A script command commonly used when an if conditional is not satisfied.
- **/etc/profile.d.** A directory with additional files commonly included in /etc/profile.
- **/etc/skel/.** A directory with files generally included in the home directories of new users.
- **fi.** A construct that closes an if loop in a script.
- **for.** A script command associated with lists.
- **FROM.** A SQL command that specifies the database to be searched.
- **function.** A command that represents others; for example, the following command creates topp as a function: topp ( ) { ps; top; }.
- **GROUP BY.** A SQL command that can organize data by common words or numbers.
- **if.** A script conditional.
- **INSERT.** A SQL command that can add a database entry.
- **ORDER BY.** A SQL command that can reorganize a database in alphabetical order.

◆ **.profile.** A configuration file in user home directories run when users log in, unless superseded by the .bash_profile or .bash_login files.

◆ **read.** A script command that prompts for user input for a variable.

◆ **SELECT.** A SQL command associated with a search.

◆ **seq.** A script command that specifies a sequence of numbers.

◆ **set.** When the export command is applied to a variable, it is set. In the bash shell, there is no set command.

◆ **SQL.** Structured Query Language, a standard language for relational database management systems such as MySQL and PostgreSQL.

◆ **test.** A script command test typically applied on files.

◆ **then.** A script command commonly used when an if conditional is satisfied.

◆ **UPDATE.** A SQL command that can change a specified entry in a database.

◆ **WHERE.** A SQL command that specifies a search parameter.

◆ **while.** A command that lists file types.

Review Questions

The number of review questions in this chapter and other chapters in this book is proportionate to each section's weight in the LPI objectives. Because this chapter covers items 105.1, 105.2, and 105.3, the weight is 10; therefore, you'll see 20 questions in this section. You'll see multiple choice single answer, fill-in-the blank, and multiple choice multiple answer questions, as you'll encounter on the exam.

1. Enter the command that creates an alias named backuphome, which backs up all files and directories from the local directory to /backup. Assume that your account has appropriate permissions to all directories. Don't forget to include hidden files.

2. Which of the following directories should not be added to the value of PATH?
   A. The current directory
   B. /usr/sbin
   C. /bin
   D. ~/sbin

3. Which of the following files is suitable to assign a function for all users?
   A. ~/.profile
   B. ~/.bashrc
   C. /etc/bashrc
   D. /etc/profile

4. You've just created the `script1` script in the local directory and given it executable permissions. Which of the following commands would execute the script? Assume that the local directory is not included in the value of PATH.

    A. script

    B. /home/michael/script1

    C. ./script

    D. ./script1

5. If you want to make sure the commands in a script are executed using the bash shell, enter the first line of the script file. The line should start with what appears to be a comment character.

    _____

6. You've just run `LINUX=great`. Which of the following commands makes that variable permanent as long as that shell or script is in operation?

    A. set LINUX

    B. perm LINUX

    C. while LINUX

    D. export LINUX

7. If you want to set up default files for new users, which of the following directories is best suited for that purpose?

    A. /etc

    B. /home

    C. /etc/skel

    D. /etc/profile

8. Which of the following commands disables an environment variable?

    A. unenv

    B. unset

    C. reset

    D. env -r

9. If you don't want to specify the full path to commands in the /usr/sbin and /sbin directories in a script, enter the appropriate line for the script.

    _____

10. Which of the following command constructs can you find at the end of an if stanza?

    A. else

    B. then

    C. done

    D. fi

11. Which of the following command constructs is equivalent to the following line in a script?

    `for n in `seq 4``

    A. for n in 4 5 6 7

    B. for n + 4

    C. for n in 4 8 12 16

    D. for n in 1 2 3 4

12. Which of the following lines checks whether /etc/profile is a regular file?

    A. if [-d /etc/profile]; then

    B. if [-r /etc/profile]; then

    C. if [-f /etc/profile]; then

    D. if [-w /etc/profile]; then

13. Which of the following command constructs checks for a value of the INPUTRC variable?

    A. if [-z "$INPUTRC"]

    B. if [-v "$INPUTRC"]

    C. if [-r "$INPUTRC"]

    D. if [-x "$INPUTRC"]

14. Which of the following files would be considered first to the exclusion of others for user-specific bash shell settings? These files are in the user's home directory.

    A. .profile

    B. .bash_profile

    C. .bash_login

    D. .bash_history

15. Enter the while command in a script that applies to a variable $n that would be true when n < 10. Do not use symbols such as <.

16. What does the `read x` command do from within a script?

    A. It reads the value of x set earlier in the script.

    B. It prompts the user to enter a value for x.

    C. It checks whether x has been set as an environment variable.

    D. It checks whether x has read permissions.

17. If you just need to change one database entry, you could `DELETE` and `INSERT`; alternatively, you could use the following command: _____

18. Which of the following SQL commands can you use to specify a database to search?

    A. `WHERE`

    B. `FROM`

    C. `UPDATE`

    D. `QUERY`

19. Which of the following SQL commands can you use to specify a search term?

    A. `WHERE`

    B. `FROM`

    C. `UPDATE`

    D. `SELECT`

20. Which of the following SQL commands can you use to organize a database in alphabetical order?

    A. `WHERE`

    B. `DESC`

    C. `ORDER BY`

    D. `GROUP BY`

Chapter 10

The GUI Desktop Environment

After completing this chapter, you will be able to

■ Install and configure an X Window and X Font Server

■ Customize display managers

■ Understand the range of accessibility technologies

Introduction

Like many of you, I began working with Linux after years of conditioning on Microsoft and Apple GUIs (graphical user interfaces). In fact, I didn't really start learning Linux until after I received my now-expired MCSE (Microsoft Certified Systems Engineer) certification.

While I learned Linux, I looked forward to those chapters related to the GUI, because it was something familiar. But the first laptop system that I tried to configure with a GUI had problems, so I had to face the seeming minutiae of the X Server configuration file.

Fortunately, the X Server configuration and GUI login managers were a lot easier to configure than I had feared. And then I learned to appreciate the elegance of Linux GUI solutions, because they more easily facilitate remote desktop environments.

As Linux has advanced on the desktop, it now includes accessibility features for the sight impaired. Some of these features are also useful for people like me who spend too much time staring at a far-too-small laptop screen every day.

 TIP

This chapter addresses three objectives in the LPI exam: 106.1 ("Install and Configure X11"), 106.2 ("Setup a Display Manager"), and 106.3 ("Accessibility").

Basic Linux GUI Configuration

Linux is built as a client-server operating system. The client-server model extends to the GUI in a way that seems counterintuitive: the GUI server is on the client, and GUI applications reside on remote systems.

Today, Linux is arguably more compatible with current hardware when compared to modern Microsoft operating systems. But Linux isn't compatible with everything. You need to know how to verify whether current hardware is supported. Once support is confirmed, you also need to understand the range of available tools that can help you configure a GUI, as well as the basics of the GUI configuration file, **/etc/X11/xorg.conf**.

NOTE

Current Linux systems generally use server software developed through the **X.org** foundation. Older Linux systems used server software developed through the XFree86 Project, Inc. For our purposes, except for the names of certain configuration tools and files, the two systems are virtually identical.

In Linux, the GUI is known as "**X**" or "**X11**." X development started in 1984 at MIT and continues today with the X.org project. X11 is the associated protocol. Just remember, X won't work on Linux without xfs, the **X Font Server**. Desktop environments such as GNOME and KDE work on top of the X server.

NOTE

Be aware: the XFS filesystem discussed in Chapter 7, "Manage and Maintain Filesystems," and the X Font Server use the same "xfs" acronym in their configuration files and commands.

Verify Support

A substantial number of packages are associated with X on a Linux system. Before installing the X or X11 server, you should verify that the hardware (graphics card and monitor) supports such an installation. Hardware compatibility lists are available from numerous sources; support contracts from vendors such as Red Hat, SUSE, or Canonical (Ubuntu) may require it. Over the past few years, problems with graphics hardware have usually related to proprietary drivers. However, even in those cases, X has generally still worked in a reduced mode such as VESA, a reference to the SVGA (Super VGA) mode of the Video Electronics Standards Association.

But compatible hardware is not limited to those configurations supported by various Linux vendors. The only way to know what hardware is supported for sure is to install the X server packages and then start the configuration process.

NOTE

The installation of text-only versions of Linux is more common than you might think. If you're working from one of these installations and want to follow along, install the X server.

Available Configuration Tools

Several Linux tools are available for graphical configuration. There is the Display Settings tool on Red Hat–style systems such as CentOS 5, which you can start with the `system-config-display` command. There is also the Screen and Graphics Preferences tool, which you can start on Ubuntu systems with the `displayconfig-gtk` command.

But because the LPI exams are "vendor neutral," the focus of the exam is on common tools, which are available from the command line. The **Xorg** `-configure` command, run with administrative privileges, can check current hardware and propose a configuration file. It writes its results to the `xorg.conf.new` file in the local directory.

If the file is acceptable, you can put it into effect by copying it to the `/etc/X11/` directory.

On most Linux distributions, the `X` command works like the `Xorg` command. In fact, the two files are linked on CentOS 5. After a working X configuration file is available in the `/etc/X11` directory, you can start a basic X server with the `X` or `Xorg` commands. The X server is so basic that all it displays is a blank screen with an "X" representing a cursor. To get a familiar GUI, you also need to install a desktop environment such as GNOME or KDE.

The xorg.conf Configuration File

The LPIC-1 objectives suggest that you need a basic understanding of the X Window configuration file. That file is `/etc/X11/xorg.conf`. Although a detailed description of this file is beyond the scope of the objectives, you do need to know the basics. The examples in this section come from different systems.

Although the organization and details of this file vary by distribution, there are some common characteristics. First, the settings are summarized in the **ServerLayout** stanza, such as that shown here:

```
Section "ServerLayout"
    Identifier    "X.org Configured"
    Screen      0  "Screen0" 0 0
    InputDevice    "Mouse0" "CorePointer"
    InputDevice    "Keyboard0" "CoreKeyboard"
EndSection
```

This stanza, which might be found at the beginning or the end of the file, includes an identifying label, as shown by the `Identifier` directive, which may be included in other stanzas. This identifier might be included in a different stanza in a multimonitor configuration. Each line that follows is from a different identifier. Look elsewhere in the file for these identifiers.

Each **InputDevice** directive is associated with some human input device, such as a mouse, keyboard, or touchpad. The keyboard stanza shown here identifies the required driver and may include options such as keyboard layout.

```
Section "InputDevice"
    Identifier  "Keyboard0"
    Driver      "kbd"
    Option      "XkbModel" "pc105"
    Option      "XkbLayout" "us"
EndSection
```

A stanza for a mouse may be just as simple. However, a stanza for a touchpad with a scroll option typically includes more information, such as the scroll configuration, as shown here. Note that the synaptics driver is also specified.

```
Section "InputDevice"
    Identifier      "Synaptics Touchpad"
    Driver          "synaptics"
    Option          "SendCoreEvents"      "true"
    Option          "Device"              "/dev/psaux"
    Option          "Protocol"            "auto-dev"
    Option          "HorizEdgeScroll"     "0"
EndSection
```

Of course, a keyboard and pointing device aren't useful for a GUI without a monitor or graphics card. That configuration comes from the Screen0 identifier, whose stanza includes references to a monitor and a graphics card (Device "Videocard0"). This particular stanza includes a default display depth of 24 bits.

```
Section "Screen"
    Identifier "Screen0"
    Monitor    "Configured Monitor"
    Device     "Videocard0"
    DefaultDepth    24
    SubSection "Display"
        Viewport   0 0
        Depth    24
    EndSubSection
EndSection
```

If some defaults are used, there may not even be a separate **Monitor** setting in the Screen stanza, much less a separate Monitor stanza like that shown here:

```
Section "Monitor"
    Identifier      "Configured Monitor"
EndSection
```

This configured video device includes a reference to the graphics driver associated with Linux installation on a VMware Server:

```
Section "Device"
    Identifier "Videocard0"
    Driver     "vmware"
EndSection
```

Less frequently seen in the xorg.conf configuration file is a stanza that specifies the location of X Font Server files. Unless those files are in nonstandard locations, a font stanza is no longer required in the xorg.conf file. Standard packages for Ubuntu and CentOS 5 (and most other Linux distributions) install fonts in standard locations.

The X Font Server

The files of the X Font Server are required for a working Linux GUI. Required packages are normally installed automatically with the installation of a GUI. But the LPIC-1 objectives specify that you need to know how to "install and configure an X Font Server."

If you need to install the X Font Server separately, the following commands would work in the Ubuntu Hardy Heron and CentOS 5 releases, respectively:

```
# apt-get install xfs
# yum install xorg-x11-xfs
```

Regular and GUI fonts are configured in the /etc/fonts directory. The fonts.conf file in this directory includes the following stanza, which may vary by distribution:

```
<!-- Font directory list -->
    <dir>/usr/share/fonts</dir>
    <dir>/usr/share/X11/fonts/Type1</dir> <dir>/usr/share/X11/fonts/OTF</dir >
    <dir>~/.fonts</dir>
```

This includes directories with available fonts. As specified at the beginning of this file, additional font directories can be added to the /etc/fonts/local.conf file. Then such directories can be activated with the mkfontdir command.

The last line suggests that user-specific fonts can even be configured in each user's home directory, in the hidden ~/.fonts file.

Test the X Server

Typically, when X is installed on a Linux system, a boot brings a user automatically to a graphical login screen, which will be discussed shortly in the "Display Manager Options" section. Once you're logged into a screen, you have several options to open a command-line text console. Although details vary, they should be elementary for the LPIC-1 candidate.

When a display manager is not configured, you may not see a login screen. If the X server is properly installed, you should still be able to start the GUI from the command line with the startx command.

However, once a command-line interface is opened in a GUI, two commands listed in the LPIC-1 objectives can help test the X server: **xdpyinfo** and **xwininfo**.

Display Server Capabilities with xdpyinfo

You can use the xdpyinfo command to find more about the capabilities of a configured X server. The first section of the output includes information about the current display, vendor, version, and color depth. For example, the following output specifies that the local system can handle 32 bits of color:

```
depth 32, bits_per_pixel 32, scanline_pad 32
```

It also includes numerous extensions to the X server. For example, if you see GLX, associated hardware includes OpenGL (open graphics library) extensions to the X server. Later sections include resolution in pixels and dots per inch.

Display Window Information with xwininfo

Run the xwininfo command. You'll see a cursor in the form of a plus sign, which allows you to click on a window. Then the xwininfo command gives you more information about that window—specifically the position, size, and color depth.

Multiple Local GUIs

On most Linux systems, the GUI is located on the seventh console. In other words, if you're in a command-line console and the X server is active, you should be able to access the GUI by pressing Ctrl+Alt+F7. Normally, six command-line consoles are available. To access these consoles, press Ctrl+Alt+F1 through Ctrl+Alt+F6.

If a GUI is not available, you can start it from a regular command-line console. Access the first command-line console by pressing Ctrl+Alt+F1, and then run the following command:

```
$ startx &
```

Although the ampersand (&) is not necessary, it allows you to run additional commands from the same prompt. You should be able to return to the first command-line console with the Ctrl+Alt+F1 command and then go back to the GUI with the Ctrl+Alt+F7 command.

You can now start a second instance of the X server. From the first command-line console, try the following command:

```
$ startx -- :1
```

This command should start an X server in the eighth virtual console. In other words, you should be able to go back and forth between this server and the first command-line console with the Ctrl+Alt+F1 and Ctrl+Alt+F8 commands.

NOTE

To simulate the effect of multiple X servers on the Hardy Heron release of Ubuntu, I had to uninstall the graphical display manager.

But wait, these X servers look identical. You can find the difference with the current value of **DISPLAY**, available with the following command:

```
$ echo $DISPLAY
```

If this is the first GUI display, available when you press Ctrl+Alt+F7, you'll see the following output:

```
:0.0
```

If this is the second GUI display, available when you press Ctrl+Alt+F8, you'll see this output:

```
:1.0
```

NOTE

On Fedora 10 and later, Ctrl+Alt+F1 opens a GUI by default; the second instance of the X server appears in the seventh virtual console, accessible with the Ctrl+Alt+F7 command.

Local Servers and Remote Clients

Remote access to the local GUI server may be available, courtesy of the **xhost** command. If you choose to allow remote access using this command, you need to allow the X server to listen for TCP connections. Such access is disabled on all current Linux distributions.

If TCP connections are allowed, you can set up a local X server to allow access for an IP address like 192.168.11.11 or a hostname like *remoteXserver* with the following commands:

```
xhost +192.168.11.11
xhost +remoteXserver
```

Then, on the local X client, enable a remote transmission of the display with the following commands:

```
DISPLAY=192.168.11.11:0.0
export DISPLAY
```

You can then run a GUI application on the local X client, which displays on the remote system with the noted IP address.

Remote access to GUI clients is also available using SSH (Secure Shell), as discussed in Chapter 15, "Security Administration." In fact, because of security issues related to the `xhost` command, SSH is the preferred method for remote GUI connections.

Display Manager Options

In this section, you'll examine how to set up and customize a display manager. The three major display managers available for Linux are **GDM** (GNOME display manager), **KDM** (KDE display manager), and **XDM** (X display manager). Sometimes a display manager is a service, activated in the `/etc/init.d` directory. Sometimes it's activated while starting the X server. In either case, the selected service is based on a configuration file, typically one of the following:

```
/etc/X11/default-display-manager
/etc/X11/prefdm
```

When current GUI desktop environments are installed, they come with a display manager. But they're not necessarily tied to that system; for example, the GDM display manager can be configured to log into the KDE desktop environment.

NOTE

Yes, the term "GDM display manager" is redundant, but so are other Linux acronyms, such as GNU (GNU's Not Unix).

NOTE

The KDM and XDM display managers are not available from CentOS 5 or Red Hat Enterprise Linux 5 repositories. The Fedora 10 version of KDM and XDM was used in this section to represent RPM-based distributions.

On the latest Red Hat–based systems, the GDM, KDM, and XDM display managers are available from the `gdm`, `kdebase-workspace`, and `xorg-x11-xdm` packages. On the Hardy Heron release, these display managers are available from the `gdm`, `kdm`, and `xdm` packages. Be aware: different distributions also configure how each display manager starts with different files and scripts.

Because the LPI exams are distribution neutral, such differences are beyond the scope of the LPIC-1 objectives. Although this chapter covers some distribution and release-unique details to help you test and learn about display managers on real systems, these details are specifically excluded from the LPIC-1 objectives. As distributions evolve, the changes specified in this section may not even work on later releases such as Fedora 10.

Unless you're installing or removing a display manager, the standard way to implement changes is to restart the display manager service. If you've made a configuration change, don't expect to see the change in the display manager until the service has been restarted.

One common way to restart a service is to find its PID (process identifier) and apply the `kill -HUP` command to that PID number. For more information, see Chapter 6, "Processes, Priorities, and Editing."

Activate (or Deactivate) the Display Manager

Activating or deactivating a display manager is straightforward. All you need to do is deactivate the appropriate setting in the applicable configuration file. You have several options in this regard. Where the **/etc/inittab** configuration file is still used (on systems like CentOS 5), that file may contain the following line:

```
x:5:respawn:/etc/X11/prefdm -nodaemon
```

Although the comment associated with this directive refers to the XDM display manager, it actually refers to the default configuration file associated with desktops and display managers. It's executed in runlevel 5. If this file is not run, the X server is never started.

In contrast, Ubuntu systems include an `/etc/X11/default-display-manager` configuration file, which executes the desired display manager, `/usr/bin/xdm`, `/usr/bin/kdm`, or `/usr/sbin/gdm`. A comment in front of the line is sufficient to disable the display manager during the boot process.

Another alternative is to uninstall the associated package; display managers can't be started if they aren't installed on a system.

Naturally, activating a display manager requires the reverse of the process; you'll need to make sure that the associated package(s) are installed and are configured properly in the noted files.

The GDM Display Manager

The GDM display manager nominally provides the default graphical login screen for many major Linux distributions. However, many developers include themes that override standard display manager settings. Standard GDM display manager configuration files are stored in the **/etc/gdm** directory.

When defaults are shown, they are made available in the **/etc/gdm/gdm.conf** configuration file. Different distributions specify another file for custom settings that are included in the GDM configuration; these files go by various names, such as `gdm.conf-custom` and `custom.conf`.

The following sections describe how to customize the display manager through the text configuration files, as discussed in the LPIC-1 objectives. In many distributions, there's a Login Window Preferences tool that can be started with the `gdmsetup` command, which is designed to help customize the GDM login screen.

Change the Display Manager Greeting

It isn't easy to customize the standard display manager greeting included with many Linux distributions, at least not with standard GDM display manager configuration options. To that end, I've customized three directives, in two categories:

```
[daemon]
Greeter=/usr/libexec/gdmlogin
[greeter]
DefaultWelcome=false
Welcome=Welcome Mike
```

The GDM display manager daemon now starts with a standard login screen. With the DefaultWelcome directive, the theme created for the distribution is disabled. Finally, the GDM display manager greeting has been customized with the Welcome directive. The results shown in Figure 10.1 respect the Ubuntu heritage as a Debian-based Linux distribution.

FIGURE 10.1 *A custom GDM display manager login screen.*

Change the Default Color for the Display Manager

It's easiest to change the default color for the GDM display manager with the GUI Login Window Preferences tool. But that tool isn't always available. Changes are implemented as a custom GDM display manager setting:

```
BackgroundColor=#82a4da
```

The BackgroundColor directive specifies three levels of red, green, and blue, in hexadecimal format. The actual color described here is not important for the LPIC-1 objectives.

Those who are paying attention might note that the LPIC-1 objectives specify that you need to know how to change the default color depth. The default color depth of the GDM display manager matches the color depth of the X server as configured earlier in this chapter, so no special customization is possible.

Configure Display Managers for Use by X-Stations

The title, which is verbatim from the LPIC-1 objectives, specifies a configuration accessible by remote stations. Remote access may require two levels of configuration changes. First, there are the changes associated with the GDM display manager, which specify the login screen shown to remote users, as well as access using the **XDMCP** (X Display Manager Control Protocol) protocol.

```
[daemon]
RemoteGreeter=/usr/libexec/gdmlogin
[xdmcp]
Enable=true
```

The second group of configuration changes relate to any firewalls that may currently exist on the local system. As shown in the /etc/services file (per Chapter 13's "Basic Networking"), the default TCP/IP port for the XDMCP protocol is 177. Any firewall that blocks access to this port prevents remote access to the GDM display manager.

The KDM Display Manager

The KDM display manager nominally provides the default graphical login screen for many major Linux distributions. However, many developers include themes that override standard display manager settings. Depending on the release, standard KDM display manager configuration files are stored in the /etc/kde/kdm, /etc/kde3/kdm, or /etc/kde4/kdm directories.

The standard KDM display manager configuration is documented in the **kdmrc** file in the configuration directory. The following sections describe how to customize the display manager through such text configuration files, as discussed in the LPIC-1 objectives. In many distributions, the KDM display manager customization tool is a Login Manager tool that can be started with the kcmshell kdm command. (The command is kcmshell4 kdm on desktops that have been upgraded to KDE version 4.) The tool is designed to help customize the GDM login screen.

Change the Display Manager Greeting

To change the display manager greeting, open the `kdmrc` file from the configuration directory. Find the `GreetString` directive, and change the greeting as desired.

Change the Default Color for the Display Manager

It's easiest to change the default color for the KDM display manager with the GUI Login Window Preferences tool. But that tool isn't always available. Changes are implemented as a custom KDM display manager configuration file, `backgroundrc`, in the configuration directory.

Those who are paying attention might note that the LPIC-1 objectives specify that you need to know how to change the default color depth. You can customize the default color depth of the KDM display manager through the `Xservers` file in the KDM configuration directory. Normally, this file has one line:

```
:0 local /usr/bin/X :0
```

As suggested by the `/usr/bin/X` command, this directive can handle the options associated with the X command. The following change specifies a color depth of 16 bits:

```
:0 local /usr/bin/X -depth 16 :0
```

Configure Display Managers for Use by X-Stations

The title, which is verbatim from the LPIC-1 objectives, specifies a configuration where remote users can log in graphically through the local login display manager. Remote access may require three levels of configuration changes. First, there are changes associated with the KDM display manager, which specify access using the XDMCP protocol.

```
[Xdmcp]
Enable=true
Willing=/etc/kde3/kdm/Xwilling
Xaccess=/etc/kde3/kdm/Xaccess
```

Be aware: the directory associated with the `Xwilling` and **Xaccess** files may vary by KDE version and distribution. Next, open the `Xaccess` file, and make sure the following directives are active:

```
*                        #any host can get a login window
*    CHOOSER BROADCAST    #any indirect host can get a chooser
```

The third group of configuration changes relate to any firewalls that may currently exist on the local system. As shown in `/etc/services` (per Chapter 13, "Basic Networking"), the default TCP/IP port for the XDMCP protocol is 177. Any firewall that blocks access to this port prevents remote access to the KDM display manager.

The XDM Display Manager

The XDM display manager provides a generic graphical login screen. Standard XDM display manager configuration files are stored in the **/etc/X11/xdm** directory. The main XDM configuration file is **xdm-config**. The following sections describe how to customize the display manager through the text configuration files, as discussed in the LPIC-1 objectives.

Change the Display Manager Greeting

The XDM display manager configuration file has a modestly different look and feel when compared to other Linux files. For example, comments in this file start with the bang character (!), also known in standard English as the exclamation point.

The display manager greeting is associated with the **Xresources** file, also in the /etc/X11/xdm directory. To change the display manager greeting for secure and unsecure configurations, modify the following directives:

```
xlogin*greeting: Welcome to CLIENTHOST, Mike
xlogin*unsecureGreeting: Welcome to CLIENTHOST, Mike
```

Change the Default Color for the Display Manager

Those who are paying attention might note that the LPIC-1 objectives specify that you need to know how to change the default color depth. The default color depth of the XDM display manager can be customized through the Xresources file in the /etc/X11/xdm directory. It includes a number of different color directives, in an ifdef - else - endif stanza. The Else stanza is a failsafe stanza.

```
#ifdef COLOR
xlogin*borderWidth: 1
xlogin*frameWidth: 5
xlogin*innerFramesWidth: 2
xlogin*shdColor: grey30
xlogin*hiColor: grey90
xlogin*background: grey
!xlogin*foreground: darkgreen
xlogin*greetColor: Blue3
xlogin*failColor: red
*Foreground: black
*Background: #fffff0
#else
xlogin*borderWidth: 3
xlogin*frameWidth: 0
xlogin*innerFramesWidth: 1
xlogin*shdColor: black
xlogin*hiColor: black
#endif
```

The color directives from the stanza just listed are described in Table 10.1, in the order they appear in the `Xresources` file. The directives that start with `xlogin` drive colors associated with the actual username/password window inside the XDM screen.

Table 10.1 XDM Xresources Color Directives

Directive	Description
`xlogin*shdColor`	Shadow color
`xlogin*hiColor`	Highlight color
`xlogin*background`	Background color
`xlogin*foreground`	Foreground color
`xlogin*greetColor`	Greeting display color
`xlogin*failColor`	Failure message color
`xlogin*greetColor`	Greeting display color
`Foreground`	Default foreground color outside the login window
`Background`	Default background color outside the login window

Configure Display Managers for Use by X-Stations

The title, which is verbatim from the LPIC-1 objectives, specifies a configuration that remote stations can access. Remote access may require three levels of configuration changes. First, to enable access through the XDMCP (X Display Manager Control Protocol) protocol, comment out the following line by adding a bang (!) in front, as shown here:

```
!DisplayManager.requestPort:    0
```

Next, this file defers to the `Xaccess` file, also in the `/etc/X11/xdm/` directory. As with the KDM display manager, you need to make sure the following directives are active:

```
*                       #any host can get a login window
*    CHOOSER BROADCAST  #any indirect host can get a chooser
```

The third group of configuration changes relate to any firewalls that may currently exist on the local system. As shown in `/etc/services` (per Chapter 13), the default TCP/IP port for the XDMCP protocol is 177. Any firewall that blocks access to this port prevents remote access to the XDM display manager.

Accessibility Options

Linux incorporates several options that are intended to help disabled users. As suggested in the LPIC-1 objectives, you need to "demonstrate knowledge and awareness of accessibility technologies." The objectives include a whole list of technologies. Their weight in the objectives is 1; in other words, you can expect to see an average of one question on LPI exam 102 on this topic. Although the descriptions in this section may seem less than complete, they go as far as needed for the LPIC-1 objectives.

This section divides current Linux accessibility technologies into three sections: keyboards, text readers, and more provisions.

Keyboards

Several keyboard accessibility options are available for Linux. Some provide custom keyboard behavior. Others provide a keyboard on-screen for mouse input and more.

AccessX is a group of keyboard options that can make life easier in certain situations. If you want to follow along with a GUI tool, open a tool named Keyboard Preferences or Keyboard Accessibility Preferences with a command like gnome-accessibility-keyboard-properties or gnome-keyboard-properties. AccessX keyboard options include the following:

◆ When **sticky keys** are enabled, you don't have to press multiple keys simultaneously. You can press Shift, release the key, press the number 7 key, and get the ampersand (&).

◆ **Repeat keys** support configuration of a delay and repeat rate. In other words, you can press a key for a certain number of milliseconds before it repeats. But once repeating keys start, it continues to repeat at some rate per second.

◆ **Slow keys** allow you to change the amount of time needed to press a key before it's accepted. However, this may slow you down if you're a fast typist.

◆ **Bounce keys** prevent "stuttering" on the keyboard. Turning this feature on ignores a second press of the same key within a given number of milliseconds.

◆ **Toggle keys** enable a beep when a keyboard feature is enabled or disabled, such as Caps Lock.

◆ When **mouse keys** are enabled, you can use the numbers on a numeric keypad to move a mouse pointer in a GUI. The numbers correspond to the movement; for example, the number 1 moves the pointer to the lower left; the number 6 moves the pointer directly right.

One option over and above the **AccessX** keyboard settings is **GOK (GNOME on-screen keyboard)**, which you can start in a GUI with the gok command. It opens the GOK main menu shown in Figure 10.2. If you click Compose from this menu, it opens an on-screen keyboard that can be run with mouse clicks. But it does more, because it supports assisted actions to launch programs, manage GUI windows, and more. Figure 10.2 includes an obscured view of GOK preferences.

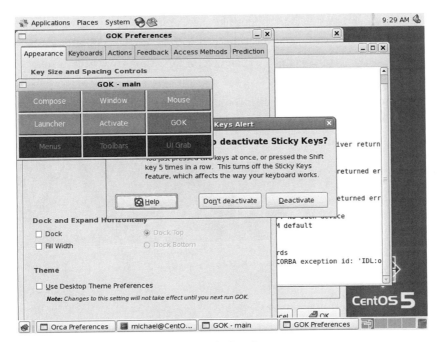

FIGURE 10.2 *The GNOME on-screen keyboard.*

Text Readers

Orca is an open source **screen reader** project that is part of the GNOME desktop environment. It includes provisions for text to speech, **braille display**, and **screen magnifiers**.

The **emacspeak** application includes a text-to-speech option for the emacs text editor. It provides audible spoken feedback for input into emacs.

More Provisions for Sight-Impaired Users

You can customize Linux desktops with appropriate themes for sight-impaired users. High-contrast themes provide color variations that are easier to see. Fonts for each element in a GUI desktop can be made as large as needed. Many of these options can be configured through the GNOME Appearance Preferences tool. For the KDE desktop environment, many of these options can be configured through the KDE Control Center or System Settings tools. Some options, based on the list shown in the LPIC-1 objectives, are shown here:

◆ **High-contrast** themes are available, which provide a more easily visible color contrast. However, such themes may not be aesthetically pleasing to some people. Of course, you can also customize contrasting colors on the desktop.

◆ **Large print** themes can be set for applications, documents, the desktop environment, window titles, and fixed width fonts.

◆ **Visual settings** include options like the Compiz compositing window manager.

◆ **Visual themes** are generally associated with individual applications.

◆ **Assistive technology** is the generic term for settings that help the disabled use computers.

Assistive technologies are also being incorporated into login screens. Figure 10.3 illustrates the Universal Access Preferences options available in the Fedora 10 GDM display manager login screen.

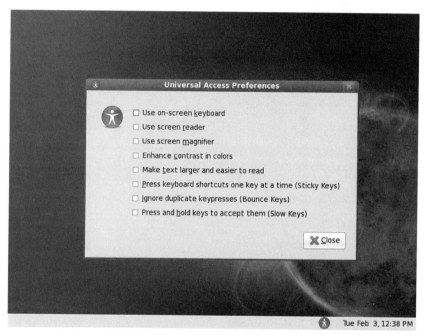

FIGURE 10.3 *Universal Access Preferences for the GDM display manager.*

Chapter Summary

This chapter provided an overview of the Linux GUI, limited to configuration tools and options common to the variety of available Linux distributions. The Linux GUI is organized in a client-server format, where the server is local, and client applications can be located on local or remote systems.

Three display manager options are available: the GDM display manager, the KDE display manager, and the XDM display manager. Each of these options can be configured with customized greetings and remote access. Of course, you shouldn't enable more than one display manager at a time.

A variety of accessibility technologies are available for Linux. The AccessX keyboard options support settings that range from sticky keys to bounce keys and even mouse control keys. Orca and emacspeak are available text-to-speech screen readers. Additional themes are available for high contrast, larger fonts, visual settings such as the Compiz window manager and more.

Key Terms

- ◆ **AccessX.** A group of keyboard options including sticky keys, repeat keys, slow keys, bounce keys, toggle keys, and mouse keys.
- ◆ **assistive technology.** The generic term for Linux settings that help the disabled use computers.
- ◆ **bounce keys.** A setting that ignores a second press of the same key within a given number of milliseconds.
- ◆ **braille display.** A display in braille format.
- ◆ **DISPLAY.** An environment variable that specifies a GUI display terminal.
- ◆ **emacspeak.** An application that incorporates text-to-speech features in the emacs text editor.
- ◆ **/etc/gdm/.** The directory with GDM display manager configuration files.
- ◆ **/etc/gdm/gdm.conf.** The main GDM display manager configuration file.
- ◆ **/etc/inittab.** The configuration file with boot settings, which may include access to a GUI display manager.
- ◆ **/etc/X11/xdm/.** The directory with XDM display manager configuration files.
- ◆ **/etc/X11/xorg.conf.** The configuration file for the X server.
- ◆ **GDM.** The GNOME display manager for graphical logins, also known as the GDM display manager.
- ◆ **GOK.** The GNOME on-screen keyboard that supports mouse actions to open programs, manage GUI windows, and more.
- ◆ **high contrast.** A term associated with GUI themes for disabled users.
- ◆ **InputDevice.** An X server configuration directive associated with keyboards and pointing devices.
- ◆ **KDM.** The KDE display manager for graphical logins, also known as the KDM display manager.
- ◆ **kdmrc.** The main KDM display manager configuration file; remote access can be configured in this file.
- ◆ **large print.** A term associated with GUI font sizes for disabled users.
- ◆ **Monitor.** An X server configuration directive associated with monitors.
- ◆ **mouse keys.** A setting that enables mouse pointer control through the numeric keypad.

- **on-screen keyboard.** A reference to keyboards such as GOK, which can be controlled with a mouse.

- **Orca.** An open-source screen reader project; the associated software includes text-to-speech, braille display, and screen magnifiers.

- **repeat keys.** A setting that configures a delay and repeat rate for a pressed key on a keyboard.

- **screen magnifier.** A reference to visual aids such as Orca, which magnify the view of a GUI screen.

- **screen reader.** A reference to text-to-speech software.

- `ServerLayout`. An X server configuration directive that encompasses other settings.

- **slow keys.** A setting that configures a delay before a pressed key on a keyboard is accepted.

- **sticky keys.** A setting that can help users avoid pressing key combinations simultaneously.

- **toggle keys.** A setting that enables a beep when a keyboard feature such as Caps Lock is enabled or disabled.

- **visual settings.** GUI options such as the Compiz window manager.

- **visual themes.** Visual settings most commonly associated with individual applications.

- `X`. A command that may be linked to `Xorg`; also a reference to the X server.

- **X11.** A reference to the X server.

- `Xaccess`. A configuration file that can allow remote access to the KDM and XDM display managers.

- **XDM.** The X display manager for graphical logins, also known as the XDM display manager.

- **XDMCP.** A network protocol associated with remote access to display managers.

- `xdm-config`. The main configuration for the XDM display manager.

- `xdpyinfo`. A command that can find more about the capabilities of a configured X server.

- **X Font Server.** The font server required for X server operation.

- `xhost`. A command that can enable remote access to X client applications.

- `xwininfo`. A command that can provide more information on an existing GUI window.

- **X.org.** The organization behind the Linux X server.

- `Xorg`. A command that can start the X server; it can also detect installed hardware and create a proposed configuration file.

- `Xresources`. A file that configures the greeting and color for the XDM display manager.

- `Xservers`. A file that specifies color depth for the XDM window manager.

Review Questions

The number of review questions in this chapter and other chapters in this book is proportionate to each section's weight in the LPI objectives. Because this chapter covers items 106.1, 106.2, and 106.3, the weight is 5; therefore, you'll see 10 questions in this section. You'll see multiple choice single answer, fill-in-the blank, and multiple choice multiple answer questions, as you'll encounter on the exam.

1. Enter the command that creates a proposed configuration file for the X server in the local directory.

   _____

2. Which of the following hardware components in the /etc/X11/xorg.conf configuration file may be associated with an InputDevice stanza? Choose two.

   A. Trackball

   B. Monitor

   C. Keyboard

   D. Graphics card

3. Which of the following commands creates an index of X font files in a directory?

   A. mkfontdir

   B. mkfont

   C. fontconfig

   D. make font

4. Which of the following commands starts a GUI in the eighth virtual console?

   A. startx -- :0

   B. startx -- :1

   C. startx -- :2

   D. startx -- :8

5. Enter the configuration file for the KDE display manager for KDE version 4. Do not include the directory path to that file. _____

6. Which of the following is the port number associated with the XDMCP protocol?

   A. 25

   B. 80

   C. 177

   D. 443

7. Which of the following files is associated with configuring remote access to both the KDM and XDM display managers?

   A. Xaccess

   B. Xwilling

   C. Xresources

   D. Xservers

8. Which of the following is the main configuration file for the XDM display manager?

   A. xorg.conf

   B. xdm-config

   C. xdmrc

   D. Xaccess

9. Which of the following features is associated with mouse keys with respect to keyboard accessibility options?

   A. Mouse-based input to a keyboard

   B. Keyboard-based input to the command line

   C. On-screen readers

   D. Keyboard-based input to a mouse

10. Which of the following options is the GNOME solution for keyboard control by a mouse?

   A. Mouse keys

   B. GOK

   C. Screen readers

   D. Bounce keys

Chapter 11

Administrative Tasks

After completing this chapter, you will be able to

- Manage local users and groups

- Work with the `cron` and `at` daemons

- Configure locales and languages

Introduction

This chapter deals with several administrative skills fundamental even to Linux power users. The configuration and management of local users and groups is important in a multiuser operating system. These skills can help you regulate access to key tools as well as help the right groups of users work together.

Linux includes two daemons designed to help run jobs on a scheduled basis. The `cron` daemon can help users run jobs regularly. The `at` daemon can help users run jobs on a one-time basis. Access to these tools can be regulated by user.

Because even two related office networks may reside in different time zones, you need to understand the basics of clock management. Multilingual enterprises may need to set up systems in different languages. Choosing a language is not enough, because there are variations in keyboards, dictionaries, and more even within a single language.

Although you may already be familiar with many of the skills in this chapter, learn them in detail. The objectives covered in this chapter have a value of 12 (out of 60 for LPI 102). In other words, expect to see the topics covered in this chapter in approximately 20% of the questions in the LPI 102 exam.

 TIP

This chapter addresses three objectives in the LPI exam: 107.1 ("Manage User and Group Accounts and Related System Files"), 107.2 ("Automate System Administration Tasks by Scheduling Jobs"), and 107.3 ("Localisation and Internationalisation"). Yes, the spelling of the title of item 107.3 in the LPIC-1 objectives is in British English.

Local Users and Groups

User and group management is a fundamental skill. Although the LPIC-1 objectives require that you know this objective in depth, the objective is limited to local users and groups. In other words, you do not need to know about networked user authentication databases such as LDAP (Lightweight Directory Access Protocol) or NIS (Network Information Service).

This section starts with a detailed analysis of the files of the **shadow password suite**. It continues with a discussion on how you can configure and add users and groups. Finally, it concludes with a related discussion on how you can manage users and groups in the authentication database.

The Shadow Password Suite

The shadow password suite includes four files: /etc/passwd, /etc/group, /etc/shadow, and /etc/gshadow. Taken together, these files are the components of the local Linux password authentication database, known as the shadow password suite.

Older versions of Linux did not have the benefits of the shadow password suite. The /etc/passwd and /etc/group files are readable by all users. Without the shadow password suite, passwords are readable from these files. Encrypted passwords in these files can be cracked.

With the shadow password suite, passwords were moved to the /etc/shadow and /etc/gshadow files, readable only by the root administrative user, and in some cases by members of the group named shadow.

The following sections describe in detail the files of the shadow password suite. Yes, you can revise individual settings using text editors. You'll also need to know how to modify each of the settings in these files using the commands described here.

/etc/passwd and Users

Before creating a user, it's helpful to review the /etc/passwd configuration file. By default, it includes seven bits of information about a user, as described in Table 11.1.

Table 11.1 Information in /etc/passwd

Column	Description
1	Username
2	Password
3	UID (user ID number)
4	GID (group ID number)
5	User information
6	Home directory
7	Login shell

You may see several things in the password column. If the column is blank, no password is required to log into the account. If there's a seemingly random bunch of letters, numbers, and punctuation, that's the password in encrypted format. If this column has an asterisk (*), the account is disabled. If this column has an x, it refers to the /etc/shadow file for more password information.

The user information column can contain more information on the user, in human-readable format.

NOTE

When the Linux kernel 2.6 was released, the effective limit on UID and GID numbers was raised from about 65,000 (2^{16}) to more than 4 billion (2^{32}). The limit was actually raised earlier, but its use was effectively stopped by a different issue beyond the scope of the LPIC-1 objectives.

/etc/group and Groups

The /etc/group configuration file includes four bits of information about a group, as described in Table 11.2.

Table 11.2 Information in /etc/group

Column	Description
1	Group name
2	Password
3	GID
4	Group members

You may see several things in the password column. If the column is blank, no password is required for the group account. If there's a seemingly random bunch of letters, numbers, and punctuation, that's the group password in encrypted format. If this column has an x, it refers to the /etc/gshadow file for more password information.

 NOTE

A group password allows a user to temporarily gain privileges as if he were a member of that group. Alternatively, the administrator could just make that user a member of the target group.

/etc/shadow and Users

The /etc/shadow configuration file includes eight bits of information about a user, as described in Table 11.3.

The information in /etc/shadow is not used unless there's an x in the password column in the /etc/passwd configuration file.

Table 11.3 Information in /etc/shadow

Column	Description
1	Username
2	Password, normally in encrypted format
3	Time since the last password change, in number of days after January 1, 1970
4	Minimum password lifetime; if greater than zero, the password can't be changed for this number of days
5	Maximum password lifetime; normally set to 99999 days, which corresponds to about 275 years
6	Warn period; users are warned this number of days before the maximum password lifetime
7	Inactivity time; an account is made inactive this number of days after a password expires
8	Time the account will be disabled, in a number of days after January 1, 1970

You may see several things in the password column. If there's a seemingly random bunch of letters, numbers, and punctuation, that's the password in encrypted format. If this column has a bang (!) or an asterisk (*), regular users won't be able to log into that account.

The observant among you might have noticed eight colons (:), which means that /etc/shadow has provisions for nine columns. However, that ninth column isn't currently in use.

/etc/gshadow and Groups

The /etc/gshadow configuration file includes four bits of information about a group, as described in Table 11.4.

Table 11.4 Information in /etc/group

Column	Description
1	Group name
2	Password
3	GID
4	Group members

You may see several things in the password column. If the column is blank, no password is required for the group account. If there's a seemingly random bunch of letters, numbers, and punctuation, that's the group password in encrypted format. If this column has an x, it refers to the /etc/gshadow file for more password information.

Add and Delete Users

You can add, delete, or modify users in the shadow password suite. In this section, you'll see how to make appropriate changes in the related files with the **useradd**, **userdel**, and **usermod** commands. Unless specifically configured otherwise, new users require a password, which can be changed with the **passwd** command. Finally, you'll see how to set up a limited account for a specialized purpose.

Add a User with useradd

Now examine what happens when you add a user. For example, review what happens when you add a user named katie.

```
# useradd katie
```

This command adds appropriate entries to the /etc/passwd configuration file, including the username, UID, GID, home directory, and default shell, such as that shown here:

```
katie:x:502:502::/home/katie:/bin/bash
```

It also adds information to the other files of the shadow password suite. But before addressing such files, examine the useradd command in more detail, as shown in Table 11.5. As you learn these commands, you'll see common switches with related commands. Some of the descriptions of other commands that follow may seem repetitive, but repetition is an effective way to learn new things.

Table 11.5 useradd Command Switches (Also Works for usermod)

Switch	Description
-c *comment*	Add comment information for the /etc/passwd user information field; multiple words should be in quotes
-d */path/to/dir*	Specify a nondefault home directory
-e *YYYY-MM-DD*	Set an expiration date for the account, in numeric year (*YYYY*), month (*MM*), and date (*DD*); it's translated into a number of days after January 1, 1970 and included in the eighth column of the /etc/shadow file
-f *num*	Assign a number of days between password expiration and when the account is to be disabled
-g *GID*	Assign a nondefault initial group by GID number

Table 11.5 Continued

Switch	Description
-G *groupa,groupb*	Specify additional groups by name
-m	Create a home directory, based on the username (default for Red Hat systems)
-s */path/to/shell*	Specify a login shell, such as /bin/bash
-u *UID*	Assign a nondefault initial UID number

As you read Table 11.5, try some of the switches with a new user. Observe the result. What does the command create in the files of the shadow password suite? Is the result what you expect? What command would you run if the home directory wasn't created (as is the default on Ubuntu systems)?

Delete a User with userdel

If you want to try another useradd command, you can delete the settings for the newly created user with the following userdel command:

```
$ userdel -r newuser
```

The userdel -r command deletes the account as well as the home directory for the new user, if it was created. As it deletes the user account information from the password authentication database, other switches are not required.

Modify a Current Account with usermod

The usermod command uses many of the same switches as the useradd command. In other words, if you want to change many of the characteristics of a user account, you can use the switches described in Table 11.5. The usermod command includes additional switches, as described in Table 11.6.

Table 11.6 Extra usermod Switches

Switch	Description
-aG *groupname*	Add the user to the specified group name; without the -a, all desired groups have to be listed
-l *newusername*	Change to the specified new username
-L	Disable the user's password
-U	Re-enable the user's password

To see the importance of the -aG switch, review the following output of the following groups command:

```
$ groups michael
michael adm dialout cdrom floppy audio dip video plugdev fuse lpadmin admin vboxusers
sambashare
```

If you wanted to add the backup group to the list of user michael's group memberships, you could run the following command:

```
# usermod -G
adm,dialout,cdrom,floppy,audio,dip,video,plugdev,fuse,lpadmin,admin,vboxusers,sambashare,
backup michael
```

But that's cumbersome. It's a lot easier to just add the backup group as follows:

```
# usermod -aG backup michael
```

Assign a Password

Every user should have a password. Fortunately, they're easy for administrators to assign. If you've just set up a new account for user garcia, you could assign that user a password with the following command:

```
# passwd garcia
New UNIX password:

Retype new UNIX password:
```

As shown, the passwd command prompts you to enter a password twice. You can then tell user garcia about the new password and advise him to log in and change it with the passwd command. Every user is allowed to change his own password with the passwd command.

An Example New User

One related task from the LPIC-1 objectives is to "create and manage special-purpose and limited accounts." As an example, assume you've accidentally deleted the user associated with UID 65534. It's a nobody account commonly used on NFS server systems.

The information as shown on a CentOS 5 system on the /etc/passwd file is as follows:

```
nfsnobody:x:65534:65534:Anonymous NFS User:/var/lib/nfs:/sbin/nologin
```

Assuming that the group account still exists, you can re-create this information with the following command. Although the full path to the useradd command is not required if /usr/sbin is in your PATH, the full path is required to any other directories.

```
# useradd -u 65534 -g 65534 -c "Anonymous NFS User" -d /var/lib/nfs -s /sbin/nologin
nfsnobody
```

The previous command leads to the following error message, because the /var/lib/nfs directory already exists. But it's not a fatal error, and it's necessary to include the /var/lib/nfs directory in the command to make sure that's set as the home directory for the nfsnobody user.

```
useradd: warning: the home directory already exists.
Not copying any file from skel directory into it
```

Note how the command specifies the UID, GID, user information, home directory, and default shell, in order. To verify, cross-check the switches against those shown in Table 11.5. If you make a mistake, substitute the usermod command. It can be used to change the noted information for existing users, based on the same command switches as found with the useradd command.

If the group doesn't exist, the user won't be created. In that case, you'd need to use the **groupadd** command, discussed next.

Add, Delete, and Modify Groups

Examine what happens when you add a group. For example, review what happens when you add a group named project.

```
# groupadd project
```

This command adds appropriate entries to the /etc/group configuration file, including the groupname and GID, such as shown here:

```
project:x:503:
```

By default, this assigns the next available GID. But because most systems specify the same UID and GID numbers to new users, this can cause problems. Generally, regular group IDs should not be assigned among those numbers reserved for services such as the Apache Web server. Depending on the distribution, the reserved range starts at 0 and ends at 100, 500, or 1000.

In addition, some versions of the Samba file server assign a range of GIDs for group members who connect from Microsoft systems.

For these reasons, many administrators prefer to assign an arbitrary GID, usually much higher than the range of standard users. The groupadd -g GID *groupname* command makes that possible. First, delete the project group with the following command:

```
# groupdel project
```

Now create the project group and assign it a GID of 50000 with the following command:

```
# groupadd -g 50000 project
```

You could have skipped a step with the help of the **groupmod** command, which uses the same -g switch. So instead of deleting and adding again as shown here, you could have run the following command:

```
# groupmod -g 50000 project
```

Two command-line methods are available to add users to the newly created group. The aforementioned usermod command, with the -G switch, adds existing users. If the target user is already a part of another group, I recommend using the -aG switch. Otherwise, you have to specify every desired group for that new user.

Alternatively, you can open the /etc/group and /etc/gshadow files in a text editor and add the usernames of desired users to the end of the line of the target group.

Manage Account Information

The LPIC-1 objectives also suggest that you need to know how to suspend and change user accounts. Some change capabilities were just documented with the usermod and groupmod commands. Additional management is possible with the **chage** command.

Suspend and Restore a User Account with usermod

You can disable and re-enable an account with the usermod -L and usermod -U commands. The -L and -U stand for lock and unlock, respectively.

For example, assume that user donna goes on vacation, and you don't want her working remotely. You can disable logins to her account with the following command:

```
# usermod -L donna
```

When user donna returns from vacation, you can re-enable her account with the following command:

```
# usermod -U donna
```

Depending on the distribution, you may also need to reset user donna's password.

Change Password Aging Information with chage

One more useful command is chage, which you can use to change aging information for user passwords. As described earlier in the discussion of the /etc/shadow configuration file, there are a number of data points on when accounts and passwords can be set to change, be made inactive, or expire.

To see the current password status for your account, run the chage -l command. With administrative permissions, you can also review the password status of other users. Important options for the chage command are shown in Table 11.7. Although chage has some similarities with useradd, the switches for the most part are different.

Table 11.7 Major chage Command Switches

Switch	Description
-d *YYYY-MM-DD*	Set the date for when the password was last changed; it can be in numeric year (*YYYY*), month (*MM*), and date (*DD*) format, or the number of days after January 1, 1970. It does not have to correspond to the actual date when the password was last changed.
-E *YYYY-MM-DD*	Set an expiration date for the account, in numeric year (*YYYY*), month (*MM*), and date (*DD*) format, or the number of days after January 1, 1970.
-I *num*	Configure a number of days between password expiration and when the account is to be disabled; if *num*=−1, the account is made active.
-l *user*	Inspect the current password settings for the *user*'s account.
-M *num*	Set the minimum number of days that a user must keep the current password to *num*.
-W *num*	Set the number of days (*num*) when a user is warned, before that user's password is set to expire.

Job Schedulers

Linux can be configured to run jobs on a regular or scheduled basis. The cron daemon can be used to run jobs at regular intervals. Administrators can set up cron jobs for administrative purposes. In fact, current Linux distributions include several preconfigured cron jobs.

But most cron jobs are, by default, scheduled to run in the middle of the night. The **anacron** service helps keep cron working, even after a system is powered up at the start of a regular workday.

Sometimes users and administrators just need to run a single job at a certain time. For example, database jobs can severely overload a system and should be run at a time of lower use, such as when no users or administrative jobs are scheduled.

The cron Daemon

As defined in its man page, the cron daemon is designed to execute scheduled commands. Two levels of cron jobs are available. The first level is based on preconfigured jobs in the /etc/crontab configuration file. The second level is based on jobs configured by individual users, courtesy of the **crontab -e** command.

Regular cron Jobs

Regular cron jobs are configured through the /etc/crontab configuration file. It includes several basic environment variables, as described in Chapter 9, "Shells, Scripting, and Data Management." It configures how cron jobs are run from several basic directories. The meat of the CentOS 5 /etc/crontab file is shown here:

```
01 * * * * root run-parts /etc/cron.hourly
02 4 * * * root run-parts /etc/cron.daily
22 4 * * 0 root run-parts /etc/cron.weekly
42 4 1 * * root run-parts /etc/cron.monthly
```

The run-parts command in each line runs the scripts in the directories that follow. Each line lists the root administrative user as the authority for each script to be run. The scripts that are shown are descriptive; for example, scripts in the /etc/cron.hourly directory are to be run on an hourly basis.

But the timing depends on the data in the first five columns, as described in Table 11.8.

Table 11.8 Time and the cron Daemon

Column	Description
1	Minute; can range between 0 and 59
2	Hour; can range between 0 and 23, where 0 is midnight and 23 is 11 p.m.
3	Day of month; can range between 1 and 31
4	Month; can range between 1 and 12, or substitute the first three letters of the month
5	Day of week; can range between 0 and 7, where 0 and 7 is Sunday; or substitute the first three letters of the day
6	Command

An asterisk in any column means the job is run every available time based on that column. For example, if there's an asterisk in the fifth column, the job may be run any day of the week.

So based on the /etc/crontab configuration shown for the CentOS 5 system, hourly jobs are run one minute after every hour. Daily jobs are run at 4:02 a.m. Weekly jobs are run at 4:22 a.m., every Sunday. Monthly jobs are run at 4:42 a.m., on the first day of every month.

Don't define too many time-based columns; otherwise, the job in question may not run when you want it to. For example, the following job runs the ls command at 2:01 a.m. on the third of April, but only when that day falls on a Friday.

```
1 2 3 4 5 /bin/ls
```

There are other ways to define the timing of a job. For example, the following line runs the noted job at 1, 5, and 43 minutes past every hour.

```
01,05,43 * * * * /home/michael/adminjob
```

Alternatively, the following line runs the noted job every third hour, at 5 minutes past the hour:

```
05 */3 * * * /home/michael/adminjob
```

Think of other iterations, and understand how to interpret them. For example, the following line runs jobs every Saturday and Sunday, every third hour, at 5 minutes past the hour:

```
05 */3 * * sat,sun /home/michael/adminjob
```

Alternatively, the following line would run jobs every weekday, at 1:05 p.m.:

```
05 1 * * 1-5 /home/michael/adminjob
```

The actual jobs are listed in the noted directories, starting with /etc/cron.hourly/. Some of these jobs were analyzed in Chapter 9.

The list of hourly, daily, weekly, and monthly jobs leaves out one standard cron directory, **/etc/cron.d**. Because jobs in that directory aren't scheduled in the /etc/crontab file, scripts in this directory require their own schedule.

User cron Jobs

One value of the administrative cron jobs just described is as a model for user-based cron jobs. Scientists, engineers, and other users may need to crunch data periodically. They may not want to burden their workstations when they have other tasks for their computers.

Authorized users can set up their own cron jobs with the crontab -e command, which opens a text editor. Once created, individual cron jobs are saved in files named after usernames in the **/var/spool/cron** directory.

For example, a user who has configured a daily job to tabulate census data with the /home/donna/censusdata script may set up the following information in her crontab file:

```
SHELL=/bin/bash
MAILTO=donna
01 23 * * * /home/donna/censusdata
```

These directives run the /home/donna/censusdata script at 11:23 p.m. every day. To configure access by regular users to both the cron and at daemons, read the "Denying and Allowing" section later in this chapter.

The anacron Service

Many administrators have to work in environments where systems are powered down at night. Perhaps you don't want to run such jobs on a laptop system while it's running on battery power. If you work under such limits, you can change the timing of cron jobs. The anacron service can help.

When the anacron service is installed, it normally doesn't run except just after Linux completes the boot process. Of course, administrators can start or restart the service with the /etc/init.d/anacron script.

As you can see from this excerpt of the Ubuntu Hardy Heron version of the /etc/crontab configuration file, the anacron service is built into standard cron jobs. (Yes, these are three lines that are wrapped.)

```
25 6    * * *    root    test -x /usr/sbin/anacron || ( cd / && run-parts --report
/etc/cron.daily )
47 6    * * 7    root    test -x /usr/sbin/anacron || ( cd / && run-parts --report
/etc/cron.weekly )
52 6    1 * *    root    test -x /usr/sbin/anacron || ( cd / && run-parts --report
/etc/cron.monthly )
```

If the /usr/sbin/anacron file exists, the job is taken by that service, as configured in the /etc/anacrontab configuration file. Otherwise, the cron service runs the jobs in the noted directories.

The anacron service is configured in the **/etc/anacrontab** configuration file. The Ubuntu Hardy Heron version of that file includes the following directives:

```
SHELL=/bin/sh
PATH=/usr/local/sbin:/usr/local/bin:/sbin:/bin:/usr/sbin:/usr/bin
# These replace cron's entries
1    5      cron.daily    nice run-parts --report /etc/cron.daily
7    10     cron.weekly   nice run-parts --report /etc/cron.weekly
@monthly    15    cron.monthly nice run-parts --report /etc/cron.monthly
```

The first two lines are standard environment variables that specify the SHELL and PATH variables. The columns specified from left to right are shown in Table 11.9.

Table 11.9 Options and the anacron Daemon

Column	Description
1	Period, in days
2	Delay, in minutes
3	/etc/ subdirectory scripts
4	Command

For example, the anacron service checks to see if scripts in the /etc/cron.weekly directory have been run in the past seven days. If not, those weekly scripts are run with the given command, 10 minutes after the anacron service was started.

The last line specifies how anacron runs with respect to jobs in the /etc/cron.monthly directory. The @monthly is needed because the number of days in a month is variable. As of this writing, there is no similar option for weekly or daily jobs.

The at Daemon

Sometimes users and administrators need to run a job on a one-time basis. Just as with many cron jobs, such one-time jobs can easily overload a system. That is the reason for the at daemon, which is designed to run a command or script at a specified time. Be aware: related commands include **atq** for system queues and **atrm** to remove queued jobs.

As such, there are no standard at system jobs. Once created, user at jobs are stored in a /var/spool/ subdirectory. As an example, assume that you're a user named scientist who wants to start the lab job from your home directory in five hours. You've already created a working script named lab and made it executable. To run that job using the at daemon, take the following steps:

1. Run the at now + 5 hours command. It opens the following prompt:

   at>

2. At the noted prompt, type in the full path to the desired script, as shown in bold:

   at> **/home/scientist/lab**

3. Press Ctrl+D to exit from the at> prompt and return to the regular command-line prompt.

4. Confirm the new job with the following command:

   $ atq

5. Review the output. The job just created should be shown as follows, which displays at job 1, which will be run on April 9, 2009, at 2:42 p.m. by user scientist.

   1 2009-04-09 14:42 a scientist

From these steps, the key to controlling the at service is the first command, where the time the job is to be run is specified. Other sample commands are shown in Table 11.10.

The teatime may seem like a strange reference, at least to users outside of the British Commonwealth, as it is specifically associated with 4 p.m.

It's easy to cancel an at job. Run the atq command, identify the job number in the left column, and run the atrm command with the job number. If the aforementioned user scientist wanted to cancel his job, he'd run the atrm 1 command.

Unlike the cron daemon, the at daemon is accessible to all users by default. But you can change defaults to both services, as is described next.

Table 11.10 at Command Samples

Sample Command	Description
at now + 5 minutes	Start the job configured at the at> prompt in 5 minutes
at now + 10 hours	Start the job configured at the at> prompt in 10 hours
at now + 2 days	Start the job configured at the at> prompt in 48 hours
at now + 1 week	Start the job configured at the at> prompt in 7 days
at **teatime**	Start the job configured at the at> prompt at 4 p.m.
at 15:00 7/13/09	Start the job configured at the at> prompt at 3 p.m. on July 13, 2009

Denying and Allowing

Access to cron and at can be regulated with the /etc/cron.allow, /etc/cron.deny, /etc/at.allow, and /etc/at.deny configuration files. These file names are intuitive; for example, users listed in the /etc/cron.allow file are allowed to create their own cron jobs.

 NOTE

Access to the cron and at daemons may also be regulated by PAM (Pluggable Authentication Modules), which is beyond the scope of the LPIC-1 objectives.

However, a specific protocol is associated with these files. By default, only the /etc/at.deny file exists. Some Linux documentation suggests that cron jobs can only be run by administrative users by default. Such jobs are accessible to regular users if the /etc/cron.deny file exists and does not include the names of target users.

If a user is listed in /etc/cron.allow, it doesn't matter if that user is listed in /etc/cron.deny. That user is allowed to create her own cron jobs. Of course, if a user is listed only in /etc/cron.deny, she gets an error message when she tries to run the crontab -e command:

```
You (donna) are not allowed to use this program (crontab)
See crontab(1) for more information
```

If neither /etc/cron.allow nor /etc/cron.deny exists, access is normally limited to the root administrative user. The exception is on Debian-based systems such as Ubuntu, where access is allowed to all users.

/etc/at.deny exists by default on our selected distributions. If your username is not listed in this file, you can use at. If the /etc/at.deny file were deleted, access to the at daemon would be denied to all but the root administrative user—assuming /etc/at.allow doesn't exist.

If a user is listed in the /etc/at.allow and /etc/at.deny files, that user can create at jobs.

Localization and Initialization

Linux is used worldwide. Its user interfaces have been translated into a number of different languages. Even the LPI exams have been translated into several languages. As suggested by the LPIC-1 objectives, you need to know how to "localize a system in a different language than English." In this section, you'll see how to change the default language of a system to German; however, you'll just examine the key files in the process.

Localization in a language is usually not enough, especially when time zones are involved. When businesses have servers in different countries, not only should they be localized with the right language, but they should be synchronized with an appropriate time server. For more information on NTP (Network Time Protocol) services, see Chapter 12, "Essential System Services."

Current Locale

The current locale of a system goes beyond a simple expression of language. That's necessary because spelling and grammar vary between dialects such as American and British English. The current **locale** variables are revealed by the `locale` command, as shown in Figure 11.1.

```
[michael@CentOS5-LPI ~]$ locale
LANG=en_US.UTF-8
LC_CTYPE="en_US.UTF-8"
LC_NUMERIC="en_US.UTF-8"
LC_TIME="en_US.UTF-8"
LC_COLLATE="en_US.UTF-8"
LC_MONETARY="en_US.UTF-8"
LC_MESSAGES="en_US.UTF-8"
LC_PAPER="en_US.UTF-8"
LC_NAME="en_US.UTF-8"
LC_ADDRESS="en_US.UTF-8"
LC_TELEPHONE="en_US.UTF-8"
LC_MEASUREMENT="en_US.UTF-8"
LC_IDENTIFICATION="en_US.UTF-8"
LC_ALL=
[michael@CentOS5-LPI ~]$
```

FIGURE 11.1 *Language from the* `locale` *command.*

As you can see in the output, the standard locale for my system is US English (en_US), with the UTF-8 (Unicode Translation Format, 8-bit) format, which goes over and above ASCII characters. But the different options shown give you information about how to further customize the locale. These variables are described in Table 11.11.

These environment variables are normally set to the same value as the language. But you can customize individual environment variables from Table 11.11. You can do this customization for all or individual users, as described in Chapter 9.

In a script, it can help to set `LANG=C sort` as a child environment variable, which sets the language for sorting to ASCII characters. If you want ASCII ordering for a script, include the following directive in that script:

`LANG=C`

Table 11.11 Locale Environment Variables

Variable	Description
LANG	Specifies the language
LC_CTYPE	Used for character types, cases, and more
LC_NUMERIC	Sets numeric formats such as commas and decimal points
LC_TIME	Specifies time and date formats
LC_COLLATE	Configures character sequences
LC_MONETARY	Sets formats for currency (money)
LC_MESSAGES	Defines the format of affirmative and negative answers
LC_PAPER	Sets the default print size
LC_NAME	Defines the format for human names, such as last name first
LC_ADDRESS	Defines how postal addresses are formatted
LC_TELEPHONE	Configures how telephone numbers are displayed
LC_MEASUREMENT	Assigns a measurement scale such as metric or nautical
LC_IDENTIFICATION	Defines the source of the code, normally the FSF (Free Software Foundation)
LC_ALL	Supersedes all other language environment variables, so normally left blank

The directive works just as if it were any other environment variable. That variable exists just for the script. If that script calls others, you can make the variable good for all child scripts with the following command:

```
export LANG
```

Over and above UTF-8 and ASCII, other formats are available. The formats listed in the LPIC-1 objectives are shown in Table 11.12.

Table 11.12 Common Character Formats

Format	Description
UTF-8	Unicode Translation Format, using 8-bit characters; inclusive of ASCII.
ISO-8859	A standard of ISO (International Organization for Standardization (the acronym doesn't match the wording) is a standard for 8-bit character encoding. Options exist for different language types from Western European through Thai.
ASCII	American Standard Code for Information Interchange; encoding for 128 characters, which include the upper- and lowercase characters of the English alphabet.

With the `iconv` command, files can be converted from one format to another. Try the `iconv --list` command. You'll find that Linux can work with more than 1,100 code formats.

For example, the following command converts the `/etc/samba/smb.conf` configuration file from UTF-8 to ASCII format, bringing the output to the screen:

```
$ iconv -f UTF-8 -t ASCII /etc/samba/smb.conf
```

Because ASCII is a subset of UTF-8, there should be no difference in the output.

Configure a Different Language

The LPIC-1 objectives suggest that you need to know how to configure a different language for a system. Assuming the appropriate language packages are installed, you can detect them among available locales with the following command:

```
$ locale -a
```

The key configuration file varies by distribution. Because distribution-specific settings are not part of the exam, these details are included just for illustrative purposes. For Red Hat–style systems such as CentOS 5, the key file is `/etc/sysconfig/i18n`. For Debian-style systems such as Ubuntu, the key file is **`/etc/default/locale`**.

In both cases, the standard German locale, based on the German dialect (as opposed to Austrian, Swiss, or other dialects) is this:

```
LANG="de_DE.utf8"
```

After the `LANG` directive is changed in the appropriate configuration file, log out of the console and log back in. You then see German in the output, in man pages, and more. One example is shown in Figure 11.2.

```
man(1)                                                                    man(1)

NAME
        man - Formatieren und Anzeigen von Seiten des Online-Handbuches (man
        pages)
        manpath - Anzeigen des Benutzer-eigenen Suchpfades für Seiten des
        Online-Handbuches (man pages)

SYNTAX
        man [-acdfhktw] [-m system] [-p string] [-C config_file] [-M path] [-P
        pager] [-S section_list] [section] name ...

BESCHREIBUNG
          man formatiert Seiten aus dem Online-Handbuch und zeigt diese an.
          Diese Version unterstützt die MANPATH und (MAN)PAGER Umgebungsvari-
          ablen, so daß Sie ihre eigenen man pages verwenden können und selbst
          wählen können, welches Programm die formatierten Seiten anzeigen soll.
          Wenn der Parameter section angegeben wird, so sucht man nur in dieser
          Sektion des Handbuchs. Sie können auch mit Hilfe von Kommando-Zeilen-
          Optionen oder Umgebungsvariablen die Reihenfolge angeben, in der die
          Sektionen nach Einträgen durchsucht werden und welche zusätzlichen Pro-
          gramme die Quelltexte bearbeiten sollen. Wenn der Parameter name das
:
```

FIGURE 11.2 *Language changes appear after the next login.*

However, translations may not be complete; for example, you may not find all man pages in a desired language other than English.

Time Zone Management

Just as it helps to customize language for different locations, it's important to customize the time zone as needed. Although the standard time zone configuration file varies by distribution, the **/etc/timezone** configuration is the standard explicitly listed in the LPIC-1 objectives. The corresponding file for CentOS 5 and similar Red Hat–based distributions is /etc/sysconfig/clock. In either case, the content of this file is simple, a line such as

```
America/Los_Angeles
```

This information comes from files in the **/usr/share/zoneinfo** directory. Explore around this directory. You might find common time zones listed as subdirectories, such as Europe/Paris, Asia/Shanghai, Africa/Cairo, and yes, America/Los_Angeles.

The selected time zone file is copied to the **/etc/localtime** configuration file. Although it's a binary file, you should be able to confirm the analysis. For example, if you're in the London time zone, try the following command:

```
$ diff /etc/localtime /usr/share/zoneinfo/Europe/London
```

The diff command displays any differences between two files. If the files are identical, there's no output.

As for time configuration, the **tzselect** command is the current standard command-line configuration tool. It's the successor to **tzconfig**. As shown in Figure 11.3, it provides prompts that can help you reconfigure the time zone for the local system.

```
michael@UbuntuHH:~$ tzselect
Please identify a location so that time zone rules can be set correctly.
Please select a continent or ocean.
 1) Africa
 2) Americas
 3) Antarctica
 4) Arctic Ocean
 5) Asia
 6) Atlantic Ocean
 7) Australia
 8) Europe
 9) Indian Ocean
10) Pacific Ocean
11) none - I want to specify the time zone using the Posix TZ format.
#?
```

FIGURE 11.3 *Time zones and the tzselect tool.*

The first 10 options are straightforward, if you want to identify the time zone by geographic location. The other option, based on the so-called **Posix TZ** format, allows you to define a time zone relative to GST (Greenwich Sidereal Time), which is an astronomical variant on GMT (Greenwich Mean Time), more frequently known in Linux as UTC.

NOTE

UTC is the atomic realization of GMT. Because the acronym is the result of a political compromise, it doesn't officially stand for anything.

The **TZ** variable can be set as an environment variable that specifies the time zone. It may be set to the time zone of your choice, such as America/Los_Angeles. A time zone in Posix TZ format may be expressed as something like GST+8. This number is counterintuitive, as this sets

```
TZ=GST+8
```

That actually corresponds to standard time in the America/Los_Angeles time zone, which is normally 8 hours behind GST.

NOTE

The numbers associated with the Posix TZ format are counterintuitive. For example, TZ=GST+8 is actually eight hours behind GST. In other words, GST+8 corresponds to the standard time zone on the Pacific coast of the USA. In contrast, TZ=GST-1 is one hour ahead of GST, which corresponds to the standard time zone for the western part of the European continent. Yes, it is a bizarre convention where + subtracts and - adds. But it's a matter of perspective, because GST is used by astronomers looking down on the earth, as opposed to the rest of us, who look up from the surface of the earth.

The final item from the LPIC-1 objectives in this section relates to the **date** command. When run by itself, date displays the current date, time, and time zone. You can set the date fairly precisely, in the following format:

```
$ date MMDDhhmm ccyy .ss
```

The letters that follow the date command set the date and time, as described in Table 11.13. All two-digit letter combinations shown are two-digit representations of the specified time period.

Table 11.13 Specification Options for the date Command

Option	Description
MM	Month
DD	Day of the month
hh	Hour
mm	Minute
CC	First two digits of the four-digit year
YY	Last two digits of the four-digit year
.ss	Seconds

Chapter Summary

User and group management is an important skill for any expert Linux user. To that end, you examined the files of the shadow password suite (/etc/passwd, /etc/group, /etc/shadow, /etc/gshadow), along with the purpose of each entry in the associated files. With that knowledge, you also ran commands to add, delete, and modify users and groups (useradd, userdel, usermod, groupadd, groupdel, groupmod)—ways that configured or modified the data in each of these files. You also explored the use of the chage command.

System administrative tasks can be simplified with the help of the cron and at daemons. Standard cron jobs are configured in the /etc/crontab configuration file and can be configured to run on a regular basis. The first five columns in a cron directive are, in order, minute, hour, day of the month, month, and the day of the week. In contrast, at jobs can be scheduled to run on a one-time basis. Access by regular users is regulated by users listed in the /etc/cron.allow, /etc/cron.deny, /etc/at.allow, and /etc/at.deny files. Current at jobs in the queue can be checked with the atq command and removed with the atrm command.

This chapter also described how you can configure a system with a different language and time zone. The locale command works with several LC_* environment variables for language dialect characteristics, such as numeric formats, measurement systems, and even the way names are specified. Time zones can be configured based on a specified location from the /usr/share/zoneinfo directory, such as America/LosAngeles or a TZ directive, which makes the local system relative to GST.

Key Terms

◆ **anacron.** Service designed to run `cron` jobs that have been delayed due to a system being powered down.

◆ **at.** Service that enables scheduled one-time jobs.

◆ **atq.** Command that displays `at` jobs in the current queue.

◆ **atrm.** Command that removes a specified `at` job, by number.

◆ **chage.** Command that can modify password aging information.

◆ **cron.** Service that runs jobs on a regular scheduled basis.

◆ **crontab -e.** Command that opens the current user's file for `cron` jobs.

◆ **date.** Command that lists the current date and time; can also be used to specify a new date and time.

◆ **/etc/anacrontab.** The configuration file for the `anacron` service.

◆ **/etc/cron.d.** Directory for administrative `cron` jobs not scheduled through `/etc/crontab`.

◆ **/etc/cron.daily.** Directory for administrative `cron` jobs scheduled to run on a daily basis through `/etc/crontab`.

◆ **/etc/cron.hourly.** Directory for administrative `cron` jobs scheduled to run on a hourly basis through `/etc/crontab`.

◆ **/etc/cron.monthly.** Directory for administrative `cron` jobs scheduled to run on a monthly basis through `/etc/crontab`.

◆ **/etc/cron.weekly.** Directory for administrative `cron` jobs scheduled to run on a weekly basis through `/etc/crontab`.

◆ **/etc/crontab.** The configuration file for the `cron` service.

◆ **/etc/default/locale.** Configuration file with the currently configured language.

◆ **/etc/group.** Configuration file for Linux groups; works with `/etc/gshadow`.

◆ **/etc/gshadow.** Configuration file for Linux groups; works with `/etc/group`.

◆ **/etc/localtime.** Configuration file copied from the `/usr/share/zoneinfo/` directory, which specifies the current time zone; also see `/etc/timezone`.

◆ **/etc/passwd.** Configuration file for Linux users; works with `/etc/shadow`.

◆ **/etc/shadow.** Configuration file for Linux users; works with `/etc/passwd`.

◆ **/etc/timezone.** A text configuration file with the currently configured time zone; also see `/etc/localtime`.

◆ **groupadd.** Command that adds a specified group to the shadow password suite.

◆ **groupdel.** Command that deletes a specified group to the shadow password suite.

◆ **groupmod.** Command that modifies specified group information in the shadow password suite.

◆ **iconv.** Command that converts encoding of a file from one type to another.

◆ **LANG.** Locale variable that specifies the language.

◆ **LC_ADDRESS.** Locale variable that defines how postal addresses are formatted.

◆ **LC_ALL.** Supersedes all other language environment variables, so normally left blank.

◆ **LC_COLLATE.** Locale variable that configures character sequences.

◆ **LC_CTYPE.** Locale variable used for character types, cases, and more.

◆ **LC_IDENTIFICATION.** Locale variable that defines the source of the code, normally the FSF (Free Software Foundation).

◆ **LC_MEASUREMENT.** Locale variable that assigns a measurement scale such as metric or nautical.

◆ **LC_MESSAGES.** Locale variable that defines the format of affirmative and negative answers.

◆ **LC_MONETARY.** Locale variable that sets formats for currency (money).

◆ **LC_NAME.** Locale variable that defines the format for human names, such as last name first.

◆ **LC_NUMERIC.** Locale variable that sets numeric formats such as commas and decimal points.

◆ **LC_PAPER.** Locale variable that sets the default print size.

◆ **LC_TELEPHONE.** Locale variable that configures how telephone numbers are displayed.

◆ **LC_TIME.** Locale variable that specifies time and date formats.

◆ **locale.** Command that specifies current language settings.

◆ **passwd.** Command that can change passwords.

◆ **Posix TZ.** A format for time zones based on an astronomical perspective, also used to define Linux locales with the locale command with the LC_TIME variable.

◆ **shadow password suite.** A group of files that specifies information on local users and groups in the /etc/passwd, /etc/group, /etc/shadow, and /etc/gshadow files.

◆ **teatime.** A reference to the at service term for 4 p.m.

◆ **TZ.** Environment variable associated with time zones, relative to GST. One example is TZ=GST-8, which is, counterintuitively, eight hours ahead of GST.

◆ **tzconfig.** Obsolete command-line utility to change the configured time zone.

◆ **tzselect.** Command-line utility to change the configured time zone.

◆ **useradd.** Command to add users.

◆ **userdel.** Command to delete users.

◆ **usermod.** Command that changes current user information.

◆ **/usr/share/zoneinfo.** Directory with available time zones.

◆ **/var/spool/cron.** Directory with user cron jobs. May include at jobs, depending on the distribution.

Review Questions

The number of review questions in this chapter and other chapters in this book is proportionate to each section's weight in the LPI objectives. Because this chapter covers items 107.1, 107.2, and 107.3, the weight is 12; therefore, you'll see 24 questions in this section. You'll see multiple choice single answer, fill-in-the blank, and multiple choice multiple answer questions, as you'll encounter on the exam.

1. Enter the full path to the directory that contains standard files for new user home directories.

   _____

2. Which of the following commands specifies a nonstandard home directory `/home/united` when creating new user enterprise?

   A. `useradd -h /home/united enterprise`

   B. `useradd -d /home/united enterprise`

   C. `useradd -s /home/united enterprise`

   D. `useradd -k /home/united enterprise`

3. When you see a number associated with the number of days since the password was last changed, what is that number based on?

   A. The date since the password was last changed

   B. The number of days since the password was last changed

   C. The number of days since January 1, 1970, that the password was last changed

   D. The number of days since January 1, 1969, that the password was last changed

4. Which of the following is a standard set of permissions for the `/etc/shadow` configuration file?

   A. `-rwxr-xr-x`

   B. `-r--r--r--`

   C. `-rw-r--r--`

   D. `-r--------`

5. Enter the command that creates a group named engineers with a GID of 444444. Do not include the full path to the command.

   _____

6. Which of the following commands disables account tempworker by disabling the password?

   A. usermod -L tempworker

   B. usermod -d tempworker

   C. usermod -l tempworker

   D. usermod -U tempworker

7. Which of the following bits of information is normally found in the /etc/passwd configuration file? Choose two.

   A. Password

   B. User home directory

   C. Password expiration date

   D. Default login shell

8. Which of the following commands sets an expiration date for existing user tempworker of January 1, 2010?

   A. usermod -E 01-01-2010

   B. usermod -e 2010-01-01

   C. useradd -E 2010-01-01

   D. usermod -e 14610

9. If user moviemaker is already a member of the audio, scanner, and cdrom groups, enter the simplest command to make that user also a member of the video group. Do not include the full path to the command, and assume that you already have administrative privileges.

   _____

10. Which of the following commands restores the account of user veteran, who has just come back from vacation? You've previously disabled logins to that account.

    A. usermod -U veteran

    B. usermod -D veteran

    C. usermod -E veteran

    D. usermod -L veteran

11. From the following line, at what time will the executable /home/michael/script be run?

    1 2 3 4 * /home/michael/script

   A. Thursday at 1:02 a.m. on the third day of the month

   B. April 3, at 2:01 a.m.

   C. March 4, at 1:02 a.m.

   D. Wednesday on the fourth day of the month, at 2:01 a.m.

12. Which of the following lines in a cron service configuration file runs the taxman job in the /home/users directory at 1 a.m. on April 15? Assume that the target user has appropriate permissions.

   A. 1 0 * 15 4 taxman

   B. 0 1 15 4 * taxman

   C. 1 0 * 4 15 taxman

   D. 1 0 4 * 15 taxman

13. Enter the directive in a cron configuration file that means you don't have to cite the full path to the /usr/sbin/adminjob script.

   _____

14. If the /etc/cron.deny file exists and is empty and the /etc/cron.allow file does not exist, what does that mean?

   A. Access is prohibited to all but the root user.

   B. Access is allowed to all users.

   C. It depends on standard options in the /etc/crontab configuration file.

   D. It depends on whether the user is a member of the cron group.

15. Enter the command that opens a user-specific cron configuration file. Assume the user has permissions to use the cron service.

   _____

16. Which of the following services checks for existing jobs when a Linux system is started?

   A. cron

   B. at

   C. anacron

   D. syslog

17. Enter the command that starts the at> prompt for a one-time job to be run in two weeks. Do not include the full path to the command.

   _____

18. If the /etc/at.deny and /etc/at.allow files do not exist on the local system, what does that say about allowed access?

    A. All users are allowed to access the at service.

    B. No users are allowed to access the at service.

    C. Only the root administrative user is allowed to access the at service.

    D. Access is not governed by the noted files.

19. Which of the following files is a specified location for the default language?

    A. /etc/locale

    B. /etc/default/locale

    C. /etc/language

    D. /etc/i18n

20. Which of the following files matches a file in the /usr/share/zoneinfo directory?

    A. /etc/timezone

    B. /etc/zoneinfo

    C. /etc/tz

    D. /etc/localtime

21. Enter the TZ directive that specifies a time zone 10 hours ahead of Greenwich Sidreal Time.

    _____

22. Which of the following commands lists all current language environment variables?

    A. locale -a

    B. locale -m

    C. locale -ck

    D. locale

23. Which of the following commands lists the current system time?

    A. date

    B. time

    C. system

    D. locale

24. Which of the following character sets is associated with the LANG=C directive?

    A. ISO8859

    B. ASCII

    C. UTF-8

    D. Unicode

Chapter 12

Essential System Services

After completing this chapter, you will be able to

■ Configure system time

■ Work with local and central log files

■ Understand basic characteristics of mail transfer agents

■ Manage basic print jobs

Introduction

This chapter addresses several system services. Enterprises with multiple servers need to keep their servers in sync, especially if they're located in different time zones. The Linux method uses the **NTP (Network Time Protocol)** service. Log files are controlled by the `syslogd` and `klogd` services, which you can configure locally or remotely.

Although detailed configuration of an **MTA (mail transfer agent)**, such as **sendmail**, **Exim**, **qmail**, and **Postfix**, are beyond the scope of the LPIC-1 objectives, a basic understanding of their capabilities is essential. Also, users still depend on their printers, so this chapter addresses the management of printers and print jobs. The standard for Linux printing services is **CUPS (Common UNIX Printing System)**.

TIP

This chapter addresses four objectives in the LPI exam: 108.1 ("Maintain System Time"), 108.2 ("System Logging"), 108.3 ("Mail Transfer Agent Basics"), and 108.4 ("Manage Printers and Printing").

Clock Management

The date and time on a computer may seem trivial. But when a customer buys a product that's actually out of stock because of an inaccurate clock, that's a problem. When a group of checks from a bank misses a deadline and doesn't clear for another day, that costs money. The problem may go further than an underpowered system clock battery; clocks on systems restored from some backups may be off by months.

To that end, LPIC-1 candidates are expected to understand the basics of the hardware clock, as well as NTP clients and servers. As suggested in the objectives, "candidates should be able to properly maintain the system time and synchronize the clock via NTP."

The Hardware Clock

The system clock specifies the time within Linux once the operating system has booted. The hardware clock, in contrast, is maintained by the internal hardware battery and can also be found in the BIOS menu.

The actual time on a hardware clock may vary from the time on a Linux system. Many standard installation programs include a reference to **UTC**, which is essentially equivalent to **GMT (Greenwich Mean Time)**, standard time in London, UK. When a Linux system boots, it takes the time on the hardware clock and translates it to local time based on the configured time zone. When a clock changes due to daylight savings time, Linux changes the system clock accordingly—if the hardware clock is set to UTC.

It's not always appropriate to set a hardware clock to UTC. Microsoft operating systems don't translate the time in the same way that Linux operating systems do. So many gurus recommend that users who "dual-boot" Microsoft and Linux operating systems on the same computer do *not* set the hardware clock to UTC.

Just to make things even more confusing, the date and time shown in the output to the `hwclock` command is the local time.

Hardware Clock Configuration Files

The `/etc/timezone` and `/etc/localtime` files were first discussed in Chapter 11, "Administrative Tasks." To review, the configured time zone is normally stored in the `/etc/timezone` file but may also be found in the `/etc/sysconfig/clock` file on Red Hat–based distributions, including CentOS 5. The correct time zone file in the `/etc/localtime` file is a copy of the actual binary time zone file in the `/usr/share/zoneinfo` directory.

As shown in Figure 12.1, the `/usr/share/zoneinfo` directory includes several unique time zones, as well as subdirectories for contiguous regions with multiple time zones, such as `Asia/`, `Atlantic/`, and `Canada/`.

```
[michael@CentOS5-LPI ~]$ ls /usr/share/zoneinfo/
Africa      Chile     Factory    Iceland     Mexico    posix       Universal
America     CST6CDT   GB         Indian      Mideast   posixrules  US
Antarctica  Cuba      GB-Eire    Iran        MST       PRC         UTC
Arctic      EET       GMT        iso3166.tab MST7MDT   PST8PDT     WET
Asia        Egypt     GMT0       Israel      Navajo    right       W-SU
Atlantic    Eire      GMT-0      Jamaica     NZ        ROC         zone.tab
Australia   EST       GMT+0      Japan       NZ-CHAT   ROK         Zulu
Brazil      EST5EDT   Greenwich  Kwajalein   Pacific   Singapore
Canada      Etc       Hongkong   Libya       Poland    Turkey
CET         Europe    HST        MET         Portugal  UCT
[michael@CentOS5-LPI ~]$
```

FIGURE 12.1 *Available time zones.*

The `/etc/adjtime` file supports systematic corrections to the hardware clock. It assumes that any drift from the actual time is predictable. If you've configured the local system as a client to synchronize with an NTP server, described later in this chapter, the `/etc/adjtime` file is less important. But the last line in this file specifies whether the hardware clock is actually set as the same time as the system clock

```
LOCAL
```

or if the hardware clock is actually set to the UTC time zone

```
UTC
```

Configuration Commands

The LPIC-1 objectives in this area suggest that you need to know how to use the hwclock and date commands, as well as how to set the hardware clock to the correct time, based on the UTC time zone.

The hwclock and date commands, by themselves, display the current system time. Although the date command was discussed in some detail in Chapter 11, there's one more option of interest:

```
$ date -u
```

With the -u switch, the date command reads the system clock and translates that to the UTC time zone. Nominally, the -u switch serves the same purpose with the hwclock command, but observe the output from the following commands, when run on my laptop in a dual-boot configuration with Windows XP:

```
$ date
Thu Feb 12 09:20:56 PST 2009
$ date -u
Thu Feb 12 17:20:58 UTC 2009
$ hwclock
Thu 12 Feb 2009 09:20:56 AM PST   -0.003150 seconds
$ hwclock -u
Thu 12 Feb 2009 01:20:58 AM PST   -0.003022 seconds
```

Both the date and the hwclock commands, by themselves, specify the same current time on the local system. However, whereas the date -u command displays the actual time in UTC, the hwclock -u command displays the wrong time in either the local or UTC time zone. Important options to the hwclock command are listed in Table 12.1. Any switches that actually change the time require administrative privileges.

In contrast, on a system that is set to UTC, the output of the following commands is identical and matches the current local time (different from UTC): date, hwclock, and hwclock -u. This is counterintuitive, because the time on the actual hardware clock is set to UTC. However, the date -u command matches the current UTC.

If the local system works alone, without the benefit of an NTP client or server, accurate time may still be important. In that case, you should run the hwclock -a command periodically to correct for time drift.

Assume that you've just corrected the time in the BIOS. In that case, you may want to make sure the system clock is changed to match the hardware clock with the hwclock -s command.

Alternatively, if you've just changed the system time, you can change the hardware clock to match that time with the hwclock -w command.

Table 12.1 Key hwclock Command Switches

Switch	Description
-a or --adjust	Adjust the hardware clock time, based on data collected in the /etc/adjtime file
-r or --show	Display the current time from the hardware clock
-s or --hctosys	Change the system clock to match the hardware clock
-u or --utc	Display the current time, based on the UTC time zone; if the hardware time is not set to UTC, this displays the wrong time
-w or --systohc	Change the hardware clock to match the system clock

A Local NTP Client

An NTP client can refer to an NTP server to adjust the time on a regular basis. Linux systems often run continuously for months at a time or more. Some distributions include both the NTP client and server on the same **ntp** package; others have a separate **ntpdate** package for the NTP client.

Once installed, the NTP client may update the local system clock based on preconfigured remote NTP servers. The list of servers may be stored in either the /etc/default/ntpdate or /etc/ntp/ntpservers files.

Generally, the ntpdate command is configured to run when Linux is started. If the local system runs for months at a time, you may want to configure a separate cron job to make sure the ntpdate command is run regularly. The basics of cron jobs were discussed in Chapter 11.

Of course, if you suspect a problem, the ntpdate command can be run on its own. As an experiment, I first set the date on one of my test systems one day into the future:

```
# date 02131343
Fri Feb 13 13:43:00 PST 2009
```

Now I can use the ntpdate command, citing an active NTP server. The noted server is from the CentOS 5 /etc/ntp/ntpservers file:

```
# /usr/sbin/ntpdate 0.centos.pool.ntp.org
Password:
12 Feb 13:35:12 ntpdate[5869]: step time server 66.187.233.4 offset -86879.562027 sec
```

The offset shown is the correction time. In other words, the command shown set the current time on my system back by more than 86,000 seconds (approximately 24 hours).

NOTE

The default NTP server for a distribution may not be appropriate for your clients. For example, the default NTP server for Ubuntu systems is ntp://ntp.ubuntu.com, which is located in the United Kingdom. If you're on another continent, the delays in transmission from the remote server may lead to errors that exceed the inaccuracies of a local system clock. For more information on publicly available NTP servers, see the NTP Pool Project at **http://www.pool.ntp.org**.

Configure an NTP Server

If you have several mission-critical, time-sensitive systems on a local network, it may be appropriate to configure a local NTP server, governed by the **ntpd** daemon. But just as NTP clients can be synchronized with a remote NTP server, local NTP servers should be synchronized with a remote NTP server. NTP options and more are normally configured in the /etc/ntp.conf configuration file.

The directives that follow appear in some form in both the CentOS 5 and Ubuntu Hardy Heron versions of the /etc/ntp.conf files, but possibly in a different order, with slightly different file names.

The **driftfile** directive shown here points to the file with the clock drift, from a standard time. The drift file might also be located in the /var/lib/ntp/ntp.drift file.

```
driftfile /var/lib/ntp/drift
```

The server directives shown specify the reference NTP servers. You can substitute the NTP servers of your choice, perhaps from the http://www.pool.ntp.org Web site.

```
server 0.centos.pool.ntp.org
server 1.centos.pool.ntp.org
server 2.centos.pool.ntp.org
```

When configuring a local NTP server, there may be times where the Internet connection from the LAN (local area network) is down. In such cases, the following server directive is a default for local NTP services:

```
server   127.127.1.0
```

The following restrict directives configure default limits for IPv4 (-4) and IPv6 (-6) communication:

```
restrict -4 default kod notrap nomodify nopeer noquery
restrict -6 default kod notrap nomodify nopeer noquery
```

The kod, notrap, and nomodify commands protect the local server from external modification. The nopeer and noquery options are used in some public NTP servers to enable sharing from other NTP servers. As a local NTP server, all that's needed is an appropriate reference to a local network address and subnet mask, such as shown in the following directive:

```
restrict -4 192.168.10.0 mask 255.255.255.0 notrap nomodify
```

You can then configure NTP clients on the 192.168.10.0/255.255.255.0 network to use this particular NTP server. Of course, the associated TCP/IP port, 123, should not be blocked by firewalls. Ports are discussed in Chapter 15, "Security Administration."

The commands associated with the NTP service are summarized in Table 12.2.

Table 12.2 NTP Service Commands

Command	Description
ntpd	Starts the NTP daemon; -g supports any degree of change
ntpdate	Acts as a client, synchronizing with a specified NTP server
ntpdc	Opens an NTP query program
ntp-keygen	Generates cryptographic keys for NTP communication
ntpq	Starts the NTP query program, similar to ntpdc
ntptime	Reads kernel time variables
ntptrace	Trace from a specified to an original NTP server
ntp-wait	Wait until the NTP server is synchronized; may be useful during the boot process

System Logs

Three types of logs are available to collect messages. Such messages can relate to system events, errors, debugging issues, and more. Logs are available for a number of individual services, but that's beyond the scope of this section. Logs are also available through the kernel (klogd) and system log (syslogd) daemons. Both are started by default during the boot process, in some cases through a combined **sysklogd** service, and they are configured through the **/etc/syslog.conf** file.

Although system logs are normally configured to send data to the local system, you can also configure them to send data to a central log server or accept logging data from other systems.

Local Log Files

Logging is configured for a number of different services in the /etc/syslog.conf configuration file. The CentOS 5 and Ubuntu versions of this file provide a variety of examples on how different messages can be logged.

But first you need to understand how logs are collected. To that end, there are facilities, priorities, and actions. The format is similar to the following line, in which `mail` is the facility, `err` is the priority, and the action is to send the log messages to the `/var/log/mail.err` file.

```
mail.err     /var/log/mail.err
```

A facility is a subsystem that produces a log message. For more information on facilities, see Table 12.3.

Table 12.3 System and Kernel Log Facilities

Facility	Description
auth, authpriv, or security	Security/authentication messages, such as logins
cron	System messages from the cron and at daemons
daemon	System messages for generic daemons without another log facility
ftp	Basic messages for FTP services; often superseded by service-specific log files
kern	Log messages related to the kernel
local0 - local7	Custom log collection
lpr	Messages related to the mostly obsolete Line Print Daemon service
mail	Messages related to mail server services
news	News server messages related to the INN (InterNetNews Usenet server) messages
syslog	Log messages from the syslogd daemon
user	User level service messages
uucp	UUCP (user to user copy) program messages

Priorities specify the level of a logging message. They are listed here in order of decreasing severity. The priorities are somewhat descriptive:

◆ **emerg** or **panic.** Show stopper issues

◆ **alert.** Important problems that require immediate attention

◆ **crit.** Critical problems that require almost immediate attention

◆ **err** or **error.** Errors related to the facility in question

◆ **warn** or **warning.** Warning messages that may not stop progress

◆ **notice.** Normal messages

◆ **info.** Information messages, often associated with smooth operation

◆ **debug.** Detailed messages for debugging purposes

Finally, there are the actions, which are the targets of a logging message. Actions are usually files to which a log is written. For example, if this line is made active (by removing the hash mark [#]), all cron messages are written to the /var/log/cron.log file:

```
#cron.*    /var/log/cron.log
```

Sometimes it helps to send the message to a specific console. For example, the following directive line sends all mail server debugging messages to the ninth virtual console, accessible by pressing Ctrl+Alt+F9:

```
mail.debug    /dev/tty9
```

If you want to send such debugging messages to a remote console, the following command sends those messages to the syslog.example.com system, where the /etc/syslog.conf file on that system handles it.

```
mail.debug    @syslog.example.com
```

System Log Configuration

Now that you've reviewed the details of the Linux system log configuration, you're ready to read and understand the /etc/syslog.conf configuration file. After reviewing some of the excerpts from both the CentOS 5 and Ubuntu versions of this file, you should understand where log messages are sent and how such messages can be reconfigured.

The following default directives from the Ubuntu version of the /etc/syslog.conf file send messages from the auth, authpriv, daemon, kern, lpr, mail, and user facilities to the noted log files. The asterisk means that related messages of all severities are sent to the noted file:

```
auth,authpriv.*    /var/log/auth.log
daemon.*           -/var/log/daemon.log
lpr.*              -/var/log/lpr.log
mail.*             -/var/log/mail.log
user.*             -/var/log/user.log
```

The following line, although controlled by the klogd daemon, is still configured in the /etc/syslog.conf file:

```
kern.*             -/var/log/kern.log
```

The following excerpt from both versions of the file suggests that all emergency-level messages are sent to the console, for all users:

```
*.emerg    *
```

The following lines associated with INN specify that only messages of a crit level of severity are sent to the /var/log/news/news.crit file, only messages of an err level of severity are sent to the /var/log/news/news.err file, and messages of a notice level of severity or higher are sent to the /var/log/news/news.notice file.

```
news.=crit      /var/log/news/news.crit
news.=err       /var/log/news/news.err
news.notice     /var/log/news/news.notice
```

The logger Command

You can use the **logger** command to set up customized messages in a generic log file. Depending on the distribution, that might be /var/log/syslog or /var/log/messages. Try the following command on both selected distributions:

```
$ logger -p auth.info -t 192.168.0.8 this is nice
```

The -p supports the use of facility and priority—in this case, auth.info. Because auth.info is separately configured in the Ubuntu version of the /etc/syslog.conf configuration file, it leads to the following log message in the /var/log/auth.log file:

```
Feb 13 12:10:17 ubuntuHHserver LABEL: this is a label
```

In contrast, there is no such configuration in the CentOS 5 version of the /etc/syslog.conf configuration file, so the log message is sent to the generic logging file, /var/log/messages:

```
Feb 13 12:11:40 CentOS5-LPI LABEL: this is a label
```

Clients and Mail Transfer Agents

An MTA, as described in the LPIC-1 objectives, relates to the variety of e-mail servers available for Linux. The objectives explicitly state that there is "no configuration" of MTAs covered on the exams. However, candidates should be aware of the commonly available MTA programs and be able to perform basic forward and alias configuration on a client host.

To that end, this section covers the basics of common mail services, the configuration of aliases, as well as files used to configure the forwarding of e-mail.

Common Mail Services

Mail services are complex. Networks may be configured with up to four major mail systems. Regular clients are normally configured with **MUAs (mail user agents)** such as Evolution and Thunderbird. Such clients use **MRAs (mail retrieval agents)** such as fetchmail to pull their e-mail from **MDAs (mail delivery agents)** such as procmail and Dovecot. When e-mail is sent, it is sent through MTAs such as Postfix, sendmail, qmail, and Exim.

NOTE

The sendmail MTA is open source, which is different from the commercial Sendmail MTA.

The following sections provide a basic overview of these MTAs. The sendmail and Postfix MTAs are described last, because they more closely relate to some of the other commands described in the LPIC-1 objectives.

In general, only one MTA should be active on any system. Multiple MTAs on the same system don't work well together.

The qmail MTA

The qmail MTA is not available from normal repositories for many Linux distributions, because it is licensed as public domain, not GPL software. If you prefer qmail, you have to download it from http://www.qmail.org/. Despite the different license, it's still a commonly used option on Linux systems.

The original developer of qmail claims that it was perhaps the first MTA developed with security in mind. Although it was designed as a replacement for sendmail, it does not work in the same way. Its relative simplicity has made it a relatively fast MTA, however.

The Exim MTA

The Exim MTA was originally developed at the University of Cambridge, using an older MTA known as Smail-3. It includes ACLs (access control lists), options for transmission and delivery, retry settings if it can't confirm that e-mail has been received, rewrite options for incoming addresses, as well as authentication.

Exim is available from many standard repositories associated with both Ubuntu and Red Hat–type distributions.

The Postfix MTA

The Postfix MTA is the default for many Linux distributions, including Ubuntu and SUSE Linux. Developed at IBM, it is released under the IBM Public License, which is approved as open source.

Postfix supports a number of desirable features, including

◆ TLS (transport layer security), the successor to SSL (secure sockets layer)
◆ A variety of database maps
◆ Options for mailboxes and virtual domains

Postfix configuration files are stored in the /etc/postfix/ directory.

The sendmail MTA

The sendmail MTA is the default for many Linux distributions. The detail available with sendmail is legendary. As such, it's the most popular MTA on the Internet. The sendmail configuration files are difficult to read. To ease the configuration process, macro files were developed. Those macro files must be processed, typically as described in the comments to the noted files.

Configuration files associated with sendmail are stored in the /etc/mail directory. The macro files that can be configured for outgoing and incoming e-mail are sendmail.mc and submit.mc.

Aliases and E-Mail Forwarding

One common file for e-mail aliases is **/etc/aliases**. Every time you change this file, you should also run the **newaliases** command to make sure the current MTA can access this database.

The Ubuntu version of this file is relatively simple, with two lines. E-mail sent to the postmaster user, the administrator for the e-mail server, is forwarded to the root administrative user. E-mail intended for that root user is forwarded to the first administrative user configured during the installation process.

```
postmaster:   root
root:   michael
```

Forwarding is often configured on a user level, courtesy of the ~/.forward file, a hidden file in each user's home directory.

To continue, an e-mail address in the .forward file forwards e-mail intended for the local user to that e-mail address.

E-Mail Management

When either the sendmail or Postfix MTA sends e-mail, it is available in a queue. Until delivery is confirmed, you can review that queue with the mailq command. For example, the following output specifies two e-mail messages with problems; the Connection timed out messages suggest that the e-mail server hasn't been able to connect to the target e-mail address.

```
-Queue ID- --Size-- ----Arrival Time---- -Sender/Recipient-------
0771272020*    354 Fri Feb 13 18:09:38  michael@example.org
            (connect to example.com[192.168.0.1]:25: Connection timed out)
                            michael@example.com
                            mjang@example.org
AAA5272024     368 Fri Feb 13 18:12:48  michael@example.org
        (connect to example.net[10.11.12.13]:25: Connection timed out)
                            mjang@example.net
        (connect to example.net[10.11.12.14]:25: Connection timed out)
                            michaeljang@example.net
```

Finally, despite the availability of MUAs such as Thunderbird and Evolution, one MUA program is listed in the LPIC-1 objectives: `mail`. It is a simple command-line program that you can use to send e-mail. To test it internally on a system, take the following steps:

1. Run the `mail root` command to set up an e-mail to the administrative `root` user.
2. When the `Subject:` prompt appears, enter an appropriate subject such as `Administrative Test`, and then press Enter.
3. Type in desired text.
4. Press Ctrl+D.
5. At the Cc: prompt, enter a second user if desired.
6. Log in as the root administrative user, and type in the mail command to confirm receipt of the message.

Basic Print Job Management

The current standard for print services on Linux is CUPS. Through **IPP (Internet Printing Protocol)**, CUPS is an excellent print solution for Linux, Apple, Microsoft, and other operating systems. Although both CentOS 5 and Ubuntu have their own GUI CUPS managers, CUPS also has an intuitive Web-based administrative interface. CUPS configuration files are primarily located in the `/etc/cups` directory.

Although detailed configuration options for CUPS are beyond the scope of LPIC-1 objectives, this section does describe the basics of key CUPS configuration files, print queues, commands that activate printers, as well as legacy commands from the LPD (Line Printer Daemon) service still in use today, which help control CUPS printers and print jobs.

Linux includes references to both the **LPD** and **LPRng** (Line Printer, Next Generation) services. Both are older services that are unavailable on some current major Linux distributions such as Red Hat.

 NOTE

CUPS was purchased by Apple, Inc., in 2007, which caused many in the open source community to be concerned for its open source license. CUPS development continues, and the open source license remains in place.

To access the basic Web-based CUPS configuration interface on a system, make sure the `cupsd` daemon is active, and navigate to **http://localhost:631**. If active, the `cupsd` daemon should appear in the output to the `ps aux | grep cupsd` command. The CUPS Web-based interface is shown in Figure 12.2.

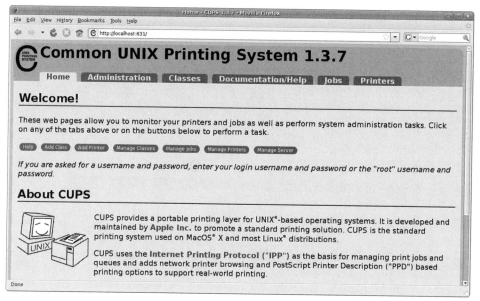

FIGURE 12.2 *CUPS Web-based interface.*

Basic CUPS Configuration

The main CUPS configuration file is **/etc/cups/cupsd.conf**. The default version of this file limits print server and administrative access to the local system, courtesy of the following directive:

```
Listen localhost:631
```

If you're setting up the local system as a print server, you'll want to change this to allow connections from remote systems, as shown here:

```
Listen 631
```

Be aware that port 631 is the default TCP/IP port for communication with CUPS printers. As described in the /etc/services file, this port is the default for IPP.

The following default stanza shares configured printers with other systems on the local network if access is also allowed per the previous **Listen** directive.

```
Browsing On
BrowseOrder allow,deny
BrowseAllow @LOCAL
```

Administrative access is normally limited to the local root administrative user. However, users who are members of a specified **SystemGroup** can also administer that print server. For example, based on the following directive, users who are members of the `lpadmin` group, as defined in the `/etc/group` and `/etc/gshadow` files, can administer printers configured through CUPS.

```
SystemGroup lpadmin
```

Although you can also configure the CUPS server for administrative access from remote systems, such details are beyond the scope of the LPIC-1 objectives.

Many Linux distributions have their own GUI configuration tools. Because Ubuntu has adapted Red Hat's Printer Configuration tool, you can open this tool with the `system-config-printer` command.

Other CUPS Configuration Files

Other important CUPS configuration files are described in Table 12.4. Unless otherwise noted, all of these files are located in the **/etc/cups** directory.

Table 12.4 CUPS Configuration Files

File	Description
`classes.conf`	Configuration file for print classes, a group of printers with a name that appears as a single printer
`cupsd.conf`	Main CUPS configuration file
`printers.conf`	Configuration file for individual printers
`ppd/`	Directory with printer drivers for configured printers
`ssl/`	Directory with SSL encryption keys for remote access
`snmp.conf`	Configuration file that regulates remote browse access
`/etc/printcap`	Legacy file, with printer names taken from `printers.conf`

The `/etc/printcap` file is less commonly used on the latest Linux distributions. However, it is sometimes used to share printers via Samba/CIFS (Common Internet File System), the Linux service for sharing files and printers on a Microsoft-style network.

Perhaps the most important of these files is `printers.conf`, because it includes configured printers and their current status. For example, the stanza shown in Figure 12.3 specifies the default printer on my laptop.

```
<DefaultPrinter LaserJet4L>
Info LaserJet4L printer
Location In the Office
DeviceURI ipp://ubuntuHHserver.mommabears.com:631/printers/LaserJet_4L
State Idle
StateTime 1221835756
Accepting Yes
Shared Yes
JobSheets none none
QuotaPeriod 0
PageLimit 0
KLimit 0
OpPolicy default
ErrorPolicy retry-job
</Printer>
```

FIGURE 12.3 *Default printer specified in /etc/cups/printers.conf.*

The printer stanza is encased between the <DefaultPrinter LaserJet4L> and </Printer> directives, a standard markup language format. The name of the DefaultPrinter as shared with CUPS clients is LaserJet4L.

Perhaps the most important directive is the **URI (uniform resource identifier)**. The URI is a "superset" of the well-known URL (uniform resource locator). In other words, although a URL such as http://www.cengagelearning.com is also an URI, an URI such as

ipp://ubuntuHHserver.mommabears.com:631/printers/LaserJet_4L

is not a URL. However, it fully defines the network location of the noted printer. Clients on Microsoft, Apple, and UNIX systems can also use this URI to connect to the noted printer. The ipp:// specifies the use of the aforementioned IPP protocol. Although port 631 is specified in the noted URI, it is not required, because that port is the default for IPP.

Following are three other important directives from Figure 12.3:

◆ State specifies the current status of the printer, normally Idle or Stopped. If Stopped, the print queue is not active. For more information, see the **cupsaccept** and **cupsreject** commands.

◆ Accepting is set to either Yes or No, which specifies whether the printer is active or disabled. For more information, see the **cupsenable** and **cupsdisable** commands.

◆ Shared is set to either Yes or No, which specifies whether the printer is accessible from other systems over the network.

Print Queues

CUPS print jobs are stored primarily in the **/var/spool/cups** directory, local to the target printer. To find current and pending print jobs, you can use the **lpq** command. To remove a print job, you can use the **lprm** command. If one printer is down temporarily, say due to a paper jam, you can move existing print jobs with the **lpmove** command.

Printers shared via Samba/CIFS may have jobs spooled in the **/var/spool/samba** directory.

The Line Print Query Command (lpq)

If you run the lpq command by itself, you'll see the current queue on the default printer, as specified in the printers.conf configuration file. For example, see the following output, which specifies one active print job:

```
LaserJet4L is ready and printing
Rank    Owner   Job     File(s)     Total Size
active  michael 516     passwd      3072 bytes
```

If more than one configured local or remote printer exists on the current system, the lpq -a command lists active and pending print jobs for all configured printers.

If you want to find the active and pending print jobs for a different printer, the lpq -P*printername* command can help. Note that the syntax of the lpq command allows you to leave out the space between the -P and the name of the printer.

The Line Print Job Removal Command (lprm)

The various lpq commands include job numbers. With the lprm command, you can remove the noted job, by number, from the print queue. For example, the following command removes job 517 from the queue:

```
$ lprm 517
```

However, if job 517 is currently active, some or perhaps all of the job may already be in the memory buffer of the printer. In that case, part or all of the job may still be printed.

Alternatively, you can cancel all print jobs in all print queues with the following command:

```
$ lprm -
```

Of course, such changes can be limited by printer; for example, the following command limits the removed jobs to the printer named color:

```
$ lprm -P color
```

The Line Print Move Command (lpmove)

As long as a queued print job has not yet entered a printer buffer, it can be moved between print queues. As an example, assume that you have access to two printers: bwprinter and colorprinter. If colorprinter is down, you can move all jobs from that printer with the following command:

```
$ lpmove colorprinter bwprinter
```

Alternatively, if you just want to move job 111 from colorprinter to bwprinter, as specified in the output to the lpq -a command, you can move that job with the following command:

```
$ lpmove 111 bwprinter
```

Printer Activation

Printers get paper jams. They run out of ink. In fact, printers may be stopped for a variety of reasons. Whenever a printer is stopped, it is deactivated. In that case, the directives in the /etc/cups/printers.conf file are updated and should appear as follows:

```
State Stopped
StateMessage Paused
```

After a printer is fixed, it can be reactivated with the cupsenable *printername* command. If a printer appears to be running out of ink or you want to deactivate it for some other reason, you can do so with the cupsdisable *printername* command.

CUPS and Queue Management

If some important pending print jobs remain in a print queue, you may not want to disable that printer. Doing so could stop a print job in mid-stream, which would be awkward. In that case, the cupsreject *printername* command might help, because it would continue processing any print job currently in the queue to the specified *printername*. However, it would reject additional print jobs.

The cupsaccept *printername* command would reverse the process.

Other LPD Commands

The CUPS configuration on Linux systems typically includes several other commands from the legacy LPD service. Those commands not already covered include:

- **lpadmin.** The lpadmin command can be used to reconfigure CUPS printers and classes.
- **lpc.** Although the CUPS version of the lpc program is much less capable, it can still be used to read the status of all locally configured printers with the lpc status command.
- **lpr.** The lpr *filename* command sends the contents of the *filename* file to the default printer. Alternatively, the lpr -P*printername* *filename* command sends the contents of the *filename* file to the printer named *printername*.
- **lpstat.** The lpstat -t command displays the default printer, the current status of the CUPS service, as well as any available printers on the network.

Chapter Summary

Linux includes a variety of system services considered essential, per the LPIC-1 requirements. NTP clients and servers can help keep system and hardware clocks in sync, if hardware clocks are set to UTC. Although the ntpdate command can synchronize a client, the hwclock command can synchronize a system to a hardware clock (or vice versa). The local NTP server configuration file is /etc/ntp.conf.

Linux log configuration is based on both the system (syslogd) and kernel log (klogd) service. Both services are configured in /etc/syslog.conf using auth, cron, daemon, ftp, kern, lpr, mail, syslog, user, and uucp facilities. Log message priorities, from least to most important, are debug, info, notice, warn or warning, err or error, crit, alert, and emerg or panic.

Linux supports various MTA mail services, including sendmail, Postfix, qmail, and Exim. Postfix configuration files are stored in the /etc/postfix directory. The configuration files for sendmail are stored in the /etc/mail directory. General aliases for both are stored in /etc/aliases and can be activated with the newaliases command. User-specific aliases are stored in user home directories, in the hidden .forward file. The e-mail client listed in the objectives is associated with the mail command.

The main Linux printing service is CUPS. Although it's the successor to LPD/LPRng, it still uses commands from the older service, including lpq, lprm, lpmove, lpadmin, lpc, lpr, and lpstat. The main CUPS configuration file is /etc/cups/cupsd.conf, but individual printers are configured in /etc/cups/printers.conf. Also, even though CUPS printers can be started and stopped with the cupsenable and cupsdisable commands, they can be configured to accept and reject queues with the cupsaccept and cupsreject commands.

Key Terms

- **alert.** Log messages that require immediate attention.
- **classes.conf.** A configuration file for printer groups in the /etc/cups directory.
- **crit.** Log messages related to critical problems that require almost immediate attention.
- **CUPS (Common UNIX Printing System).** The standard printing service for Linux; uses the IPP protocol.
- **cupsaccept.** A command that can accept future print jobs to a specified printer.
- **cupsd.** The CUPS daemon.
- **cupsdisable.** A command that can disable a specified printer.
- **cupsenable.** A command that can enable a specified printer.
- **cupsreject.** A command that can reject future print jobs to a specified printer.
- **debug.** Detailed log messages related to the normal operation of a service.
- **driftfile.** An NTP directive that specifies the measured clock drift.
- **emerg.** Show-stopper log messages.
- **err, error.** Log messages that specify errors related to a specific log facility.
- **/etc/adjtime.** A file that supports systematic corrections to the hardware clock.
- **/etc/aliases.** A file with user aliases for e-mail delivery.
- **/etc/cups.** The directory with CUPS configuration files.
- **/etc/cups/cupsd.conf.** The main configuration file for CUPS.

- **/etc/printcap.** A legacy printer configuration file, with printer names taken from the /etc/cups/printers.conf file. May be used to share printers on a Samba/CIFS server.

- **/etc/syslog.conf.** Standard configuration file for system and kernel logging.

- **Exim.** An MTA e-mail service for outgoing e-mail.

- **GMT (Greenwich Mean Time).** A standard time zone that many Linux hardware clocks are based on.

- **http://localhost:631.** The URL for the CUPS Web-based administrative tool, if the CUPS service is running.

- **http://www.pool.ntp.org.** The URL for the NTP Pool Project, with a list of publicly available NTP servers.

- **hwclock.** A command that relates and can synchronize the hardware and system clocks.

- **info.** Log informational messages related to the normal operation of a service.

- **IPP (Internet Printing Protocol).** A standard protocol for CUPS, which communicates over TCP/IP port 631.

- **klogd.** The kernel log daemon.

- **Listen.** A directive in the CUPS configuration file that specifies communication for CUPS.

- **logger.** A command to set up custom log messages.

- **lpadmin.** A command that can configure CUPS printers and print classes.

- **lpc.** A control command that can read the status of existing printers.

- **LPD (Line Print Daemon).** An older printing service for Linux.

- **lpmove.** A command that can move existing jobs in a print queue to a different printer.

- **lpq.** A command that can list current jobs in a print queue.

- **lpr.** A command that can send a text file as a job to an existing printer.

- **lprm.** A command that can remove a current print job.

- **LPRng (Line Printer, Next Generation).** An older printing service for Linux.

- **lpstat.** A command that displays the default printer and status of the CUPS service.

- **mail.** A basic text-based e-mail client.

- **mailq.** A command that lists current messages in an outgoing e-mail queue.

- **MDA (mail delivery agent).** Mail services that can forward e-mail to a client, such as procmail and Dovecot.

- **MRA (mail retrieval agent).** Mail services that can pull e-mail from an MDA.

- **MTA (mail transfer agent).** Mail services that can forward e-mail from a client, such as Postfix, sendmail, qmail, and Exim.

◆ **MUA (mail user agent).** Mail client services such as `mail`, Evolution, and Thunderbird.

◆ `newaliases`. A command that processes the `/etc/aliases` file for e-mail aliases.

◆ `notice`. Log messages related to the normal operation of a service.

◆ **ntp.** The package associated with the NTP service.

◆ **NTP (Network Time Protocol).** The protocol associated with synchronizing system clocks over a network.

◆ `ntpd`. The daemon associated with the NTP service.

◆ `ntpdate`. A client command that synchronizes the local system clock with a remote NTP server.

◆ `ntpdc`. A command that opens an NTP query program.

◆ `ntp-keygen`. A command that generates cryptographic keys for NTP communication.

◆ `ntpq`. A command that starts the NTP query program.

◆ `panic`. Show-stopper log messages.

◆ **Postfix.** An MTA e-mail service for outgoing e-mail, with configuration files in the `/etc/postfix/` directory.

◆ `printers.conf`. A configuration file for printers in the `/etc/cups/` directory.

◆ **qmail.** An MTA e-mail service for outgoing e-mail, released under a public domain license.

◆ **sendmail.** An MTA e-mail service for outgoing e-mail, with configuration files in the `/etc/mail/` directory.

◆ `syslogd`. A combined system and kernel log daemon service.

◆ `syslogd`. The system log daemon.

◆ `SystemGroup`. A CUPS directive that specifies one or more groups of printer administrative users, as defined in the `/etc/group` and `/etc/gshadow` files.

◆ **URI (uniform resource identifier).** A superset of the URL, which includes constructs such as `ipp://cups.example.com:631/printers/LaserJet_4L`.

◆ **UTC.** Essentially equivalent to Greenwich Mean Time. It is standard to set the hardware clocks on Linux systems to UTC.

◆ `/var/spool/cups`. The directory for CUPS print jobs.

◆ `/var/spool/samba`. The directory for jobs for CUPS printers shared via Samba and CIFS.

◆ `warn, warning`. Log messages that warn of a noncritical problem.

Review Questions

The number of review questions in this chapter and other chapters in this book is proportionate to each section's weight in the LPI objectives. Because this chapter covers items 108.1, 108.2, 108.3, and 108.4, the weight is 10; therefore, you'll see 20 questions in this section. You'll see multiple choice single answer, fill-in-the blank, and multiple choice multiple answer questions, as you'll encounter on the exam.

1. Enter the full path to the directory with time zone files.

   _____

2. Which of the following files supports corrections to the hardware clock?
   - **A.** /etc/hwclock
   - **B.** /etc/adjtime
   - **C.** /etc/ntp.drift
   - **D.** /etc/ntpdate

3. Which of the following commands changes the system clock to match the hardware clock?
   - **A.** hwclock -s
   - **B.** hwclock -r
   - **C.** hwclock -w
   - **D.** hwclock -a

4. Which of the following commands synchronizes the local clock as a client with a remote NTP server at 0.centos.pool.ntp.org?
   - **A.** ntp 0.centos.pool.ntp.org
   - **B.** ntpclock 0.centos.pool.ntp.org
   - **C.** ntptime 0.centos.pool.ntp.org
   - **D.** ntpdate 0.centos.pool.ntp.org

5. Enter the name of the NTP server configuration file. Include the full path to the file.

   _____

6. Which of the following files may include NTP configuration options? Choose two.
   - **A.** /etc/default/ntpserver
   - **B.** /etc/default/ntpdate
   - **C.** /etc/sysconfig/ntpd
   - **D.** /etc/sysconfig/clock

7. Enter the name of the standard kernel log configuration file. Include the full path to the file.

_____

8. Which of the following log options has the highest priority?

   A. alert

   B. crit

   C. warn

   D. debug

9. Which of the following directives specifies kernel messages solely of a notice level?

   A. kern.note

   B. kern.=note

   C. kern.notice

   D. kern.=notice

10. Which of the following log files includes boot messages?

   A. /var/log/syslog

   B. /var/log/user.log

   C. /var/log/kern.log

   D. /var/log/dmesg

11. Enter the full path to the directory with sendmail configuration files.

_____

12. Which of the following services is not an MTA?

   A. sendmail

   B. Dovecot

   C. Exim

   D. qmail

13. Which of the following files can include mail forwarding information? Choose two.

   A. ~/.aliases

   B. ~/.forward

   C. /etc/aliases

   D. /etc/forward

14. Which of the following macro files is associated with sendmail configuration? Choose two.

   A. sendmail.mc

   B. master.mc

   C. submit.mc

   D. main.mc

15. Enter the command that processes aliases. Do not include the full path, and assume that you already have administrative privileges.

_____

16. Which of the following commands starts a mail client?

   A. exim

   B. sendmail

   C. mail

   D. newaliases

17. Which of the following directories includes print jobs on a local system?

   A. /var/cups

   B. /var/spool/cups

   C. /var/cups/spool

   D. /var/spool

18. Which of the following commands specifies the current status of CUPS printers? Choose two.

   A. lpstat -t

   B. cupsstat -t

   C. lpc status

   D. lpq -a

19. Enter the full URL for the CUPS Web-based interface on the local system. Do not use an IP address.

_____

20. Which of the following commands allows a printer to start again after a printer jam is fixed?

   A. cupsenable

   B. cupsaccept

   C. lpenable

   D. lpaccept

Chapter 13

Basic Networking

After completing this chapter, you will be able to

- Understand the fundamentals of internet protocols

- Work with basic network configuration files

Introduction

This chapter describes the fundamentals of several TCP/IP protocols. The **TCP/IP protocol suite** is named for two of its many protocols: **TCP (Transmission Control Protocol)** and **IP (Internet Protocol)**. You'll learn a bit about several of the components of the TCP/IP protocol suite.

With this knowledge, you can, in the words of the LPIC-1 objectives, "view, change, and verify" network configuration settings. To that end, you'll look at those commands and files that support viewing, changing, and verifying the network configuration on a local system.

 TIP

This chapter addresses two objectives in the LPI exam: 109.1 ("Fundamentals of Internet Protocols") and 109.2 ("Basic Network Configuration").

Fundamentals of Internet Protocols

Although there are others, the TCP/IP protocol suite is the language of the Internet. As a suite of protocols, it defines communication over a number of ports. It includes specific ports reserved for specific services, from **FTP (File Transfer Protocol)** through SMTP (Simple Mail Transfer Protocol) and much more.

You need to understand a few of the major differences between the two primary internet addressing protocols: **IPv4** (IP version 4) and **IPv6** (IP version 6). However, because most systems still use IPv4, you only need to understand network masks, private IP networks, and routing tables using that address system. Fortunately, when most of the Internet finally does convert to IPv6, an understanding of the concepts and commands described in this chapter will serve you well.

In my opinion, one item listed in this 109.1 LPIC-1 objective belongs in, and I therefore cover with, Objective 109.2 later in this chapter: "Setting a Default Route."

NOTE

The terms "IPv4 address" and "IP address" are often used interchangeably, here and elsewhere. In contrast, references to IPv6 information are specific, such as "IPv6 address."

Common TCP/IP Ports

TCP/IP ports are analogous to the channels on a cable TV box—if cable TV enabled two-way communication. Although 65,000 TCP/IP ports are available, only a few hundred are actually dedicated to specific services. Dedicated ports are defined in the /etc/services file. The LPIC-1 objectives explicitly define 16 ports.

Be aware: there are two types of data communicated over each port. Data transmitted using TCP packets uses confirmed delivery. Data transmitted using **UDP (User Datagram Protocol)** packets is sent with "best effort." In other words, although TCP data transmission is more certain, UDP data transmission may be faster. As discussed later in this chapter, the ping command uses a third alternative: **ICMP (Internet Control Message Protocol)**. TCP, UDP, and ICMP data works at the same level of the TCP/IP protocol suite.

Because there's no way around it, be prepared to memorize the 16 ports listed in Table 13.1. To help you remember these ports, they're also listed in the Key Terms section at the end of this chapter.

Table 13.1 Common TCP/IP Ports

Port Number	Description	TCP	UDP
20	ftp-data; used for FTP server data transmission. Enables downloads from FTP servers.	x	
21	ftp; used for FTP connections. Supports login access to FTP servers.	x	
22	ssh; reserved for SSH secure shell communication.	x	x
23	telnet; configured for cleartext network connections.	x	
25	smtp; designed for SMTP (Simple Mail Transfer Protocol) server connections from MTAs (mail transfer agents) such as sendmail, Postfix, qmail, and Exim.	x	
53	domain; reserved for DNS (domain name system) communication.	x	x

Table 13.1 Continued

Port Number	Description	TCP	UDP
80	www; for HTTP (Hypertext Transfer Protocol) communication.	x	x
110	pop3; reserved for POP3 (Post Office Protocol, version 3).	x	x
119	nntp; configured for NNTP (Network News Transfer Protocol).	x	
139	netbios-ssn; reserved for file and printer sharing over a Microsoft network.	x	x
143	imap2; reserved for IMAP2 and IMAP4 (Internet Message Access Protocols version 2 and 4).	x	x
161	snmp; configured for SNMP (Simple Network Management Protocol) for network monitoring.	x	x
443	https; for HTTPS (Hypertext Transfer Protocol-Secure) communication.	x	x
465	smtps; designed for SMTP (Simple Mail Transfer Protocol) server connections, over SSL (Secure Sockets Layer) from MTAs such as sendmail, Postfix, qmail, and Exim.	x	
993	imaps; reserved for IMAP2 and IMAP4, over SSL.	x	x
995	pop3s; reserved for POP3, over SSL.	x	x

Typical Linux firewalls block all but a few essential TCP/IP ports. Related commands such as iptables are covered in the LPIC-2 objectives.

The list of ports shown in this table is just a start. If you administer a network, scan the /etc/services file. You'll see some additional port numbers of interest, such as 123 for the NTP servers; 631 for CUPS print services discussed in Chapter 12; 1214 for Kazaa music file sharing; 1352 for Lotus Notes; 5190 for AOL Instant Messenger communication; and much more.

IPv4 Addressing

It was once believed that IPv4 addressing would provide more than enough IP addresses for the Internet. And it was easy to believe that 32 bits, which provide 2^{32}—or more than 4 billion—IP addresses, would be sufficient. But 32-bit IP addresses are not enough for all of the computers, phones, servers, and so on. Part of the difficulty lies in the way IPv4 addresses are organized. As a result, experienced network administrators need to be ready for an IPv6 world.

However, IPv4 addresses are still in common use today, especially in the United States of America. In fact, they are still used for about 99% of Internet traffic. So it makes sense that IPv4 is still the primary version of IP addressing associated with the LPIC-1 objectives. To find the route to the public IPv4 address of a Web site, apply the **traceroute** command to it by running the following command:

```
$ traceroute www.cengage.com
```

Because there aren't enough IPv4 addresses, there are several options that help administrators ration these addresses. They include DHCP (Dynamic Host Configuration Protocol) servers, which are not covered in the LPIC-1 objectives.

But to continue, the following sections break down the basics of IPv4 addressing and various address classes.

Basic IPv4 Addressing

When you think about IPv4 addresses, think about 32 bits. They correspond to 32 binary digits of 0s and 1s. Because there are eight bits in a byte, that's four bytes of information.

If you already understand IPv4 addressing, you understand that the following binary address corresponds to an IP address of 192.168.0.50:

```
11000000 10101000 00000000 00110010
```

There are four groups of eight bits—or four bytes in the address. Each byte corresponds to a decimal number, per Table 13.2.

Table 13.2 Decimal Byte Equivalents

Byte	Decimal Equivalent
10000000	128
01000000	64
00100000	32
00010000	16
00001000	8
00000100	4
00000010	2
00000001	1

To convert each byte into an IPv4 address, add the decimal equivalent of each of the bits in each byte. Take the first byte from the address shown in Table 13.2.

```
11000000
```

The first number is equivalent to the first and second entries from Table 13.2, 128 + 64 = 192. Now take the four bytes of binary digits shown in the table and convert them in the same way:

```
128 + 64    128 + 32 + 8    0    32 + 16 + 2
```

The totals give us our dotted-quad IP address:

```
192    168    0    50
```

The way IP addresses are depicted, in numbers such as 192.168.0.50, is known as **dotted-quad** notation.

For one more exercise, take this common combination of bits:

```
11111111 11111111 11111111 00000000
```

The following line converts that address, based on the information from Table 13.2.

```
128+64+32+16+8+4+2+1 128+64+32+16+8+4+2+1 128+64+32+16+8+4+2+1 0
```

The result, in dotted-quad notation, is this:

```
255.255.255.0
```

IPv4 Address Classes

To enable configuration as networks of various sizes, IPv4 addresses are organized by **address classes** and **network masks**. Network masks and private IP addresses are discussed in later sections. The five IPv4 address classes specified in Table 13.3 include public, private, and otherwise reserved IP addresses. Many of the addresses in the noted classes cannot be assigned to specific systems.

Table 13.3 IPv4 Address Classes

Class	Address Range
Class A	1.0.0.0–127.255.255.255
Class B	128.0.0.0–191.255.255.255
Class C	192.0.0.0–223.255.255.255
Class D	224.0.0.0–239.255.255.255
Class E	240.0.0.0–255.255.255.255

Generally, IP addresses for regular systems can be assigned in classes A, B, and C. Class D IPv4 addresses are configured for multicasts, and Class E IPv4 addresses still have not been assigned except for experimental purposes.

IPv4 Address Exceptions

Several IPv4 addresses are reserved for various purposes. Private IPv4 networks are described in the next section. Reserved IP addresses are listed in Table 13.4.

Table 13.4 Reserved IPv4 Addresses

Address	Description
0.0.0.0	Specifies the default IP address
127.0.0.1	Loopback IP address
255.255.255.255	Universal broadcast address

Generally, the 127.0.0.0 network, with an address range to 127.255.255.255, is reserved for loopback purposes. One example discussed in Chapter 12, "Essential System Services," for NTP specifies an IP address of 127.127.1.0 for the local clock.

The first and last IPv4 addresses in a network range also qualify in part as "reserved" addresses. They're not officially reserved, because they vary. However, the first address in a range is known as the **network address**. The last address in a range is known as the **broadcast address**. You'll see how these addresses are used later in this chapter.

Private IPv4 Networks

Several groups of IPv4 addresses are reserved for private networks and can't be assigned on the Internet. However, as **private IP addresses**, they can be set up on home or corporate networks. All systems on that network may connect to the Internet through one (or a few) public IP addresses. There's a private IPv4 network available for Class A, B, and C addresses, as described in Table 13.5.

Table 13.5 Private IPv4 Address Networks

Class	Network	Description
A	10.0.0.0–10.255.255.255	May contain 2^{24} IP addresses, or more than 16 million total
B	172.16.0.0–172.31.255.255	May contain 2^{20} IP addresses, or more than 1 million total
C	192.168.0.0–192.168.255.255	May contain 2^{16} IP addresses, or more than 65,000 total

The first address in each of these networks is commonly used as a network address. In other words, typical private network addresses include 10.0.0.0, 172.16.0.0, and 192.168.0.0.

I use the 192.168.0.0 private network for my home systems. Because such IP addresses are not public, other home and business users can use the same private network on their own systems.

One other group of IP addresses falls into the same category, known as APIPA (Automatic Private IP Addressing). Some Microsoft systems automatically assign addresses in this range, for networks where IP address information hasn't been already assigned. This range of IP addresses is

```
169.254.0.1 - 169.254.255.254
```

Network Masks and CIDR Notation

A network mask helps define the number of available IP addresses on a network. Network masks go by other names, including subnetwork mask, subnet mask, or netmask. Default network masks are available for Class A, Class B, and Class C addresses. These default network masks can also be expressed in **CIDR (Classless Inter-Domain Routing)** notation, which specifies the number of bits occupied by a network mask.

Default network masks are based on the associated IP address class. The default class A netmask is 255.0.0.0; the default class B netmask is 255.255.0.0; and the default class C netmask is 255.255.255.0. These network masks support networks of 16 million, 65,000, and 254 IP addresses, respectively.

However, there is no requirement to use a default network mask, as you'll see shortly in the "Put It All Together" section.

Network masks are often depicted in CIDR notation, which depicts the number of bits in a netmask. For example, the default class A netmask can be depicted in bits as follows:

```
11111111 00000000 00000000 00000000
```

Because the first eight bits of this address are used, the address is represented by a /8 in CIDR notation. Sometimes networks and netmasks are combined in various configuration files. For example, the following lines depict typical Class A, Class B, and Class C private network IP addresses with their default netmasks:

```
10.0.0.0/255.0.0.0
172.16.0.0/255.255.0.0
192.168.0.0/255.255.255.0
```

These same network address/netmask combinations can be written like this:

```
10.0.0.0/8
172.16.0.0/16
192.168.0.0/24
```

Other network masks are possible. For example, one common network mask for smaller networks is 255.255.255.128. Because that's associated with 25 bits, one possible network may be depicted by either of the following combinations:

```
192.168.0.0/255.255.255.128
192.168.0.0/25
```

Network Addresses and Broadcast IPs

A network address is an IP address that represents all of the systems on a network. A broadcast IP address sends a message to all systems on that network.

The first assignable IP address typically comes right after the network IP address. For example, my home network has a network IP address of 192.168.0.0. The first assignable IP address on that network is 192.168.0.1.

In contrast, the broadcast address is the last available IP address on that network. Because I use a standard Class C netmask of 255.255.255.0, the broadcast address for my home network is 192.168.0.255.

These are private IP addresses, so you won't be able to directly access the Internet using any of those addresses.

Put It All Together

A network isn't fully defined without a network address and network mask. Each network has a broadcast IP address that can be used to send a message to every system on that network. For example, the private IP network address that I use is 192.168.0.0, with a network mask of 255.255.255.0 and a broadcast address of 192.168.0.255.

The network address and netmask, taken together, define a network. Routers send information to a network address, as discussed in the "Routing Tables" section later in this chapter. The netmask literally masks out those addresses that are not part of the network. For the example described, the first line specifies the IP network address; the second line specifies the netmask:

```
11000000 10101000 00000000 00000000
11111111 11111111 11111111 00000000
```

All but the last eight bits are masked. Available network addresses come from those last eight bits, the last number in a dotted-quad address. So the addresses that are part of my home network range from 192.168.0.0 to 192.168.0.255.

However, the network and broadcast IP addresses are dedicated as such. They are reserved addresses, which means they can't be assigned to individual systems. As such, the addresses that can be assigned to systems on my network are these:

```
192.168.0.1 - 192.168.0.254
```

In other words, although there are 256 IP addresses on my network, there are only 254 assignable IP addresses.

In a similar fashion, a bigger business might use a class B netmask. If you run such a business, you can set it up with the 192.168.0.0 network address, a netmask of 255.255.0.0, and a broadcast address of 192.168.255.255. Although that encompasses $2^{16} = 65{,}536$ IP addresses, the network and broadcast IP addresses are dedicated as such, so there are 65,534 assignable IP addresses on that network.

Here's one more example. Based on the previously mentioned 192.168.0.0/25 network, the network IP address is 192.168.0.0. Because the network mask is 255.255.255.128, we can break it down to its bits:

```
11000000 10101000 00000000 00000000
11111111 11111111 11111111 10000000
```

In this case, all but the last seven bits are masked. Available network addresses come from those last seven bits, the last number in a dotted-quad address. So the addresses that are part of that network range from 192.168.0.0 to 192.168.0.127. The first address, 192.168.0.0, is the network address. The last address, 192.168.0.127, is the broadcast address. Assignable IP addresses in that network range from 192.168.0.1 through 192.168.0.126.

Because that leaves free the IP addresses between 192.168.0.128 and 192.168.0.255, you can set up a second network for those addresses, with the same netmask. That network may be depicted by either of the following lines:

```
192.168.0.128/255.255.255.128
192.168.0.128/25
```

For that second network, the network IP address would be 192.168.0.128. The netmask would be 192.168.0.255. Assignable IP addresses on that network are 192.168.0.129 through 192.168.0.254.

IPv6 Addressing

The basic difference between IPv4 and IPv6 is in the number of bits associated with the IP address. Although there are 32 bits in an IPv4 address, there are 128 bits in an IPv6 address.

IPv6 addresses are typically depicted in hexadecimal notation, also known as base 16. In contrast, standard decimal numbers follow a base 10 format; binary numbers follow a base 2 format. In base 16, standard numbers are as follows:

```
0, 1, 2, 3, 4, 5, 6, 7, 8, 9, a, b, c, d, e, f
```

As shown in the output to the **ifconfig** command, the following lists the IPv6 address on my desktop system:

```
inet6 addr: fe80::240:f4ff:fe3c:558/64 Scope:Link
```

With so many IPv6 addresses available, there's an IPv6 address for every current IPv4 address. For example, the following IPv4 address

```
192.168.0.50
```

can be converted to the hexadecimal notation of an IPv6 address. First, convert the IPv4 address to binary format, split out by bytes.

```
11000000 10101000 00000000 00110010
```

But because $16 = 2^4$, there are four bits in every hexadecimal number. So break down the binary format into groups of four. (Believe it or not, the technical term for a group of four bits, or half a byte, is a "nibble.")

```
1100 0000 1010 1000 0000 0000 0011 0010
```

Now convert these nibbles back to decimal numbers:

```
12 0 10 8 0 0 3 2
```

Convert each decimal number to a hexadecimal number, based on the hexadecimal numbering system defined earlier (12=c and 10=a):

```
c 0 a 8 0 0 3 2
```

To configure it in a standard IPv6 format, now group these hexadecimal numbers by four (which isn't a nibble):

```
c0a8:0032
```

Now you can express the IPv6 translation of the 192.168.0.50 IPv4 address as follows:

```
0000:0000:0000:0000:0000:0000:c0a8:0032
```

In other words, there's an IPv6 address for every existing IPv4 address, and it's included in the last eight hexadecimal numbers in that IPv6 address. That address can also be expressed as follows, where the first colons (:) substitute for all the 0s at the beginning of the address.

```
::c0a8:0032
```

The IPv6 loopback address (::1) is different from its IPv4 equivalent (127.0.0.1). The ::1 would translate to a 0.0.0.1 IPv4 address. Conversely, the 127.0.0.1 would translate to an ::8f00:0001 IPv6 address.

 NOTE

Because my home routers can't handle IPv6 addresses, I registered at http://go6.net/ for the purpose of this chapter, using the instructions at https://wiki.ubuntu.com/IPv6.

Basic Network Commands

Several basic network commands are listed in the LPIC-1 objectives for this section. For the most part, these commands test and trace connections, as well as translate FQDNs (fully qualified domain names) such as www.courseptr.com and IP addresses such as 69.32.142.109.

The commands described in this section include `ftp`, `telnet`, `host`, `dig`, `ping`, `traceroute`, and `tracepath`. For IPv6 addresses, the last three commands are replaced by the `ping6`, `traceroute6`, and `tracepath6` commands.

If there are DNS servers that do not provide output as suggested, a list of the root DNS servers for the Internet is available in the output to the `dig` command. Alternatively, many routers on home networks have the same functionality. The IP address of your home router should correspond to the gateway address `route -n` command described later in this chapter.

Connect with ftp

The `ftp` command is a standard client command for connections to FTP servers. For example, the following command is perhaps the simplest way to connect to the Debian FTP server:

```
$ ftp ftp.debian.org
```

Connections to FTP servers may require a regular username and password. Many FTP servers support connections based on an anonymous username and a random password. Some FTP administrators still request that people who connect enter their e-mail address as the password.

Once a connection is made, note the `ftp>` prompt. Many FTP servers support Linux-style commands and listings at that prompt, as shown in Figure 13.1. Other `ftp` client commands may be listed with the `help` command. To exit from the client, use the `quit` or `exit` commands.

Generally, local commands can be run from the `ftp>` prompt with the bang (!) preface. For example, whereas the `ls` command at the `ftp>` prompt lists files on the local FTP server directory, the following command lists files in the local system directory:

```
ftp> !ls
```

Remote Logins with telnet

The traditional command tool for remote logins is `telnet`. Because it transmits all information in cleartext, it's a simple tool, and it's not normally encumbered by encryption schemes. However, it even transmits passwords in cleartext, so it is less frequently used, especially when compared to the remote `ssh` command logins described in Chapter 15, "Security Administration."

When enabled on a host system, `telnet` command logins are simple. For the purpose of this chapter, I've temporarily enabled a Telnet server on my CentOS 5 system and logged into that server, as shown in Figure 13.2.

```
michael@ubuntuHHserver:~$ ftp ftp.debian.org
Connected to ftp.debian.org.
220 ftp.debian.org FTP server
Name (ftp.debian.org:michael): anonymous
331 Please specify the password.
Password:
230 Login successful.
Remote system type is UNIX.
Using binary mode to transfer files.
ftp> ls
200 PORT command successful. Consider using PASV.
150 Here comes the directory listing.
drwxr-xr-x    8 1176      1176         4096 Feb 24 15:23 debian
226 Directory send OK.
ftp> cd debian
250 Directory successfully changed.
ftp> ls
200 PORT command successful. Consider using PASV.
150 Here comes the directory listing.
-rw-r--r--    1 1176      1176         1060 Feb 14 14:06 README
-rw-r--r--    1 1176      1176         1290 Dec 04  2000 README.CD-manufacture
-rw-r--r--    1 1176      1176         2581 Feb 14 14:05 README.html
-rw-r--r--    1 1176      1176       120941 Feb 23 13:52 README.mirrors.html
-rw-r--r--    1 1176      1176        60724 Feb 23 13:52 README.mirrors.txt
drwxr-xr-x   11 1176      1176         4096 Feb 14 14:12 dists
drwxr-xr-x    4 1176      1176         4096 Feb 24 13:52 doc
drwxr-xr-x    3 1176      1176         4096 Feb 24 14:55 indices
-rw-r--r--    1 1176      1176      4765965 Feb 24 14:55 ls-lR.gz
-rw-r--r--    1 1176      1176       137496 Feb 24 14:55 ls-lR.patch.gz
drwxr-xr-x    5 1176      1176         4096 Dec 19  2000 pool
drwxr-xr-x    4 1176      1176         4096 Nov 17 23:05 project
drwxr-xr-x    2 1176      1176         4096 Feb 07 00:33 tools
226 Directory send OK.
ftp> exit
```

FIGURE 13.1 *An* ftp *client session.*

```
michael@UbuntuHH:~$ telnet CentOS-5
Trying 192.168.0.11...
Connected to CentOS-5.mommabears.com.
Escape character is '^]'.

    CentOS5-LPI (Linux release 2.6.18-92.1.22.el5 #1 SMP Tue Dec 16 12:03:43 EST
 2008) (1)

login: michael
Password:
Last login: Tue Feb 24 14:39:46 from 192.168.0.8
You have new mail.
[michael@CentOS5-LPI ~]$ []
```

FIGURE 13.2 *A* telnet *client session.*

After a connection is made via telnet, all you need to do to log into a remote system is enter a username and password configured for that remote system.

TIP

The telnet command is frequently used for network troubleshooting. The telnet 10.0.0.1 123 command checks for an available connection to port 123 on the noted IP address. As noted earlier, port 123 is associated with NTP services.

Look Up Address Information with host

DNS servers provide the database of FQDNs, such as www.cengage.com, and IP addresses, such as 69.32.133.79. The host and dig commands use this database in different ways.

The host command, when applied to an FQDN, finds basic information about that domain, as it is stored in available DNS servers. For example, see what happens when I run the host command on www.cengage.com.

 NOTE

Normal formatting conventions for this book would require the use of the http:// in front of associated URLs. However, the http:// does not work with the host, dig, or nslookup commands. Furthermore, it does not work with some of the URLs described in this chapter and Chapter 14, because they communicate based on other TCP/IP protocols.

```
$ host www.cengage.com
www.cengage.com is an alias for cengage.com.
cengage.com has address 69.32.133.79
cengage.com mail is handled by 5 mail123.cengage.com.
```

 NOTE

The output from the host cengage.com command includes an e-mail server URL that we believe to be unused, as of this writing. A simulated URL was substituted, because the associated databases are being changed. Therefore, the actual output of the host www.cengage.com or the host cengage.com commands is different from what you see in this book.

The first line, which specifies an alias, sends data directed at www.cengage.com to cengage.com. The second line specifies the IP address. The third line specifies the URL of the associated MTA e-mail service.

The search can also work in reverse. When applied to the noted IP address, it identifies the DNS server that serves the domain in question, in this case:

```
host -1 69.32.133.79
79.133.32.69.in-addr.arpa domain name pointer academic.cengage.com.
```

The DNS data shows the IP address, in reverse, followed by the pointer directive, which actually points to academic.cengage.com, the FQDN of the authoritative DNS server for the cengage.com domain.

To see the full capabilities of the `host` command, try it by itself. You'll see a summary of available switches. Then try the `host -v cengage.com` command. You'll see the data listed in associated DNS servers, specified in the section marked `AUTHORITY`, with an `SOA` label.

The information in this section is made available from DNS servers. If I have doubts about those DNS servers, I could try the root DNS servers described earlier, or possibly even the IP address of a home gateway router. The IP address of my home gateway router is 192.168.0.1. I read its information about `cengagelearning.com` with the following command:

```
$ host cengagelearning.com 192.168.0.1
```

Look Up Address Information with dig

The `dig` command provides similar information to `host`, but in a different format. From Figure 13.3, you can see the output to the `dig www.cengage.com` command. The www.cengage.com FQDN is shown as an alias; the `CNAME` directive specifies that www.cengage.com is a canonical name for cengage.com. In other words, the output says that cengage.com is the real FQDN for www.cengage.com. Yes, the 192.168.0.1 IP address is on my local network; it is the DNS server for my network.

```
michael@UbuntuHH:~$ dig www.cengage.com

; <<>> DiG 9.4.2-P2 <<>> www.cengage.com
;; global options:  printcmd
;; Got answer:
;; ->>HEADER<<- opcode: QUERY, status: NOERROR, id: 16061
;; flags: qr rd ra; QUERY: 1, ANSWER: 2, AUTHORITY: 0, ADDITIONAL: 0

;; QUESTION SECTION:
;www.cengage.com.               IN      A

;; ANSWER SECTION:
www.cengage.com.        542     IN      CNAME   cengage.com.
cengage.com.            542     IN      A       69.32.133.79

;; Query time: 10 msec
;; SERVER: 192.168.0.1#53(192.168.0.1)
;; WHEN: Wed Feb 25 09:02:34 2009
;; MSG SIZE  rcvd: 63

michael@UbuntuHH:~$ []
```

FIGURE 13.3 *dig for DNS information.*

Try the `dig` command by itself. You'll see the list of root DNS servers for the Internet. Although DNS is a distributed database, these root servers contain the information required to identify the FQDN and IP addresses on every properly published system on the Internet. Because it's not possible for a single DNS server to contain information on every Internet host, the root DNS servers know where to find other DNS servers authoritative for every Internet domain.

If I wanted to use a different DNS server (on IP address 192.168.0.2), I would run the following command:

```
$ dig @192.168.0.2 courseptr.com
```

If your local gateway router (or locally configured DNS server) is on a different IP address, substitute that address for 192.168.0.2. If allowed by your ISP (Internet service provider), you could also substitute the IP address of one of its DNS servers.

Test a Connection with ping

The ping command is also known as the packet internet groper. It uses ICMP packets for data transmission, which works at the same level as TCP and UDP.

You can use the ping command to confirm connectivity to available Web sites and IP addresses. For example, if you believe that a Web site such as www.cengage.com might be down, try the following command:

```
ping -c1 www.cengage.com
```

The -c1 switch looks for one response. If you forget the -c1, the responses continue until you log out of the console or press Ctrl+C. If the connection is good, you should see output similar to the following:

```
PING www.cengage.com (69.32.133.79) 56(84) bytes of data.
64 bytes from academic.cengage.com (69.32.133.79): icmp_seq=1 ttl=111 time=103 ms
```

The first line confirms a connection to a DNS server, which translates www.cengage.com to the noted IP address. The second line specifies the name of the server, academic.cengage.com, which in this case is another alias for www.cengage.com. It also confirms that the response was received in 103 milliseconds.

Even on an IPv4 network, you should be able to try the ping6 command on the IPv6 local-host address:

```
$ ping6 ::1
```

If you've registered at http://go6.net, as described earlier in this chapter, you should be able to access IPv6-capable sites, such as ipv6.google.com.

The ping command is also useful for troubleshooting. You'll read more about such features in Chapter 14, "More Network Fundamentals."

Trace a Network Route with traceroute

Larger networks, including the Internet, are filled with routers. Any time data moves from one network to another, it passes a router. The traceroute command finds each of the routers between you and the destination and identifies each of those routers when possible.

As a tool that traces a path through networks, the traceroute command can diagnose problems on larger groups of networks. Even if you don't have access to a larger network, you can still test the traceroute command on the largest network group of them all: the Internet. For example, if you run the traceroute canonical.com command, you'll see a series of domain names and IP addresses. Although there are no guarantees, many domain names are descriptive of their locations.

However, it takes time to find those domain names. Sometimes a traceroute command can find the IP address but cannot find the associated domain name—at least not fast enough to avoid timeouts that can stop a route from being traced. If you have a problem with the traceroute *domainname* command, try the traceroute -n *domainname* command.

The IPv6 version of traceroute is the traceroute6 command. If you've registered at http://go6.net, as described earlier in this chapter, you should be able to run commands such as this:

```
$ traceroute6 ipv6.google.com
```

Trace a Network Route with tracepath

At the level of the LPIC-1 user, the tracepath command is subtly different from the traceroute command. Figure 13.4 lists the path taken from my laptop on IP address 192.168.0.8, through my router on 192.168.0.1, through locations in Seattle, Denver, Chicago, New York, and to the Canonical offices in London, UK. (Canonical, Ltd., is the corporate sponsor of the Ubuntu distribution.)

The subtle difference is in the cited MTU, the size of the network packet sent and received from responding routers.

```
michael@UbuntuHH:~$ tracepath ubuntu.com
 1:  192.168.0.8 (192.168.0.8)                                    0.292ms pmtu 1500
 1:  192.168.0.1 (192.168.0.1)                                    2.859ms
 1:  192.168.0.1 (192.168.0.1)                                    3.530ms
 2:  no reply
 3:  no reply
 4:  no reply
 5:  no reply
 6:  te-0-4-0-5-cr01.seattle.wa.ibone.comcast.net (68.86.90.237)  14.440ms asymm
 7:  te-3-3.car1.Seattle1.Level3.net (4.79.104.109)               30.754ms asymm  6
 8:  ae-31-51.ebr1.Seattle1.Level3.net (4.68.105.30)              18.452ms asymm  7
 9:  ae-1-100.ebr2.Seattle1.Level3.net (4.69.132.18)              21.809ms asymm  7
10:  ae-2.ebr2.Denver1.Level3.net (4.69.132.54)                   42.644ms asymm  8
11:  ae-3.ebr1.Chicago2.Level3.net (4.69.132.62)                  67.235ms asymm  9
12:  ae-6.ebr1.Chicago1.Level3.net (4.69.140.189)                 74.293ms asymm 10
13:  ae-2.ebr2.NewYork1.Level3.net (4.69.132.66)                 105.180ms asymm 11
14:  ae-62-62.csw1.NewYork1.Level3.net (4.69.134.82)              94.673ms asymm 10
15:  ae-61-61.ebr1.NewYork1.Level3.net (4.69.134.65)              94.676ms asymm 11
16:  ae-43-43.ebr2.London1.Level3.net (4.69.137.73)              166.804ms asymm 12
17:  ae-1-100.ebr1.London1.Level3.net (4.69.132.117)             171.150ms asymm 13
18:  ae-2.ebr2.London2.Level3.net (4.69.132.145)                 179.886ms asymm 14
19:  ae-26-54.car2.London2.Level3.net (4.68.117.112)             166.235ms asymm 16
20:  195.50.121.2 (195.50.121.2)                                 165.709ms asymm 17
21:  gw0-0-gr.canonical.com (91.189.88.10)                       165.165ms asymm 17
22:  no reply
23:  no reply
```

FIGURE 13.4 *The tracepath command specifies a network route.*

As with the traceroute command, trouble may happen when translating IP addresses to domain names. If you have a problem with the tracepath *domainname* command, you can avoid DNS server issues with the tracepath -n *domainname* command.

The IPv6 version of tracepath is the tracepath6 command. If you've registered at http://go6.net, as described earlier in this chapter, you should be able to run commands such as the following:

```
$ tracepath6 ipv6.google.com
```

Basic Network Configuration

With an understanding of the TCP/IP protocol suite described in the first part of this chapter, you have the tools to understand the basic network configuration of a Linux system. That configuration is driven by several text files in the /etc directory and several related commands that can configure local network and routing interfaces.

Once you understand these basic network configuration files and commands, you'll have the tools to troubleshoot most Linux network problems.

Network Configuration Files

Four network configuration files are listed in the LPIC-1 objectives: **/etc/hostname**, **/etc/hosts**, **/etc/resolv.conf**, and **/etc/nsswitch.conf**. Taken together with distribution-specific network configuration files, they fully define how a system communicates online. For more information on /etc/resolv.conf and /etc/nsswtich.conf, see Chapter 14. This chapter is focused on /etc/hostname, /etc/hosts, and related files.

The Local Host in /etc/hostname

Although the LPIC-1 objectives specify the /etc/hostname configuration file, this file isn't part of standard Red Hat–style distributions such as CentOS 5. But it's a simple file, designed to include just the hostname for the local system. On Red Hat–based systems, the hostname is stored in the /etc/sysconfig/network configuration file.

The hostname of the local system can be called with the hostname command, from the /bin directory.

A Database in /etc/hosts

The precursor to the Internet was the ARPAnet (Advanced Research Projects Agency Network). The ARPAnet started with four nodes, at UCLA, Stanford, UC Santa Barbara, and the University of Utah. At that point, it would have been possible and practical to store the information for each node in a single file.

On a Linux system, that file is /etc/hosts. Today, it's often used to store the hostnames and IP addresses of all systems on small local networks. If you don't have a DNS server for the local network, you can set the hostname/IP address database in that file, in the following format:

```
127.0.0.1       localhost
192.168.0.11    CentOS-5.mommabears.com CentOS-5
```

Note how it includes the IP address, the FQDN, and the hostname of the noted CentOS 5 system, along with the well-known IP loopback address for the localhost system.

To configure an /etc/hosts file for a network, you need to do two things:

1. Add the IP address and hostname of each system to a separate line in /etc/hosts. You can also add the FQDN to each line.
2. Copy the /etc/hosts file to each system on the local network.

The /etc/hosts file is a static database. Any changes to this database are made "by hand." In contrast, DNS servers can dynamically update their databases, with the help of other more authoritative DNS servers.

I keep the IP address of a couple of FQDNs on my /etc/hosts file. That allows me to have a minimal level of connectivity if configured DNS servers are unavailable or down.

The /etc/hosts files can also be configured for IPv6 addresses. One default IPv6 address is the localhost address:

```
::1          localhost6.localdomain6 localhost6
```

Other Network Configuration Files

Although there are other important network configuration files, they're not listed in the objectives covered in this chapter. However, you might need to change some essential configuration files for the CentOS 5 distribution: /etc/sysconfig/network and /etc/sysconfig/network-scripts/ifcfg-eth0. Yes, if your network device name is other than eth0, substitute appropriately for ifcfg-eth0.

The functionally similar file on the Ubuntu distribution is /etc/network/interfaces. These configuration files set basic network parameters during the boot process, whenever the network process is started. If there's a problem with networking on either distribution, it might be due to an error in these files.

Routing Tables

A routing table determines the path of a network message. To see the routing table for the local system, run the **route** command from the /sbin directory. When run by itself, it specifies the networks to which a network message may be sent. Take this excerpt from the output from the route command from my CentOS 5 system:

```
Kernel IP routing table
Destination     Gateway         Genmask         Flags Metric Ref    Use Iface
192.168.20.0    0.0.0.0         255.255.255.0   U     0      0        0 eth1
192.168.0.0     0.0.0.0         255.255.255.0   U     0      0        0 eth0
default         192.168.0.1     0.0.0.0         UG    0      0        0 eth0
```

Now interpret the relevant parts of this output. The first line specifies the path for messages that are sent to systems on the 192.168.20.0/255.255.255.0 network, as specified by Destination and Genmask, which specify the network address and network mask. Messages to that network are sent through the second Ethernet card on the local system, designated eth1.

The second line specifies the path for messages that are sent to systems on the 192.168.0.0/255.255.255.0 network. Messages to that network are sent through the first Ethernet card on the local system, designated eth0.

The third and final line specifies the path for messages that are sent to other systems. The default setting is also known as IP address 0.0.0.0. When the routing table is read in this order, the address of all network packets is read. If the network packet is not destined for the 192.168.20.0/255.255.255.0 or the 192.168.0.0/255.255.255.0 networks, it is sent to the address named default, through the specified Gateway, also using the first Ethernet card on the local system, eth0.

One possible problem with the route command is that it checks available DNS servers and /etc/hosts configuration files for hostnames and domain names. That process can take time; if a DNS server is down, it can even keep the route command from working. One popular option is the following:

```
$ route -n
```

Functionally equivalent to route is the netstat -r command. The netstat command is a more generic network status command, not included in the LPIC-1 objectives. But the -n switch can be helpful there as well, because the netstat -nr command is equivalent to route -n. Both commands provide the same routing table without having to look to a DNS server for help.

Network Management Commands

Several network configuration commands are associated with Objective 109.2. You can use the ifconfig, **ifup**, and **ifdown** commands to configure and control specific network cards. In contrast, you can use the route command to set up paths to different networks. You can also use the ping command to verify a local interface.

ifconfig

The ifconfig command is powerful. Not only does it reveal the current state of network connections, it allows you to configure each of these connections. The ifconfig command by itself reveals the state of all connections on the local system. A simple output is shown in Figure 13.5.

The ifconfig command reveals two devices: the loopback device (lo) and the Ethernet card (eth2). Normally, the first and only Ethernet device on a system is designated as eth0, but that is not always the case. But when devices eth0, eth1, and eth2 exist, they're designated as the first, second, and third Ethernet network cards, respectively.

```
michael@ubuntuHHservervm:~$ ifconfig
eth2      Link encap:Ethernet  HWaddr 00:0c:29:64:d9:1e
          inet addr:192.168.0.205  Bcast:192.168.0.255  Mask:255.255.255.0
          inet6 addr: fe80::20c:29ff:fe64:d91e/64 Scope:Link
          UP BROADCAST RUNNING MULTICAST  MTU:1500  Metric:1
          RX packets:105 errors:0 dropped:0 overruns:0 frame:0
          TX packets:146 errors:0 dropped:0 overruns:0 carrier:0
          collisions:0 txqueuelen:1000
          RX bytes:16952 (16.5 KB)  TX bytes:22129 (21.6 KB)
          Interrupt:16 Base address:0x1400

lo        Link encap:Local Loopback
          inet addr:127.0.0.1  Mask:255.0.0.0
          inet6 addr: ::1/128 Scope:Host
          UP LOOPBACK RUNNING  MTU:16436  Metric:1
          RX packets:66 errors:0 dropped:0 overruns:0 frame:0
          TX packets:66 errors:0 dropped:0 overruns:0 carrier:0
          collisions:0 txqueuelen:0
          RX bytes:5248 (5.1 KB)  TX bytes:5248 (5.1 KB)

michael@ubuntuHHservervm:~$ []
```

FIGURE 13.5 *The* ifconfig *command reveals current network devices.*

The ifconfig command output provides a lot of other information, including that specified in Table 13.6. Data transfer information is specified in packets, the term associated with Ethernet network transmissions. The list includes those options relevant to the LPIC-1 objectives. You might notice that the capitalization in the labels is inconsistent, but most Linux geeks are not English majors.

Table 13.6 Command Output from ifconfig

Label	Description
Link encap	Network type
HWaddr	Hardware address of the network card, in hexadecimal notation
inet addr	IPv4 address
Bcast	IPv4 Broadcast address
Mask	Network mask, also known as the subnet mask or netmask
inet6 addr	IPv6 address
Scope	May be Link for local addresses or Global if there's an IPv6 router
UP	Only if the network device is up
BROADCAST	Only if broadcasts are enabled
MULTICAST	Only if multicasts are enabled
MTU	Maximum transmission units in packets
RX packets	Number of packets received through the network interface
TX packets	Number of packets transmitted through the network interface

A number of the items shown in Table 13.6 can be modified with the ifconfig command. Perhaps most important is an IP address; for example, the following command sets a static private IP address for the first Ethernet adapter:

```
ifconfig eth0 172.16.0.55
```

However, that command assumes a default network mask, as reflected in the following excerpt from the output to the ifconfig eth0 command:

```
inet addr:172.16.0.55  Bcast:172.16.255.255  Mask:255.255.0.0
```

Because the noted address is a Class B IP address, the default network mask is 255.255.0.0. You can set up the same address with a nonstandard network mask with the netmask switch, as shown here:

```
ifconfig eth0 172.16.0.55 netmask 255.255.255.0
```

There are additional options that can be customized. Sometimes user subscriptions through an ISP (Internet service provider) are tied to a specific hardware address on a network card. If that network card goes down, the following command can be used to set up a new network card with the old hardware address:

```
ifconfig eth0 hw ether 00:0c:29:a3:fc:4f
```

The command retains the designation of eth0 as an Ethernet card and assigns the noted hardware address in hexadecimal notation.

ifdown

The ifdown command is straightforward. You can use it to deactivate the network interface of your choice. For example, the ifdown eth0 command deactivates the eth0 network interface. Alternatively, the ifdown -a command deactivates all configured network interfaces.

ifup

The ifup command also is straightforward; it works almost as a mirror image to the ifdown command. You can use this command to activate any network interfaces that are currently down. For example, the ifup eth1 command activates the eth1 network interface. The ifup -a command activates all network interfaces configured in distribution-specific configuration files, such as /etc/network/interfaces and /etc/sysconfig/network-scripts directory files associated with each interface.

route

As described earlier, the route command displays the currently configured routing table for the system and determines where network packets are sent. There are times when you'll want to change the routing table and the route command. The following exercise assumes a system with a single configured network card. On such a system, take the following steps:

1. To simplify the commands to be run, log in as the root user.

2. Run the `route -n` command to review the current routing table. Write down the value of the gateway IP address and `Iface` device associated with the default route, to the destination network 0.0.0.0.

3. Delete the default route with the `route del default` command.

4. Review the routing table again. What happened to the route to the destination network 0.0.0.0?

5. Add a new default route with the `route add default gw gateway dev device` command, where `gateway` is the gateway IP address and `device` is the `Iface` device identified in step 2.

6. Rerun the `route -n` command. Is there a difference with the routing table identified in step 2?

7. Rerun steps 3 through 6, except substitute 0.0.0.0 for `default` in the `route` commands.

If the routing table isn't restored, or if there are other network problems, try the aforementioned `ifdown -a` and `ifup -a` commands. Alternatively, restart network services with the `/etc/init.d/network restart` or `/etc/init.d/networking restart` commands; the actual network service script name depends on the distribution.

ping

When I run the `ifconfig` command on my system, it reveals an IP address of my network card of 192.168.0.8. That network card happens to be wlan1, which is the second wireless card on my laptop system.

To confirm that the noted IP address works, I run the `ping` command on that address. If it doesn't work and the network card is properly configured, there may be a second system on the local network with the same IP address. Now see what happens when the network is deactivated with the `ifdown dev` command, where *dev* is the network device such as `eth0` or `wlan1`.

Then try the `ping` command on the noted IP address—in my case, 192.168.0.8. It should still work, which demonstrates that the IP address is bound to the network card. The network card can respond, because it doesn't have to communicate over the network. If I tried to run the `ping` command on the IP address on a different system on the network, I would get the following message:

```
connect: network is unreachable
```

As suggested earlier in this chapter, the troubleshooting features associated with the `ping` command are covered in Chapter 14.

Chapter Summary

In this chapter, you examined some of the fundamentals of the TCP/IP protocol suite, as well as basic network configuration files. The knowledge in this chapter provides tools to understand and configure basic networking on a Linux system.

Although there are more than 65,000 TCP/IP ports, the LPIC-1 objectives suggest that you need to memorize the purpose of only a few, including ports 20 (ftp-data), 21 (ftp), 22 (ssh), 23 (telnet), 25 (smtp), 53 (domain), 80 (http), 110 (pop3), 119 (nntp), 139 (netbios-ssn), 143 (imap), 161 (snmp), 443 (https), 465 (smtps), 993 (imaps), and 995 (pop3s). These ports communicate via TCP and often UDP packets. The ping command uses ICMP packets.

This chapter also examined the basics of IPv4 addressing, including the dotted-quad IP address notation, network addresses, network masks, as well as basic differences between IPv4 and IPv6 addressing. Although a few of the associated commands, such as ftp, telnet, host, dig, ping, traceroute, and tracepath, were designed for IPv4, they have IPv6 counterpart commands.

You examined some common basic network configuration files, including /etc/hostname /etc/hosts, /etc/resolv.conf, and /etc/nsswitch.conf. You also learned to use the route command to delete and add options to a routing table. You examined the use of the ifconfig, ifup, and ifdown commands to configure, activate, and deactivate network cards.

Key Terms

♦ **20 (TCP/IP port).** The port number used for FTP server data transmission. Enables downloads from FTP servers.

♦ **21 (TCP/IP port).** The port number used for FTP connections. Supports login access to FTP servers.

♦ **22 (TCP/IP port).** The port number reserved for SSH (secure shell) logins and communication.

♦ **23 (TCP/IP port).** The port number configured for cleartext network logins via telnet.

♦ **25 (TCP/IP port).** The port number reserved for SMTP server connections from MTAs such as sendmail, Postfix, qmail, and Exim.

♦ **53 (TCP/IP port).** The port number reserved for communication with DNS servers.

♦ **80 (TCP/IP port).** The port number used for HTTP communication, normally with Web browsers.

♦ **110 (TCP/IP port).** The standard port number used for connections to POP3 servers.

♦ **119 (TCP/IP port).** nntp, configured for the NNTP (Network News Transfer Protocol) protocol.

◆ **139 (TCP/IP port).** `netbios-ssn`, reserved for file and printer sharing over a Microsoft network.

◆ **143 (TCP/IP port).** `imap2`, reserved for the IMAP2 and IMAP4 (Internet Message Access Protocols, versions 2 and 4).

◆ **161 (TCP/IP port).** `snmp`, configured for SNMP (Simple Network Management Protocol) for network monitoring.

◆ **443 (TCP/IP port).** `https`, for HTTPS (Hypertext Transfer Protocol-Secure) communication.

◆ **465 (TCP/IP port).** `smtps`, designed for SMTP (Simple Mail Transfer Protocol) server connections, over SSL (Secure Sockets Layer) from MTAs such as sendmail, Postfix, qmail, and Exim.

◆ **993 (TCP/IP port).** `imaps`, reserved for the IMAP2 and IMAP4 (Internet Message Access Protocols, versions 2 and 4), over SSL.

◆ **995 (TCP/IP port).** `pop3s`, reserved for the POP3 (Post Office Protocol, version 3) protocol, over SSL.

◆ **address class.** Reference to a series of IPv4 addresses.

◆ **broadcast address.** Reference to an IP address that sends messages to all IP addresses on a network, normally the last IP address assigned to that network. May also refer to the universal broadcast IP address, 255.255.255.255.

◆ **CIDR (Classless Inter-Domain Routing).** Specifies an IP address network mask by its number of bits.

◆ **Class A.** Reference to a series of IPv4 addresses, between 1.0.0.0 and 127.255.255.255.

◆ **Class B.** Reference to a series of IPv4 addresses, between 128.0.0.0 and 191.255.255.255.

◆ **Class C.** Reference to a series of IPv4 addresses, between 192.168.0.0 and 223.255.255.255.

◆ **Class D.** Reference to a series of IPv4 addresses, between 224.0.0.0 and 239.255.255.255.

◆ **Class E.** Reference to a series of IPv4 addresses, between 240.0.0.0 and 255.255.255.255.

◆ `dig.` Command that accesses information from a DNS server.

◆ `dotted-quad.` Reference to the format of IPv4 addresses such as 127.127.1.0.

◆ `/etc/hostname.` Standard file with the local system hostname; may be called with the `hostname` command.

◆ `/etc/hosts.` Configuration file with a static database of hostnames and IP addresses.

◆ `/etc/nsswitch.conf.` Configuration file that specifies the name service switch order, including the `/etc/hosts` and DNS databases.

◆ `/etc/resolv.conf.` Configuration file with the IP addresses of DNS servers.

◆ **FTP (File Transfer Protocol).** One protocol of the TCP/IP protocol suite, associated with IP addressing.

◆ `ftp.` Command that connects as a client to an FTP server.

◆ `host.` Command that accesses information from a DNS server.

◆ **ICMP (Internet Control Message Protocol).** One protocol of the TCP/IP protocol suite, commonly used for the `ping` command, and an alternative to TCP and UDP.

◆ `ifconfig.` Command that reveals the current IP address configuration; may also be used to reconfigure individual network devices.

◆ `ifdown.` Command that deactivates a specific network device; with the `-a` switch, it deactivates all configured network devices.

◆ `ifup.` Command that activates a specific network device; with the `-a` switch, it activates all configured network devices.

◆ **IP (Internet Protocol).** One protocol of the TCP/IP protocol suite, associated with IP addressing.

◆ **IPv4 (IP version 4).** One protocol of the TCP/IP protocol suite, associated with IPv4 addresses, which have 32 bits and are formatted in dotted-quad notation such as 192.168.0.50.

◆ **IPv6 (IP version 6).** One protocol of the TCP/IP protocol suite, associated with IPv6 addresses, which have 128 bits and are expressed in hexadecimal format.

◆ **loopback IP address.** Reference to IP address of the local system, used to confirm proper installation of network software. The IPv4 loopback address is 127.0.0.1; the IPv6 loopback address is ::1.

◆ **MTU (maximum transmission unit).** Specifies the size of a network packet.

◆ **network address.** An IP address that signifies the network, normally the first IP address for the series of addresses assigned to that network.

◆ **network mask.** Reference to an IP address that masks the network address, leaving the bit components of IP addresses used for the network.

◆ `ping.` Command that sends an ICMP message to a target host or IP address; the IPv6 version is `ping6`.

◆ **private IP address.** Reference to IP addresses reserved for private networks. Private IP addresses cannot be assigned or used on the Internet.

◆ `route.` Command that lists, adds to, or deletes from a routing table.

◆ **TCP/IP protocol suite.** The group of protocols associated with communication on Linux networks and the Internet.

◆ **TCP (Transmission Control Protocol).** One protocol of the TCP/IP protocol suite, commonly used for data transmission for services listed in the `/etc/services` configuration file, and an alternative to UDP and ICMP.

◆ `telnet.` Command that connects as a client to a Telnet server.

◆ **tracepath.** Command that checks the response from each intermediate router on the way to a given destination host or IP address. The difference is the use of MTUs. The IPv6 version of this command is tracepath6.

◆ **traceroute.** Command that checks the response from each intermediate router on the way to a given destination host or IP address. The IPv6 version of this command is traceroute6.

◆ **UDP (User Datagram Protocol).** One protocol of the TCP/IP protocol suite, commonly used for data transmission for services listed in the /etc/services configuration file, and an alternative to TCP and ICMP.

Review Questions

The number of review questions in this chapter and other chapters in this book is proportionate to each section's weight in the LPI objectives. Because this chapter covers items 109.1 and 109.1, the weight is 8; therefore, you'll see 16 questions in this section. You'll see multiple choice single answer, fill-in-the blank, and multiple choice multiple answer questions, as you'll encounter on the exam.

1. Enter the port number associated with the sendmail MTA.

   _____

2. Which of the following commands gets information from a DNS server? Choose two.
   A. ping 192.168.0.1
   B. host courseptr.com
   C. dig 69.32.133.79
   D. traceroute -n 69.32.133.79

3. Which of the following port numbers is associated with secure IMAP services?
   A. 25
   B. 110
   C. 143
   D. 993

4. Which of the following statements differentiates TCP messages from UDP messages?
   A. Both TCP and UDP messages are best effort.
   B. TCP messages are best effort; UDP messages include confirmed delivery.
   C. UDP messages are best effort; TCP messages include confirmed delivery.
   D. Both TCP and UDP messages include confirmed delivery.

5. Enter the protocol acronym associated with the `ping` command.

_____

6. Which of the following port numbers is associated with secure shell connections?

   A. 21

   B. 22

   C. 23

   D. 25

7. Which of the following is a standard private IP address?

   A. 1.2.3.4

   B. 10.20.30.40

   C. 100.200.100.200

   D. 255.255.255.0

8. Which of the following IP addresses can be assigned to a computer as part of the 192.168.0.0/24 network?

   A. 192.168.24.0

   B. 192.168.0.24

   C. 192.168.0.255

   D. 192.168.0.0

9. Which of the following files includes the IP addresses of DNS servers?

   A. `/etc/hosts`

   B. `/etc/resolv.conf`

   C. `/etc/dnssvr`

   D. `/etc/search`

10. Which of the following directives in the `/etc/nsswitch.conf` file specifies the name search order?

   A. `hosts`

   B. `dns`

   C. `files`

   D. `resolv`

11. Enter the full path to the file with a static database of hostnames and IP addresses.

_____

12. Which of the following commands would help you identify the loopback IP address? The local system has an IP address of 192.168.0.100.

   A. `ping loopback`

   B. `ping localhost`

   C. `ping 192.168.0.100`

   D. `ping 192.168.0.0`

13. Which of the following commands configures the first Ethernet device with IP address 192.168.10.20, with a network mask of 255.255.255.0?

   A. `ifconfig eth0 192.168.10.20`

   B. `ifconfig eth1 192.168.10.20`

   C. `ifconfig eth0 192.168.10.20 submask 255.255.255.0`

   D. `ifconfig eth1 192.168.10.20 netmask 255.255.255.0`

14. Which of the following commands configures the second Ethernet device with IP address 192.168.10.20, with a Class B network mask?

   A. `ifconfig eth1 192.168.10.20 netmask 255.255.0.0`

   B. `ifconfig eth2 192.168.10.20 submask 255.255.0.0`

   C. `ifconfig eth1 192.168.10.20 netmask 255.255.255.0`

   D. `ifconfig eth2 192.168.10.20 submask 255.255.255.0`

15. Enter the command that adds eth1 as the route to the 192.168.1.0 network. Do not include the full path, and assume that you already have administrative privileges.

   _____

16. Which of the following entries in a routing table is associated with the network mask?

   A. `netmask`

   B. `submask`

   C. `genmask`

   D. `network`

Chapter 14

More Network Fundamentals

After completing this chapter, you will be able to

■ Troubleshoot basic network problems

■ Configure a basic DNS client

Introduction

This chapter is in many ways a continuation of Chapter 13, "Basic Networking." Although it covers troubleshooting skills and the configuration of a DNS (domain name system) client, just about every key term listed in the associated objectives for this chapter was also covered in Chapter 13. So this chapter goes into more depth regarding how you can use each of the noted commands for troubleshooting and how you can further customize name resolution for DNS clients.

TIP

This chapter addresses two objectives in the LPI exam: 109.3 ("Basic Network Troubleshooting") and 109.4 ("Configure Client Side DNS").

Basic Network Troubleshooting

The ability to connect to a network is fundamental on today's computers. Therefore, qualified Linux professionals like you need to know how to troubleshoot networking issues on Linux clients. To that end, you need to know how to configure, debug, and change network interfaces, as well as manage the routing table for the local system.

Important commands for network troubleshooting include `ifconfig`, `ifup`, `ifdown`, `route`, **netstat**, `ping`, and `traceroute`. All but the `netstat` command are in the Key Terms list in Chapter 13.

LPIC-1 objective 109.3 is specific; you need to know how to "manually and automatically configure network interfaces and routing tables," including the process of "adding, starting, stopping, restarting, deleting or reconfiguring network interfaces." You'll examine each of these actions in the following sections.

Actions on Network Interfaces

In this section, you'll review the actions that you can take on a network interface. First, review the current network configuration with the following command:

```
$ ifconfig -a
```

The -a switch reads the current status of all configured network interfaces even if they're currently down. In the following subsections, you'll examine what it takes to add, delete, start, stop, and restart network interfaces. You'll also look at how to manually and automatically reconfigure such network interfaces.

Add a Network Interface

The commands associated with this section were first discussed in Chapter 1, "System Architecture." In most cases, Linux detects and configures newly installed network interfaces automatically. Often, you can find more information with the lspci or lsusb command.

If a device driver is loaded, it shows up in the output to the lsmod command, in a list of loaded modules. You can load modules manually with the insmod or modprobe command.

However, if you're configuring a new network interface for the first time, you'll want to find the key configuration file for your distribution. For Ubuntu systems, the file is /etc/network/interfaces. For Red Hat systems including CentOS 5, the file is ifcfg-*dev*, where *dev* is a device name such as eth0. You can find that file in the /etc/sysconfig/network-scripts/ directory.

Delete a Network Interface

Just as Linux automatically detects most network interfaces, it should automatically delete any network interfaces physically removed from a system. Network interfaces, like any other hardware that has been removed, should no longer show up in the output to a command like lspci or lsusb.

However, problems happen. Network interfaces that have been removed may still show up in a list of modules. In most cases, that's not a problem. You might see one or two extra modules loaded out of hundreds on a Linux system. It's possible that a different hardware component may still require a module. But if needed, you can remove modules with commands such as rmmod or modprobe -r, as discussed in Chapter 1.

Start a Network Interface

Once network interfaces are installed, they may already be running and configured on your system. If so, they may appear in the output to the ifconfig command.

If not, there are three basic ways to start a newly installed network interface. For example, assume that you've just installed a new network card. From the output to the ifconfig -a command, assume that you see a new Ethernet interface eth1. In that case, you can start that network card based on existing configuration files with either of the following commands:

```
# ifconfig eth1 up
# ifup eth1
```

Alternatively, you can activate all current network interfaces with the ifup -a command.

There is one more option to start network interfaces: use the network service script in the /etc/init.d/ directory. Because it varies by distribution, the following commands provide two examples of how that service, along with configured network cards, can be started:

```
# /etc/init.d/network start
# /etc/init.d/networking start
```

Stop a Network Interface

There may be several reasons to stop a network interface. You may want to limit access to a specific network. Or perhaps you want to disconnect other users. Or maybe you want to continue working without interference from instant messages. There are other possibilities, too.

The following commands can stop a specific network interface, in this case, eth1:

```
# ifconfig eth1 down
# ifdown eth1
```

Alternatively, you can stop networking on the local system completely with the following command:

```
# ifdown -a
```

Of course, you can also use the appropriate network service script in the /etc/init.d directory to stop all networking on the local system. Examples of distribution-specific stop commands follow:

```
# /etc/init.d/network stop
# /etc/init.d/networking stop
```

Restart a Network Interface

There are two ways to think about restarting a network interface. First, you can stop and then start one or more network interfaces, using the ifconfig, ifup, and ifdown commands just described. Alternatively, you can use the distribution-specific scripts in the /etc/init.d directory to restart networking on a system. The command may look like one of the following:

```
# /etc/init.d/network restart
# /etc/init.d/networking restart
```

Manually Configure a Network Interface

Network interfaces can be reconfigured temporarily with commands such as ifconfig. Some of the commands used to assign different IP addresses and related information were described in Chapter 13. To review, the following command specifies an IPv4 address with a non-standard network mask to what may be the second Ethernet card on the local system:

```
# ifconfig eth1 192.168.20.30 netmask 255.255.0.0
```

The eth1 device is normally the second Ethernet card, but that depends on the existence of an eth0 device. In addition, the following command deactivates the eth1 interface while assigning it a new hardware address:

```
# ifconfig eth1 down hw ether 00:0c:29:a3:fc:55
```

The hardware address of the Ethernet card is in hexadecimal notation, also known as base 16.

Manually Configure a Network Interface

However, to make a change permanent, you need to change the text configuration file directly. Because such files are distribution specific, those details—at least currently—are beyond the scope of the LPIC-1 objectives. However, that is always subject to change, so review the following excerpts from the /etc/network/interfaces file used on Ubuntu systems:

```
iface eth0 inet static
address 192.168.0.50
netmask 255.255.255.0
gateway 192.168.0.1
auto eth0
```

The directives shown specify a static IP address for device eth0. To make this device look to a DHCP (Dynamic Host Configuration Protocol) server for address information, you can change these lines to

```
iface eth0 inet dhcp
```

Alternatively, the Red Hat method used on CentOS 5 is fairly straightforward. The following excerpt from the ifcfg-eth0 file in the /etc/sysconfig/network-scripts directory includes a number of descriptive directives:

```
DEVICE=eth0
BOOTPROTO=none
BROADCAST=192.168.0.255
HWADDR=00:0C:29:A3:FC:4E
IPADDR=192.168.0.11
IPV6INIT=yes
IPV6_AUTOCONF=yes
NETMASK=255.255.255.0
NETWORK=192.168.0.0
ONBOOT=yes
GATEWAY=192.168.0.1
TYPE=Ethernet
```

Of course, if you're willing to accept DHCP-based configuration of this eth0 device, you can change BOOTPROTO to dhcp and then omit those directives otherwise assigned by a DHCP server.

Troubleshoot Networking

Problems happen with networks. The ping and traceroute commands can help identify problems with a network connection. For example, if you are responsible for some of the routers on the Internet, you may want to make sure that those routers aren't causing problems.

Before starting this process, run the ifconfig command to find the IP address associated with the local network card. For example, the following output excerpt suggests that the network card device is eth0 and lists its IPv4 and IPv6 addresses:

```
eth0    Link encap:Ethernet  HWaddr 00:0C:29:A3:FC:4E
        inet addr:192.168.0.11  Bcast:192.168.0.255  Mask:255.255.255.0
        inet6 addr: fe80::20c:29ff:fea3:fc4e/64 Scope:Link
```

The IPv4 address of this network card is 192.168.0.11. The IPv6 address shown, with the Scope:Link, suggests that no IPv6 hardware has been detected. If your system includes Scope:Global in this location, you should also be able to carry out the commands shown starting with step 3 with IPv6 addresses.

In addition, you'll want the IP address of another system on the local network. If it's a Linux system, just run the ifconfig command on that system. In this section, I use the IP address of my desktop system for this purpose. It's 192.168.0.50.

The first steps in this process involve the ping command, which sends messages using ICMP (Internet Control Message Protocol), discussed in Chapter 13. If you don't include the -c1 (or another number), which transmits one ICMP packet, the ping command sends packets continuously. You can then stop the ping command by pressing Ctrl+C.

1. Run the following command to make sure networking software is properly installed on the local system:

   ```
   $ ping -c1 127.0.0.1
   ```

   You should recognize 127.0.0.1 as the IPv4 localhost address. In fact, the first line in /etc/hosts should confirm that association. You should also be able to run the ping6 command on the IPv6 localhost address, ::1.

2. Run the following command, based on the information from your network card. Substitute accordingly for 192.168.0.11. The output should confirm that the IPv4 address is properly bound to that card. The IPv4 address shown here is based on the output to the ifconfig command shown earlier.

   ```
   ping -c1 192.168.0.11
   ```

   Alternatively, run the following ping6 command, using the IPv6 address shown from the ifconfig output. Be aware: the -I specifies access from the noted eth0 interface:

   ```
   ping6 -I eth0 -c1  fe80::20c:29ff:fea3:fc4e
   ```

3. Assuming that you've found the IP address of another system on the local network, run the ping command on that IP address. The following command specifies the IP

address of my desktop system, reachable from the 192.168.0.11 system. (Substitute accordingly on your network.)

```
ping -c1 192.168.0.50
```

If successful, this confirms a proper connection across the local network. Unless your network has IPv6-capable hardware, the ping6 command won't work from a remote system.

4. Finally, apply the ping command on the broadcast address for the local network. Chapter 13 described how you can identify the broadcast address for a local network—normally the last IP address in the associated range of addresses. For example, 192.168.0.255 is the last IP address; thus, it's the broadcast address for the private IP network range I use in my home network, 192.168.0.0/255.255.255.0. The -b switch sends a broadcast message. The -c10 sends 10 ICMP packets to all systems, which may be answered by individual systems on the local network. Of course, if the broadcast address on your system is different, substitute accordingly.

```
ping -b -c10 192.168.0.255
```

If all of these commands are successful, you've confirmed connectivity at least on the local network. The next step in networking is routing.

Analyze the Routing Table

When a message is sent between networks, it is routed. When a message is sent in a bigger multinational enterprise, it is often routed through multiple networks. If you're the administrator of such a network, you need to be able to identify where a problem stops a message. Perhaps that router has lost power, needs to be rebooted, or even needs to be replaced.

In preparation for the following steps, run the route -n command. Then run the netstat -nr command. The output from both commands should be identical. Take the following example output from a system connected to two different networks through the first (eth0) and second (eth1) adapters.

```
Kernel IP routing table
Destination     Gateway         Genmask         Flags   MSS Window  irtt Iface
192.168.20.0    0.0.0.0         255.255.255.0   U         0 0          0 eth1
192.168.0.0     0.0.0.0         255.255.255.0   U         0 0          0 eth0
169.254.0.0     0.0.0.0         255.255.0.0     U         0 0          0 eth1
0.0.0.0         192.168.0.1     0.0.0.0         UG        0 0          0 eth0
```

Network messages are sent in units known as packets. The header of each message includes information about the destination address. That destination address is compared against the destination listed in the routing table.

The destination address is compared against the destinations shown in each line, from first to last. So if the destination address is in the 192.168.0.0/255.255.255.0 network, the packet is sent through the eth1 network device. If the destination is not in that network, the system proceeds to the next line in the routing table. If the destination address is in the 192.168.0.0/255.255.255.0 network, the packet is sent through the eth0 network device. If the destination is not in that network, the system proceeds through the routing table until it reaches the default address, 0.0.0.0.

Messages to the default address are sent through the eth0 network device, via 192.168.0.1.

Now that you understand the current routing table, you should have a better feel for when network routes need to be changed. But for now, assume the routing table is good, as it is in most situations on a Linux system.

Trace a Network Route

In most cases, networking on individual Linux systems rarely poses problems. But when systems are put together in networks, more can go wrong. Cables can become disconnected. As suggested earlier, routers can break down or even lose power. To identify where a network stops transmitting messages, the traceroute command can help.

You can use the traceroute command on the biggest network of all: the Internet. The simplest expression of that command is on a distant Web site, preferably on another continent. Choose an appropriate site on the other side of the globe from you, based on the following model.

I target a connection on the other side of the globe, in this case the government of Australia. First, I run the dig command on the appropriate Web site to find the associated IP address:

```
$ dig www.australia.gov.au
```

The output identifies an IP address of 152.91.62.145. Now I apply the traceroute command to the noted URL (uniform resource locator) or IP address. Like the ping command, traceroute sends ICMP packets. The difference is that traceroute sends ICMP packets to each router between your system and the Web site of the Australian government. If successful, the note IP address is identified in the last output line. If not, you'll see three asterisks after the last successful ICMP message to a router, which may look similar to this:

```
15  CyberTrustAustraliaPtyLtd.sb5.optus.net.au (61.88.128.38)  205.281 ms   204.943 ms
199.768 ms
16  * * *
```

In this case, if there is a problem, it may be in the router, which would otherwise show up in line 16. To compare, you could run the traceroute command to the Web site of an organization closer to you.

Change Network Routes

Based on the routing table shown previously, assume that you've done the physical work to rewire a network. Perhaps you've changed Internet providers. For the purpose of this section, assume that the new gateway to other unspecified networks is 192.168.20.1. The easiest way to set this up on a test system is on a virtual machine. Yes, your networks will vary, so substitute accordingly.

To delete the old gateway and create a new one, take the following steps:

1. Run the following command to delete the current default gateway. In this case, you can substitute 0.0.0.0 for `default`.

   `# route del default`

   Confirm the result with the `route -n` command.

2. Add the new gateway as specified. The `dev eth1` part is not required unless multiple network devices are connected to the same network.

   `# route add 0.0.0.0 gw 192.168.20.1 dev eth1`

   Confirm the result with the `route -n` command. In my case, this command confirms problems, with the following output excerpt. The Genmask of 255.255.255.255 suggests that the given gateway address doesn't lead to other networks.

   ```
   Destination Gateway       Genmask          Flags MSS Window  irtt Iface
   0.0.0.0     192.168.20.1 255.255.255.255 U       0 0          0 eth1
   ```

   If you see the route shown above, you need to delete it and then find the default route through the `eth1` device. The gateway through that device happens to be 192.168.20.254.

3. Delete the faulty route and create the new one with the following commands:

   ```
   # route delete 0.0.0.0 gw 192.168.20.1 dev eth1
   # route add default gw 192.168.20.254 dev eth1
   ```

   Confirm the result with the `route -n` command.

To make sure changes survive a reboot or even a restart of network services, add the changes to distribution-specific configuration files. For Ubuntu, it's `/etc/network/interfaces`; for Red Hat systems including CentOS 5, it's `route-`*dev* in the `/etc/sysconfig/networking/devices` directory, where *dev* is the name of the network device, such as `eth1`.

Local Network Troubleshooting

Now you'll debug various network-related issues. To that end, you'll use a variety of commands to see the current status of the network. The `traceroute` command was used earlier to identify problems that may exist on remote networks. In this section, you'll examine other possible network problems.

On occasion, the given hostname of the local system differs from that available in databases such as the /etc/hosts file or an authoritative DNS server for the local network. Differences can prevent services from connecting. Problems could arise if any of the following four files or systems doesn't have the same hostname:

◆ The output of the hostname command

◆ The contents of the /etc/hostname file, if it exists on the local system

◆ The /etc/hosts configuration file

◆ For any authoritative DNS server on the local network, the host command, when run on the local IP address

The output of each of these options should match. If it doesn't, there may be problems.

As discussed in Chapter 13, you can use the ifconfig command to verify the following:

◆ The current status of configured network cards

◆ The IP address configuration on each network card

There's one more bit of information from the ifconfig output that may be helpful, based on data packets transmitted and received through the network device. Take the following excerpt from the ifconfig eth0 command output:

```
RX packets:20371580 errors:0 dropped:0 overruns:0 frame:0s
TX packets:13178476 errors:0 dropped:0 overruns:0 carrier:0
```

It documents the millions of network packets received (RX) and transmitted (TX) through the eth0 network device, which confirms that the device is actually networking data. If this output specifies an RX or TX of 0 or is suddenly not changing, there may be a problem with this specific network card.

At that point, you can run the ifup and ifdown commands described in Chapter 13 to activate and deactivate a specific network card with commands such as these:

```
# ifdown eth0
# ifup eth0
```

Alternatively, the ifup -a and ifdown -a commands activate and deactivate all network devices on the local system.

Open Ports and netstat

As discussed earlier, the netstat -nr command can identify the contents of the local routing table, in the same way as the route -n command. However, the netstat command can do more. It can identify remote connections, as well as ports that are open to remote connections. By itself, the netstat command identifies established connections. For example, run the netstat | less command on a system connected to the Internet—and if possible, other systems on the local network. You should see the hostnames of other local systems and the Web sites and IP addresses of remote connections.

Now go a bit further. One command I run to diagnose network problems is this:

```
$ netstat -atun | less
```

This command shows all (-a) network sockets, for connections that use both TCP (-t) and UDP (-u) packets, in numeric (-n) format. As discussed in Chapter 13, TCP/IP services, as listed in the /etc/services file, may transmit data using TCP and UDP packets. One sample result from my home server is shown in Figure 14.1.

```
tcp    0    0 0.0.0.0:902          0.0.0.0:*              LISTEN
tcp    0    0 127.0.0.1:3306       0.0.0.0:*              LISTEN
tcp    0    0 0.0.0.0:139          0.0.0.0:*              LISTEN
tcp    0    0 0.0.0.0:45967        0.0.0.0:*              LISTEN
tcp    0    0 0.0.0.0:111          0.0.0.0:*              LISTEN
tcp    0    0 0.0.0.0:80           0.0.0.0:*              LISTEN
tcp    0    0 0.0.0.0:6000         0.0.0.0:*              LISTEN
tcp    0    0 192.168.20.1:53      0.0.0.0:*              LISTEN
tcp    0    0 192.168.10.1:53      0.0.0.0:*              LISTEN
tcp    0    0 0.0.0.0:21           0.0.0.0:*              LISTEN
tcp    0    0 192.168.122.1:53     0.0.0.0:*              LISTEN
tcp    0    0 192.168.0.50:53      0.0.0.0:*              LISTEN
tcp    0    0 127.0.0.1:53         0.0.0.0:*              LISTEN
tcp    0    0 0.0.0.0:631          0.0.0.0:*              LISTEN
tcp    0    0 0.0.0.0:25           0.0.0.0:*              LISTEN
tcp    0    0 127.0.0.1:953        0.0.0.0:*              LISTEN
tcp    0    0 0.0.0.0:59513        0.0.0.0:*              LISTEN
tcp    0    0 127.0.0.1:4700       0.0.0.0:*              LISTEN
tcp    0    0 0.0.0.0:445          0.0.0.0:*              LISTEN
tcp    0    0 192.168.0.50:902     192.168.0.8:39938      ESTABLISHED
tcp    0    0 192.168.0.50:902     192.168.0.8:46592      ESTABLISHED
tcp    0    0 192.168.0.50:902     192.168.0.8:46591      ESTABLISHED
tcp6   0    0 :::6000              :::*                   LISTEN
tcp6   0    0 :::53                :::*                   LISTEN
tcp6   0    0 :::22                :::*                   LISTEN
tcp6   0    0 :::631               :::*                   LISTEN
tcp6   0    0 ::1:953              :::*                   LISTEN
tcp6   0 1920 192.168.0.50:22      192.168.0.8:46834      ESTABLISHED
udp    0    0 0.0.0.0:2049         0.0.0.0:*
udp    0    0 192.168.10.1:137     0.0.0.0:*
udp    0    0 192.168.20.1:137     0.0.0.0:*
:
```

FIGURE 14.1 *The netstat command and active connections.*

Note that the first column may specify TCP or UDP connections. For example, the first line suggests that the local system listens on the default IP address (0.0.0.0), using port 902. If you've installed VMware server, this port is listed in /etc/services for remote connections. And in fact, as shown in three of the ESTABLISHED connections listed in the middle of the figure, the netstat output identifies the three virtual machines that I'm running on my home server and have connected to from my laptop system on IP address 192.168.0.8.

Note the other ports listed. If you don't recognize some of the port numbers, look them up in the /etc/services file. They should provide hints as to services running on the local server, accessible to other systems. For example, the listing for 0.0.0.0:80 near the top of the figure suggests that I have a Web server, running on TCP/IP port 80, accessible to any IP address.

Of course, access may be further limited by provisions such as firewalls, but that is beyond the scope of the LPIC-1 objectives.

A DNS Client

This section is another continuation of Chapter 13, because it covers the /etc/hosts, /etc/resolv.conf, and /etc/nsswitch.conf configuration files. DNS clients are configured in these files. Once configured, the host and dig commands may be used as DNS client commands.

DNS Client Configuration

To configure a DNS client, you should include the IP addresses of DNS servers in the /etc/resolv.conf configuration file. A properly configured /etc/resolv.conf file looks like the following:

```
search mommabears.com
nameserver 192.168.0.1
```

The search directive adds the noted name to the end of hostnames. For example, if I run the ping ubuntuHHserver command, the search directive appends the mommabears.com domain name. The ping command then searches for the ubuntuHHserver.mommabears.com FQDN (fully qualified domain name). But if neither the ubuntuHHserver nor the FQDN exist in the /etc/hosts or DNS databases, it will still reveal an error message.

If you're working with utilities that add the FQDN of a DNS server to the /etc/resolv.conf configuration file, you may need to replace the FQDN with an IP address.

Host Resolution Files

As suggested in the LPIC-1 objectives, two other files relate to the configuration of a DNS client: /etc/hosts and /etc/nsswitch.conf. As discussed in Chapter 13, the standard /etc/hosts file includes the localhost address, 127.0.0.1, and possibly the hostname and IP address of the local system.

The /etc/hosts file can also be configured for IPv6 addresses. One default IPv6 address is the localhost address:

```
::1             localhost6.localdomain6 localhost6
```

But you can do more. To configure an /etc/hosts file for a network, you need to do two things:

1. Add the IP address and hostname of each system to a separate line in /etc/hosts. You can also add the FQDN to each line.
2. Copy the /etc/hosts file to each system on the local network.

The /etc/hosts file is a static database. Any changes to this database are made manually. In contrast, DNS servers can dynamically update their databases, with the help of other more authoritative DNS servers.

I keep the IP address of a couple of FQDNs on my /etc/hosts file. That allows me to have a minimal level of connectivity if configured DNS servers are unavailable or down for some reason.

Name Service Switch Order

As discussed in Chapter 13, the /etc/nsswitch.conf configuration file normally contains the following line, which points a DNS client first to the /etc/hosts file and then to DNS servers specified in the /etc/resolv.conf file.

```
hosts: files dns
```

Other databases may be used for name service support, including those based on Microsoft Windows, NIS (Network Information Service), and LDAP (Lightweight Directory Access Protocol) name services. You might see the following line in some versions of /etc/nsswitch.conf, associated with

```
hosts:    files mdns4_minimal [NOTFOUND=return] dns mdns4 mdns
```

The several references to **mdns4** in this line relate to APIPA (Automatic Private IP Addressing), first described in Chapter 13. In other words, the mdns4 directives search for IP addresses that would be assigned via APIPA. The mdns directive is associated with IPv6 addressing.

The host and dig Commands

There was a brief reference in Chapter 13 to the host -v command for more information. Try it on an FQDN such as www.cengage.com as well as an IP address such as 69.32.146.50. It reveals several different types of DNS database information, known as resource records, including those specified in Table 14.1.

Table 14.1 Selected DNS Database Information

Resource Record	Description
A	Specifies an IPv4 address associated with a domain name
AAAA	Specifies an IPv6 address associated with a domain name
CNAME	Lists a canonical name, a reference from an FQDN such as www.cengage.com to a domain name such as cengage.com
MX	Lists the name of a mail exchanger, normally a mail server that communicates using SMTP such as sendmail, Postfix, qmail, or Exim
PTR	Associates an IP address with a domain name, which supports reverse searches
SOA	Lists the start of authority record, which cites the FQDN of the DNS server, as well as contact e-mail information for the administrator

Beyond the options described in Chapter 13, the `host` and `dig` commands can test the DNS database from the servers of your choice. For example, if you've just configured a DNS server on the local network, on a system with IP address 192.168.0.1, the following commands use that server to search for DNS database information associated with the courseptr.com domain:

```
$ host courseptr.com 192.168.0.1
$ dig @192.168.0.1 courseptr.com
```

Chapter Summary

This chapter continued the coverage of networking fundamentals. In this chapter, you learned the basic troubleshooting features of various network configuration commands, including `ifconfig`, `ifup`, and `ifdown`. You reviewed commands including `lsmod`, `lsusb`, `lspci`, `rmmod`, and `modprobe`, which relate to how network hardware is detected and associated driver modules are loaded.

You examined how to use the `ping` command to test the proper installation of network software as well as connectivity with other systems on the local network. It's related to the `traceroute` command, because it also uses ICMP packets; however, `traceroute` can help identify where network messages may run into problems. You also looked at various `route` commands to identify and modify routing tables, as well as the `netstat` command, which can identify open ports.

The last part of the chapter reviewed the configuration of a DNS client and related files such as `/etc/hosts`, `/etc/nsswitch.conf`, and `/etc/resolv.conf`. It also reviewed the use of the `host` and `dig` commands to query related DNS databases.

Key Terms

◆ **mdns4.** Reference to a directive in the `/etc/nsswitch.conf` configuration file, related to APIPA.

◆ **netstat.** Reference to a series of IPv4 addresses, between 1.0.0.0 and 127.255.255.255.

Review Questions

The number of review questions in this chapter and other chapters in this book is proportionate to each section's weight in the LPI objectives. Because this chapter covers items 109.3 and 109.4, the weight is 6; therefore, you'll see 12 questions in this section. You'll see multiple choice single answer, fill-in-the-blank, and multiple choice multiple answer questions, as you'll encounter on the exam.

1. Enter the command that sets the first Ethernet adapter to an IP address of 10.20.30.40, with a network mask of 255.255.0.0. Do not include the full path to the command, and assume that you have administrative privileges.

   _____

2. Which of the following commands removes the route to all other IP addresses?

   A. route del default

   B. route del 255.255.255.255

   C. route del eth0

   D. route del 0.0.0.0

3. Which of the following commands specifies open TCP ports?

   A. netstat

   B. netstat -nr

   C. netstat -au

   D. netstat -at

4. Which of the following IP addresses is a loopback address? Choose two.

   A. 192.168.0.1

   B. 127.0.0.1

   C. ::1

   D. ffff:ffff:ffff:ffff

5. Enter the command that deactivates all current network interfaces. Do not include the full path to the command, and assume that you have administrative privileges.

   _____

6. Which of the following protocols does the traceroute command use?

   A. TCP

   B. UDP

   C. SMTP

   D. ICMP

7. Which of the following commands adds a default route to the 192.168.20.0 network using the second Ethernet adapter?

   A. route add default

   B. route add default gw eth1

   C. route add 192.168.20.0 dev eth1

   D. route add 192.168.20.0 dev eth2

8. Which of the following commands reviews the current routing table?

   A. ping -r

   B. hostname -ar

   C. netstat -nr

   D. ifconfig -r

9. Which of the following files includes the name of the local system? Choose two.

   A. /etc/hostname

   B. /etc/resolv.conf

   C. /etc/hosts

   D. /etc/nsswitch.conf

10. Which of the following directives in the /etc/resolv.conf file specifies the address of a DNS server?

    A. bind

    B. dns

    C. nameserver

    D. search

11. Enter the full path to the file that specifies the order of databases associated with name resolution.

    _____

12. Which of the following commands searches through the DNS server at 192.168.0.1 for information on IP address 69.32.142.109? Assume that a DNS server has been configured on the system with that IP address.

    A. host 192.168.0.1 69.32.142.109

    B. dig 69.32.142.109

    C. traceroute 69.32.142.109

    D. host 69.32.142.109 192.168.0.1

Chapter 15

Security Administration

After completing this chapter, you will be able to

- Regulate access to administrative accounts, groups, and files

- Set up basic host security with passwords and TCP wrappers

- Configure encrypted connections with SSH and set up GPG keys

Introduction

Because the objectives covered by this chapter are dedicated to security, this chapter includes diverse, seemingly unrelated topics. The next section, "Various Administrative Tasks," is associated with a variety of security policies, from administrative access through port management. The "Basic Host Security" section relates to security policies on passwords and services and through **TCP wrappers**. Finally, the "Encryption Management" section describes **SSH (Secure Shell)** connections as well as **GPG (GNU Privacy Guard)** keys.

TIP

This chapter addresses three objectives in the LPI exam: 110.1 ("Perform Security Administration Tasks"), 110.2 ("Setup Host Security"), and 110.3 ("Securing Data with Encryption").

Various Administrative Tasks

This section includes a variety of security-related administrative tasks. The su and sudo commands define how users may get administrative access. Passwords can be regulated in different ways. Security is enhanced when you know and regulate configured open ports. Resources can be regulated by user. One final security issue relates to the SUID (Super User ID) and SGID (Super Group ID) bits.

Limits with su

The su command allows a regular user to temporarily assume administrative privileges. The action requires the user to enter the administrative root password. For example, the following command runs the fdisk -l command with root administrative privileges:

```
$ su -c 'fdisk -l'
Password:
```

Double quotes work equally well. Other su command switches are less frequently used.

The su command doesn't work unless there is a password for the root administrative account. On some distributions, namely Ubuntu Linux, the root administrative user is not usually (but can be) assigned a password. However, regular users can be given administrative privileges. For that purpose, users can be added to the /etc/sudoers configuration file, described next.

> ### THE DANGERS OF ROOT
>
> Although the LPIC-1 exams assume that you're logged in as the root user, many Linux experts believe that's a dangerous practice in real life. They encourage newer Linux users to do everything possible as a regular user. That practice allows the safeguards built into Linux to work.
>
> As an example, assume that you want to delete all files related to a download of VMware server, unpacked to the /home/michael/VMware directory. Assuming that you have permissions to this directory, you can perform this task with the following command:
>
> `$ rm -rf /home/michael/VMware`
>
> If you accidentally press the spacebar at the wrong moment, you might end up running the following command:
>
> `$ rm -rf /  home/michael/VMware`
>
> This command tries to delete all files and directories in the top-level root directory (/) before trying to delete all files in the home/michael/VMware subdirectory. If run as a regular user, this command just deletes those files for which that user has access. If run as the root administrative user, this command immediately begins to delete files critical to the continued operation of Linux.

Limits with sudoers

The **/etc/sudoers** file configures administrative access by regular users. If properly authorized in this file, you can access administrative commands by prefacing them with the sudo command.

For example, regular users aren't allowed to open the /etc/shadow configuration file. Try the less /etc/shadow command. Unless you're logged into the root administrative account, you get a Permission denied message. However, users who are properly authorized in the /etc/sudoers file can read that file with the sudo less /etc/shadow command after entering their own regular user password. Access is not required to the root administrative password.

The Ubuntu version of this file is relatively simple. First, the following directive includes minimal environment variables, including the LOGNAME, SHELL, USER, and USERNAME in the context of the sudo command:

```
Defaults    env_reset
```

Next, the following line gives the root administrative user sudo privileges.

```
root    ALL=(ALL) ALL
```

The lines in /etc/sudoers follow this format:

```
user system=authuser command
```

In other words, the root administrative user is authorized on ALL systems, as ALL users, to run ALL commands. The parentheses around ALL in the *authuser* setting indicate that it isn't required. Ubuntu systems also include the following line, which gives members of the admin group (the % defines the variable that follows as a group) the same privileges:

```
%admin ALL=(ALL) ALL
```

And yes, any account that is a member of the admin group can get administrative privileges by prefacing administrative requests with the sudo command. One interesting option from CentOS 5 is based on the following line:

```
%sys ALL = NETWORKING, SOFTWARE, SERVICES, STORAGE, DELEGATING, PROCESSES, LOCATE, DRIVERS
```

In other words, members of the sys group have access to all commands associated with the noted variables, starting with NETWORKING. Of course, such variables also must be defined in the /etc/sudoers file; the CentOS 5 version of this file defines it as follows:

```
Cmnd_Alias NETWORKING = /sbin/route, /sbin/ifconfig, /bin/ping, /sbin/dhclient,
/usr/bin/net, /sbin/iptables, /usr/bin/rfcomm, /usr/bin/wvdial, /sbin/iwconfig,
/sbin/mii-tool
```

Alternatively, you can give just one specific user the same sudo privileges as the root user by adding the following line:

```
username     ALL=(ALL) ALL
```

The sudo Command

The sudo command is perhaps most frequently used in the Ubuntu distribution. The root administrative user is not normally assigned a password in this distribution. The first regular account configured during the Ubuntu installation process gets administrative privileges documented in its /etc/sudoers file, as a member of the admin group.

So a member of the admin group on an Ubuntu system can run administrative commands such as fdisk /dev/sda. When user michael runs that command, he sees the following:

```
$ sudo fdisk /dev/sda
[sudo] password for michael:
```

In other words, because user michael is a member of the admin group, he just has to enter his own password to run administrative commands in this way. He doesn't need to know the root administrative password.

Unless you use the sudo -k command, the timestamp associated with this command lasts 15 minutes. To change this default, you can add a timestamp_timeout=*time* directive to the Defaults line, described earlier in the /etc/sudoers file.

Password Security

All users should change passwords frequently. If a cracker discovers the password to your bank account and it happens to be the same password associated with your credit cards, you may be in trouble. But if there's a discrepancy in your account, many financial institutions ensure the security of your account.

However, if you're a system administrator and a cracker discovers the password to your Linux account, that cracker will have access to everything administered on your network. That information could easily include personal financial information for the employees in the organization. Your bosses and coworkers would not be pleased, to put it mildly.

The best solution is to have a "strong" password, a seemingly random mix of upper- and lowercase letters, along with numbers and punctuation. I encourage users to set up passwords based on a favorite sentence. For example, 0T,Ia3ck! could stand for the first letters of each word, along with the punctuation in the following sentence: "On Tuesday, I ate 3 computer keyboards!"

If a cracker finds the encrypted packet with your password, he'll eventually be able to decrypt it with readily available tools. But that takes time.

If you change your password on a regular basis, a cracker who finds and decrypts your password will be disappointed the next time he tries to log into your account. The three commands to this end listed in the LPIC-1 objectives are passwd, chage, and usermod.

Because these commands were previously discussed in Chapter 11, "Administrative Tasks," the following provides just a brief review of these commands.

The passwd Command

The passwd command, run by itself, supports changes to the password of the currently logged in user. On a standard Ubuntu system, the root administrative user is not assigned a password. To temporarily assign a password to root on Ubuntu, take the following steps:

1. Log in as the first regular user on an Ubuntu system. Normally, that user account is a member of the admin group in /etc/group.

2. If your user account is a member of the admin group, you should be able to connect indirectly into the root administrative account with the sudo su command.

3. Enter your regular user account password when prompted.

4. Back up the current /etc/shadow file with the cp /etc/shadow /etc/shadow.bak command.

5. Run the passwd command. Enter the desired password for the root user when prompted. Confirm by typing in the same password again when prompted.

6. Open a different virtual console; they're normally available when you press Ctrl+Alt+F*x* where *x* is a number between 1 and 6.

7. Log in as the root user, entering root at the login: prompt and the password created in step 5.

8. Log out of the root administrative account with the exit command; the Ctrl+D key combination works in the same way.

9. If you don't want a password assigned to the root account, restore the original /etc/shadow file with the cp /etc/shadow.bak /etc/shadow command. Alternatively, replace the numbers, letters, and punctuation in the second column with a single asterisk (*).

The passwd username command, when run with administrative privileges, supports changes to the passwords of the accounts of your choice.

The usermod Command

Several usermod command switches relate to password security. Because some of these switches were discussed in Chapter 11, this section, including the switches described in Table 15.1, is somewhat repetitive. But since the usermod command is also listed in this part of the LPIC-1 objectives, do expect to see additional questions based on usermod on your exam.

Table 15.1 Password Management usermod Switches

Switch	Description
-p "encryptedpassword" username	Specifies a password, in encrypted format. If encryptedpassword is blank, it disables the password for that username.
-L	Disable the user's password.
-U	Re-enable the user's password.

The effect of the -p switch has been modified on Red Hat distributions. If used on CentOS 5, the usermod -p username command disables the username account.

The chage Command

Several chage command switches relate to password security. Because some of these switches were discussed in Chapter 11, this section is repetitive. The chage command is also listed in this part of the LPIC-1 objectives, so expect to see additional questions based on chage on your exam. As you can see in Table 15.2, several chage command switches relate to password aging information, which sets rules for when passwords have to be changed.

Table 15.2 Password Management chage Switches

Switch	Description
-d YYYY-MM-DD	Set the date for when the password was last changed; it can be in numeric year (*YYYY*), month (*MM*), and date (*DD*) format, or the number of days after January 1, 1970. It does not have to correspond to the actual date when the password was last changed.
-E YYYY-MM-DD	Set an expiration date for the account, in numeric year (*YYYY*), month (*MM*), and date (*DD*) format, or the number of days after January 1, 1970.
-I num	Configure a number of days between password expiration and when the account is to be disabled; if *num*=-1, the account is made active.
-l user	Inspect the current password settings for the *user*'s account.
-m num	Set the minimum number of days that a user must keep the current password to *num*.
-M num	Set the maximum number of days that a user must keep the current password to *num*.
-W num	Set the number of days (*num*) that a user is warned before his password is set to expire.

Open Ports

The LPIC-1 objective related to open ports specifically cites the **nmap** and netstat commands. The nmap command is a port scanner. The port-related features of the netstat command were described in Chapter 14, "More Network Fundamentals." Closely related is the **lsof** command, which can identify whether a specific port is open.

 CAUTION

Per the developers of nmap (http://nmap.org/book/legal-issues.html), the unauthorized use of the nmap command "can (in rare cases) get you sued, fired, expelled, jailed, or banned by your ISP."

When you identify an open port, cross-check that port number against the /etc/services file. If the port number is not in that file, check the IANA (Internet Assigned Numbers Authority) Web site at http://www.iana.org/assignments/port-numbers. That should help you identify the associated service, such as FTP (File Transfer Protocol). If you're actively running that service, great! You're probably up to speed on related security issues.

However, if you're not running that service, consider uninstalling the associated packages. The action of uninstalling a service normally closes access to a port. For example, if you see an open port 21 in the output to any of the following commands, check for the installation of an FTP server. If you uninstall that server, it becomes more difficult for a cracker to break into the local system.

Review Open Ports and Established Connections with netstat

A review of open ports with the netstat command can help secure a system. Because netstat was discussed in Chapter 14, this section is somewhat repetitive. Note that the netstat command is also listed in this part of the LPIC-1 objectives, so expect to see additional questions based on that command on your exam.

To review, you can use the netstat -atun command to identify open ports on all (-a) network sockets, based on both the TCP (-t) and UDP (User Datagram Protocol (-u) protocols, in numeric (-n) format. The following output is based on a virtual system that I've configured with few open ports:

```
Active Internet connections (servers and established)
Proto Recv-Q Send-Q Local Address        Foreign Address     State
tcp      0      0 0.0.0.0:21            0.0.0.0:*           LISTEN
tcp      0      0 127.0.0.1:25          0.0.0.0:*           LISTEN
tcp      0      0 192.168.0.203:41865   91.189.90.220:80    TIME_WAIT
tcp6     0      0 :::22                 :::*                LISTEN
tcp6     0      0 192.168.0.203:22      192.168.0.8:37028   ESTABLISHED
udp      0      0 0.0.0.0:68            0.0.0.0:*
```

I've configured an FTP server on this system, which accounts for why port 21 is open to the default IP address of 0.0.0.0. Based on a default installation of the Exim mail server, e-mails are limited to the local system, based on the 127.0.0.1 loopback address through port 25. Although the connection from IP address 91.189.90.220 may seem ominous, a quick check via a Web browser (using port 80) reveals it to be a connection to a Landscape server, the Canonical (Ubuntu) version of the Red Hat Network, also similar to SUSE's Zenworks server.

The TCP6 connections through port 22 may appear unexpected, especially because the local network has no IPv6-capable hardware components. However, as noted in Chapter 13, "Basic Networking," every IPv4 address has a place in an IPv6 network, which explains the connection from my laptop system from an IPv4 address of 192.168.0.8. Finally, port 68, as listed in /etc/services, is specified as a BOOTP (Bootstrap Protocol) client, which is the same port as that used by a DHCP (Dynamic Host Configuration Protocol) client.

To further secure a system in this configuration, you can set up a relatively simple firewall. It would only need to be based on rules associated with these port numbers. One method is based on TCP wrappers, using the **/etc/hosts.allow** and **/etc/hosts.deny** files described later in this chapter.

Port Scanning and nmap

The nmap command can be used to find TCP/IP port numbers from other systems on a network. The command lists only those services that are running and are available to those external systems.

If you're just learning about the nmap command, limit its use to systems under your control, on your local network. Otherwise, you might be subject to the risks (lawsuits, arrests, and so on) described in the Caution earlier in this chapter.

If a cracker were to run the nmap command on the system described earlier, this is what he would see:

```
Starting Nmap 4.53 ( http://insecure.org ) at 2009-03-09 13:03 PDT
Interesting ports on 192.168.0.203:
Not shown: 1712 closed ports
PORT   STATE SERVICE
21/tcp open  ftp
22/tcp open  ssh
```

Note that the port associated with the Exim e-mail server (25) is not visible through nmap; the netstat -atun command described previously confirmed that its configuration is limited to the localhost system.

If a cracker were determined to break into that system, he would then know that the only network avenues available are through an FTP and a SSH server. An administrator could reduce these vulnerabilities even further by stopping or uninstalling the associated services. However, you may want to run FTP and SSH servers on such a system.

List Open Files and Ports with lsof

The lsof command is normally used to list the open files associated with a process. For example, the following command, when run with administrative privileges, illustrates several instances of the SSH service daemon:

```
# lsof /usr/sbin/sshd
```

The full path to the desired service script or device file is required. However, in the context of network security, the -i switch provides more information about exposed and connected network services. Based on the system described previously, the lsof -i command, run with administrative privileges, leads to the output shown in Figure 15.1.

The output confirms the open ports described in the output to the netstat -atun command. Where possible, it refers to /etc/services and substitutes the name of the protocol such as ssh for the port number, such as 22.

The expression associated with certain default IP addresses differs slightly; for example, localhost is substituted for 127.0.0.1, and * is shown in place of the default address of 0.0.0.0.

```
michael@ubuntujeos:~$ sudo lsof -i
COMMAND    PID       USER  FD   TYPE DEVICE SIZE NODE NAME
sshd      4260       root  3u   IPv6 11834       TCP *:ssh (LISTEN)
exim4     4521 Debian-exim  3u   IPv4 12057       TCP localhost:smtp (LISTEN)
dhclient  4771       dhcp  6u   IPv4 13007       UDP *:bootpc
sshd      5109       root  3r   IPv6 14338       TCP 192.168.0.203:ssh->192.168.0.8:46461 (ESTABLISHED)
sshd      5112    michael  3u   IPv6 14338       TCP 192.168.0.203:ssh->192.168.0.8:46461 (ESTABLISHED)
vsftpd    5198       root  3u   IPv4 15143       TCP *:ftp (LISTEN)
michael@ubuntujeos:~$ []
```

FIGURE 15.1 *The lsof command and active connections.*

Resource Limits

Resource limits by users, processes, and memory usage can be configured globally courtesy of PAM (Pluggable Authentication Modules). Specifically, the **pam_limits** module uses the options configured in the **/etc/security/limits.conf** configuration file. There's actually a man page for the pam_limits module that describes some of the options.

Additional system-wide resource limits by users, processes, and memory usage can be configured in the /etc/profile file. User-specific resource limits are normally configured in the ~/.bash_profile file in each user's home directory.

Limits on user logins can be configured through /etc/security/limits.conf.

Resource Limits with ulimit

Review the default resource limits, available in the output to the **ulimit** -a command. The output as shown in Figure 15.2 illustrates the options and associated switches. The more important options are further described in Table 15.3.

The concepts of soft and hard limits were described earlier in Chapter 8, "File Permissions and More." Although those limits related to quotas, the concepts are the same. Soft resource limits are never greater than hard limits. To see the current hard limits on a system, run the ulimit -aH command.

```
[root@CentOS5-LPI ~]# ulimit -a
core file size          (blocks, -c) 0
data seg size           (kbytes, -d) unlimited
scheduling priority             (-e) 0
file size               (blocks, -f) unlimited
pending signals                 (-i) 4096
max locked memory       (kbytes, -l) 32
max memory size         (kbytes, -m) unlimited
open files                      (-n) 1024
pipe size            (512 bytes, -p) 8
POSIX message queues     (bytes, -q) 819200
real-time priority              (-r) 0
stack size              (kbytes, -s) 10240
cpu time               (seconds, -t) unlimited
max user processes              (-u) 4096
virtual memory          (kbytes, -v) unlimited
file locks                      (-x) unlimited
[root@CentOS5-LPI ~]# []
```

FIGURE 15.2 *The ulimit -a command lists resource limits.*

Table 15.3 Limiting Resources with ulimit Switches

Switch	Description
-c	Sets a limit for the size of core files, in blocks; normally set to 0 to disable core dumps. May be enabled for debugging.
-d	Limits the amount of memory that can be allocated to a process, in KB; normally unlimited.
-f	Configures a maximum file size that can be created; normally unlimited.
-H	Specifies a hard limit; used with another switch.
-l	Limits the maximum amount of memory that can be locked.
-S	Specifies a soft limit; used with another switch.
-t	Sets a maximum amount of CPU time per user, in seconds.
-u	Limits the number of processes, per user.
-v	Configures maximum virtual memory for a command-line shell.

To configure nonstandard limits for a system, you need to add appropriate commands to the /etc/profile file. For example, the following command is included in the standard CentOS 5 version of this file:

```
ulimit -S -c 0 > /dev/null 2>&1
```

To interpret, the ulimit command sets a soft limit (-S) for core files (-c) of 0. The output from this particular command is sent to /dev/null, which essentially keeps the output from appearing on-screen during the boot process. However, the 2>&1 merges both standard and error messages to the screen.

Other limits can be set in /etc/profile. Individual limits can be set in the hidden .bash_profile or .bashrc files in each user's home directory. However, you can't set all such limits with the ulimit command.

Resource Limits in /etc/security/limits.conf

To see how limits are set on user logins, processes, and more, examine the /etc/security/limits.conf configuration file. By default, the file includes a number of useful comments, which specify limits in the following format:

```
domain    type    item    value
```

Examine the sample limits that are included in comments from this file. To activate any of these limits, delete the comment character (#) at the beginning of the line.

```
#*    soft    core    0
```

The asterisk in the domain field means this limit applies to all users. As described earlier, limits can be soft or hard, as specified in the type field. The core setting in the item field limits the core file size, equivalent to the ulimit -c command. The value is set to 0.

The interesting variations are in the domain and type fields. Examples in the domain field are shown in other comment lines. For example, @student applies to all users who are members of the hypothetical student group, as documented in the /etc/group file. To limit the setting to my username, set michael in the domain field.

Several major item field settings are listed in Table 15.4. Be aware: you can configure only some of these options with the aforementioned ulimit command.

Table 15.4 Major /etc/security/limits.conf Configuration Items

Item	Description
core	Limits the size of core files, in blocks; corresponds to ulimit -c
data	Limits the memory for a process, in KB; corresponds to ulimit -d
fsize	Sets a maximum file size; corresponds to ulimit -f
memlock	Notes a maximum amount of memory that can be locked; corresponds to ulimit -l
cpu	Sets a maximum amount of CPU time per user; corresponds to ulimit -t
nproc	Limits the number of processes, per user; corresponds to ulimit -u
maxlogins	Configures the maximum number of simultaneous logins per user
maxsyslogins	Configures the maximum number of simultaneous logins for the system

File Audits

The file audits specified in the LPIC-1 objectives relate to the SUID (Superuser ID) and SGID (Supergroup ID) bits described in Chapter 8. Files with such permissions can be security risks because they can be run as scripts by users who don't own the file, either as the owner or possibly as a member of the group that owns the file.

To identify files with SUID and SGID permissions, you need a couple of specialized options of the find command. For example, the following command, run as root, starts in the top-level root directory and identifies all files with SUID permissions:

```
# find / -perm -u=s
```

If you're paying attention to detail, you might note the difference between the comparable command listed in Chapter 8. That command

```
# find / -perm /o+t
```

identified all files with the sticky bit enabled. Here's another variation that looks for all files with the SGID bit enabled:

```
# find / -perm /g+s
```

Try some of these variations for yourself. The forward slash or dash (–) in front of the specified permissions is critical. Without it, the search identifies only those files with the specified permission—in the latest case, the SGID bit. With the forward slash or dash, the command identifies those files with the SGID bit and other read, write, and execute permissions.

In general, these commands are superior in file audits to numeric permissions in octal format. For example, the following command

```
# find / -perm 2755
```

identifies those files with the SGID bit enabled, and with 755 permissions set on the file. It omits those files with 744 permissions (or any other octal representation of their permissions).

Basic Host Security

Those who are paranoid about the risks of networks can just disconnect their systems. But few stand-alone computer systems are useful today. Anyone who administers Linux computers has to deal with networks. For that reason, the LPIC-1 objectives suggest that candidates need to "know how to set up a basic level of host security."

Perhaps the most straightforward host security measure relates to unused network services. For example, if you're not setting up a Web server on the local system, uninstall related packages. Unless such packages are installed, a cracker can't break in and use them as a way to steal your data. The techniques described in Chapter 3, "Package Management Systems," can help.

This section assumes that services remain installed. In that case, you can turn off network services not in use. You can work to secure local user passwords. You can protect services that are installed with TCP wrappers. With systems associated with the **super servers**, custom security measures are available.

 NOTE

This chapter covers two super servers, known as `inetd` and `xinetd`. These commands refer to the "super server daemon" and the "internet super server daemon." I use "internet" in lowercase, to differentiate a group of networks from the Internet.

Basic Service Security

Many Linux users like to experiment with different services. A lot of services you may not need are installed by default on Linux distributions. But for those concerned with security, it's best to keep those services turned off until they're ready for production use. The simplest way to deactivate a service is to use the associated service script in the **/etc/init.d** directory. For example, the following command deactivates the sendmail e-mail server on our selected distributions:

```
# /etc/init.d/sendmail stop
```

But that action doesn't survive a reboot or even a change in runlevel. It's possible to set up a custom runlevel with desired services. Suitable runlevels for this purpose are runlevel 3 on Ubuntu-style systems and runlevel 4 on Red Hat-style systems. Whatever runlevel is selected, you should set it as the default. Based on the files cited in the LPIC-1 objectives, the key file is /etc/inittab, first covered in Chapter 1, "System Architecture." The default runlevel cited in older Ubuntu and CentOS 5 versions of this file is

```
id:2:initdefault:
id:5:initdefault:
```

If you choose to keep the default runlevel, you can configure services not to start in that runlevel. On Red Hat–type distributions such as CentOS 5, you can make that happen for the sendmail service with the following command:

```
# chkconfig --level 5 sendmail off
```

Alternatively, the following command keeps the sendmail service from starting in any runlevel:

```
# chkconfig sendmail off
```

In contrast, Ubuntu uses different commands. The following commands retain the start script for sendmail just in runlevel 2. The numbers 21 and 19 are based on the default service scripts in the /etc/rcx.d directories, where x corresponds to the runlevel.

```
# update-rc.d -f sendmail remove
# update-rc.d sendmail start 21 2 . stop 19 0 1 3 4 5 6 .
```

Of course, if you don't want sendmail to be active in any runlevel, you wouldn't run the second command.

Users and Passwords

Users and passwords are governed on standard Linux systems through the shadow password suite. The files in this suite were first discussed in Chapter 11, "Administrative Tasks." The objectives associated with this chapter suggest that you need to have an "awareness of shadow passwords and how they work."

To review, the second column in the /etc/passwd file was the original location for passwords. But the x in the second column, as shown in the excerpt for my account

```
michael:x:1000:1000:,,,:/home/michael:/bin/bash
```

points the system to the /etc/shadow file for the password. Configured passwords are stored in the second column of user entries for that file, in a seemingly random series of letters, numbers, and punctuation. But it isn't random. It's encryption, using the MD5 (Message-Digest algorithm 5) algorithm.

Given enough time and access to /etc/shadow, a cracker can decrypt such passwords. That is why read access to this file is limited to the root administrative user (and on some distributions, members of the shadow group).

 TIP

If you need to test a system without regular users, you can boot or move into runlevel 1. However, that runlevel is not suitable for all tests. In that case, make sure all users are logged off, and run the touch /etc/nologin command. When **/etc/nologin** exists, regular users aren't allowed to log into the local system. If the root user doesn't have a password, you have to boot into recovery mode to access that system. However, a reboot automatically deletes the /etc/nologin file.

Regulation with TCP Wrappers

Although firewalls such as those associated with iptables are not part of the LPIC-1 objectives, TCP wrappers arc. These "wrappers" use rules configured in the /etc/hosts.allow and /etc/hosts.deny configuration files to regulate access to many but not all network services that communicate with TCP packets.

Services Regulated by TCP Wrappers

Depending on the configuration, these services may be documented in one of four places: the **/etc/inetd.conf** file, the **/etc/inetd.d** directory, the **/etc/xinetd.conf** file, or the **/etc/xinetd.d** directory. These "super servers" are defined in the section that follows.

TCP wrappers can also protect those services associated with the libwrap.so.0 library file. You can identify such services with the lsof command described earlier, based on the full path to the library file. Depending on the distribution, you might be able to find that file in the /lib or /usr/lib directories. The locate command described in Chapter 4, "Command Lines and Files," can help.

In other words, TCP wrappers can be used to protect services shown in the output to a command such as one of the following:

```
# lsof /lib/libwrap.so.0
# lsof /usr/lib/libwrap.so.0
```

The output only includes those services that are currently running. For example, it would not include the Red Hat vsFTP service if it were not active. Nevertheless, if it were active, it would be included in the output, and the vsFTP service could be protected by TCP wrappers. In addition, the output should include either the inetd or xinetd super server, as defined in the aforementioned /etc/inetd.conf and /etc/xinetd.conf configuration files.

Configuration Files for TCP Wrappers

Now you can configure the /etc/hosts.allow and /etc/hosts.deny files to control access to these services. But because the rules in these files may conflict, TCP wrappers consider the rules in these files in the following order:

1. The rules configured in /etc/hosts.allow are considered. If a rule in this file explicitly allows access to the service in question, access is granted, control is passed back to the service, and the /etc/hosts.deny file is ignored.

2. The rules configured in /etc/hosts.deny are considered. If a rule in this file explicitly denies access to the service in question, access is denied. A message may be sent to the client, depending on how the rule is configured.

3. If there is no rule in either /etc/hosts.allow or /etc/hosts.deny related to the service in question, access is granted, and control is passed back to the service.

Directives in TCP Wrappers Configuration Files

The directives in the TCP wrappers configuration files, /etc/hosts.allow and /etc/hosts.deny, follow a specific format:

```
daemons : clients [ : command ]
```

In other words, no command is required as part of the line. If you want to disable access to all services regulated by TCP wrappers, add the following line to the /etc/hosts.deny file, which sets the rule for access to all services from all clients:

```
ALL : ALL
```

However, if this same line is also found in the /etc/hosts.allow file, access is automatically granted by TCP wrappers, per the configuration order described previously.

Of course, most TCP wrappers configuration files include more specific rules. For example, the following directive limits the rule to the SSH server, for systems on the 192.168.0.0/24 network:

```
sshd : 192.168.0.
```

The service listed is based on its name in the /usr/sbin directory. Note the difference in the way the IP network address is presented. The 192.168.0. represents all systems with IP addresses that start with those numbers. Of course, the rule works differently depending on whether the line shown is in /etc/hosts.allow or /etc/hosts.deny.

Further customization is possible. For example, the following line applies to both the noted FTP service, vsftpd, as well as SSH. The rule applies to all systems on the 192.168.0.0/24 network except 192.168.0.111:

```
vsftpd, sshd : 192.168.0. EXCEPT 192.168.0.111
```

The Super Servers

Several services are associated with the super server. The original super server was configured in the /etc/inetd.conf file. However, current super servers are configured in the /etc/xinetd.conf file and are known as "extended internet super servers" (xinetd). Both super servers may refer to files in the /etc/inetd.d and /etc/xinetd.d directories for more information. The regular "super server" has not been used on Red Hat–based distribution since about 2000; Debian-based distributions including Ubuntu have converted most related services to xinetd as well.

If both super servers are configured on a system, make sure that options like Telnet aren't configured in both sets of configuration files.

The Original Super Server

The original super server configured access to services through /etc/inetd.conf. Services can be configured collectively in this file or by service in unique files in /etc/inetd.d.

Because the super server is no longer in use on Red Hat–based distributions, you may want to follow along on an Ubuntu system. For the purpose of this section, make sure the inetutils-inetd and swat packages are installed.

/etc/inetd.conf used to contain configuration information for a dozen services or more. Based on the noted packages, my version configures one service with the following directive:

```
swat    stream   tcp   nowait.400   root   /usr/sbin/tcpd   /usr/sbin/swat
```

If /etc/inetd.conf is overloaded with services, create an /etc/inetd.d/swat file and move the directive shown to that file. The column meanings are described in Table 15.5.

To disable a service in the /etc/inetd.conf file, comment it out by adding a hash mark (#) in front. Then make the super server reread the configuration file with the following command:

```
# /etc/init.d/inetutils-inetd reload
```

Sometimes, the /etc/init.d script that controls the services configured in /etc/inetd.conf is /etc/init.d/openbsd-inetd. If neither of these scripts exist, you likely don't have a service configured in the /etc/inetd.conf configuration file.

Table 15.5 Super Server /etc/inetd.conf Options

Column	Description
Service	Service by name (in /etc/services) or TCP/IP protocol number
Socket	Connection type, normally stream (generally a reliable TCP connection) or dgram (generally a best-effort UDP connection)
Protocol	Protocol type, such as TCP, UDP, or ICMP (Internet Control Message Protocol); for more options, see /etc/protocols
Wait/No wait	Connection type for the socket; nowait.400 frees the socket and allows a maximum of 400 instances of the server
User	User who is authorized; may also specify the group in a user.group format
Server program	Full path to the server daemon, normally in the /usr/sbin directory
Arguments	Options to be passed to the server program when it starts; the man page for the target server may have more information

Alternatively, you can send the HUP (hangup) signal to the associated service with the following command:

```
# kill -HUP inetutils-inetd
```

As described in Chapter 6, "Processes, Priorities, and Editing," the kill -HUP command is equivalent to kill -1.

The Extended Internet Super Server

The xinetd service is commonly used on all current Linux systems. The basic configuration file is /etc/xinetd.conf. The standard version of this file for both Ubuntu and CentOS 5 includes two key directives:

```
defaults
includedir /etc/xinetd.d
```

The defaults directive refers to a number of options documented in the xinetd.conf man page. It also supports the use of default ports for individual services, as documented in /etc/services. Some of the more interesting default and other options are included in the CentOS 5 version of the file, which will be reviewed here. After defaults, that file specifies logging through the syslog daemon specified in Chapter 12, "Essential System Services," at the info level.

```
log_type = SYSLOG daemon info
```

The line that follows specifies the information that is logged if an attempt to connect to an xinetd service fails, which includes hostname or IP address information of the remote system:

`log_on_failure = HOST`

The next line specifies the logging information associated with a successful connection, in this case, the PID (process identifier), the hostname or IP address, the amount of time the remote user is connected, and the time the user exits the connection:

`log_on_success = PID HOST DURATION EXIT`

The following line prevents a connection flood; if there are more than 50 attempts to connect in one second, remote users have to wait at least 10 seconds before trying again:

`cps = 50 10`

The instances directive specifies the number of allowed simultaneous connections:

`instances = 50`

But the number of connections is further limited per IP address:

`per_source = 10`

Unless every system on your network and all related hardware are IPv6 capable, you shouldn't change this directive:

`v6only = no`

Next, examine the /etc/xinetd.d/rsync file, which configures an rsync server through xinetd:

```
service rsync
{
    disable = yes
    socket_type    = stream
    wait           = no
    user           = root
    server         = /usr/bin/rsync
    server_args    = --daemon
    log_on_failure += USERID
}
```

Just about all the directives shown here were also used in the /etc/inetd.conf file. The additional directives show that the service is currently disabled, and the user ID is logged when a connection attempt fails.

You can activate this service directly by changing `disable = yes` to `disable = no`. A couple of additional options related to security are `only_from` and `no_access`. For example, the following directives support access from all systems on the 192.168.0.0/24 network, except 192.168.0.13:

```
only_from = 127.0.0.1 192.168.0.0/24
no_access = 192.168.0.13
```

Encryption Management

This section is focused on two types of encryption that can help secure your communication. SSH communication can encrypt remote connections. GPG keys can create digital signatures, which others can use to verify the authenticity of transmitted information, such as packages and e-mails.

A Secure Shell Server

In this section, you'll learn how to set up SSH communication between two Linux systems. Specifically, you'll go through the process of creating an SSH server on one system and an SSH client on a second system. On the selected distributions, these packages include `openssh` in their names. Although appropriate SSH packages are normally installed by default on Linux systems, you should make sure that the latest versions of these packages are installed, using the commands described in Chapter 3.Although the LPIC-1 objectives are focused on SSH as a client, it's not possible to demonstrate how such connections work without configuring SSH as a server. So in this section, examine some critical directives in the main SSH server configuration file, **/etc/ssh/sshd_config**. Many of these directives may be commented out on your system, but they generally represent the defaults, unless otherwise noted.

 CAUTION

The SSH random number generator for login keys used on some older Ubuntu and Debian releases wasn't really random. For more information, see the Ubuntu Security Notice at http://www.ubuntu.com/usn/usn-612-2. The problem even affects the first release of Ubuntu Hardy Heron. Fortunately, updates are available using the normal update systems documented in Chapter 3.

The following directive uses the default port for SSH, 22:

```
Port 22
```

Although it's not always necessary, I find it helpful to activate the following directive, because it limits communication to IPv4 networks. If no `ListenAddress` directive is active, SSH tries to connect to both IPv4 and IPv6 networks. I have not installed IPv6 network hardware, so it at least avoids unneeded network communication.

```
ListenAddress 0.0.0.0
```

If the local system has multiple network adapters, you can specify the IP address of the adapter of your choice.

The following directive limits connections to **SSH protocol 2**, which is more secure than SSH protocol 1. The default is `Protocol 2,1`; it's insecure because it accepts communication from SSH 1 clients.

```
Protocol 2
```

The generic host keys associated with SSH connections are as listed:

```
HostKey /etc/ssh/ssh_host_rsa_key
HostKey /etc/ssh/ssh_host_dsa_key
```

Check the permissions associated with these files. You'll note that they're readable (and writable) only by the root administrative user. These are private keys, which may be paired with public keys in the same directory. The matching public keys have the same file name, with a `.pub` extension. If used, they're paired with an `ssh_known_hosts` file in the `/etc` or `/etc/ssh` directories.

However, I recommend that you go further than these key pairs, because they do not take advantage of the **passphrases** described shortly. Those passphrases store different versions of these files in secure subdirectories of user home directories, so they can be customized by a user.

In the following section, you'll create a private/public key pair for an individual user. You'll also set up a system that requires password authentication only once. After they're configured on the client and server systems, users can log in securely, without transmitting passwords over the network.

Privilege separation, as configured in this directive, enhances SSH security:

```
UsePrivilegeSeparation yes
```

The `KeyRegenerationInterval` and `ServerKeyBits` directives are not relevant, because this system is configured for SSH version 2. The next directives configure logins; the first directives disconnect clients if a login isn't complete in 120 seconds. Logins by the root administrative user are enabled. The `StrictModes` setting checks for appropriate permissions on user encryption keys:

```
LoginGraceTime 120
PermitRootLogin yes
StrictModes yes
```

Consider changing the `PermitRootLogin` directive to no. Disabling root administrative logins denies access to even valid attempts to log in with the root account. However, regular users can still access root administrative privileges after connecting via SSH.

Although this particular RSA directive applies only to SSH protocol 1, RSA public/private key pairs are still allowed for both SSH protocols, as long as `PubkeyAuthentication` is set to yes.

```
RSAAuthentication yes
PubkeyAuthentication yes
```

The following directive allows password authentication. Keep it as is, at least until public and private keys are established later in this chapter.

```
PasswordAuthentication yes
```

The following commands are essential if you want to tunnel GUI tools through the SSH connection:

```
X11Fowarding yes
X11DisplayOffset 10
```

Secure Shell Connections

The default configuration of an SSH server enables connections to local accounts remotely. The process is straightforward; either of the following two command options starts the connection process to the SSH server on the 192.168.0.50 system on my account:

```
$ ssh -l michael 192.168.0.50
$ ssh michael@192.168.0.50
```

If this is the first time for an SSH connection between a client and server, you'll see a message similar to the following:

```
The authenticity of host '192.168.0.50 (192.168.0.50)' can't be established.
RSA key fingerprint is 84:68:ab:80:1e:89:14:a3:89:c4:49:7c:41:dc:f8:1a.
Are you sure you want to continue connecting (yes/no)?
```

To continue, enter `yes` at the prompt as shown. At that point, information from that host is added to the end of the `known_hosts` file in the `/home/michael/.ssh` directory.

To enable **X11 tunnels** for GUI services, you can use the `-X` switch; for example, if you connected remotely to the noted system with the following command

```
$ ssh -l michael -X 192.168.0.50
```

you could then start GUI tools such as the Red Hat/CentOS 5 `system-config-securitylevel` tool or the Ubuntu `network-admin` tool. These tools would appear on the local system, and any changes would affect the remote server. (The `ssh -X michael@192.168.0.50` would work equally well to create the X11 tunnel.)

Two other related commands are available through SSH services: scp and sftp. Both commands require an SSH server on the target system. The scp command is typically used to encrypt and copy a file; for example, you could copy the local 1p15.doc file to the remote ubuntuserver system with the following command:

```
$ scp lp15.doc ubuntuserver:
```

By default, this copies the 1p15.doc file to the home directory of the current user on the remote ubuntuserver system. If desired, and if you have permissions to that directory, it can be specified as shown:

```
$ scp lp15.doc ubuntuserver:/tmp
```

Finally, the default SSH server configuration supports encrypted FTP-style access to user home directories. For example, the following command connects to my home directory on the noted CentOS5-LPI system, with access to standard FTP commands:

```
$ sftp michael@CentOS5-LPI
```

Authorized Login Keys and Passphrases

The encryption keys used for SSH are associated with **RSA** and **DSA** cryptographic algorithms. RSA is named for its developers, Rivest, Shamir, and Adleman; DSA stands for the Digital Signature Algorithm. Whichever encryption scheme is used, encryption keys make it much more difficult for a cracker to read the communication between your system and an SSH server.

Users who connect to the default SSH server send their passwords over the network. Even when the connection is encrypted, a cracker can look at the beginning of an encrypted connection for the data associated with the username and password and eventually decrypt that information.

For that reason, SSH connections commonly use passphrases. Because a passphrase can be a complete sentence, such phrases are much more difficult to decrypt. When entered, they provide access to the private key stored locally, which is then matched with a public key stored on a remote system, the SSH server.

The command that creates the private/public key pair is **ssh-keygen**. Based on SSH protocol 2, you can create key pairs based on the RSA or DSA algorithms with one of the following commands:

```
$ ssh-keygen -t rsa
$ ssh-keygen -t dsa
```

Although DSA keys use a standard 1,024 bit hash for encryption, RSA key hashes are variable, ranging from 768 to 2,048 bits. For example, the following command creates an RSA key pair based on a 2,048 bit hash:

```
$ ssh-keygen -t rsa -b 2048
```

In the following steps, you'll learn how to set up an authentication private/public key pair with the passphrase of your choice. For the purpose of this exercise, I demonstrate with my account on two different systems, named ubuntuhardy3 and CentOS5-LPI on IP addresses 192.168.0.219 and 192.168.0.11, respectively. The following steps configure the CentOS5-LPI system as an SSH server.

1. Run the ssh-keygen command with the encryption scheme and bit hash of your choice. For demonstration purposes, 2,048 bits are listed here:

    ```
    $ ssh-keygen -t rsa -b 2048
    ```

2. Accept the default location for the private key when the key pair is generated. This location is in my home directory:

    ```
    Generating public/private rsa key pair.
    Enter file in which to save the key (/home/michael/.ssh/id_rsa):
    ```

3. Enter an appropriate passphrase, which can and should be something complex like a full sentence, complete with uppercase, lowercase, numbers, and punctuation. The actual passphrase is not shown in the prompt:

    ```
    Enter passphrase (empty for no passphrase):
    ```

4. Enter the same passphrase a second time. Once saved, you'll see the following output, which specifies the location of both the private and public keys. (This system is named ubuntuhardy3.)

    ```
    Enter same passphrase again:
    Your identification has been saved in /home/michael/.ssh/id_rsa.
    Your public key has been saved in /home/michael/.ssh/id_rsa.pub.
    The key fingerprint is:
    f3:ab:9d:6a:70:37:79:0c:5e:86:6b:e6:fb:05:70:ac michael@ubuntuhardy3
    ```

5. Send the public key to the appropriate file on the remote SSH client system. The following command copies it over a network; if network security is a concern, you could even copy it to media such as a USB key and then append it to the end of the authorized_keys file in the remote .ssh subdirectory.

    ```
    $ ssh-copy-id -i .ssh/id_rsa.pub 192.168.0.11
    ```

    If you don't use the ssh-copy-id command, make sure to append the id_rsa.pub key (or possibly the id_dsa.pub key) to the **~/.ssh/authorized_keys** file with a command like cat id_rsa.pub >> .ssh/authorized_keys. When run with the double forward arrows (>>), the command doesn't overwrite existing public keys.

6. If this is the first time you're connecting, you'll see the authenticity message shown in the last section; otherwise, you're taken to the following password prompt:

    ```
    michael@192.168.0.11's password:
    ```

    This transmits the password over the network, which is why you may prefer to copy the public key (id_rsa.pub) to the remote system with a USB key.

7. The message that follows documents that the information from the `ubuntuhardy3` `id_rsa.pub` file, the public authentication key, has been added to the `CentOS5-LPI`'s `/home/michael/.ssh/authorized_keys` file.

   ```
   Now try logging into the machine, with "ssh '192.168.0.11'", and check in:
     .ssh/authorized_keys
   to make sure we haven't added extra keys that you weren't expecting.
   ```

8. Try logging in to the `CentOS5-LPI` system. You should be prompted for the passphrase that was created:

   ```
   $ ssh -l michael 192.168.0.11
   Enter passphrase for key '/home/michael/.ssh/id_rsa':
   ```

9. If successful, the private key on the local system verifies the public key on the remote SSH server, and you're logged in!

To review, the private key is created in user home directories, in the `.ssh/` subdirectory, in file `id_rsa` for RSA keys and `id_dsa` for DSA keys. In other words, these are the private keys on the local system, the SSH client:

```
~/.ssh/id_dsa
~/.ssh/id_rsa
```

The public keys, with `.pub` extensions, are transmitted to the server. In other words, these are the public keys sent to the remote system, the SSH server:

```
~/.ssh/id_dsa.pub
~/.ssh/id_rsa.pub
```

These keys are appended to the `authorized_keys` file on the remote SSH server, also in the target user's home directory, in the `.ssh/` subdirectory:

```
~/.ssh/authorized_keys
```

The Authentication Agent

Passwords and passphrases can be a pain, especially if you have passphrases for several SSH servers. The **ssh-agent** command is an authentication agent, used to start a "child shell." At that point, you can use the **ssh-add** command to add appropriate authentication keys.

To get the authentication agent working, the following command starts a "child" bash shell. It's known as a child shell because it's started from a shell command line.

```
$ ssh-agent /bin/bash
```

In that child shell, you can then add the private key from your home directory with the following command:

```
$ ssh-add ~/.ssh/id_rsa
```

Of course, if there are also DSA keys, you have to add the id_dsa private key from the same subdirectory.

GPG Keys

GPG keys are the Linux implementation of **PGP (Pretty Good Privacy)** keys. They're already used on most Linux systems to verify package signatures. If a problem arises when downloading a package from a repository, there will be an error message, related to a bad GPG signature. In most cases, that means the maintainer of the package mirror described in Chapter 3 has not updated his package signature. However, it could also mean that a cracker has substituted his own package in a third-party repository.

You can create your own GPG key with the **gpg --gen-key** command. As with the SSH keys just created, this command creates private and public keys that can be used to encrypt files and e-mails. It performs the actions listed in Figure 15.3.

```
michael@ubuntuhardy3:~$ gpg --gen-key
gpg (GnuPG) 1.4.6; Copyright (C) 2006 Free Software Foundation, Inc.
This program comes with ABSOLUTELY NO WARRANTY.
This is free software, and you are welcome to redistribute it
under certain conditions. See the file COPYING for details.

gpg: directory `/home/michael/.gnupg' created
gpg: new configuration file `/home/michael/.gnupg/gpg.conf' created
gpg: WARNING: options in `/home/michael/.gnupg/gpg.conf' are not yet active during this run
gpg: keyring `/home/michael/.gnupg/secring.gpg' created
gpg: keyring `/home/michael/.gnupg/pubring.gpg' created
Please select what kind of key you want:
   (1) DSA and Elgamal (default)
   (2) DSA (sign only)
   (5) RSA (sign only)
Your selection? []
```

FIGURE 15.3 *The gpg --gen-key command generates GPG keys.*

The message lists keys and configuration files created in my home directory, in the **.gnupg/** subdirectory. It includes three options for encryption; DSA and RSA are the same schemes described earlier for SSH connections. The **Elgamel** option is a probabilistic scheme described by Taher ElGamel in 1984.

Whichever scheme you select, you need to be prepared with the following answers:

◆ The size of the encryption keys: if you choose the RSA or ElGamel schemes, the encryption keys between 1,024 and 4,096 bits can be created.

◆ The lifetime of the keys in a number of days, weeks, months, or years—or a key that does not expire.

◆ A name, e-mail address, and comment. In practice, there are few restrictions on entries; even abcd@efgh works in the e-mail address entry.

◆ A passphrase (entered twice).

The process takes some time. If there's an error message about not enough random bytes being available, run some other programs in other consoles. To demonstrate this process, you need two systems, each configured with SSH servers. For the purpose of the following exercise, I've created a GPG key pair on a CentOS 5 system and exported the associated public key to an Ubuntu server system. When exported, the gpg --list-keys command displays the output shown in Figure 15.4. The sub line specifies a key imported from another source, normally a second system.

```
michael@ubuntuHHserver:~$ gpg --list-keys
/home/michael/.gnupg/pubring.gpg
-------------------------------
pub   2048R/06755ECD 2009-03-16 [expires: 2009-03-23]
uid                 Mike Jang (This is a second test) <mike@example.com>

pub   1024D/4A605C7A 2009-03-16 [expires: 2009-03-17]
uid                 Michael Jang (This is a test) <michael@example.com>
sub   2048g/62DE99BC 2009-03-16 [expires: 2009-03-17]

michael@ubuntuHHserver:~$
```

FIGURE 15.4 gpg --list-keys *displays GPG public keys.*

I used that public key to encrypt a file from that Ubuntu server system, transmitted that file to the CentOS 5 system, and then decrypted the file with the private GPG key. The following is a step-by-step breakdown of the process:

1.   On the CentOS 5 system, I generated the GPG keys with the gpg --gen-key command. I was ready when prompted for the choices; I selected the default DSA and Elgamel scheme, the default 2,048 bits for the Elgamel keysize, a key that expires in one day with the 1d entry, my real name, an e-mail address, and an appropriate comment.

2.   I listed the current public keys with the gpg --list-key command, which helps me remember the name associated with the GPG keys. One example is shown in Figure 15.4.

3.   With the following command, I exported the public key just created and revealed in the output to the gpg --list-key command. Substitute the real name for name; based on Figure 15.4, that's Mike Jang. No quotes are required here.

     gpg --export Mike Jang > gpg.pub

4.   I copied the public key to a remote system, my Ubuntu server with the scp command associated with the SSH service, described earlier in this chapter.

     $ scp gpg.pub ubuntuHHserver:/home/michael

5.   I logged into the remote Ubuntu server system and listed current public keys with the gpg --list-keys command.

6.   I imported the public GPG key file copied from the CentOS 5 system with the gpg --import gpg.pub command, and then verified the import with the gpg --list-keys command.

7. I encrypted a file for later transmission to the CentOS 5 system; in this case, the quotes around the username are required. Note also that the username is different—based on the private key on the file recipient.

```
$ gpg --out kickstartfile --recipient 'Michael Jang' --encrypt ks.cfg
```

You may need to confirm the key fingerprint if prompted.

8. I copied the encrypted file to the original system:

```
$ scp kickstartfile CentOS5-LPI:/home/michael
```

9. I then returned to the original system and decrypted the file:

```
$ gpg --out ks.cfg --decrypt kickstartfile
```

10. Enter the passphrase of the local user when prompted.

11. The ks.cfg should now be decrypted and ready on the local system.

Chapter Summary

This chapter provided an overview of the variety of LPIC-1 topics associated with security. Because the topics are diverse, the sections covered in this chapter do not include consistent themes.

Security is enhanced with appropriate use of the su command and the appropriate configuration of the /etc/sudoers file. Security is also enhanced when users configure complex passwords and change them frequently. Administrators can use the netstat, nmap, and lsof commands to check for open ports, where the risks of break-ins are greatest. Resources can be limited with the ulimit command, coupled with options in /etc/security/limits.conf and ulimit options in the /etc/profile and ~/.profile files. Finally, file audits can help identify those risky files with the SUID and SGID bits set.

A service is most secure when it isn't installed. The next best is a service that isn't active, courtesy of its script in the /etc/init.d directory. You can use the chkconfig and update-rc.d commands to keep undesired services from starting in the default runlevel, as defined in the /etc/inittab file. Although host security is enhanced with shadow passwords in /etc/shadow, you can enhance regular user logins if the /etc/nologin file exists. TCP wrappers support regulation of related services through the /etc/hosts.allow and /etc/hosts.deny files. Related are the regular and extended super servers, inetd and xinetd, with configuration files in /etc/inetd.conf and /etc/xinetd.conf, along with service specific configuration files in the /etc/inetd.d and /etc/xinetd.d directories.

Linux encryption security is enhanced with SSH protocol 2 connections, using RSA and DSA encryption. The use of host public and private keys such as ssh_host_rsa_key and ssh_host_dsa_key, with and without the .pub extension in the /etc/ssh directory, does not provide adequate security. However, the use of the equivalent id_rsa and id_dsa private and public keys in each user's ~/.ssh subdirectories does more. Key pairs can be created with the ssh-keygen command; the public keys can then be transmitted with the ssh-copy-id command. When transmitted, public keys are stored in the remote user's ~/.ssh/authorized_keys file. Linux encryption also covers GPG keys, which can encode files for secure transmission.

Key Terms

- ◆ **DSA.** The Digital Signature Algorithm, used for encryption.
- ◆ **Elgamel.** Probabilistic encryption algorithm first described by Taher ElGamel in 1984.
- ◆ **/etc/hosts.allow.** Security configuration file for TCP wrappers–related services; directives in this file are considered before those in /etc/hosts.deny.
- ◆ **/etc/hosts.deny.** Security configuration file for TCP wrappers–related services; directives in this file are considered after those in /etc/hosts.deny.
- ◆ **/etc/inetd.conf.** The main configuration file for the super server, inetd.
- ◆ **/etc/inetd.d.** Configuration directory for inetd services.
- ◆ **/etc/init.d.** Directory with service scripts.
- ◆ **/etc/nologin.** If this file exists on a system, logins by regular users are not allowed.
- ◆ **/etc/security/limits.conf.** Configuration file for user resource limits; can work with ulimit commands in /etc/profile and ~/.bash_profile or ~./bashrc.
- ◆ **/etc/ssh/ssh_host_dsa_key.** File for host-based SSH private encryption keys using the DSA algorithm.
- ◆ **/etc/ssh/ssh_host_rsa_key.** File for host-based SSH private encryption keys using the RSA algorithm.
- ◆ **/etc/ssh/sshd_config.** The main configuration file for an SSH server.
- ◆ **/etc/sudoers.** The main configuration file for sudo command access.
- ◆ **/etc/xinetd.conf.** Configuration file for the xinetd service.
- ◆ **/etc/xinetd.d.** Configuration directory for xinetd service.
- ◆ **gpg.** Command to create, import, and export GPG keys, as well as encrypt and decrypt files for secure transmission.
- ◆ **GPG (GNU Privacy Guard).** The Linux implementation of PGP.
- ◆ **~/.gnupg/.** The subdirectory with GPG configuration files.
- ◆ **inetd.** The super server for some services; may be superseded by xinetd, the extended internet super server.
- ◆ **lsof.** A command that lists open files to help identify open ports and services associated with libraries, such as those associated with TCP wrappers.
- ◆ **nmap.** A port scanning tool for remote systems. May not be legal when used without authorization.

◆ **pam_limits.** Pluggable Authentication Module related to the ulimit command and the /etc/security/limits.conf configuration file.

◆ **passphrase.** A more secure password, which can be a complete sentence.

◆ **PGP (Pretty Good Privacy).** A standard for cryptographic privacy; the Linux implementation is GPG.

◆ **RSA.** An algorithm used for encryption. It's named after its developers, Rivest, Shamir, and Adleman.

◆ **SSH (Secure Shell).** Service that enables remote connections, including X11 tunneling with the ssh -X command.

◆ **SSH Protocol 2.** The more secure version of the SSH protocol.

◆ **~/.ssh/authorized_keys.** File for public keys for SSH connections from remote systems.

◆ **~/.ssh/id_dsa.** File for a private SSH key using DSA encryption.

◆ **~/.ssh/id_dsa.pub.** File for a public SSH key using DSA encryption.

◆ **~/.ssh/id_rsa.** File for a private SSH key using RSA encryption.

◆ **~/.ssh/id_rsa.pub.** File for a public SSH key using DSA encryption.

◆ **~/.ssh/known_hosts.** File for previously connected and known hosts.

◆ **ssh.** Command that connects to remote systems.

◆ **ssh-add.** Command that can add authentication identities.

◆ **ssh-agent.** Command that can hold authentication keys.

◆ **ssh-copy-id.** Command that can copy public keys to remote systems for authentication.

◆ **ssh-keygen.** Command that can generate a private/public RSA or DSA key pair for SSH connections.

◆ **su.** Command that enables login as another user, including the root administrative user; it requires an appropriate password. Regular users can run the su -c command to temporarily assume administrative permissions.

◆ **sudo.** Command that enables an authorized regular user to temporarily assume administrative privileges, as limited by /etc/sudoers.

◆ **super server.** The inetd service for other network services; may be superseded by xinetd, the extended internet super server.

◆ **TCP wrappers.** The security option associated with /etc/hosts.allow and /etc/hosts.deny for services that use TCP wrappers libraries.

◆ **ulimit.** Command that can limit user access to resources.

◆ **X11 tunnel.** Reference to an SSH connection that can connect GUI applications; implemented with the ssh -X command.

◆ **xinetd.** The extended internet super server; may supersede inetd.

Review Questions

The number of review questions in this chapter and other chapters in this book is proportionate to each section's weight in the LPI objectives. Because this chapter covers items 110.1, 110.2, and 110.3, the weight is 9; therefore, you'll see 18 questions in this section. You'll see multiple choice single answer, fill-in-the blank, and multiple choice multiple answer questions, as you'll encounter on the exam.

1. Enter the command that starts in the top-level root directory and searches for all files with the SGID bit set. Do not specify the full path to the command, assume you have administrative permissions, and keep the options to a minimum.

   _____

2. Which of the following commands lists the date of the last password change for user elizabeth?
   A. chage -l elizabeth
   B. usermod -l elizabeth
   C. passwd -l elizabeth
   D. ulimit elizabeth

3. Which of the following commands is capable of scanning remote systems for open network ports?
   A. netstat
   B. route
   C. nmap
   D. lsof

4. Which of the following commands, when used to run an administrative command, requires the root administrative password?
   A. sudo
   B. su - administrator
   C. sudo -k
   D. su -c

5. Enter the full path to the file that configures administrative access for regular users from their own accounts.

   _____

6. Which of the following files can be used to configure resource limits associated with the ulimit command? Choose two.

    A. /etc/profile

    B. /etc/passwd

    C. ~/.bash_profile

    D. ~/.bash_history

7. Which of the following files, by its very existence, can prevent logins by all but the root administrative user?

    A. /etc/login

    B. /etc/nologin

    C. /etc/shadow

    D. /etc/passwd

8. Which of the following directories includes a script that can control the super server?

    A. /etc

    B. /etc/init.d

    C. /etc/inet.d

    D. /etc/inetd.d

9. Which of the following lines is appropriate for a TCP wrappers /etc/hosts.allow file?

    A. ALL : ALL

    B. disable = yes

    C. 9572 stream tcp nowait nobody /usr/sbin/tcpd /usr/sbin/nbdswapd

    D. defaults

10. If you want to turn off a service, which of the following files specifies the target run-level?

    A. /etc/xinetd.conf

    B. /etc/inetd.conf

    C. /etc/hosts.allow

    D. /etd/inittab

11. Enter the full path to the configuration file that controls the super server.

12. Which of the following files is considered first when restricting access to certain TCP wrappers–capable services?

    A. `/etc/hosts`

    B. `/etc/hosts.allow`

    C. `/etc/hosts.deny`

    D. `/etc/inittab`

13. What are appropriate permissions, in octal format, for private SSH keys?

    A. 644

    B. 655

    C. 600

    D. 440

14. Which of the following commands attempts to log in to the account named `history` on the `remoteserver` system, with access to GUI options on the remote system?

    A. `ssh -l history remoteserver`

    B. `ssh -lX history remoteserver`

    C. `ssh -l history -X remoteserver`

    D. `ssh -X history -l remoteserver`

15. Enter the full path to the directory with user linux's SSH keys. Assume a standard home directory.

    _____

16. Which of the following directives in the SSH server configuration file is not secure?

    A. `HostbasedAuthentication no`

    B. `PubkeyAuthentication yes`

    C. `Protocol 2,1`

    D. `PermitRootLogin no`

17. Enter the command that lists currently loaded GPG keys. Do not use the full path to the command.

    _____

18. Which of the following are not associated with GPG keys?

    A. Debian-based packages

    B. Red Hat–based packages

    C. The `gpg.pub` file in the `gpg --import gpg.pub` command

    D. None of the above

PART III

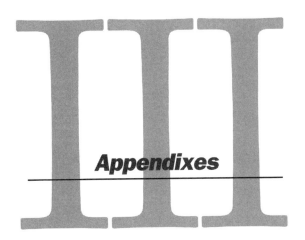

Appendixes

Appendix A

Chapter 1

1. C
2. D
3. `lsmod`
4. D
5. A
6. `/var/log/dmesg`
7. B
8. A, C
9. B
10. C
11. B
12. C
13. `init 1`; `telinit 1` is also acceptable
14. B; answer A would kick off users
15. D
16. B, C

Chapter 2

1. `/home`; the key reference is to "user files"; don't let the reference to network file systems confuse you
2. C; the standard rule of thumb is 2x RAM
3. D; the use of a virtual machine says nothing about the size or type of the drive
4. A, C, D
5. `grub-install /dev/sda`; `grub-install (hd0)` may also work, depending on whether a PATA hard drive is installed
6. B
7. B; although `/boot/grub/grub.conf` and `/etc/grub.conf` may be documented and configured as options in some distributions, `/boot/grub/menu.lst` is the default GRUB boot loader configuration file
8. A
9. `/etc/ld.so.conf`
10. D

Chapter 3

1. D
2. B
3. C, D
4. C
5. `apt-file`; `apt-file search` should also be acceptable
6. D
7. A
8. `rpm -V bigpkg`
9. B, C; although the `yum list` command includes uninstalled packages, it does classify packages by their installation status
10. A
11. `yumdownloader`; remember, the objective is just to download a package
12. B

Chapter 4

1. C, D
2. `~/.bashrc`; `.bashrc` is also acceptable based on the wording of the question. Other hidden `.bash*` files in user home directories are sometimes used.
3. A
4. B; other answers won't find all commands in the `PATH` that starts with `gnome-`
5. B
6. C
7. A
8. `pwd`
9. D; remember, the `!` refers to anything but
10. C; the `-a` includes hidden files, and the `-t` is associated with modification time
11. A
12. `mkdir -p /united/states/of/america`
13. `-type f`
14. C
15. D
16. C, D

Chapter 5

1. C
2. B
3. `tail -n14 /etc/passwd`; although a space is acceptable between the `-n` and 14, the original version of this command didn't work with a space
4. `/etc/init.d/good 2> gooderror`
5. A
6. D; although the `more` command also supports a minimal type of search, it is less extensive than the search tools available with the `less` command
7. B
8. A, C
9. B, C
10. `unexpand -t4 tabby`
11. D
12. C
13. B
14. `sed 's/Solaris/Linux/g' UnixOS`; the `g` is required to change all instances of `Solaris` on each line in the `UnixOS` file
15. C, D
16. A
17. D
18. A

Chapter 6

1. B, C
2. C
3. B
4. `?passwd`
5. A
6. B
7. `renice -20 -p 25`
8. C
9. A; the command is run in the `top` command task browser
10. C; the `ps a` and `ps x` commands, by themselves, may not include the noted process

11. A
12. A, B
13. B
14. nohup
15. A, C
16. B
17. B
18. &

Chapter 7

1. A
2. fdisk -l; do not confuse the question with partitions that have been configured in /etc/fstab or otherwise mounted
3. C
4. tune2fs -j /dev/hda2; the tune2fs -O has_journal /dev/hda2 command is also acceptable
5. A, C
6. C; every now and then, you'll encounter a question where everything appears to be wrong. Problems with a partition suggest that you should run the fsck command on that partition. However, even in single user mode, the partition is mounted. If you try to run the fsck command on that partition, you'll get a warning about "severe filesystem damage." Nevertheless, it is still the best available answer. To run the fsck command on such a partition, you need to either boot into rescue mode with distribution-specific rescue media or boot with a Live CD/DVD available from many Linux distributions.
7. df -i
8. B; there is no XFS filesystem type available with the fdisk command
9. B
10. umount -l; you actually need to apply the command to the partition or device file, but as that's not provided by the question, umount -l is as far as you can go
11. A, D; unless otherwise changed, default settings apply
12. B
13. /mount/cdrom; although some distributions provide DVD-specific device files such as /dev/dvd, such media, when automatically mounted, still is made available on a directory such as /mount/cdrom
14. B

Chapter 8

1. `grpquota`
2. C
3. A, B
4. D
5. `chmod u+s big`
6. A
7. D
8. C
9. `ln /etc/httpd/conf/httpd.conf apache`
10. B
11. B
12. A
13. C; although it's possible to identify the man page for `fstab` with the `locate` command, it's much less efficient
14. `/etc`
15. B
16. A; the `mlocate` file is actually a script that calls the `updatedb` command

Chapter 9

1. `cp -ar . /backup/`; the dot includes hidden files
2. A
3. C
4. D
5. `#!/bin/bash`; the `#!/bin/sh` found in many scripts is insufficient, because it refers to the dash shell on some distributions
6. D; the `set` command doesn't apply in the default bash shell
7. C
8. B
9. `PATH=/usr/sbin:/sbin`
10. D
11. D
12. C

13. A
14. B
15. `while [ $n -lt 10 ]`
16. B
17. `UPDATE`
18. B
19. A
20. C

Chapter 10

1. `Xorg -configure`; although the `X -configure` command may work, `Xorg` is the command that controls the X server
2. A, C
3. A
4. B; this assumes default virtual consoles, where the first GUI is assigned the seventh virtual console
5. `kdmrc`
6. C
7. A
8. B
9. D
10. B

Chapter 11

1. `/etc/skel`
2. B
3. C
4. D
5. `groupadd -g 444444 engineers`
6. A
7. B, D; the password is in `/etc/passwd` only if the Shadow Password Suite is disabled
8. B
9. `usermod -Ga video moviemaker`

10. A
11. B
12. B; yes, the only way this works is if /home/users is in the PATH. Nevertheless, B is the best available answer.
13. SHELL=/usr/sbin
14. B
15. crontab -e
16. C
17. at now + 2 weeks
18. C
19. B
20. D
21. TZ=GST-10; remember, Greenwich Sidreal Time has a different perspective from Greenwich Mean Time
22. A
23. A
24. B

Chapter 12

1. /usr/share/zoneinfo; although actual time zone files are in subdirectories, that varies
2. B; don't confuse C with the /var/lib/ntp/ntp.drift file
3. A
4. D
5. /etc/ntp.conf
6. B, C
7. /etc/syslog.conf; don't let the "kernel log" term confuse you. Fedora 10 and above use /etc/rsyslog.conf.
8. B
9. D
10. D; although other log files noted may contain some boot messages, the kernel ring buffer, /var/log/dmesg, is dedicated to this purpose
11. /etc/mail
12. B
13. B, C
14. A, C

15. `newaliases`
16. C
17. B
18. A, C
19. http://localhost:631; of course, this works only if CUPS is running on the local system
20. A

Chapter 13

1. 25
2. B, C
3. D
4. C
5. ICMP
6. B
7. B
8. B
9. B
10. A
11. `/etc/hosts`
12. B
13. A; the default network mask for Class C addresses is already 255.255.255.0
14. A
15. `route add 192.168.1.0 dev eth1`
16. C

Chapter 14

1. `ifconfig eth0 10.20.30.40 netmask 255.255.0.0`
2. A; the `default` route normally refers to all other IP addresses, if a match to other routes is not found. Although 0.0.0.0 is often known as the default IP address, a route to that address doesn't necessarily follow a defined gateway.
3. D
4. B, C
5. `ifdown -a`

6. D
7. C; don't let the word "default" deceive you, as in this case, it's just the default route to the noted network
8. C
9. A, C
10. C
11. `/etc/nsswitch.conf`
12. D

Chapter 15

1. `find / -perm -g=s`
2. A
3. C
4. D
5. `/etc/sudoers`
6. A, C
7. B
8. B; the `openbsd-inetd` or `inetutils-inetd` script in the `/etc/init.d` directory controls the super server; in contrast, the `/etc/inetd.d` directory may include scripts for individual super server services
9. A
10. D
11. `/etc/inetd.conf`; don't confuse this with the configuration file for the extended internet super server, `/etc/xinetd.conf`
12. B
13. C
14. C
15. `/home/linux/.ssh`
16. C
17. `gpg --list-keys`
18. D; both Red Hat– and Debian-based packages have GPG signatures

Appendix B

The latest versions of the LPIC-1 exams include 60 questions each for Exam 101 and 102. As you can see in the LPIC-1 objectives, the total weight of objectives for Exam 101 is 60. In other words, you'll see approximately one question on the exam for each objective weight. Variations are possible on every exam, because questions are taken from an exam pool. If this were a real LPI exam, you would have 90 minutes to answer the following questions.

1. Enter the name of the system that creates devices when hardware is detected.

   _____

2. If /dev/sda2 is a SATA device, which of the following statements best describes this device file?

   A. Second partition of the first hard drive

   B. Third partition of the second hard drive

   C. Second partition of the primary master hard drive

   D. First partition of the second hard drive

3. If you see the root (hd1,1) in a GRUB stanza, what does that mean?

   A. Boot files are on the second partition of the second hard drive.

   B. Boot files are on the first partition of the first hard drive.

   C. The top-level root directory is on the first partition of the first hard drive.

   D. The top-level root directory is on the second partition of the second hard drive.

4. Which of the following commands lists boot messages?

   A. grub-boot

   B. cat /var/log/boot

   C. bootmsg

   D. dmesg

5. Enter the full directory path to the initial RAM disk file.

   _____

6. Which of the following commands may be used to change the default runlevel? Choose two.

   A. runlevel

   B. init

   C. inittab

   D. telinit

7. Which of the following files may include the default runlevel?

   A. /etc/init

   B. /etc/inittab

   C. /etc/runlevel

   D. /etc/default/runlevel

8. Which of the following directories includes service scripts that can work with the stop and start commands?

   A. /etc/

   B. /etc/default/

   C. /etc/init.d/

   D. /etc/rcS.d/

9. On older systems, which of the following directories should be located within the first 1,024 cylinders of the first two hard drives?

   A. /

   B. /boot

   C. /etc

   D. /var

10. Which of the following partition types cannot be mounted? Choose two.

   A. Primary partition

   B. Extended partition

   C. Logical partition

   D. Swap partition

11. Enter the command that installs the GRUB boot loader on the MBR of the first SCSI drive.

   _____

12. Which of the following files is the standard location for the GRUB boot loader?

   A. /etc/grub.conf

   B. /boot/grub.conf

   C. /boot/grub/menu.1st

   D. /grub.conf

13. Which of the following commands reads the list of libraries stored in the current cache? Assume that you're running with administrative privileges.

   A. ldd

   B. ldd -p

   C. ldconfig

   D. ldconfig -p

14. Which of the following commands deletes a Debian package, along with the associated configuration files?

    A. dpkg -r *packagename*

    B. dpkg -v *packagename*

    C. dpkg -P *packagename*

    D. dpkg -u *packagename*

15. Enter the full path to the configuration file for apt-* commands.

    _____

16. Which of the following commands installs the package named bigwig with dependencies? Assume that you have administrative privileges on the current account. Choose two.

    A. apt-get install bigwig

    B. apt install bigwig

    C. dpkg -i bigwig

    D. aptitude install bigwig

17. Which of the following commands identifies the package associated with the /etc/samba/smb.conf file?

    A. rpm -qf /etc/samba/smb.conf

    B. rpm -ql /etc/samba/smb.conf

    C. rpm -qa /etc/samba/smb.conf

    D. rpm -q /etc/samba/smb.conf

18. Which of the following commands downloads an RPM package named bigtest without installing it? You may assume that the package is downloaded to the local directory.

    A. rpm -it bigtest

    B. yum install bigtest

    C. yum download bigtest

    D. yumdownloader bigtest

19. Enter the full path to the directory where the configuration files with yum repositories are usually stored.

    _____

20. Which of the following commands lists commands recently entered at the command-line interface?

    A. type

    B. history

    C. recent

    D. env

21. Enter the command that moves to the next higher level directory.

    _____

22. Which of the following is the advantage of directories in the PATH?

    A. It prevents crackers from maliciously running programs from the noted directories.

    B. It allows you to run commands directly from directories listed in the PATH, without entering that directory path.

    C. It allows you to run commands directly from directories not listed in the PATH, without entering that directory path.

    D. It supports access to user home directories.

23. Which of the following commands lists the kernel version number? Choose two.

    A. uname -i

    B. uname -r

    C. uname -v

    D. uname -a

24. Which of the following commands lists files in the current directory so the newest files are listed last?

    A. ls -lr

    B. ls -tr

    C. ls -r

    D. ls -lt

25. Enter the minimum command that extracts and uncompresses the test.tar.gz archive.

    _____

26. Which of the following commands can be used to copy the contents of a partition?

    A. dd

    B. tar

    C. cpio

    D. gzip

27. Which of the following commands removes all directories and subdirectories from the /path/to/file/ directory? Assume that these directories are not empty, and you have permissions to remove all of these files and directories.

    A. rm -rf /path/to/file

    B. rmdir -p /path/to/file

    C. rm -af /path/to/file

    D. rmdir -rf /path/to/file

28. Which of the following commands adds error messages from the executable dataprocessor script in the local directory to the end of the file named results?

    A. cat dataprocessor -e >> results

    B. ./dataprocessor >> results

    C. ./dataprocessor 2> results

    D. ./dataprocessor 2>> results

29. Which of the following commands displays the number of lines in the current directory?

    A. ls | wc -l

    B. ls > wc -l

    C. wc -l < ls

    D. wc -l .

30. Which of the following commands takes the contents of the databasefile as input to the dataprocessor script? Both files are in the local directory.

    A. databasefile > dataprocessor

    B. databasefile | dataprocessor

    C. ./dataprocessor < databasefile

    D. ./dataprocessor | databasefile

31. Enter the cat command that appends the contents of the /etc/passwd file to the local file named authentication.

32. Which of the following commands substitutes spaces for tabs in a text file?

   A. fmt

   B. expand

   C. unexpand

   D. od

33. Which of the following commands lists the contents of the fifth column of the file named securedata? Columns from this file are separated with colons (:).

   A. cut -d: -c 5 securedata

   B. cut -s: -f 5 securedata

   C. cut -r, -c 5 securedata

   D. cut -d: -f 5 securedata

34. Which of the following commands reads a file and removes duplicate lines?

   A. sort

   B. remove

   C. uniq

   D. undup

35. Enter the simplest command that finds all lines in the local text file named OperatingSystems with the term Linux.

_____

36. Which of the following commands is the simplest way to substitute the term "Open Source" for "Secret Code" from the local text file named licenses?

   A. sed 's/Secret Code/Open Source/g' licenses

   B. sed 's/"Secret Code"/"Open Source"/g' licenses

   C. sed 's/"Secret Code'/'Open Source'/g' licenses

   D. sed 's/`Secret Code'/'Open Source'/g' licenses

37. Which of the following directories includes print jobs on a local system?

   A. /var/cups/

   B. /var/spool/cups/

   C. /var/cups/spool/

   D. /var/spool/

38. Which of the following commands exits from the vi editor without saving changes that have been made?

  A. w!

  B. Z!

  C. e!

  D. q!

39. If you're in command mode in the vi Editor, enter the command that lists files in the local directory.

  _____

40. Which of the following vi commands starts insert mode, with a line above the current cursor?

  A. a

  B. A

  C. o

  D. O

41. Enter the command that lists running processes with the resources it uses. Make sure the data is refreshed on a regular basis. Do not include the path to the command.

  _____

42. Which of the following numbers represents the highest available process execution priority?

  A. 19

  B. 20

  C. −19

  D. −20

43. Which of the following, when added to the end of a command, returns to the command-line interface even if the command is still running?

  A. $

  B. #

  C. &

  D. bg

44. Which of the following commands would automatically restart the `cupsd` server daemon? Assume that you have logged in with administrative privileges and `cupsd` has a PID of 2222.

   A. `/etc/cupsd restart`

   B. `kill -9 2222`

   C. `/etc/kill 2222 restart`

   D. `kill -1 2222`

45. Enter the command that runs the local executable `databasejob` script, so it continues to run in the background after you log out of the local console.

   _____

46. Which of the following commands identifies the amount of used and free RAM and swap memory? Choose two.

   A. `mem`

   B. `free`

   C. `swap`

   D. `top`

47. Which of the following commands activates journaling on the `/dev/hda2` partition? Assume that the partition is not currently mounted. Choose two.

   A. `tune2fs /dev/hda2`

   B. `tune2fs -O ^has_journal /dev/hda2`

   C. `tune2fs -j /dev/hda2`

   D. `tune2fs -O has_journal /dev/hda2`

48. Which of the following commands formats the empty partition `/dev/sdc1`?

   A. `fsck /dev/sdc1`

   B. `mkfs /dev/sdc1`

   C. `fmt /dev/sdc1`

   D. `tune2fs /dev/sdc1`

49. Which of the following commands lists configured partitions on all connected storage devices? Assume that you're connected with administrative permissions.

   A. `fdisk -la`

   B. `fdisk -a`

   C. `fdisk -lv`

   D. `fdisk -l`

50. On what directory should you mount a standard swap partition?
    A. /
    B. /swap
    C. /sys
    D. None of the above

51. Enter the command that mounts every configured mount point in the /etc/fstab configuration file. Assume that you're connected with administrative permissions. Do not include the path to the command.

    _____

52. Which of the following characteristics of a mount point is not included in the /etc/fstab file?
    A. Format
    B. Mount order
    C. Journaling
    D. Mount directory

53. Which of the following commands can be used to revise the quota file for user michael? Assume that quotas have been properly configured on the applicable filesystem.
    A. revquota -u michael
    B. edquota michael
    C. quota michael
    D. quotacheck michael

54. Enter the command that activates write permissions on the file named sharedfile for all users. Do not include the full path, and assume that you already have appropriate privileges. Make sure no other existing permissions are changed.

    _____

55. Which of the following commands changes the user and group owner to michael and engineers, respectively? Do not include the full path, and assume that you already have administrative privileges. Assume the stated user and group exist.
    A. chgrp michael.engineer
    B. chown michael:engineer
    C. chmod michael.engineer
    D. chmask michael:engineer

56. Which of the following octal permissions includes the SGID and sticky bits?

    A. 3744

    B. 4755

    C. 5766

    D. 6777

57. Which of the following characteristics is associated with hard-linked files on the same partition? Choose two.

    A. The same file size

    B. Identical soft links

    C. The same inode number

    D. The deletion of one linked file leads to the deletion of the file

58. Enter the command that creates a soft link named `currentchapter` connected to the `lp12.doc` file in the `LPIbook/Ch12/` subdirectory?

    _____

59. Which of the following commands identifies the full path to the `ls` command? Choose two.

    A. `whereis ls`

    B. `which ls`

    C. `man ls`

    D. `updatedb ls`

60. Which of the following commands identifies a file from a database that is normally updated daily?

    A. `find`

    B. `locate`

    C. `whichis`

    D. `updatedb`

Appendix C

The latest versions of the LPIC-1 exams include 60 questions each for Exam 101 and 102. As you can see in the LPIC-1 objectives, the total weight of objectives for both exams is 120. In other words, you'll see approximately one question on the exam for each objective weight. Variations are possible on every exam, because questions are taken from an exam pool. If this were a real LPI exam, you would have 90 minutes to answer the following questions.

1. Enter the command that lists devices connected as PC cards. Do not include the full path to the command.

   _____

2. If /dev/sdb1 is a SCSI device, which of the following statements best describes this device file?
   A. Second partition of the first hard drive
   B. Third partition of the second hard drive
   C. Second partition of the primary master hard drive
   D. First partition of the second hard drive

3. If you see root (hd0,2) in a GRUB stanza, what does that mean?
   A. Boot files are on the second partition of the first hard drive.
   B. Boot files are on the first partition of the second hard drive.
   C. Boot files are on the third partition of the first hard drive.
   D. The top-level root directory is on the third partition of the first hard drive.

4. Which of the following commands specifies the kernel ring buffer?
   A. grub-boot
   B. cat /var/log/boot
   C. bootmsg
   D. dmesg

5. Enter the full directory path to the kernel used by the Linux operating system.

   _____

6. Which of the following runlevels is associated with a system reboot?
   A. 0
   B. 1
   C. R
   D. 6

7. Which of the following commands moves to the default runlevel on Ubuntu?
   A. init 2
   B. telinit 3
   C. init 1
   D. telinit 5

8. Which of the following directories includes service scripts that can work with the `reload` and `restart` commands?

   A. `/etc/`

   B. `/etc/default/`

   C. `/etc/init.d/`

   D. `/etc/rcS.d/`

9. Which of the following directories is appropriate to mount on a separate partition or volume?

   A. `/etc`

   B. `/sbin`

   C. `/root`

   D. `/var`

10. Which of the following volumes cannot contain a regular data mount point? Choose two.

    A. Primary partition

    B. Extended partition

    C. Logical partition

    D. Swap partition

11. Enter the command that installs the LILO boot loader on the MBR of the first PATA drive. Do not include the full path to the command.

    _____

12. Which of the following files is the standard location for the LILO boot loader configuration file?

    A. `/etc/lilo.conf`

    B. `/boot/lilo.conf`

    C. `/boot/grub/lilo.conf`

    D. `/lilo.conf`

13. Which of the following files or variables may store directories of currently installed program libraries? Choose two.

    A. `/etc/ldd.conf`

    B. `/etc/ld.so.conf`

    C. `LD_LIBRARY_PATH`

    D. `LD_LIBRARY`

14. Which of the following commands installs but does not upgrade an already existing Red Hat package?

    A. rpm -i *packagename*

    B. rpm -U *packagename*

    C. rpm -F *packagename*

    D. rpm -u *packagename*

15. Enter the full path to the directory with other configuration files associated with yum.conf.

    _____

16. Which of the following commands lists all currently installed Debian-style packages?

    A. dpkg -qa

    B. dpkg -l

    C. dpkg -i

    D. dpkg -li

17. Which of the following commands identifies the package associated with the /etc/samba/smb.conf file?

    A. dpkg -s /etc/samba/smb.conf

    B. dpkg -S /etc/samba/smb.conf

    C. dpkg -qf /etc/samba/smb.conf

    D. dpkg -sf /etc/samba/smb.conf

18. Which of the following commands updates the local database of Debian-style packages?

    A. apt-cache update

    B. apt-get update

    C. apt-get upgrade

    D. apt-get dist-update

19. Enter the command associated with Debian-style source code packages, commonly found in the main update configuration file.

    _____

20. Which of the following files lists commands recently typed in at the command-line interface?

    A. ~/.history

    B. ~/.command

    C. ~/.bash_history

    D. ~/.bashrc

21. Enter the command that moves up two directory levels.

    _____

22. Which of the following should not be included in the PATH?
    - **A.** /usr/bin
    - **B.** /sbin
    - **C.** /usr/sbin
    - **D.** .

23. Which of the following commands lists the hostname? Choose two.
    - **A.** uname -h
    - **B.** uname -n
    - **C.** uname -r
    - **D.** uname -a

24. Which of the following commands lists hidden files in the current directory?
    - **A.** ls -a
    - **B.** ls -t
    - **C.** ls -r
    - **D.** ls -l

25. Enter the minimum command that extracts and uncompresses the test.tar.bz2 archive.

    _____

26. Which of the following commands creates a new empty file named abc?
    - **A.** dd abc
    - **B.** vi abc
    - **C.** touch abc
    - **D.** cp abc

27. Which of the following commands removes all directories and subdirectories from the path/to/file/ directory? Assume that these directories are empty and you have permissions to remove all of these files and directories.
    - **A.** rm -f path/to/file
    - **B.** rmdir -p path/to/file
    - **C.** rm -af path/to/file
    - **D.** rmdir -rf path/to/file

28. Which of the following commands adds regular messages from the executable dataprocessor script in the local directory and overwrites the file named results?

    A. cat dataprocessor -e >> results

    B. ./dataprocessor >> results

    C. ./dataprocessor 2> results

    D. ./dataprocessor 2>> results

29. Which of the following commands displays the number of lines in the /etc/samba/smb.conf configuration file?

    A. cat /etc/samba/smb.conf | wc -l

    B. cat /etc/samba/smb.conf > wc -l

    C. wc -l < cat /etc/samba/smb.conf

    D. wc -l | cat /etc/samba/smb.conf

30. Which of the following files is part of the output to the ls figure[!2-4].tif command?

    A. figure2.tif

    B. figure2-4.tif

    C. figure4.tif

    D. figure1.tif

31. Enter the less command that takes the contents of the /etc/group file and adds them to the end of the local file named authentication.

    _____

32. Which of the following commands substitutes tabs for spaces in a text file?

    A. fmt

    B. expand

    C. unexpand

    D. od

33. Which of the following commands lists the contents of the second column of the /etc/shadow file? Assume that you've logged in with administrative permissions.

    A. cut -d: -c 2 /etc/shadow

    B. cut -s: -f 2 /etc/shadow

    C. cut -r, -c 2 /etc/shadow

    D. cut -d: -f 2 /etc/shadow

34. Which of the following commands reorders the lines from a text file in alphabetical order?

    A. sort

    B. order

    C. uniq

    D. tr

35. Enter the simplest command that finds all lines in the /etc/group file with the term admin.

    _____

36. Which of the following commands substitutes the term "Open Source" for all instances of "Secret Code" in the local text file named licenses?

    A. sed 's/Secret Code/Open Source/' licenses

    B. sed 's/Open Source/Secret Code/' licenses

    C. sed 's/Secret Code/Open Source/g' licenses

    D. sed '/Secret Code`/Open Source/g' licenses

37. Which of the following commands in the vi editor puts five lines into the local cache?

    A. 5pp

    B. 4yy

    C. 5yy

    D. 4pp

38. Which of the following commands exits from the vi editor while saving changes that have been made?

    A. :w!

    B. :Z!

    C. :wq!

    D. :q!

39. If you're in command mode in the vi editor, enter the command that lists files in the /etc directory.

    _____

40. Which of the following vi commands starts insert mode, with a line below the current cursor?

    A. a

    B. A

    C. o

    D. O

41. Enter the command that lists running processes limited to the current console. Do not include the path to the command.

   _____

42. Which of the following numbers represents the lowest available process execution priority?
   - **A.** 19
   - **B.** 20
   - **C.** –19
   - **D.** –20

43. Which of the following key combinations suspends a currently running process in the console?
   - **A.** Ctrl+Z
   - **B.** Ctrl+C
   - **C.** Ctrl+X
   - **D.** Ctrl+H

44. Which of the following commands would kill the `cupsd` server daemon uncleanly? It may be necessary if other commands can't stop that process. Assume that you have logged in with administrative privileges and `cupsd` has a PID of 2222.
   - **A.** `kill -HUP 2222`
   - **B.** `kill -9 2222`
   - **C.** `kill -15 2222`
   - **D.** `kill -1 2222`

45. Enter the command that lists just used and free RAM and swap space memory, without reference to currently running processes. Do not include the path to the command.

   _____

46. Which of the following commands can be used to start a job and keep it running after you log out of the current console?
   - **A.** `hup`
   - **B.** `&`
   - **C.** `nohup`
   - **D.** `free`

47. Which of the following commands deactivates journaling on the /dev/hda2 partition? Assume that the partition is not currently mounted.

    A. `tune2fs /dev/hda2`

    B. `tune2fs -O ^has_journal /dev/hda2`

    C. `tune2fs -j /dev/hda2`

    D. `tune2fs -O has_journal /dev/hda2`

48. Which of the following commands repairs the filesystem on the partition /dev/sdc1? Assume that it's not currently mounted.

    A. `fsck /dev/sdc1`

    B. `mkfs /dev/sdc1`

    C. `dumpe2fs /dev/sdc1`

    D. `tune2fs /dev/sdc1`

49. Which of the following commands lists configured partitions on the second SATA drive?

    A. `fdisk /dev/sda`

    B. `fdisk /dev/sdb`

    C. `fdisk -l /dev/sda`

    D. `fdisk -l /dev/sdb`

50. Which of the following commands formats a swap partition on the second partition of the first PATA drive?

    A. `mkfs.swap /dev/hda2`

    B. `mkswap /dev/hdb1`

    C. `mkswap /dev/hda2`

    D. `mkfs.swap /dev/hda2`

51. Enter the option in /etc/fstab for a partition to be configured with user quotas.

    _____

52. Which of the following variables is not used as the device to be mounted in /etc/fstab?

    A. UUID

    B. LABEL

    C. Partition device file

    D. Mount directory

53. Which of the following commands can be used to revise the quota file for group admin? Assume that quotas have been properly configured on the applicable filesystem.

    A. revquota -g admin

    B. edquota -g admin

    C. quota -g admin

    D. quotacheck -g admin

54. Enter the command that activates executable permissions for all users on the file named sharedfile. Do not include the full path, and assume that you already have appropriate privileges. Make sure no other existing permissions are changed.

    _____

55. Which of the following commands changes the user and group owner to guest and admins, respectively? Do not include the full path, and assume that you already have administrative privileges. Assume the stated group exists.

    A. chgrp guest.admins

    B. chown guest:admins

    C. chmod guest.admins

    D. chmask guest:admins

56. Which of the following octal permissions includes the SUID and sticky bits?

    A. 3744

    B. 4755

    C. 5766

    D. 6777

57. Which of the following commands creates a hard-linked file /tmp/test2 based on file ~/test1? Assume that both the current home directory and the /tmp directory are mounted on the same partition.

    A. ln -h ~/test1 /tmp/test2

    B. ln /tmp/test2 ~/test1

    C. ln -s ~/test1 /tmp/test2

    D. ln ~/test1 /tmp/test2

58. Enter the command that creates a soft link named /etc/bootfile connected to the /boot/grub/menu.1st file.

    _____

59. Which of the following commands identifies the full path to the man command? Choose two.

    A. whereis man

    B. which man

    C. man man

    D. updatedb man

60. Which of the following commands updates a database of currently loaded files?

    A. find

    B. locate

    C. whichis

    D. updatedb

Appendix D

LPIC-1 101, Sample Exam 1 and 2 Answers

Exam 101: Answers from Appendix B, "LPIC-1 101, Sample Exam 1"

1. `udev`
2. A
3. A
4. D
5. `/boot/`
6. B, D
7. B
8. C
9. B
10. B, D
11. `grub-install /dev/sda`
12. C
13. D
14. C
15. `/etc/apt/sources.list`
16. A, D
17. A
18. D
19. `/etc/yum.repos.d/`
20. B
21. `cd ..`
22. B
23. B, D
24. B
25. `tar xzf test.tar.gz`
26. A
27. A
28. D
29. A
30. C

31. `cat /etc/passwd >> authentication`
32. B
33. D
34. C
35. `grep Linux OperatingSystems`
36. A
37. B
38. D
39. `:!ls`
40. D
41. `top`
42. D
43. C
44. D
45. `nohup ./databasejob &`
46. B, D
47. C, D
48. B
49. D
50. D; swap partitions or volumes aren't mounted
51. `mount -a`
52. C; although journaling is implicit in the specified format, it's not explicitly cited in `/etc/fstab`
53. B
54. `chmod a+w sharedfile`
55. B
56. A
57. A, C
58. `ln -s LPIbook/Ch12/lp12.doc currentchapter`
59. A, B
60. B

Exam 101: Answers from Appendix C, "LPIC-1 101, Sample Exam 2"

1. `lspcmcia`
2. D
3. C
4. D
5. `/boot`
6. D
7. A
8. C
9. D
10. B, D
11. `lilo /dev/hda`
12. A
13. B, C
14. C
15. `/etc/yum.repos.d`
16. B
17. B
18. B
19. `deb-src`
20. C
21. `cd ../..`
22. D
23. B, D
24. A
25. `tar xjf test.tar.bz2`
26. C; the `vi abc` command doesn't create a file until it's written from within the editor
27. B
28. B
29. A
30. D

31. `less /etc/group >> authentication`

32. C

33. D

34. A

35. `grep admin /etc/group`

36. C

37. C

38. C

39. `:!ls /etc`

40. C

41. `ps`

42. A

43. A

44. B

45. `free`

46. C; although the ampersand (&) at the end of a command has the same effect, the ampersand itself is not a command

47. B

48. A

49. D

50. C

51. `usrquota`

52. D

53. B

54. `chmod a+x sharedfile`

55. B

56. C

57. D

58. `ln -s /boot/grub/menu.lst /etc/bootfile`

59. A, B; the `whereis man` command also includes the location of the full path to the command

60. D

Appendix E

LPIC-1 102,
Sample Exam 1

The latest versions of the LPIC-1 exams include 60 questions each for Exam 101 and 102. As you can see in the LPIC-1 objectives, the total weight of objectives for Exam 102 is 60. In other words, you'll see approximately one question on the exam for each objective weight. Variations are possible on every exam, because questions are taken from an exam pool. If this were a real LPI exam, you would have 90 minutes to answer the following questions.

1. Enter the directive that adds the `/opt/bin/` directory to the current `PATH`.

   _____

2. Which of the following files is appropriate for aliases shared by all users?
   - **A.** `~/.profile`
   - **B.** `/etc/bashrc`
   - **C.** `./bashrc`
   - **D.** `/etc/profile`

3. Which of the following directories includes files normally added to the home directories of all new users?
   - **A.** `/etc/profile/`
   - **B.** `/home/`
   - **C.** `/etc/default/`
   - **D.** `/etc/skel/`

4. Which of the following commands sets up a function?
   - **A.** `psls { ps; ls; }`
   - **B.** `psls ( ) { ps; ls; }`
   - **C.** `psls ( ps; ls; )`
   - **D.** `psls { } { ps; ls; }`

5. Enter the line in a script that specifies the use of the bash shell. Do not use the `SHELL` variable.

   _____

6. If you see an `if [ -f /path/to/file ];` in a script, when is the conditional satisfied?
   - **A.** If the `/path/to/file` is a directory
   - **B.** If the `/path/to/file` file exists
   - **C.** If the `/path/to/file` is writable
   - **D.** If the `/path/to/file` is readable

7. Which of the following directives in a script is associated with user input?
   - **A.** `while`
   - **B.** `seq`
   - **C.** `read`
   - **D.** `test`

8. If you see an `if [ $value -le 100 ];` in a script, when is the conditional satisfied?

   A. When `value = 100`

   B. When `value <= 100`

   C. When `value >= 100`

   D. When `value` is not 100

9. Which of the following SQL commands is most efficient if you want to change a database entry?

   A. `INSERT`

   B. `DELETE`

   C. `REPLACE`

   D. `UPDATE`

10. In a SQL search, which of the following SQL commands specifies the search parameter?

    A. `WHERE`

    B. `SELECT`

    C. `FROM`

    D. `ORDER BY`

11. Enter the standard X server configuration file with the full directory path.

    _____

12. If you need more information about the GUI capabilities of the current system, which of the following commands can help?

    A. `xwininfo`

    B. `xdpyinfo`

    C. `Xorg`

    D. `X`

13. Which of the following commands opens a tool that can customize the GNOME display manager?

    A. `gdmconfig`

    B. `gdm-setup`

    C. `gdm-config`

    D. `gdmsetup`

14. Which of the following directories may include configuration files for the KDE display manager?

    A. `/etc/`

    B. `/etc/kdm/`

    C. `/etc/kde/kdm/`

    D. `/etc/X11/kdm`

15. Which of the following features means that you don't have to press the keys of a combination such as Ctrl+Alt simultaneously?

    A. Bounce keys

    B. Sticky keys

    C. Repeat keys

    D. Toggle keys

16. Enter the full path to the shadow password suite file that normally contains user passwords.

_____

17. Which of the following commands specifies that a new user `guest` is set to be a member of group `nobody`? Assume that you're connected with administrative permissions.

    A. `useradd -g nobody -u guest`

    B. `useradd nobody guest`

    C. `useradd -g nobody guest`

    D. `useradd -g guest nobody`

18. Which of the following commands displays the current user's password status and aging information?

    A. `chage -l`

    B. `chage -d`

    C. `chage -s`

    D. `chage -p`

19. Which of the following commands disables logins to the account of user `tempworker`?

    A. `usermod -U tempworker`

    B. `usermod -D tempworker`

    C. `usermod -E tempworker`

    D. `usermod -L tempworker`

20. Enter the command that specifies group memberships for the current user. Do not use the full path to the command.

_____

21. If you see 12 4 12 * * root run-parts /etc/cron.monthly in /etc/crontab, when are jobs in the /etc/cron.monthly/ directory run?
    A. 4:12 a.m. on the 12th day of the month
    B. 4:12 p.m. on the 12th day of the month
    C. 12:12 a.m. on the 4th day of the month
    D. 12:04 a.m. on the 1st day of December

22. Which of the following directories contains files associated with user cron jobs?
    A. /etc/cron.d/
    B. /var/cron/
    C. /var/spool/cron/
    D. /etc/crontab/

23. Which of the following commands returns a list of pending one-time jobs?
    A. cronq
    B. atq
    C. /var/spool/cron/atjobs/
    D. atrm

24. What time is teatime, to the at daemon?
    A. 2:00 p.m.
    B. 3:00 p.m.
    C. 4:00 p.m.
    D. 5:00 p.m.

25. Enter the command that sets the local system clock to 1:45 p.m. on October 30, 2009. Assume that you're logged into an administrative account.

    _____

26. Which of the following commands specifies all current LC_* environment variables?
    A. locale
    B. locale -a
    C. locale -e
    D. env | grep locale

27. Which of the following configuration files may include the default language for the system?
    A. /etc/default/language
    B. /etc/default/locale
    C. /etc/default/i18n
    D. /etc/default

28. Which of the following commands synchronizes the local clock with
`0.centos.pool.ntp.org`?

   A. `ntp 0.centos.pool.ntp.org`

   B. `ntpd 0.centos.pool.ntp.org`

   C. `ntptime 0.centos.pool.ntp.org`

   D. `ntpdate 0.centos.pool.ntp.org`

29. Which of the following features is not normally available in Linux unless the local
hardware clock is set to UTC?

   A. Time changes for daylight savings time

   B. Synchronized time between the system and hardware clocks

   C. Configuration of the local system as an NTP client

   D. Configuration of the local system as an NTP server

30. Which of the following files is a copy of the binary file that represents the configured
time zone?

   A. `/etc/timezone`

   B. `/etc/default/localtime`

   C. `/etc/default/timezone`

   D. `/etc/localtime`

31. Enter the full path to the standard kernel log configuration file.

   _____

32. Which of the following logging priorities is lowest?

   A. `notice`

   B. `warn`

   C. `debug`

   D. `info`

33. Which of the following MTAs includes configuration files in the `/etc/mail/` directory?

   A. sendmail.

   B. Postfix.

   C. Exim.

   D. All MTAs include configuration files in the `/etc/mail/` directory.

34. Which of the following configuration files is associated with sendmail? Choose two.

   A. `sendmail.cf`

   B. `master.cf`

   C. `submit.cf`

   D. `main.cf`

35. Which of the following MTAs is not released under an open source license?

   A. sendmail

   B. Postfix

   C. qmail

   D. Dovecot

36. Enter the command that lists pending print jobs on the printer named `office`. Do not include the full path to the command.

   _____

37. Which of the following configuration files may be used as a list of printers?

   A. `/etc/cups/cupsd.conf`

   B. `/etc/printcap`

   C. `/etc/printers`

   D. `/etc/cups/classes.conf`

38. Which of the following TCP/IP port numbers is associated with secure IMAP?

   A. 25

   B. 110

   C. 143

   D. 993

39. Enter the command that can help identify the network route between the local system and a remote URL. Do not include a switch or the full path to the command.

   _____

40. Which of the following addresses may be assigned as a public IP address?

   A. 172.16.1.11

   B. 10.11.12.13

   C. 127.0.0.1

   D. 192.16.11.12

41. Which of the following commands automatically searches a DNS database? Choose two.
   A. host
   B. traceroute
   C. dig
   D. ping

42. Enter the full command that assigns an IP address of 192.168.0.50 and a network mask of 255.255.0.0 to network device eth0. Do not include the full path to the command, and assume that you're connected with administrative privileges.

   _____

43. Which of the following files contains a local database of hostnames and IP addresses?
   A. /etc/default/hostname
   B. /etc/hostname
   C. /etc/hosts
   D. /etc/resolv.conf

44. Which of the following files may include information about a DNS server?
   A. /etc/nsswitch.conf
   B. /etc/hostname
   C. /etc/hosts
   D. /etc/resolv.conf

45. Enter the command that configures a default gateway route through IP address 172.16.1.1. Do not include the full path to the command, and assume that you're connected with administrative privileges.

   _____

46. Which of the following commands activates the wlan0 interface? Choose two.
   A. ifup wlan0
   B. ifconfig wlan0
   C. ifconfig wlan0 start
   D. ifconfig wlan0 up

47. Which of the following commands can give you more information about the DNS information associated with the IP address of the Cengage Learning Web site, 69.32.133.79?
   A. ping 69.32.133.79
   B. host 69.32.133.79
   C. route 69.32.133.79
   D. netstat 69.32.133.79

48. Which of the following commands can provide geographic information about a remote IP address?

   A. netstat

   B. traceroute

   C. ping

   D. route

49. Which of the following commands specifies the current routing table, in numeric format? Choose two.

   A. route -n

   B. route -r

   C. netstat -nr

   D. netstat -n

50. Which of the following files determines whether a local system searches first through a local database or a DNS server for IP address resolution?

   A. /etc/hosts

   B. /etc/resolv.conf

   C. /etc/nsswitch.conf

   D. None of the above

51. Enter the command that specifies the name of the local system. Do not include the path to the command.

   _____

52. Which of the following commands sets June 17, 2009, as the date when account katie is disabled?

   A. usermod -f 2009-06-17 katie

   B. usermod -e 2009-06-17 katie

   C. usermod -E 2009-06-17 katie

   D. usermod -U 2009-06-17 katie

53. Which of the following commands can open /etc/sudoers for editing, in a mode other than read-only?

   A. vi /etc/sudoers

   B. visudo /etc/sudoers

   C. visudo

   D. vi sudoers

54. Which of the following commands can be used to find open ports?

    A. netstat

    B. nmap

    C. lsof

    D. route

55. One file, if it exists on a system, can prevent logins by all regular users. Enter the full path to that file.

    _____

56. Which of the following files relates to security based on TCP wrappers?

    A. /etc/hosts

    B. /etc/cron.deny

    C. /etc/hosts.allow

    D. /etc/iptables

57. Which of the following directories includes services that may be easily deactivated?

    A. /usr/sbin/

    B. /etc/

    C. /etc/init.d/

    D. /sbin/

58. Which of the following commands generates a public/private key pair for SSH connections?

    A. ssh

    B. ssh-add

    C. ssh-agent

    D. ssh-keygen

59. Enter the full path to the directory with authorized server host keys for account michael.

    _____

60. Which of the following files is a standard system private key for SSH authentication?

    A. /etc/ssh/ssh_dsa_key

    B. /etc/ssh_dsa_key

    C. /etc/ssh/ssh_host_dsa_key

    D. /etc/ssh_host_dsa_key

Appendix F

LPIC-1 102,
Sample Exam 2

The latest versions of the LPIC-1 exams include 60 questions each for Exam 101 and 102. As you can see in the LPIC-1 objectives, the total weight of objectives for Exam 102 is 60. In other words, you'll see approximately one question on the exam for each objective weight. Variations are possible on every exam, because questions are taken from an exam pool. If this were a real LPI exam, you would have 90 minutes to answer the following questions.

1. Enter the command that lists all aliases for the current user.

   _____

2. Which of the following files is most appropriate for custom PATH settings for a specific user?
   A. ~/.bash_history
   B. ~/.bashrc
   C. ~/.path
   D. ~/.etc/profile

3. Which of the following files would not contain typical generic profile settings associated with the bash shell?
   A. /etc/profile
   B. /etc/profile.d
   C. /etc/bash_profile
   D. /etc/bash_history

4. Which of the following commands sets up a function?
   A. lspw { ls; pw; }
   B. lspw ( ) { ls; pw; }
   C. lspw (ls; pw;)
   D. lspw { } { ls; pw; }

5. Enter a line in a script that includes the /bin, /usr/bin, and /sbin directories (in that order) in the PATH. Assume that there's no currently existing value of PATH.

   _____

6. If you see an if [-d /path/to/file]; in a script, when is the conditional satisfied?
   A. If the /path/to/file is a directory
   B. If the /path/to/file file exists
   C. If the /path/to/file is writable
   D. If the /path/to/file is readable

7. Which of the following directives in a script is normally a conditional for a loop?
   A. while
   B. seq
   C. read
   D. test

8. If you see an if [$value !100]; in a script, when is the conditional satisfied?

   A. When value = 100

   B. When value <= 100

   C. When value >= 100

   D. When value is not 100

9. Which of the following SQL commands sorts output in alphabetical order?

   A. SORT BY

   B. ORDER BY

   C. OUTPUT BY

   D. UNIQ BY

10. When specifying information to enter into a database, which of the following SQL commands is used?

    A. WHERE

    B. SELECT

    C. INSERT

    D. INCLUDE

11. Enter the directory with X configuration files.

    _____

12. Which of the following files may include information about GUI fonts for all users?

    A. /etc/X11/fonts.conf

    B. /etc/fonts.conf

    C. /etc/fonts/fonts.conf

    D. ~/.fonts

13. Which of the following commands may support GUI displays on remote systems?

    A. xrandr

    B. xdpyinfo

    C. xhost

    D. xwininfo

14. Which of the following directories may include configuration files for the XDM display manager?

    A. /etc/

    B. /etc/xdm

    C. /etc/X11/xdm

    D. /etc/X11

15. Which of the following features can help when a keyboard is not available?
   A. Toggle keys
   B. Braille display
   C. Repeat keys
   D. On-Screen Keyboard

16. Enter the full path to the shadow password suite file where password aging information is stored.

_____

17. Which of the following commands specifies that a new user nobody is set to be a member of group guest? Assume that you're connected with administrative permissions.
   A. `useradd -g nobody -u guest`
   B. `useradd nobody guest`
   C. `useradd -g nobody guest`
   D. `useradd -g guest nobody`

18. Which of the following commands on the tempworker account means that user's password will expire on June 1, 2010?
   A. `chage -d 2010-06-01 tempworker`
   B. `chage -d 06-01-2010 tempworker`
   C. `chage -E 06-01-2010 tempworker`
   D. `chage -E 2010-06-01 tempworker`

19. Which of the following commands re-enables logins to the account of user tempworker?
   A. `usermod -U tempworker`
   B. `usermod -D tempworker`
   C. `usermod -E tempworker`
   D. `usermod -L tempworker`

20. Enter the full path to the directory to add files, if you want those files to be included in the home directory of all new users.

_____

21. If you see `4,44 4 12 * * root run-parts /etc/cron.monthly` in `/etc/crontab`, when are jobs in the `/etc/cron.monthly/` directory run?
   A. 4:44 a.m. on the 12th day of the month
   B. 4:04 a.m. and 12:44 a.m. on the 4th day of the month
   C. 4:04 a.m. and 4:44 a.m. on the 12th day of the month
   D. 12:04 a.m. and 12:44 a.m. on the 4th day of the month

22. Which of the following directories contains files associated with system cron jobs?

    A. /etc/cron.d

    B. /var/cron

    C. /var/spool/cron

    D. /etc/crontab

23. Which of the following commands lists jobs to be run for the current account?

    A. cronq

    B. atq

    C. atc

    D. atrm

24. Which of the following commands sets the local system clock to 2:15 p.m. on April 13, 2010?

    A. date 101514113

    B. date 13451030090413021510

    C. date 10300913451304141510

    D. date 0413141510

25. Enter the command that starts the at> prompt for jobs to be run at 1:45 p.m. on October 30, 2010.

    _____

26. Which of the following commands is associated with language and country settings?

    A. date

    B. timezone

    C. locale

    D. tzselect

27. Which of the following directories includes standard time zone information?

    A. /etc/share/zoneinfo

    B. /usr/share/zoneinfo

    C. /etc/zoneinfo

    D. /usr/zoneinfo/share

28. Which of the following files may include the addresses of remote NTP servers?

    A. /etc/ntpdate.conf

    B. /etc/ntp.conf

    C. /etc/pool.conf

    D. /etc/ntp.org.conf

29. Which of the following files is related to deviations from a hardware clock? Choose two.

    A. `/etc/ntp.conf`

    B. `/etc/adjtime`

    C. `/var/lib/ntp/ntp.drift`

    D. `/etc/hwclock`

30. Which of the following files configures standard log files?

    A. `/etc/log.conf`

    B. `/etc/syslog.conf`

    C. `/etc/kernlog.conf`

    D. `/etc/stanlog.conf`

31. Enter the command that can synchronize the system and hardware clocks. Do not use the full path to the command.

    _____

32. Which of the following logging priorities is highest?

    A. `notice`

    B. `warn`

    C. `debug`

    D. `info`

33. Which of the following is not an MTA?

    A. sendmail

    B. Postfix

    C. Exim

    D. procmail

34. Which of the following configuration directories is associated with sendmail?

    A. `/etc/mail`

    B. `/etc/sendmail`

    C. `/etc/mta`

    D. `/etc/Sendmail`

35. Which of the following directives in a CUPS configuration file specifies printer administrators?
    A. `PrintGroup`
    B. `SystemGroup`
    C. `AdminGroup`
    D. `Admin`

36. Enter the command that moves all pending print jobs from the printer named `office` to the printer named `remoteoffice`. Do not include the full path to the command.

    _____

37. Which of the following files normally includes information on CUPS-configured printers?
    A. `/etc/cups/printers.conf`
    B. `/etc/printers.conf`
    C. `/etc/cups/printers`
    D. `/etc/cups/cupsd.conf`

38. Which of the following TCP/IP port numbers is associated with SMTP?
    A. 25
    B. 110
    C. 143
    D. 993

39. Enter the simplest IPv4 command that can help verify a working connection between the local system and a remote URL. Do not include a switch or the full path to the command.

    _____

40. Which of the following addresses is the loopback IP address?
    A. 172.16.0.1
    B. 10.0.0.1
    C. 127.0.0.1
    D. 192.168.0.1

41. Which of the following commands searches a DNS database for the domain associated with an IP address? Choose two.
    A. `host course.com`
    B. `host -1 69.32.142.109`
    C. `dig 69.32.142.109`
    D. `ping 69.32.142.109`

42. Enter the full command that assigns an IP address of 10.11.12.13 and a network mask of 255.255.255.0 to network device eth0. Do not include the full path to the command, and assume that you're connected with administrative privileges.

_____

43. Which of the following commands does not provide a continuous series of ICMP messages to a remote system?

    A. ping -b www.cengage.com

    B. ping -c1 www.cengage.com

    C. ping -d www.cengage.com

    D. ping -n www.cengage.com

44. Which of the following files specifies the order in which databases of hostnames and IP addresses are searched?

    A. /etc/nsswitch.conf

    B. /etc/hostname

    C. /etc/hosts

    D. /etc/resolv.conf

45. Enter the command that deletes an existing default gateway route through IP address 172.16.1.1. Assume that it's the only default route. Do not include the full path to the command, and assume that you're connected with administrative privileges. Make sure to make the command as simple as possible.

_____

46. Which of the following commands deactivates the wlan0 interface? Choose two.

    A. ifdown wlan0

    B. ifconfig wlan0 halt

    C. ifconfig wlan0 stop

    D. ifconfig wlan0 down

47. Which of the following commands, when directed at a remote system, confirms if a network is properly connected?

    A. ping

    B. host

    C. route

    D. ifconfig

48. Which of the following commands can help identify a problem router on a large network?

    A. netstat

    B. traceroute

    C. ping

    D. route

49. Which of the following commands specifies the current routing table, in nonnumeric format? Choose two.

    A. route -n

    B. route

    C. netstat -ar

    D. netstat -n

50. Which of the following port numbers is associated with secure SMTP services?

    A. 25

    B. 443

    C. 465

    D. 995

51. Enter the full path to the file with the name of the local system.

    _____

52. Which of the following commands connects and logs into to the root user account?

    A. su -c

    B. sudo

    C. su

    D. su - admin

53. Which of the following characters, in front of a name in /etc/sudoers, specifies a group?

    A. #

    B. &

    C. %

    D. $

54. Which of the following commands can be used to limit the number of logins per user?

    A. ulimit

    B. usermod

    C. chage

    D. su

55. Enter the full path to the directory with configuration files for extended internet super server services.

    _____

56. Which of the following files is considered first by TCP wrappers libraries when it secures services?

    A. /etc/hosts

    B. /etc/hosts.deny

    C. /etc/hosts.allow

    D. /etc/xinetd.conf

57. Which of the following configuration files is associated with the older super server?

    A. /etc/xinetd.conf

    B. /etc/inetd.conf

    C. /etc/hosts.allow

    D. /etc/init.d/xinetd

58. Which of the following commands adds SSH keys to enable logins?

    A. ssh

    B. ssh-add

    C. ssh-agent

    D. ssh-keygen

59. Enter the full path to the directory with GPG configuration files for account michael.

    _____

60. Which of the following files includes public SSH keys from remote systems?

    A. ~/.ssh/id_rsa.pub

    B. ~/.ssh/id_dsa.pub

    C. ~/.ssh/known_hosts

    D. ~/.ssh/authorized_keys

Appendix G

LPIC-1 102, Sample
Exam 1 and 2
Answers

Exam 102: Answers from Appendix E, "LPIC-1 102, Sample Exam 1"

1. `PATH=$PATH:/opt/bin/`
2. B
3. D
4. B
5. `#!/bin/bash`
6. B; although the condition would also be satisfied if the `/path/to/file` is readable or writable, B is the most precise answer
7. C
8. B
9. D
10. A
11. `/etc/X11/xorg.conf`
12. B
13. D
14. C
15. B
16. `/etc/shadow`
17. C
18. A
19. D
20. `groups`
21. A
22. C
23. B
24. C
25. `date 1030134509`
26. A
27. B
28. D
29. A
30. D

31. `/etc/syslog.conf`; this file configures both the system and kernel log services
32. C
33. A
34. A, C
35. C
36. `lpq -Poffice`; `lpq -P office` is also acceptable
37. B; this file is less commonly used on current Linux systems
38. D
39. `route`; `netstat` is also acceptable
40. D
41. A, C
42. `ifconfig eth0 192.168.0.50 netmask 255.255.0.0`
43. C
44. D
45. `route add default gw 172.16.1.1`
46. A, D
47. B
48. B
49. A, C
50. C
51. `hostname`
52. B
53. C
54. B
55. `/etc/nologin`
56. C
57. C
58. D
59. `/home/michael/.ssh/`
60. C

Exam 102: Answers from Appendix F, "LPIC-1 102, Sample Exam 2"

1. `alias`
2. B
3. D
4. B
5. `PATH=/bin:/usr/bin:/sbin`
6. A
7. A; although `seq` can be part of a conditional for a loop, it is not the conditional
8. D
9. B
10. C
11. `/etc/X11`
12. C; `~/.fonts` is limited to the specified user
13. C
14. C
15. D; yes, the question is a bit misleading, but you have to be ready for slightly misleading questions on the exam
16. `/etc/shadow`
17. D
18. D
19. A
20. `/etc/skel`
21. C
22. A; the `/var/spool/cron` directory includes user cron jobs; `/etc/crontab` is a file
23. B
24. D
25. `at 13:45 10/30/2010`
26. C
27. B
28. B
29. B, C
30. B

31. `hwclock`

32. B

33. D

34. A

35. B

36. `lpmove office remoteoffice`

37. A

38. A

39. `ping`; although the `traceroute` command can also confirm connections, it's not as simple as `ping`

40. C

41. B, C

42. `ifconfig eth0 10.11.12.13 netmask 255.255.255.0`

43. B

44. A

45. `route del default`; as there is only one default route, no reference to a gateway is required

46. A, D

47. A

48. B

49. B, C

50. C

51. `/etc/hostname`

52. C

53. C; the % makes a name a group in other configuration files

54. A

55. `/etc/xinetd.d`

56. C

57. B

58. B

59. `/home/michael/.gnupg`

60. D

Appendix H

The CD includes four videos from CBT Nuggets that provide one more perspective on the LPIC-1 exams. These videos cover topics that have not changed from the previous LPIC exams and are part of their courses originally recorded in 2004.

Three of the videos cover the command-line interface; the final video is associated with the SSH (Secure Shell) service. Although the final video was originally developed for the LPIC-2 exams, the associated topics are now incorporated into the 2009 revision to the LPIC-1 exams.

CBT Nuggets has graciously decrypted these videos for use on Linux systems, converting them to the .mov format. In this appendix, I describe how you can configure the Linux MPlayer Movie Player to play these videos (which CBT Nuggets calls "nuggets").

This appendix assumes that you've installed the GUI (graphical user interface) on either the Ubuntu Hardy Heron or CentOS 5 Linux releases used throughout this book.

CAUTION

Use of the videos on your specific software may require the use of additional decryption and/or codecs software packages from other sources. Although CBT Nuggets has explicitly granted permission to use any software necessary for viewing the videos under its copyright with this book, these packages and others referenced in this appendix may not be available in all countries.

The CD Media

Depending on your distribution, the CD may be automatically mounted. To reveal the mount directory, run the mount command. For example, on CentOS 5, when the CD is inserted in the default configuration, it's automatically mounted on the following directory:

```
/media/Linux Demo
```

Alternatively, on the Ubuntu Hardy Heron release, insert the CD. You'll likely need to mount the CD with the following command:

```
$ mount /dev/cdrom
```

The video files referenced in the appendix can be found in the Files to be run directly subdirectory. In other words, to list the video files provided by CBT Nuggets on the CentOS 5 and Ubuntu Hardy Heron releases, run one of the following commands. (The backslashes escape the meaning of the space, making the space a part of the directory.)

```
$ ls /media/Linux\ Demo/Files\ to\ be\ run\ directly/
$ ls /media/cdrom/Files\ to\ be\ run\ directly/
```

You don't need to type in all of these backslashes. Remember, with command completion, you don't need to type in the whole command. Just type in

```
$ ls /media/Linux\ Demo/F
```

or

```
$ ls /media/cdrom/F
```

and then press the Tab key to reveal the rest of the directory.

Install and Configure MPlayer

Although the CBT Nuggets videos may work with numerous Linux video players, the one I use is MPlayer, developed in Hungary. It is a GPL (General Public License) video player that is readily available from both the Ubuntu Hardy Heron and CentOS 5 repositories. Depending on the distribution, you can install MPlayer from the Ubuntu multiverse repositories or third-party repositories designed for Red Hat Enterprise Linux 5 and CentOS 5, available from https://rpmrepo.org. For more information on repository management, see Chapter 3, "Package Management Systems."

On CentOS 5, you'll need to install the rpmforge-release RPM package, per the instructions listed at https://rpmrepo.org/RPMforge/Using. That installation adds references to associated third-party repositories in the /etc/yum.repos.d directory. At that point, you can download and install the MPlayer video player with the following command:

```
# yum install mplayer
```

On Ubuntu Hardy Heron, you'll need to activate the multiverse repositories in the /etc/apt/sources.list configuration file. To do so, look for the following lines in that file:

```
deb http://mirrors.kernel.org/ubuntu/ hardy universe
deb-src http://mirrors.kernel.org/ubuntu/ hardy universe
deb http://mirrors.kernel.org/ubuntu/ hardy-updates universe
deb-src http://mirrors.kernel.org/ubuntu/ hardy-updates universe
```

Then add a reference to the multiverse repositories to the end of each of these lines, so they read as follows:

```
deb http://mirrors.kernel.org/ubuntu/ hardy universe multiverse
deb-src http://mirrors.kernel.org/ubuntu/ hardy universe multiverse
deb http://mirrors.kernel.org/ubuntu/ hardy-updates universe multiverse
deb-src http://mirrors.kernel.org/ubuntu/ hardy-updates universe multiverse
```

Then run the `apt-get update` command. At that point, you can install the MPlayer video player with the following command:

```
# apt-get install mplayer
```

However, even after decryption by CBT Nuggets, MPlayer requires additional codecs, which code and decode sound and video to digital data. Such codecs are available from the MPlayer Web site in Hungary, at http://www.mplayerhq.hu/design7/dload.html. Select a binary codec package that's appropriate for your system. They're packaged in `tar.bz2` format, described in Chapter 4, "Command Lines and Files."

Once you've downloaded the package, you should be able to prepare it; the one available as of this writing is named `essential-20071007.tar.bz2`. You can prepare the package with the following command:

```
$ tar xjvf essential-20071007.tar.bz2
```

The command unpacked the package into the `essential-20071007/` subdirectory. As directed by the `README` file in that directory, you can then, with administrative privileges, copy the contents of that directory to the `/usr/lib/codecs` directory.

Playing the CBT Nuggets Videos

The directions in this section are based on the use of MPlayer in a GUI, based on an available command-line console. MPlayer is typically also available from a GUI menu, but the directions vary by distribution and version. This assumes that you've installed the `mplayer` package designed for your distribution and have copied the needed codec files to the `/usr/lib/codecs` directory. It also assumes that you know how to open a command-line terminal in your selected Linux GUI. To play the CBT Nuggets videos, take the following steps:

1. Log into a GUI.
2. Insert the CD into the drive. Some Linux GUIs are configured to automatically mount the CD mounted in a drive. As noted earlier, on a CentOS 5 system, the CD may be mounted in the `/media/Linux Demo` directory. If this does not happen, run the `mount /dev/cdrom` command; depending on the local configuration, you may need to run this command with administrative privileges.
3. Enter the `gmplayer` command.
4. Right-click in the main body of the MPlayer window that appears. In the pop-up menu, select Open, Play File.
5. Navigate to the directory with the CBT Nuggets videos. It should be in a subdirectory where the CD is mounted. Based on the previous discussion, that may be `/media/cdrom` or `/media/Linux Demo`.

6. Select the CBT Nuggets video of your choice. If necessary, right-click in the main body of the MPlayer window again, and select Playing, Play.

7. Adjust the volume and size of the window as desired. Some options to this end are available in the noted MPlayer pop-up menu.

8. When you're finished, close the MPlayer window.

One common problem relates to the `vo_driver` directive in a couple of configuration files in the `~/.mplayer` directory: `config` and `gui.conf`. In these files, you may need to set the following:

```
vo_driver = "x11"
```

On systems with some graphics cards, you may still see the following error message:

```
Error opening/initializing the selected video_out (-vo) device.
```

In that case, you could try a different video device. For a list of available video devices, run the following command:

```
$ mplayer -vo help
```

For example, I run the following command to play a video on the Ubuntu Hardy Heron release installed in a VMware virtual machine:

```
$ mplayer -vo x11 /media/cdrom/Files\ to\ be\ run\ directly/lpi01.mov
```

Remember, with command completion, you don't need to type in the whole command. Just type in

```
$ mplayer -vo x11 /media/cdrom/F
```

and then press the Tab key to reveal the rest of the directory.

If the `x11` device doesn't work for you, some trial and error with the other video devices revealed with the `mplayer -vo help` command may be required. Once an appropriate device is found, it can be incorporated into the aforementioned configuration files in the `~/.mplayer` directory.

You can find additional hints and options for configuring MPlayer for CBT Nuggets `.mov` files at http://www.ubuntugeek.com.

Index

Special Characters

! (bang), 127, **131**, 233
#! expression, 127, **132**
$ expression, 127, **131**
& (ampersand), 127, **131**, 153, **158**
&& operator, 234
. (dot), 82, **102**
.. (double dots), **82**, **102**
. switch, 177
/ (forward slash), 379
/ (top-level root directory), **33**, **46**
/ directory, FHS, 209
[] (brackets), 127, 131
\ (backslash), 127–128, **131**
^ (carat), 127, **131**
` (back quote), 126–127, **131**
{} (braces), 127, 131
| (pipe character), 111–112
|| operator, 234
~ (tilde), 127, 139
< redirection arrow, **131**
> redirection arrow, **131**
>> redirection arrow, **131**
– (dash), 379
" (double quote), 126–127, **131**
' (single quote), 126–127, **131**
-1 switch, 157
1G (gg) command, 140
2> redirection arrow, 110–111, **131**
2>> redirection arrow, **131**
2x command, 142
5 rpm -V Failure Code, 65
6 code, 172
7 code, 172
8e code, 172
-9 switch, 157
-15 switch, 157
20 (TCP/IP port), **323**, **344**
21 (TCP/IP port), **323**, **344**

22 (TCP/IP port), **323**, **344**
23 (TCP/IP port), **323**, **344**
25 (TCP/IP port), **323**, **344**
53 (TCP/IP port), **323**, **344**
80 (TCP/IP port), **324**, **344**
82 code, 172
83 code, 172
85 code, 172
110 (TCP/IP port), **324**, **344**
119 (TCP/IP port), **324**, **344**
139 (TCP/IP port), **324**, **345**
143 (TCP/IP port), **324**, **345**
161 (TCP/IP port), **324**, **345**
443 (TCP/IP port), **324**, **345**
465 (TCP/IP port), **324**, **345**
993 (TCP/IP port), **324**, **345**
995 (TCP/IP port), **324**, **345**

A

A command, 141
a command
   fdisk commands, 169
   insert mode, 141
   vi editor, **158**
A resource record, 363
-a switch
   cp command, 92
   hwclock command switches, 301
   ls command, 91
   mount and unmount commands, 189
   ps command, 144
   uname command, 86
-A switch, cpio command, 98
a switch, ps command, 144
AAAA resource record, 363
absolute path, **82**, **102**
Accepting directive, 312
access control lists (ACLs), 307

Bold text indicates page where indexed terms are defined.

Bold text indicates page where indexed terms are defined.

Bold text indicates page where indexed terms are defined.

Bold text indicates page where indexed terms are defined.

Bold text indicates page where indexed terms are defined.

Bold text indicates page where indexed terms are defined.

Bold text indicates page where indexed terms are defined.

Bold text indicates page where indexed terms are defined.

Bold text indicates page where indexed terms are defined.

Bold text indicates page where indexed terms are defined.

Bold text indicates page where indexed terms are defined.

Bold text indicates page where indexed terms are defined.

Bold text indicates page where indexed terms are defined.

Bold text indicates page where indexed terms are defined.

Bold text indicates page where indexed terms are defined.

Bold text indicates page where indexed terms are defined.

Bold text indicates page where indexed terms are defined.

Bold text indicates page where indexed terms are defined.

Bold text indicates page where indexed terms are defined.

Bold text indicates page where indexed terms are defined.

Bold text indicates page where indexed terms are defined.

Bold text indicates page where indexed terms are defined.

Bold text indicates page where indexed terms are defined.

License Agreement/Notice of Limited Warranty